T0322362

The Pleasant Profession of
ROBERT A. HEINLEIN

Also by the author

Fiction

Spring Flowering

Non-fiction

Children's Fantasy Literature: An Introduction
(with Michael M. Levy)

A Short History of Fantasy (with Edward James)

The Cambridge Companion to Fantasy Literature
(ed. with Edward James)

*The Inter-Galactic Playground: A Critical Study of Children's
and Teen's Science Fiction*

On Joanna Russ

Rhetorics of Fantasy

Foundation 100 (ed. with Graham Sleight)

*Diana Wynne Jones: Children's Literature and
the Fantastic Tradition*

Glorifying Terrorism: An Anthology of Science Fiction Stories

Polder: A Festschrift in Honour of John Clute and Judith Clute

The Cambridge Companion to Science Fiction
(ed. with Edward James)

The True Knowledge of Ken MacLeod (ed. with Andrew M. Butler)

Quaker Relief in the Spanish Civil War

Terry Pratchett: Guilty of Literature
(ed. with Andrew M. Butler, Edward James)

The Parliament of Dreams: Conferring on Babylon 5
(ed. with Edward James)

The Pleasant Profession of

ROBERT A. HEINLEIN

Farah Mendlesohn

Unbound

This edition first published in 2019

Unbound
6th Floor Mutual House, 70 Conduit Street, London W1S 2GF

www.unbound.com

Text design by PDQ Digital Media Solutions, Bungay, UK

A CIP record for this book is available from the British Library

ISBN 978-1-78352-678-9 (hardback)
ISBN 978-1-78352-680-2 (ebook)

Printed in Great Britain by CPI Group (UK) Ltd.

1 3 5 7 9 8 6 4 2

Edited by Edward James

This book owes a few debts.

To George Slusser, who suggested to a first-year Ph.D. student in
1993 that she should write a book on Heinlein.

To Edward James, who, when twenty years later that ex-Ph.D.
student was pondering the open invitation from Illinois,
reminded her of this.

To Bill Patterson, whose biography of Heinlein has rendered
this project ever so much more feasible.

To the fans who have made my life so much easier with
online concordances.

And finally . . .

To everyone who makes science fiction and its communities.

Contents

Preface

The origins of this book lie at the very beginning of my career. I began reading science fiction in the 1980s, with a suitcase full of books given to me by my father's best friend. I quickly found more of Heinlein's juvenile novels in the library. In 1988, as a second-year undergraduate, my tutor persuaded me that instead of writing on the history of romance I should take a look at the history of science fiction. His was not an entirely disinterested position: he had recently become involved with the Science Fiction Foundation, had through that organisation aided the establishment of the Arthur C. Clarke Award and become one of the first judges, and had also become the editor of *Foundation: the International Review of Science Fiction.* When I walked through his door in October 1986, noted his bookshelves and said, 'Oh, you read science fiction?', I suspect my dissertation fate was sealed. In 1988 I accepted his suggestion and embarked on a study of six science-fiction writers over a twenty-year period (1965–1985), considering how their portrayal of women had shifted and changed. This was a fairly standard approach to material at the time. As I was in a history department, Marxist social and cultural theory had far more influence than any interest in literary quality, and as those who know my work will recognise, this has barely shifted in almost thirty years. I have always been interested in the *typical* rather than the ground-breaking, in a body of work rather than single texts.

The effect of this approach was to produce a different outcome and assessment than a literary scholar might expect. Because of the nature of the study I needed a set of people who had written continuously across the period I had chosen: for the women, I selected Ursula K. Le Guin, Marion Zimmer Bradley and James Tiptree, Jr. (I would have liked to include Joanna Russ, but she was not prolific enough); for the men I chose Harry Harrison, Samuel R. Delany and Robert A. Heinlein.

At the end of the study (an abbreviated version of which can be read in *Foundation* 53, Autumn 1991) I had reached an unexpected conclusion. Of the six authors considered, five showed very little change in their attitudes: whether radical (Delany) or liberal (Bradley), where they began was more or less where they ended. The exception was Heinlein. Over a period of twenty years, Heinlein's attitudes had shifted noticeably. Were one to include the twenty years previous to that, the word would be 'dramatically'. This was not always (from my 1980s feminist point of view) a good shift, but it was there, and I was fascinated. Here was a person sometimes ahead of his time, sometimes crosswise, and, towards the end, in retrenchment. As a historian how could I not be entranced? I have never lost my love of Heinlein's work. Because I am not strictly a literary critic, it bothers me not one bit that he is not the greatest of stylists (although the playfulness and serviceability of Heinlein's prose is often overlooked).

It is not terribly clear how much more influential Heinlein will become. The critical voices are getting louder, and although as a historian I frequently want critics to have a stronger sense of context (as I note in Chapter 7, Heinlein's most controversial comment on slavery is actually a quote from Booker T. Washington) we live now, in our context, and what was radical once we can recognise as problematic, and something to be argued against. For all I value Heinlein I do not require him to continue to be read or valued as contemporary fiction. Because I am a historian, discussing the really terrible Heinlein works can be enfolded into a discussion of his limitations (both rhetorical and political) and understood without serving as some kind of justification. As a historian, I am perfectly happy to know that I like Heinlein without feeling that it is essential that newcomers to science fiction need to read him. I like 1930s pulp magazines as well and I wouldn't wish those on any but the most serious of historians.

The purpose of this book is to tease out what I find fascinating about Heinlein, good, bad and reprehensible, and to understand his work as a close-to-fifty-year-long argument with himself and those he admired.

NB. In what follows, since I am aware that there are many editions of most of these novels, I have cited quotations by chapter number. I have assumed that people do not need page references to the short stories or articles.

Introduction

When Robert A. Heinlein was first published in 1939, the magazine science-fiction field was entering what would later be termed by many 'the Golden Age'. In the late 1920s and early 1930s the magazines had been supplied by writers who worked in multiple genres. Much science fiction was thinly glossed empire romance, or invention stories in which little about the world fundamentally changed. By 1939 however, new writers who had 'grown up' with the magazines were emerging, and activist editors such as Raymond Palmer and John W. Campbell, Jr. argued in editorials and through editorial choices what science fiction should be.[1]

Heinlein's very earliest contribution to this field, 'Life-line', mimicked the earlier narratologies: an inventor announces an invention that threatens to rupture industrial peace, and is quietly disposed of, if only by fate. His stories 'The Roads Must Roll' and 'Blowups Happen' take the conventional focalising view of a journalist

---

1 Only one title founded during the war, *Science Fiction Quarterly*, had a substantial run into the 1950s.

or anthropologist. Quite quickly, however, Heinlein began to shift the nature of the field. A key change was in his insistence that the consequence of change was more interesting than the change itself. In stories such as 'The Roads Must Roll', 'Misfit' and 'Coventry' we are introduced to the changes in the world long after they have taken place. The stories are about the psychological and social effect on human beings. Heinlein helped to move the field away from stories about the future to stories set in the future.

Heinlein produced twenty-nine stories before his engagement in the war, and another thirty-two between 1946 and 1962. He wrote thirty-one novels in total, of which thirteen are usually listed as juveniles (I will be suggesting that we might add at least two more titles to the list). Add in all the essays and collections (which often contain interesting contextual reading) and there are 129 titles.

Heinlein brought to his writing a number of sensibilities and positions. He was the middle child of a middle-class but not wealthy mid-western family; he had entered the navy to get an education and had enjoyed both the process of education and the absorption into a larger body. He brought to his writing the interest in and knowledge of engineering that gave his early stories such heft: Robert W. Bly cites Heinlein's technological engagement with the invention of atomic bombs, computers, dimensional theory, exoskeletons, generational space ships, genetic engineering, hyperspace, longevity studies, space, asteroid mining, mutation, nuclear warfare, suspended animation and time travel. Heinlein's work, particularly everything before 1960, is a part of what Paul Boyer in his book *By the Bomb's Early Light*, calls 'Fantasies of a Techno-Atomic Utopia' (p. 107) in which atomic power could fuel cars, change the polar ice coverage (melt it for a warmer climate, without worrying about polar bears), control the weather and generally perform miracles (pp. 107–122). Heinlein was never really a hard SF writer: he was always more interested in the human than the machine, more interested in the use of invention than the invention itself. Peter Nicholls, in his essay 'Robert A. Heinlein', in *Science Fiction Writers: Critical Studies*, offers an accurate assessment when he maintains that the 'emotional centre of his work has always been the political and social satire of man, and the cultures he builds and lives in' (p. 63). Alfred Berger, in his book *The Magic that Works*, argues persuasively that it is in this way that Heinlein contributed to the feel that there was a 'science of society' (p. 91).

After leaving the navy Heinlein became involved in Californian politics both as a grass-roots campaigner and a participant in classic block politics; he enjoyed a radical open marriage with Leslyn MacDonald. He had already written a lightly fictionalised utopian manifesto that did not see the light of day while he was alive. His stories were startlingly political compared to those of his contemporaries (they share interests more common to the utopian-inflected writers of the 1920s and early 1930s). They have a clear cinematic arc, and tuck sexual and social radicalism into their corners and then, as Heinlein moved into adult novels in the 1960s, bring them up front as the primary interest. He understood science fiction as part of the historical process and as part of preparing for the future. 'There won't always be an England – nor a Germany, nor a United States, nor a Baptist Church, nor the Democratic Party, nor the superiority of the white race...' (GoH Speech at Denvention 1941, in *Requiem: New Collected Works*, p. 156).

Although it is not really helpful to think of SF writers as predictors, for all Heinlein that never successfully predicted technological change (although there is Matt Dodson's mobile phone in *Space Cadet*), it is amusing that he predicted the President's wife consulting an astrologer (*Stranger in a Strange Land*), an actor becoming President while controlled by his PR staff (*Double Star*), gender-neutral bathrooms (*Friday*), a demagogic presidential candidate ('Revolt in 2100'), and gender fluidity (*I Will Fear No Evil*). His futures are politicised in complex ways over and above the stories he tells. This is not always successful and this book will tackle the failures as well as the successes but it is in those complex backgrounds that the truth in Peter Nicholls' summation lies: 'Although most of his themes were not new to science fiction, Heinlein was often the first writer to render them solidly believable rather than merely mind-boggling' (p. 185).

Heinlein also brought to science fiction a genuine interest in the *craft* of the form which he may well have acquired from Leslyn MacDonald, who brought her experience of cinema and knowledge of script doctoring to their relationship. He wrote one of the earliest essays to contribute to a study of SF's narratology,[2] 'On the Writing of Speculative Fiction' in Arthur Lloyd Eshbach's *Of Worlds Beyond: The Science of Science Fiction Writing* (1947), and was often open as to his influences in interviews and in letters. This is reflected in the difficulty of describing Heinlein's work as a single body. Many of his short stories show what we now think of as the slingshot ending of the classic SF short story, but one of his very best stories, '"All You Zombies—"' does not. Several of his novels, from *Stranger in a Strange Land* onwards through *The Number of the Beast*, are constructed as epics; others are political thrillers such as *Between Planets, Double Star, Puppet Masters*. He uses the juvenile adventure, the bildungsroman, the romance and the picaresque.

Yet one of the problems in Heinlein studies is the strength of the overarching narratives that have formed around his writings. You can see these narratives at work in the entry on Heinlein in *The Encyclopaedia of Science Fiction*. There is a tendency to dismiss Heinlein's literary skills; to dismiss Heinlein's characters as examples of

---

2   An area which has been relatively neglected until recently: see the work of Susan Mandala and Istvan Csiscery-Ronay Jr.

the 'competent man'; to assume that dogmatic characters are *ipso facto* the authorial voice; and there is an often presumptive division of novels into major and minor, reliant on immediate reception and nostalgia. This tendency has emerged both from fan and academic response.

The fan response is complicated because Heinlein in some ways served (less so today) as a man for all seasons: most people of most political persuasions had at least one text they enthused over, one they hated and several they had never read. Relatively few fans had read the entire body of work. So when there are discussions of Heinlein's work online they rapidly become heated and as new fans are less familiar with his work, arguments in the comments threads can become astonishingly second-hand.[3] At the same time it is often fans who have undertaken the very detailed dissection of Heinlein's work, as at the Heinlein archive (https://www.heinleinarchives.net/), and in James Gifford's *Robert A. Heinlein: A Reader's Companion* (2000).

Academic approaches to Heinlein have often been rather simplistic, and as I refreshed my reading I found myself having some sympathy for Heinlein's complaints: Heinlein's attitudes to sexuality have been most to the fore here – his relative willingness to even envisage sex, compared to the writings of most pre-New Wave writers (Sturgeon may be the exception), made him an open target, and it is very noticeable that Alexei Panshin, who describes him as naive (*Heinlein in Dimension,* 1968) and George Slusser (*The Classic Years of Robert A. Heinlein,* 1977) who categorises him as a Calvinist (for both the depictions of sex and for his tendency to laud educated elites, and education as a route to salvation) rarely consider the context in which he is writing. H. Bruce Franklin, like Panshin and Slusser,

---

3   Contrary David Brin, 'Looking Back at Heinlein's Future History – Coming True before Our Eyes', 18 March 2017, https://medium.com/@david.brin/heinleins-future-history-coming-true-before-our-eyes-10356a95556a

focuses on sex and sexuality and assumes that sexual performativity and representation can be divided into adult or juvenile, acceptable or sexist. Neither they nor Warren Rochelle ('Dual Attractions', 1999) nor Chris West ('Queer Fears and Critical Orthodoxies', 2002) (who focuses on homosexuality) ground their critiques in the periods in which Heinlein was writing, the editors he was writing for, or the librarians who could decide whether books did or did not make it onto the shelves in a period in which libraries were only just starting to retreat from the position of major purchasers. Oddly, Leon Stover, in *Robert A. Heinlein*, one of the best close readers in other ways, comes away with the idea that Heinlein 'defends the traditional ethics of Christian civilisation' (p. 61) which is a hard argument to make given the amount of out-of-wedlock sex in his work and the satirisation of so much Christian practice in *Stranger in a Strange Land* and *Job*.

Often the reading is just sloppy. Slusser makes several mistakes – Maggie in 'Coventry' is not 'pure'; Jubal Harshaw in *Stranger in a Strange Land* does *not* sleep with his secretaries (it is made explicit in Chapter 10, and in Chapter 30 we are even told that people make this mistake); there is no hyperfertility in *I Will Fear No Evil*, and the twins Laz and Lor are not test-tube babies with 'no biological contact with women at all': if anything, they are many-mothered.

The best of the historicist criticism comes from H. Bruce Franklin. His classically Marxist approach positions Heinlein along a trajectory which includes many white male Democrats who found themselves at sea in the 1970s party. For all Heinlein's commitment to equality, his futures deliberately erased such political identities in search of this equality. Leon Stover was the first to be able to consider Heinlein's entire oeuvre and to chart properly and conclusively the same outline Franklin proposed in 1980. It is a tribute to Franklin's acuity that Stover, while far more sympathetic to Heinlein's politics, comes to very similar conclusions. As I will also argue in this book, Stover also concludes that Heinlein was far from being the stark individualist that Panshin and Slusser and (to a degree) Franklin paint.

Heinlein did not write in a vacuum and we are lucky enough to know from his commentaries, letters, friendships and from the fiction texts themselves who his key influences were (they are scattered in mentions across the fiction and summarised in *To Sail Beyond the Sunset* in Maureen's youthful reading). These were the satirical fiction writers Jonathan Swift, Mark Twain, Upton Sinclair, Rudyard Kipling and James Branch Cabell, along with political activists and theorists Thomas Jefferson, Thomas Paine, Patrick Henry and the developer of General Semantics, Alfred Korzybski. The fiction writers crop up over and over again and I will discuss them where relevant: we need to remember them because there was a chasm between what Heinlein thought he was doing – writing satire – and the ways in which his works were often received by readers. Whether readers loved or loathed a book, whether reading for pleasure or for criticism, there has been a repeated tendency to take the strongest character voice in a Heinlein novel as an authorial voice, as in *Stranger in a Strange Land* (1961), or in *Time Enough for Love* (1973); or to read a political system as either flawless and to be taken as a political rallying cry for libertarianism, as in *The Moon is a Harsh Mistress* (1966), or as a rallying cry for white supremacy, as in *Farnham's Freehold* (1964). Neither extreme is true.

Heinlein lacked both the technique of the writers he admired, and to a very large extent their political subtlety. His attempts at satire often don't work or backfire, in part because his authorial voice is the same *writer from conviction* that we see in the juvenile novels. Heinlein's earnestness is an asset when he is being earnest, a hindrance when he is attempting something more acerbic. This is connected to the politicians he admired: Jefferson, Paine and Henry, all of whom, although in many ways having very little in common, were men with very clear visions. It is noticeable that the great compromiser Benjamin Franklin never once crops up as either a reference or a character name.

Peter Nicholls perhaps best summed up Heinlein's work, describing him as 'not a conventional conservative', 'consistently iconoclastic about our most hallowed institutions'. This has been my experience. When I returned to Heinlein's work I tried very hard to read the texts with fresh eyes, choosing to read them in order, and without initial reference to critical works. Returning to my own early criticism it is noticeable how harsh I was. Crucially I replicated many of the criticisms I am lodging here, in particular projecting my own values. In addition I was like others swayed by the tendency to focus on only certain novels without considering how they fitted together, and, one of the key influences on this book, how they spoke to each other. This is what will distinguish this book from perhaps the best critical study on Heinlein so far. Thomas Clareson and Joe Sanders' *The Heritage of Heinlein* is a careful, text-by-text discussion which begins at the beginning and ends at the end. It is weak on the short stories but is probably the best guide to his novels, even where I disagree with its tendency to dismiss Heinlein's polemical work. Its strength is the willingness to understand Heinlein as an experimental writer (if not always a successful experimenter) and I hope to build on this argument. Its weakness is precisely that each text is approached in turn, resulting in a false sense of linear progression, rather than an ongoing and tangled exploration of a set of ideas and themes.

Heinlein's influence has been twofold: he has been influential in the political sphere and in the development of science fiction. In politics he had little formal influence despite appearances before Senate committees on ageing and on space defence, but his informal influence is far more extensive; socially on the left, economically on the right. On the left, as is often noted, *Stranger in a Strange Land* became one of the bibles of the counterculture. His sexual radicalism is often cited by SF fans who identify as polyamorous; his female characters are often cited by older female fans for being easily the best on offer for that time,[4] and his use of non-white characters and non-Christian characters stands out in a sea of 1950s whiteness and default Christianity. But equally, all of these areas have provoked reaction: not all readers feel the sexual radicalism is without prejudice, with issues arising around heteronormativity, homophobia and male-centred sexuality; the characters of colour are too often erased, lacking any culture that might indicate another ethnic identity. Moreover, Heinlein's failure to comprehend institutionalised discrimination and the relationship of economic practice to discrimination has become an ever greater issue, rendering even his juvenile novels increasingly naive and perhaps irrelevant.

On the right, Heinlein's most influential works are a single line from late in *Beyond This Horizon* ('an armed society is a polite society') and the novel *The Moon is a Harsh Mistress* with its anarcho-syndicalist, or libertarian society in captivity. Perhaps also influential is the philosophy of Lazarus Long, which forms the interludes in *Time Enough for Love*. The 'notebooks' are a series of epigrams, which crop up regularly in conversation with Heinlein fans. At the time of writing there are two clear 'wings' in science fiction, a group who see themselves as traditionalists, self-named the Sad Puppies, and a group that the Sad Puppies have termed social justice warriors, which some have embraced ironically. Writers on

4   Male critics, in contrast, often rush to tell women that Heinlein is sexist. For example: Slusser on Anne, Dorcas and Miriam in *Stranger in a Strange Land*: 'In spite of this they remain the same faceless automata, varieties of sexual experience rather than persons' (*Robert A. Heinlein*, 1977a p. 27); Franklin on Podkayne: 'Throughout the book, Poddy is inept at everything except taking care of babies and some social relations' (*Robert A. Heinlein*, 1980 p. 142). She learns astrogation and is rather good at it.

both sides cite the influence of Heinlein. But it is often a different Heinlein (and a different set of texts) to whom they are referring. This is possible because Heinlein's attitudes to 'a life well lived', which crop up throughout his work from the juvenile novels onwards – and make clear statements about what honour and bravery are, what one owes to one's society, and what one owes other people – are more generically influential than his political statements.

Heinlein's political influence melds with his structural influence on the field. As far as technique is concerned, once SF writers learned to embrace the future the most adventurous of them ran in other directions: even if the New Wave owes something to Heinlein's sexual radicalism it owes nothing to his technique, although stories such as Ted Chiang's 'Story of Your Life' (1998) (now filmed as *Arrival*) clearly take something from the time-travel structures Heinlein developed. If anything the New Wave was in search of an alternative to the 'good stories, well told' approach to literature that Heinlein preferred. Similarly much of his political influence is in the reaction to his work: Joe Haldeman's *The Forever War* is an acknowledged riposte to *Starship Troopers* as is John Varley's *Steel Beach* and perhaps Samuel R. Delany's *The Towers of Toron* (see David Higgins, 'Psychic Decolonization in 1960s SF'), while Haldeman's *All My Sins Remembered* is in part a response to *Double Star*. Ken MacLeod's *Fall Revolution* sequence is clearly influenced by *The Moon is a Harsh Mistress*, not only in its series of revolutions but in its insistence on a polysemy Heinlein avoids. Authors such as Greg Benford, C. J. Cherryh and Charles Stross all acknowledge his influence in terms of the futures they created. Perhaps the most successful 'Heinleinian' writer is Lois McMaster Bujold as demonstrated in her Vorkosigan series; from the construction of her galaxy, the absence of aliens, to a badly damaged hero, a fascination with both diplomacy and engineering, a conviction that family is the most valuable thing in the world and a fascination with reproduction and gender performativity, Heinlein's legacy is evident.

No book on Heinlein can do justice to all of his work. His publishing career ran from 1939 to 1987; he wrote few sequels and although there is some repetition of form there is relatively little subgenre consistency outside Heinlein's construction of his Future History and later his alternatives to that history. This book tries to deal with that by taking a very loosely thematic approach. Chapter 1 begins with a potted biography, heavily indebted to Bill Patterson's two-volume epic, which tries to situate Heinlein's work in his own life. In Chapter 2 I offer an overview which looks at the genres and movements in Heinlein's work, reinforcing some narratives and arguing for other stories we can tell about his work. Chapter 3 is concerned with technique, arguing that in dismissing Heinlein as a solid writer, we often miss what it was he tried to achieve in each work. This is extended in Chapter 4 with a discussion of Heinlein's rhetoric, how he is such a *convincing* writer with whom the reader nods right along up until the moment when they do not. Chapters 5, 6, 7 and 8 are more conventionally thematic, but consider the issues of gender, race and sexuality within a wider argument about Heinlein's concern with what I have called the right ordering of self and society. The book concludes with a short epilogue on one of the things Heinlein cared most about.

1

Biography

All studies of individual authors need a sense of where they came from. However, the general outline of Robert A. Heinlein's career is well known, and for those interested in the details of his life there is the two-volume biography by William H. Patterson Jr. (*Robert A. Heinlein In Dialogue with his Century*). This opening chapter therefore offers a relatively short summary of Heinlein's life, drawn almost entirely from Patterson's biography, striving to highlight key events and themes in Heinlein's life.

Robert Anson Heinlein was born 7 July 1907 in Butler, Missouri, and died 8 May 1988. He was the third child (and third son) of a family of seven. His family were members of the Methodist Episcopal Church, which appeared to have little impact on Robert Heinlein's ability to believe in God, but a profound and long-lasting effect on his deep-down belief in justice and in sexual and racial equality. His parents moved to Cleveland and then to Kansas City, where they were involved in the Democratic political machine. They lived on the edge of the white district, and Heinlein's two closest friends were Jewish boys; they later turn up in *Rocketship Galileo* (1947).

One needs to be cautious about suggesting, as Bill Patterson does, that Heinlein lived in a multicultural environment, for this was a period in which segregation was fierce, but he grew up aware that the world was neither monochrome nor religiously homogenous.

As a boy in a large and not prosperous middle-class family he was inculcated into the classic American-child work culture of the period – unhindered by child labour laws – and spent much of his teen years hustling as a newspaper delivery boy, a vacuum cleaner (he and a friend hired a machine and rented out their services), and whatever else was available. This sense that people should be able to turn a hand to whatever they could to earn a living crops up in much of his work.

Heinlein seems to have been studious, but interested in the knowledge, not necessarily the grades; he inherited or was acculturated to a love of reading from his family and demonstrated the kind of mind that explored any area of interest that crossed his path, whether stage magic, woodwork or chemical engineering. His interests, spurred by the popular-science magazines, drifted towards astronomy, but there was no money for college and this was before the scholarship industry was in place. His family wanted Robert to go into medicine – a classic route into the more settled middle classes – but Robert was not attracted to medicine at this time, although later it becomes clear that medical advances fascinated him, and are often the key to his fictions: *Methuselah's Children* (1941) and *I Will Fear No Evil* (1970) to give just two examples.

However, the family had an association with military service – Heinlein more than once stated that his family had served in every war since the Spanish American War – and Heinlein's older (second) brother Rex Ivar was at Annapolis Naval Academy, where a degree-level education could be received. This was a period, however, when gaining such places rested on influence, not ability – Ivar's place had been secured by a family friend – and by distributed patronage held by congressmen who each took turns to make appointments. Without that patronage a place at Annapolis was impossible.

Heinlein's actions to secure a place are often seen as evidence of his determination, and that is undisputable, but it is also the first sense we get of Heinlein as a consummate political campaigner. We don't know if he was active in the party machine with his parents, but it is very clear that he had watched and learned, for he spent almost two years writing letters to congressmen, explored loopholes in the process and eventually applied for and secured a place in the Civilian Military Training Camp at Fort Leavensworth, Kansas, which was a way to secure the recommendation letters he needed. When a place came up, Heinlein tapped fifty people he had previously written to or worked with for recommendation letters.

Heinlein's drive, admirable though it was, would alienate those who resented his self-containment; others, however, would regard him as supportive and loyal. His school ROTC (Reserve Officers' Training Corps) colleagues disliked his leadership, and made complaints. His classmates saw him as a 'grind'. One of his female classmates on the other hand remembered him as 'the sweetest boy in the class' (Patterson, vol. 1, p. 44).

Heinlein was part of the class of '29 at Annapolis, one of 409 boys to enter and 243 to graduate. Patterson gives a very detailed account of Heinlein's time at the college. Heinlein seems to have shown the same virtues and faults as he had in the ROTC, a dogged persistence and determination that failed to inspire others and frequently left them feeling rather used. His drive alienated other men because they knew it was essentially self-centred.

Heinlein also learned self-study, that being the mode of teaching at the academy in his day[1] – reported faithfully in the accounts in

---

1   Education continually reinvents itself: see an article on self-study at MIT in 2017 in *Times Higher Education*, 23 March 2017.

both *Space Cadet* (1948) and *Starship Troopers* (1959) – and the art
of dealing with the trick-question modes of hazing, detailed in 'The
Man Who Was Too Lazy to Fail'. This latter is one of the scheherazade
tales in *Time Enough for Love* (1973), and almost certainly based on
Heinlein's classmate Delos Wait, the captain of the fencing team
(see Patterson, vol. 1, p. 101). Heinlein's tendency to introversion was
reflected in his choice of fencing as his academy sport: it allowed him
to succeed on his own drive and merit without worrying too much
whether his team mates would follow him or like him. It would later
give him material for Oscar in *Glory Road* (1963).

Heinlein made friends enough that his reading was influenced
by them. Barrett 'Cal' Laning gave him James Branch Cabell's
Jurgen: A Comedy of Justice (1919), traces of which can be seen in
some of Heinlein's earliest stories and also in almost all of his later
novels. Heinlein served his cruise tours, became engaged with his
engineering and aviation work but failed the depth perception test
for flying, to his everlasting regret (and he was to have problems with
his eyesight from 1928 onwards). But he stayed with the course, and
graduated twentieth in his class.

Through most of his time at Annapolis, Heinlein was broke
and had to scrounge for money. He was dependent on friends for
loans and on his eldest brother Larry for support. It is worth being
aware of this because although Heinlein's rhetoric is often fiercely
individualistic, one thing that this book will be arguing throughout
is that this is an individualism tempered by an understanding of how
networked communities function, and of John Donne's argument
that no man is an island – everyone's success is built on the support
and compassion of others. It is probably what lay behind Heinlein's
own legendary personal generosity to writers in need and his
philosophy, expressed in both life and in his books, of *pass it forward*.
Loans from strangers to strangers crop up in a number of books and

are key to the plot in *The Door Into Summer* (1957) and to the story in *Job* (1984).

Staying in the navy was not required of an Annapolis graduate. Several of Heinlein's friends left of their own accord, and Heinlein appears to have flirted with this to the extent of applying for the first Rhodes scholarship for which the Academy was to be eligible. Patterson thinks this would have allowed Heinlein to pursue his interest in astronomy, but in the meantime he pursued his interest in sex, with an encounter with a Mary Briggs on his way home to Kansas City that seems to have had a major impact on the understanding of sex as *healthy play* that emerges very early in Heinlein's work. Unfortunately it also revived his interest in access to sex. Returning home reintroduced him to his high-school girlfriend Elinor Curry. We would normally assume that they married because in 1929 a respectable boy and a respectable girl could only have sex if they were married, but the motive for the marriage seems in part to have been to give Elinor cover for her other affairs. It is notable mostly because, for all the marriage failed, it does not seem to have soured Heinlein on the idea of flexible and open marriages.

The marriage lasted only a year, but as a married man Heinlein was no longer eligible for the Rhodes scholarship. Instead, ruled out for flight training because of his poor depth perception, he ended up in the administrative office of the USS *Lexington*. He stayed there initially for less than a year and was then despatched to Long Island City to attend the Ford Instrument Company school and learn how to operate electromechanical computers. He then spent seven weeks in New York (Elinor refused to join him) and appears to have had a very good time in the more bohemian hangouts of Greenwich Village but had to leave and return to his ship. There he would find the new captain was an Ernest J. King, a man who was hugely influential on Heinlein and clearly the model for a number of characters in his military and scouting stories. King was stern, by the book, noted for being just and with 'an ironclad sense of duty' (Patterson, vol. 1, p. 129). Speculation is always problematic but it may have been the experience of working for King that reshaped Heinlein's self-aggrandising need to excel into something wider and more all-encompassing.

What comes over clearest in Patterson's biography is that Heinlein's time on the *Lexington* was a period of continual learning: training courses were supplemented by tasks – sketching engineering systems – and tests. Some stand-out moments or issues for his future career include Heinlein's assignment to the assistant editorship of the ship's newspaper, *The Observer*; his role as an on-ship Defender for those accused of infractions of military discipline (apparently he had a reputation for winning); and his brush with some kind of medical issue. At some point in March 1931 he was diagnosed with 'nonspecific urethritis' (Patterson, v1: 137). This reappeared in the autumn and was diagnosed as Myxococcus catarrhalis. Patterson insists that this was not a venereal disease, but this was 1931. The diagnosis of 'nonspecific urethritis' only means 'not gonorrhoea' but this leaves several other possible causes, including herpes and chlamydia. The spread of venereal disease among troops was of high concern to the military authorities and at various times led to a crackdown on port prostitutes. It could also lead to officers being disciplined or discharged from the service. Given that nonspecific urethritis was to be a recurring issue for Heinlein, along with problems with his rectum, kidneys and other areas, and his apparent infertility, it may be that someone was covering up.

In the *Lexington* Heinlein sailed by Seattle, San Francisco, Ecuador and Peru and was sent to Panama City to compete in a pistol competition. Late in 1932, he took part in the war games in Hawaii – what has become known as the Fleet Problem XIII – the results of which should have but did not change the defensive tactics at Pearl Harbor.

During 1932 Heinlein met up with his friend Cal Laning, and pinched Cal's girlfriend, Leslyn MacDonald (always referred to by her own name), actor, writer, philosopher, then working as Assistant Director of the Music Department at Columbia Pictures with a sideline as a story doctor. Unusually for the period she had a Masters degree. She was also a liberal and a Republican (the two parties were only then in the process of swapping their positions on the liberal-conservative axis). They slept together – Patterson thinks Laning may have wanted Heinlein's opinion on the woman he was about to propose to (Patterson, vol. 1, p. 146) – and Heinlein offered marriage immediately. Leslyn accepted, gave up her job and followed Heinlein back to Washington for the layover while the ship was refitted. Leslyn, and Heinlein's feelings of failure around this marriage, would prove central to the story told in *Farnham's Freehold* (1964).[2]

During this time Heinlein was reading science fiction (he was particularly fond of the work of E. E. 'Doc' Smith whom he would grow to admire in person), and was probably introduced to modern philosophy and theosophy by Leslyn, whose mother was a practising theosophist. He also took and passed his examination for promotion to lieutenant, received his promotion and was transferred to the destroyer *Roper*. He and Leslyn moved to a new home in the port of San Diego but this was to be the end of his naval career. By the end of 1932 it was clear Heinlein was very ill, losing weight rapidly and suffering night sweats. He had tuberculosis. Heinlein was lucky: this

---

2 See Robert James, 'Regarding Leslyn', 2001 for a consideration of Leslyn's role. We differ in our interpretation. In new transcripts of the Denvention speech James notes that Heinlein said, 'I wanted to make a little aside to the effect that Mrs Heinlein and I are in almost complete collaboration on everything. She never signs any of the stories, but I do better if she's there.' James writes: 'What this reveals, in my opinion, are Heinlein's constant efforts to make Leslyn feel wanted and included in this new career' (p. 22). I think it reveals an editorial role, and the shift in style away from the cinematic, discussed in Chapter 1, is correlative evidence.

was still the period of sanatoria, bed rest and lung inflation/artificial pneumothorax. His brother Ivar also had TB and recounted to him the incident he turned into the story 'No Bands Playing, No Flags Flying' (1947, published 1974). Heinlein had six months' sick leave, towards the end of which he was well enough that he and Leslyn explored a nudist club, something he would continue doing, first with then without Virginia (Ginny) Heinlein, in later life. Then he returned to the navy, where he was assigned as a patient to the Naval Hospital in Denver. But the treatment there was casual; continued urinary tract infections went untreated and he became ill again. He discharged himself and found a new doctor who operated on him for cysts. This resolved the immediate problem but by March 1934 it was clear his naval career was over. He reported for an examination for retirement and the process was duly completed. Heinlein was now a civilian, in the middle of the Great Depression.

Once out of the navy Heinlein had to find something else to do. He investigated silver mining but his backer turned out to be Johnny Lazzia of the Chicago mob, and when he was gunned down the backing dried up. But Heinlein's pension amounted to two-thirds of his full service pay – not a huge amount and one that would diminish with inflation, though it always ensured a small level of independence. It gave him time to look around. He and Leslyn returned to West Hollywood with the intention that he would enrol for a Masters degree. The snag was that his class at Annapolis was one of the last to graduate without a Bachelors degree so his choice was limited. What Heinlein did instead was audit classes in the physics and maths department at the University of California at Los Angeles (UCLA). This would stand him in good stead for his writing but did not in the end lead to a place. Instead, Heinlein became entranced with politics.

Heinlein in the 1930s was possibly a socialist and definitely a liberal. However he was an *American* socialist – bred on *Looking Backwards* and the Bellamy Club tradition rather than the new Marxism that was entering America along with new immigrant groups. Like many from the small-business class, Marxism's doctrine of class warfare felt alien to Heinlein. Upton Sinclair, to whose platform Heinlein was to tie his colours, thought communism 'the sabotage of civilisation by the disappointed'.[3] Sinclair was more closely aligned to co-operatism which can be understood as a collective business ethic: the EPIC (End Poverty in California) programme he espoused involved buying up repossessed businesses and farms and rebooting them with state hired labour. Realistically, the only difference between this and communism is the decision to take advantage of failing capitalism rather than to destroy it directly with repossessions. Private business recognised this, and by the time Heinlein wrote 'The Devil Makes the Law' in 1940, he may have recognised it too. But Sinclair's proposals were among the few proactive moves on the table and Heinlein supported him in the California primary for the Democratic nomination for governor. It is here that Heinlein got his major experience in formal politics and ended up on the West Hollywood Democratic Club's board of directors.

The experience of Sinclair's failed gubernatorial campaign, its aftermath and his move towards a Presidential run, left a number of legacies. First, it taught Heinlein how to organise a campaign; second, it taught him the limits of grassroots democracy when faced with party machines, the press and the apathy of much of the American electorate (something he would have done well to remember during his later 'Patrick Henry' campaign; see his *How to Be a Politician*). Finally, it seems to have been the beginning of Heinlein's intense dislike for communism.

---

3   Actually a quotation from H. G. Wells, *The World of William Clissold*, 1926: Chapter 9.

Heinlein saw communism and communists as a fifth column within American socialism. Their danger was not as opposition: in *How to Be a Politician* he notes that communists act as an early warning system, warning the nation of injustices that need rectifying.[4] 'Any real local success on their part is a sure sign that some group of Americans are in such dire straits as to need emergency help – not punitive action!' (p. 207) and 'we are more prone to ignore the sick spots thus disclosed and content ourselves with calling out more cops.' Their danger was as allies, for they hollowed out the Americanness of a movement. Sinclair would eventually distance himself from EPIC because he felt it had been co-opted by communists. Heinlein's experience of the Communist Popular Front and its collapse in 1939 almost certainly reinforced this belief but he himself stayed with EPIC into the 1938 elections.

Heinlein came to believe that the Democratic party itself was thoroughly infested by communists (quite how many members he thought they had is unclear). His feelings were intense:

> I regard communism as expressed by the U.S.S.R. and its friends here and elsewhere as a grisly horror, a tyranny maintained by force and terror, utterly subversive of human liberty, freedom of thought and dignity. I regard it as Red Fascism. (Letter to Robert Bloch, 03/18/49; Patterson, v1: 198)

However, this letter is from 1949, at the height of the Cold War and Stalin's regime. It is not clear that he was as vitriolic in 1938.

4   The edition used is the retitled *Take Back Your Government*, with an introduction by William H. Patterson Jr. 2012. I have chosen to use the original title throughout, because the new title – chosen, as the introduction discusses, by Virginia Heinlein and Jerry Pournelle – carries with it a weight of political ideologies and attitudes that it is unclear Heinlein would have supported.

Heinlein's involvement with EPIC led him into a brief engagement with the Works Progress Administration (WPA), the results of which can be seen in the early scenes of 'Misfit' (1939). It also took him far enough into Democrat politics that he was asked to be a candidate for the 59th Assembly District seat in the California State Assembly in 1938. This was a Republican seat but was on EPIC's target list. Heinlein lost, of course, and that was the end of his life in active politics.

During 1938, Heinlein started casting around for work and, cushioned by that military pension, decided to try fiction. His first attempt, *For Us, the Living*, was an Edward Bellamyesque utopia, loosely plotted and heavy on the lectures, which never reached the public during his lifetime. However, for the rest of his life he would mine this unpublished manuscript for ideas, so that we can see the working and reworking of the thoughts of the young Heinlein using the skill and critical eye (and sometimes mature cynicism) of the older Heinlein. While it did the rounds of publishers Heinlein embarked on his first venture into the pulp magazines.

The standard account of this period is that Heinlein saw a competition in *Thrilling Wonder Stories* and realised that the prize did not match the going rate, and decided instead to target the market. But Patterson notes that Heinlein had already read Jack Woodford's *Trial and Error: A Key to the Art of Writing and Selling* (1937), and his background in business, his habit of meticulously researching everything with which he became engaged and his general business-like approach to writing were there from the very beginning. It is probable that the magazine market was always his aim. This impression is reinforced by Patterson's observation that Heinlein already had a raft of incidents from his navy years noted down as possible plots.

Heinlein submitted his first story 'Life-Line' in April 1939. As a professional writer in training, his intention was to target the slicks (glossy magazines). Stories were sent first to Colliers, then to the science fiction magazines. However, as Patterson and many others have noted, Heinlein quickly established a firm relationship with John W. Campbell, the interventionist editor of *Astounding*, who was determined to create a stable of authors who could produce the fiction he wanted to buy.

Up to 1942 (when there was a war-created hiatus), Heinlein published twenty-seven stories and two serialised novels (*Methuselah's Children*, 1941, and *Beyond This Horizon*, 1942). During this time he spent the late part of 1939 in California in one last outing as a (paid) political campaigner, fighting to persuade Californians to vote for an oil conservation initiative. The failure of that initiative may explain the corporatist, technocratic approach of 'The Roads Must Roll' which contains a fairly accurate prediction of the state of California roads in the Age of the Car. It certainly did nothing for Heinlein's faith in 'the masses', however liberal his ideals were to remain (as late as 1939 he denounces technocracy in a letter to Robert A. W. Lowndes: Patterson, vol. 1, p. 257), and in that sense, this small distraction may be a crucial element in explaining the tension in Heinlein's work that argues, increasingly as the years go on, for an elitist process and radical outcome.

The other events that shaped Heinlein were the salons he and Leslyn began which eventually transformed into writers' groups. Heinlein was and remained in many ways an essentially private person, and one who seems to have distinguished carefully between acquaintances and *friends* (both Bruce Yerke and Forrest J. Ackerman were to discover that friends were expected to honour the Heinleins' privacy and loyalty), but as in the navy he learned to perform as a public person. One way in which he would do so was in gatherings at home, and later at parties at conventions, and eventually in the community he and his third wife Ginny would create at Bonny Doon.

This first set of gatherings was notable for the presence of Jack Williamson, Henry Kuttner, C. L. Moore and a nineteen-year-old Ray Bradbury.

In May 1939 Heinlein and Leslyn travelled to New York where he met John W. Campbell, Willy Ley, Fletcher Pratt, L. Sprague de Camp and L. Ron Hubbard. After that he travelled to Chicago for Korzybski's General Semantics Convention (Kate Gladstone, in 'Words, Words, Words', 2002, thinks their route to the conference was via Stuart Chase, *A Tyranny of Words*, 1938), and in July he attended the Democratic Convention as a press officer. Here he found himself disturbed by Roosevelt's hints of conscription and involvement in a European war. In words he later put into the mouth of Lazarus Long in the final sections of *Time Enough for Love*, Heinlein understood the draft as a *semi-totalitarian condition*. Even in the heat of war Heinlein would feel the same way. For him the health of a nation lay precisely in its ability to inspire people to volunteer, even as he castigated those who declined, a principle reflected in the social structure of *Starship Troopers*.

In August 1939 Heinlein and Leslyn met E. E. 'Doc' and Jeanne Smith, and Heinlein established what was to be a lifelong friendship with Smith. In a field in which his peers were significantly younger than him, and as a person who conspicuously advocated vertical mentorship in his work, Heinlein may have particularly welcomed the friendship of an older colleague and mentor. Later in the year the Heinleins committed to be potential foster parents for the Campbells' baby in the event of any serious incident. Heinlein was already showing signs of building the fictive family that he would later create in real life and on the page. At the same time there were the first hints that this might be all the family he would have: Leslyn had not conceived and Heinlein thought it might be due to his TB (a distinct possibility as it can cause scarring of the reproductive organs). A high note of the year was meeting H. G. Wells at a signing at a Pasadena bookshop.

In 1941 Heinlein was Guest of Honour at Denvention, the 1941 World Science Fiction Convention, held in Denver. This was not the huge event it is today: with only ninety members, Heinlein thrived at what was effectively a family reunion. Between covering the cost of an award that had failed to materialise, behaving like a civilised human being to the black bellman (as Ackerman noted, not the norm in 1941) and taking part in the masquerade, Heinlein made an impression. This was only the third World Convention to have been held and there was still room to lay down custom and practice for guests of honour. In the event that would have to wait. On 7 December 1941 the Japanese attacked Pearl Harbor.

Some events are such strong breaches in the narrative that they are impossible to avoid in any biography, and Pearl Harbor is one of those for all Americans alive in 1941. For Heinlein there was a strong personal connection. The *Oklahoma*, on which Heinlein made his 1927 practice cruise, was sunk, with more than four hundred men killed. Leslyn's brother-in-law, nephews and sister were on the Philippine island of Luzon. Her brother-in-law would eventually be executed there. Heinlein reported for active duty and waited. In the event, no immediate assignment was forthcoming. One of the consequences of the Annapolis system, in which students graduated and then left immediately or after one or two years, was that there were plenty of reserve officers, most in better health than Heinlein. Eventually he was recruited to civilian service through a friend, Buddy Scoles, a lieutenant commander in charge of the Aeronautical Materials Laboratory in Philadelphia, but despite much agitation Heinlein could never get his retired status revoked, possibly because of his health, possibly because he remained on a blacklist on the basis of an ill-advised newspaper letter written in the 1930s. After a number of hitches Heinlein moved to Philadelphia. While at the Laboratory, Heinlein supervised the cold and pressure chambers for high-altitude projects and became involved in overturning the block on taking women into the engineering school at the University of Delaware. Eventually he ended up at the NAES Materials Laboratory, Plastics and Adhesives. However, Heinlein hated Philadelphia, and complained about backache and kidney problems the entire time he was there. It is one of the confusions in the Heinlein record that when asked directly he understood himself as intensely healthy, but that the actual record says quite otherwise.

Leslyn, meanwhile, had signed up as a factory mechanic: she was regularly promoted and ended up managing several machine shops. But she was constantly anxious about her sister and family. Her sister and the boys were finally rescued in 1944 but by this time Heinlein was seriously ill and having rectal surgery, and there were growing signs that Leslyn was not coping. Her weight was fluctuating (mostly downwards) and she was sleeping ten to twelve hours a day. Patterson argues that Heinlein's turn to Campbell as his writing partner excluded Leslyn, but so too did the war years during which much of his writing was on hiatus. Certainly if we use the account of Grace in *Farnham's Freehold* as a guide – arguments for which I will return to in another chapter – Leslyn was someone for whom boredom was near-fatal. The marriage was still an open one. Patterson – who was writing while Ginny was still alive – tends to be rather coy on these matters, but he thinks Leslyn was active, while Heinlein, who was in very poor physical shape, was not. It was in this atmosphere of overwork, stress, and the loss of the thing that had held them together (Heinlein's writing), that Lieutenant Virginia Gerstenfeld came on the scene.

Heinlein quickly became friends with Lieutenant Gerstenfeld. Gerstenfeld was a chemist, she had the desk behind Heinlein, she had lost her brother in submarine warfare and had herself volunteered the moment the WAVES (Women Accepted for Volunteer Emergency Service) were set up. When Heinlein was asked to take on a new project he took Ginny with him as his most dependable engineer. Her politics were much more conservative than Heinlein's (she hated the Soviet Union) and when she read *Beyond This Horizon* she repudiated his ideas on Social Credit. Her influence was to show up in the books Heinlein wrote in the 1980s but it is not until *The Cat Who Walks Through Walls* in 1985 that I would argue Heinlein becomes wholly convinced by her economic arguments. In terms of her attitude to life however, Gerstenfeld shared at least some aspects of Heinlein's social radicalism. Virginia Gerstenfeld was, in retrospect, the wrong person to show up at a time when Heinlein's home life was becoming difficult. Or the right one.

At home Leslyn was beginning to fall apart. Her mother had died of 'food fads' (possibly anorexia) and the news of her brother-in-law's brutal execution came through. She was sleeping too much and exhibiting rapid mood swings. There was no money, and Heinlein was increasingly unhappy to find himself enmeshed in naval bureaucracy when he was asked to pass shoddy goods at the Naval Air Factory (Ginny had approached him for back-up). He ended up so angry that he had to seek medical sedatives. It's worth noting that his own good experience with medical sedatives is reflected in his rather casual use of them in his fiction.

Heinlein too had losses to deal with. Around two-thirds of his naval class of '29 were dead. On the writing front little was happening. Reprint sales became caught up in arguments with the magazine publisher, Street & Smith, and, by extension, Campbell. Heinlein began to plan a move back to California and before he went, said goodbye to Ginny.

Meanwhile America dropped the atomic bombs on Hiroshima and Nagasaki, and Heinlein, like most science-fiction fans, was caught up in the wonder of it all. It is interesting to summarise the three positions he considered 'dunderheaded' however, for it is a reminder that whatever Heinlein was, he was neither 'America First' nor a militarist.

1. 'We got it. We'll hang on to it. From now on they got to do what we tell them to.'
2. The second crazy viewpoint regards the atomic bomb as just another weapon, powerful but bound to be subject in time to an effective counter-weapon . . .
3. There is a third reaction, one of deploring the whole thing, of passing resolutions expressing that we ever used so barbarous a weapon, apologising to the poor mistreated Japs, and calling on Congress to do away with the whole thing . . . forever proscribed as forbidden knowledge. (RAH to John Arwine, 09/15/45; Patterson, vol. 1, p. 359)

In terms of the debate that was to take place over the next twenty years, it might be best to regard Heinlein as 'unaligned'. If he agreed with anyone, it was with the scientists who wanted to go public. He felt the only possible route forward was to be friends with Russia although 'Russia has reason to be suspicious of us. Twice since World War I the United States has invaded her for the open purpose of overthrowing the present government.' (RAH to E. E. 'Doc' Smith, 10/17/45; Patterson, vol. 1, p. 362). This comment is worth being aware of: Heinlein is often presented as anti-Soviet but there are too many such comments in his Cold War period writing, and in his memoir *Tramp Royale*, for this to hold water. What Heinlein was, was intensely hostile to American communism, expressed in his contribution to founding Americans for Democratic Action, dedicated to purging the party of communists.

Leslyn and Robert arrived back in LA in September 1945. It took them several months to displace their tenant and longer to fix up the house. Heinlein spent the waiting time writing, focusing on injecting his beliefs into the political debate. The stories and essays he wrote between 1946 and 1947 reflected this; at that stage they were presumably too polemical to find a publisher (Heinlein did not become less polemical, of course; he just earned the right to be polemical in fiction). *How to Be a Politician* did not get taken up. It may have been too cynical for the times. He also paid attention to developments in atomics, rocketry and radar, and particularly to ideas for a space station in orbit to bounce signals; he remained committed to world government and also to the sense of 'we are all in this together', writing to his representatives in 1946 to argue that America should adopt food rationing so that it could support famine-stricken states (Patterson vol. 1, p. 389).

The one new development was the offer from the publisher, Westminster, to write a juvenile novel. Heinlein hesitated: he did not have children and he did not know children. Science fiction was already fighting to distance itself from the epithet of *kids' stuff*. Fritz Lang, a family friend, persuaded him that writing for children was a chance to do something Heinlein desperately wanted to do, influence people (Patterson, vol. 1, p. 380). He considered it, began taking notes and working towards a novel which would eventually be picked up by Alice Dalgliesh at Scribner. He planned to call it *Young Atomic Engineers*, revealing a life-long tin ear for titles: almost all of his novels would be renamed, either by Ginny or by his editor. He also broke into the *Saturday Evening Post*, with 'The Green Hills of Earth' and 'Space Jockey' (both 1947). Sadly, he was to place only four stories there before the editors decided to discontinue their interest in science fiction. It casts some doubt on the popular narrative that the publication in the *Saturday Evening Post* was his breakthrough.

The real problem in Heinlein's life was Leslyn. Clearing up a long-term sinus problem (possibly caused by the poor air in Philadelphia) meant that he could now smell the alcohol on her breath. For a short while they had as a companion (one can never be sure what this means; Heinlein was always very discreet) a young woman named Vida Jameson, daughter of naval officer and science-fiction writer Malcolm Jameson who had died of cancer in 1944.[5] When she left to go back to New York both Heinleins felt that she left a hole in their lives. Into that space stepped Ginny Gerstenfeld, newly demobbed, no longer engaged and with a place at UCLA where she could bypass taking a Master's degree and, as a veteran, go straight for a Ph.D.

Ginny initially lived in a boarding house. She was a skater and when the Heinleins saw her skate they were enthralled and asked her to teach them. They became closer and when the Heinleins were away they wrote. Ginny dated the writer Cleve Cartmill (famous for writing a story, 'Deadline' (1944) which provoked a visit from the FBI, fearful he had been stealing nuclear secrets). When the Heinleins returned the friendship resumed but Vida also came back. Ginny dropped out of their lives for a while, in part due to financial worries but quite clearly also because Vida was competition and Leslyn had to some degree warned her off. By mid-1943 it was clear Leslyn's drinking problem was worse. The Heinleins vacationed, and when they wrote to Ginny, Heinlein added an intimate note. When they returned Ginny informed Robert that Leslyn was drinking heavily and thus began a period of failed interventions during which Robert and Ginny became ever closer. By the middle of June and after a

5   See https://thatsideofthefamily.wordpress.com/category/people/vida-jameson-ii/

suicide attempt by Leslyn, Heinlein had decided on a divorce and registered the separation documents. In 1948 after completing the rewrite (typed up by Ginny) of *Beyond This Horizon* (a fictionalised version of *For Us, the Living*) for Lloyd Eshbach's Fantasy Press, Heinlein purchased a trailer and began travelling with Ginny. One reason for travel was to keep their names out of the papers and avoid any link of his name with Ginny's. It would taint his work if he were to be thought of as an adulterer before the divorce was through, and it could wreck his emerging career as a juvenile writer (*Space Cadet* had just been commissioned).

They drove across Arizona and New Mexico. Heinlein's health improved – it always would in dry climates – and he began to sell again to the adult market: *Methuselah's Children* was bought by Shasta Press, and 'Gentlemen, Be Seated' sold to *Argosy*. Ginny acquired the first of a series of cats, Pixel – who would be left behind in Mississippi – and Heinlein began his period of protesting he was not a 'cat person'. The continued relationship with Ginny was not guaranteed. Many adulterous relationships *do not* continue beyond a divorce. This one was under pressure from the start because Heinlein needed to keep it secret, doubly so when offered work in Washington by an old friend of Leslyn's, and work in Hollywood with Fritz Lang (this fell through due to personal and professional differences) so he and Ginny briefly split up, and Ginny went to New York. They exchanged letters, Heinlein wrote 'Our Fair City' and a film treatment, almost got himself killed in a diving suit, and finally proposed to Ginny in a letter in August 1948. It is noteworthy that in her acceptance letter Ginny agreed to an open marriage but also framed it entirely in terms of Heinlein's behaviour. This was not the radical arrangement Heinlein had had with Leslyn.

They agreed to settle in Colorado Springs, and in September 1948 Ginny flew up to meet him. They acquired two kittens and otherwise laid low until the divorce came through, then married two days later, on 21 October 1948. After the marriage they settled in Colorado Springs which proved excellent for Heinlein's health but, as it would later turn out, not for Ginny's. Eventually altitude sickness would force them to move on, but for now it was a true settling down, perhaps for the first time. This move away from either American coast had another consequence however, in that it isolated Heinlein from active politics, and from the political radical movements that had shaped his earlier career. From the 1950s onwards, the flow of information shaping Heinlein's worldview would be more restricted. But for now, he reflected that restriction in actual construction.

Heinlein decided that if he wanted a house of the future, he needed to build it himself, so that is precisely what he set out to do in 1950. The house was hermetically sealed (which ironically may have contributed to health issues later on as sick building syndrome was unknown in 1950), and everything that could be built into the house, or built to store and roll out, was made to do so. Heinlein went for as much automation, and time and motion analysis, as he could. He also spent a lot of time fuming that many modern materials were ruled out by local building regulations. Heinlein wanted the most up-to-date and efficient house he could build for himself and Ginny. What he built looks, from the specifications, like a cross between a camper van and a space vehicle: everything is built in, sealed, portable and multi-functional.[6] However, although early Heinlein works, from *For Us, the Living* onwards, are absolutely fixated on food and the perfect meal, the food detailed is always incredibly low-maintenance, boring and terribly 1940s American – steak, rolls, butter and orange juice were the height of Heinlein's gustatory ambition. These don't

6   Cover story, *Popular Mechanics*, June 1952, Vol. 97, number 6.

need much of a kitchen.[7] Thus the kitchen is small and a bit cramped (although Ginny had a desk there that could be rolled away into an alcove, which this enthusiastic cook/writer envies); on the other hand, Ginny's bath (not pictured) was apparently heated, deep and faced a picture window (Patterson, vol. 2, p. 56).

The period up to 1953 lacked any momentous events but it did create an arc for Heinlein's career. This was the period in which he tried to break into the movies, but his experiences with scriptwriters and the option system were as unhappy as they were for many writers, and only *Destination Moon* would make it to production. Heinlein's involvement in the *Tom Corbett* television series did little for his reputation. On the other hand he thoroughly enjoyed his time on the set of *Destination Moon* and in Hollywood during 1949; it was almost ruined, however, by arguments over screen credits, all too familiar to many writers. He did do better with a CBS adaptation of 'Ordeal in Space' however (in which an agoraphobe cures himself when he rescues a kitten from a ledge).

At the same time Heinlein published a number of very effective short stories, including 'The Long Watch' (1949) which would eventually form an arc with 'Requiem' and *Space Cadet,* and also 'Delilah and the Space Rigger' (1949), the first of what we might want to think of as the 'Ginny' stories, which feature a redhead demonstrating to the men around her that she is smarter and tougher than they are.

Heinlein revised some of his work in this period. 'Gulf' was revised extensively for Shasta Press to remove or at least reduce the racism that was inherent to his storyline (see the discussion in Chapter 3). And he worked on constructing a Future History that

---

7   See Harvey Levenstein, *Revolution at the Table: The Transformation of the American Diet* (Berkeley: University of California Press, 2003) for a discussion of the dismal state of middle-class American eating in the 1930s and 1940s, pp. 60–72. Robert James says Ginny used to brag that she taught Heinlein what real food tasted like (pers. comm.).

linked his stories (and which leaned heavily on *For Us, the Living*). But the key idea at the back of Heinlein's head was a Mowgli-inspired story, set on Mars. It was to be many years before this saw fruition (as *Stranger in a Strange Land*, 1961); at this stage it was a larger story than Heinlein had the skills to handle. In the 1991 edition, which presented Heinlein's original version, Virginia Heinlein claims credit for the idea, but Heinlein's love of Kipling and Burroughs was deep, and I find her claim unconvincing.

The 1950s is, more significantly, the period of the classic Heinlein juvenile novels. Although he regularly argued with Alice Dalgliesh at Scribner over levels of violence and romance in his books this was a highly effective collaboration that secured Heinlein a new market. As the hardback books were very acceptable to schools and libraries they almost certainly helped to create the field as it was to exist in the next fifteen to twenty years. Heinlein himself was delighted to discover that his co-educational approach in most of the later titles (far more unusual then) had secured him a female fan-base.

Heinlein did not really like large, group gatherings, full of people he did not know, unless they were purposeful (Ginny was later to take him to square dances and ice-skating, social activities with design). Probably thanks to his time in the Academy Heinlein knew the rules of engagement in large groups and could perform the bonhomie that collective endeavours required. Yet, although he was to gain a reputation as a gracious host, the impression he creates as a younger man is of an expressive introvert, someone who very much preferred the company of people in ones and twos, always with strong, close friends and very much enjoying the kind of couples-socialising that was such a strong feature of American social life in the 1950s.[8] Heinlein's

---

8   See Beth Bailey, *From Front Porch to Back Seat* (Baltimore: Johns Hopkins University Press, 1989).

life with Ginny enabled him to strengthen this. His letters are full of the couples he and Ginny met and socialised with, and through this kind of relationship and through extensive letter writing he created and nurtured relationships with other writers that lasted a lifetime. He was occupied with such work for much of this period and we see exchanges between him, John W. Campbell and E. E. 'Doc' Smith.

Heinlein's interactions with fandom during this period were complex. His appearances at conventions in the 1950s were infrequent but welcomed. Unfortunately, much of his connection with fandom was initially mediated by Forrest J. (Forry) Ackerman. Bill Patterson offers the excruciating details but a fair summary might be that Ackerman saw himself as a kind of John the Baptist for science fiction; whatever he did to promote it *ought* to endear him to the writers he felt that he served. On a number of occasions this appears to have involved him giving away rights and reprints without authorisation, or at times claiming that he could speak for Heinlein. However, Heinlein was simultaneously generous and protective: his protection of his intellectual property was precisely what liberated him emotionally to give so much away.

The move to Colorado took Heinlein away from California, and politics was changing anyway. It was not only that anti-communism was on the rise, of which more in a moment, but that the focus of politics in America was undergoing a shift in that the bread-and-butter politics which had united left and right in conversation, was moving slowly towards a new kind of non-conversation, in which the Democrats would be engaged and challenged by the rise of identity politics, first in the form of the civil rights movement, and in which the Republicans would, until the 1980s, become ever more associated with foreign policy.

Heinlein went into the 1948 election voting Truman for his commitment to civil rights. He wrote to Virginia, 'What I do like is the fact that Truman stood up to the southern "gentlemen" white racists and told them to go pee up a rope' (RAH 07/22/48; Patterson, vol. 2, p. 16), but with an increasing conviction that communists were a genuine threat to the American body politic. He wrote a statement to support his friend Robert Cornog when the Department of the Navy suspended him, but it did not occur to him that he might have defended someone's *right* to be a communist. He seems to have been alert to communist propaganda everywhere, objecting to James O'Hanlon's script for *Destination Moon*, partially (Patterson thought) because as well as objecting to the comic scenes he felt it was imbued with Communist Party propaganda (Patterson, vol. 2, p. 35). However, we do need to be careful not to confuse Patterson's commentary with Heinlein's thinking. Patterson felt the adaptation placed too much emphasis on *collective effort*, but this is quite unlikely to have come from Heinlein's pen: even as a capitalist Heinlein was almost always a collectivist capitalist for whom groups of people were far more effective than individuals, as I shall be arguing throughout.

The Puppet Masters (1951) reflects the paranoia rampant in the US at the time, but critics rarely note that the book retains its sexual radicalism, perhaps because they are working from the original, cut-down version. This book uses the later reissue from Del Rey as this is the one now most commonly in circulation. Heinlein's anti-communism, however virulent it became, never acquired the paratext of sexual illiberalism or gender policing that characterised the wider world. Nor did he ever get locked into seeing communism as the *only* threat. *Between Planets*, also published in 1950 when the US was a year into its Korean engagement, is firmly anti-imperialist in the old, anti-expansionist model that fundamentally saw extensive expansion as anti-democratic.[9]

9   B. Perkins, *The Cambridge History of American Foreign Relations, Volume II: The Creation of a Republican Empire, 1776–1865* (Cambridge: Cambridge UP, 1993), p. 172.

Perhaps the most significant event in terms of Heinlein's relationship to the field was the publication in 1950 of L. Ron Hubbard's *Dianetics: The Modern Science of Mental Health*. In theory Heinlein should have been extremely enthusiastic about Dianetics. He and Hubbard were at this stage friends of a sort (though Heinlein was always suspicious of Hubbard's schemes). Hubbard was a chancer; Heinlein a rigorous creator of business plans from his teens. But they shared a strong interest in Alfred Korzybski's General Semantics. However Heinlein was short of time and when Ginny – a much more pragmatic and empirical thinker who was rather suspicious of mysticism – suggested he stay away from it all for five years until he could judge the response, he was probably glad of the excuse. Furthermore, he had had out-of-body experiences as a boy and had already processed and rationalised them. Heinlein was constitutionally oriented to *seeking out the testable*. Dianetics seemed like a backward move.

The difficulty of course was that John W. Campbell signed on to Dianetics the way Raymond A. Palmer had once signed on to the Shaver Mysteries. It didn't last long and by 1953 Campbell had broken with Hubbard. The problem then was that Campbell went on to develop his own mode of mysticism and when Heinlein did not buy into it, accused him of a lack of 'social purpose', which may be one of the most ludicrous insults of all time. Campbell also seems to have gone further and affixed this lack of purpose to Heinlein's lack of children (RAH to Harry Stine, 07/18/54; Patterson, vol. 2, p. 118). The friendship never seems to have been so close again.

It was towards the end of 1950 that Heinlein began to move away from writing short stories. Always the commercial writer, it only took Ginny noting that he had spent more time on his short stories per word than on his novels and earned far less for them, to bring him to the conclusion that the market had changed and it was time to change direction. Heinlein would publish his final short story in a science-fiction magazine in 1959, and it would be a fine story to go out on, the stunning "'All You Zombies—'".[10]

Sadly, their attempts to start a family came to nothing. A possible pregnancy was a false alarm: investigations of Ginny showed a possible problem, but Ginny reported much later that she was shown Heinlein's sperm and 'There were no wigglers living in it at all' (Paterson, vol. 2, p. 119). Heinlein himself seems to have been unaware of this at this stage, although by the 1920s it was known that poor sperm count could be a factor in a failure to conceive. It is quite possible that there was damage as a consequence of Heinlein's earlier wartime treatment, or the 'nonspecific urethritis' from his service days, or the TB, or given that at least one other brother was sterile, a wider family issue resulting from a bout of mumps affecting all the brothers. There is some confusion over how seriously the Heinleins approached adoption: in 1950 Heinlein noted he was too old to adopt in the state of Colorado, but in 1953 he appears to have been negotiating for a private adoption, despite simultaneously planning an extensive (but not fully round-the-world) cruise tour with Ginny. Later, they would consider overseas adoption (from Switzerland), but this idea was also dropped. As far as we can tell from Paterson's biography, an impression reinforced by Heinlein's fiction, the desire was predominantly his. Ginny may have simply been more reticent but there is nothing in the records Patterson reprints to indicate a great drive towards parenthood on her part. (I would usually skip over personal matters such as fertility and vacations but *both* of these would leave traces in Heinlein's work.)

Heinlein was baby-hungry. Patterson records how fond a fictive uncle he was: every close friend's child was adored. He mourned that

10 In 1962, Heinlein published a short-short, 'Searchlight', in an advertisement for Hoffman Electronics in *Scientific American*, August.

there were few children in the family and loved his brother's adopted children. This hunger is there as early as *Beyond This Horizon*, but from *Stranger in a Strange Land* onwards, book after book after book will emphasise the importance of babies to both society and family. Heinlein, as we shall see, believed in many types of sexual and loving relationship, but underneath it all he clearly came to believe that the point of *family* was to nurture children. His saving grace will be that he never suggested that the point of family was to bio-parent them. It is a subtle but important distinction.

The lengthy overseas trip Ginny and Heinlein took in 1953 was also immensely significant. Patterson notes that *The Star Beast* (1954) was 'his last visualization of the peaceful world-state ideal of his socialist youth' (Patterson, vol. 2, p. 99) suggesting that this was due to America's changing role in the world. In the account of the trip in *Tramp Royale*, however, it is clear that the Heinleins went out into the world and discovered that the 'other nations are just like us' liberalism in which Heinlein had been reared did not hold water.

The Heinleins sailed from New Orleans, spending two days there before taking the *Gulf Shipper* (a passenger-freighter) to the Atlantic side of the Panama Canal and then sailing through the canal to Buenaventura, Colombia. From there they went to Peru. From Lima they went to Valparaiso in Chile, where they left the ship. They enjoyed Chile enormously, and went on from there to Argentina, which they found less oppressive than they had expected. Thence to Brazil (Rio de Janeiro), and on to Cape Town. They had an unscheduled stop on the isolated island of Tristan da Cunha (where the ship infected the inhabitants with the cold virus, and four died). They spent ten days in South Africa, took in a safari, and generally felt deeply uncomfortable with the racial politics (*Tramp Royale*, Chapter 8). This may have led to the decision to make Mannie in *The Moon is a Harsh Mistress* (1964) the descendant of a South African terrorist. Heinlein was relieved in many ways to leave and head for Singapore, a place the couple thoroughly enjoyed, thanks to an entrée with a business connection of Heinlein's father's (they worried about racism when they invited him to dine with them at Raffles but it did not arise). They then travelled through Jakarta and on to Brisbane, and from there to New Zealand, which they flat-out detested.

Judging from the Heinleins' description of their Auckland experience, New Zealand in the 1950s was doing its utmost to imitate the worst of British cooking, boarding-house culture and stifling rules. Heinlein was bitterly disillusioned at what he felt was 'a semi-socialism which does *not* work and which does not have anything like the degree of civil liberty we have' (RAH to Robert Lowndes, 03/13/56; Patterson, vol. 2, p. 111). When a year later Heinlein visited Britain (RAH to Alfred Bester, 10/17/55; Patterson, vol. 2, p. 129) he came to similar conclusions: he did not like the bureaucratic state of post-war Britain (which had only just come off rationing, of course, so there were still many shortages). But even then Heinlein did not become a full-blown libertarian. He wrote:

> I have come to believe that we here are usually better off with private ownership government policed than we are when the government owns the deal and a bored clerk looks at you and sneers when you complain. (To Lowndes, 03/13/56; Patterson, vol. 2, p. 116)

From New Zealand the Heinleins travelled to Hawaii, visiting the Pearl Harbor Memorial, and finally back to Denver.

Heinlein had learned that however much he *liked* the people of different cultures – and he particularly enjoyed visiting Latin America and Singapore – they were, quite simply, not Americans. Furthermore, it was one thing to admire another system from outside but he preferred the one he lived in. His dislike of the intense British culture of New Zealand may have been the worst shock: the people who most looked like him and sounded like him, were the least like him. The idea of even a pan-Anglo alliance suddenly felt insecure, and this is reflected in *Double Star* (1956) where his world government is a far more fractious thing than he had previously envisaged, and in *The Moon is a Harsh Mistress* (1966) where Heinlein is far less optimistic about the development of a universal liberal culture in the future.

One consequence of this trip is that the Heinleins were out of the country at the height of McCarthyism. Heinlein is on record as despising McCarthy – 'a revolting son of a bitch with no regard for truth, justice, nor civil rights' – but Heinlein's contempt and absence combined means that he seems to have underrated the effect of McCarthyism (*Tramp Royale*, pp. 63–4). He repeatedly found himself trying to explain to non-Americans why congressional investigations were *not* punitive. 'The idea that a private citizen can answer or refuse to answer a series of questions put to him by a senator ... and then get up and walk out a free man – is so foreign to most other people that they simply cannot believe it' (RAH to Thomas B. Buell, 10/03/74; Patterson, vol. 2, p. 102) Heinlein is of course correct as far as he goes. For Heinlein the *outcome* of the McCarthyite hysteria proved that liberty could be sustained, but despite his own experience of writing to defend a colleague's job, he seems to have been blissfully unconscious of the degree to which McCarthyism was wrecking lives as people rushed to comply lest they be targeted. The ripple effect passed him by: of his books, only *The Puppet Masters* depicts the kind of paranoia that McCarthy triggered and in this novel it is viewed approvingly. This kind of insulated commentary is worth noting because it becomes an increasingly significant element in Heinlein's social politics in the 1980s. Heinlein, the man of *facts*, rarely seems to have paused to wonder if he had *all* the facts. This is not an uncommon position among the politically engaged of any orientation, but I would tentatively suggest that the generation that lived through America's golden age of news media may not have been intellectually equipped for the much more partisan reporting which became a hallmark of the 1980s and onwards. His isolated locale in this period may also have shielded him from political complexity. Heinlein did relatively little travelling within America, and little to cities. In addition, he was constitutionally and culturally inclined to believe certain kinds of authority.

The most problematic and most significant incident reflecting Heinlein's tendency to trust authority, because it had very long-lasting consequences, was his acceptance as gospel of Admiral Robert A. Theobald's *The Final Secret of Pearl Harbor: The Washington Background of the Pearl Harbor Attack*, published in 1954. We are used to thinking of Watergate as the moment of American disillusionment, but for Heinlein it was clearly this book. In it Theobald not only accused Roosevelt of failing at Pearl Harbor, but tried to argue that he had deliberately engineered it. This is not the place to go into the details of the event but while there has been much criticism since of Roosevelt's ineptitude regarding naval strategy, there has never been any evidence provided to show that it was a deliberate attempt to bring America into the war (as a conspiracy theory it fails quickly on the grounds of the sheer cost of the ordinance lost).

It is easy to forget that Heinlein was almost a classic 1930s *pacificist*. This is not a word much used now but it once described the classic American non-interventionist, keen on defence, committed to a *military defence*, but utterly opposed to *military engagement* overseas. Committed as Heinlein was to the war once it started, it is deeply unlikely that he would ever have actively supported entering the war (and Lazarus Long repeats this position in the last segment of *Time Enough for Love*). He was horrified, during his trip to Europe in 1955, to see America hand tanks to Marshall Tito, because he disliked interventionist America as much as he disliked communism. Even Heinlein's signature on the notorious pro-Vietnam war petition (co-ordinated by Poul Anderson and printed on the opposite page to an anti-war petition in *Galaxy*, June 1968) was privately couched in terms of supporting the President and *denying aid and comfort to the enemy* while deploring any overseas involvement so unpopular as to need conscription.

> No, I don't like this war. It's a proxy war, and I don't like proxy wars. It's a war fought with conscripts, and I don't like conscription at any time under any pretext ... Slavery is not made any sweeter by calling it 'selective service'. (unsent to Judith Merril, 11/01/67; Patterson, vol. 2, p. 291).

The political stance taken against war and involvement in war in *For Us, the Living* – like his sexual radicalism – remained with him his whole life.

But Heinlein's narrowing experience of the world led him to become increasingly defensive of American culture and in the process rather blind to its complexities.

> ... in the wider sense we have made the greatest cultural contribution of any society to date, by demonstrating that 160,000,000 people can live together in peace *and* freedom. Nothing else in all history even approached this cultural accomplishment, and sneers at *our* 'culture' are both laughable and outrageously presumptuous when emanating from a continent that habitually wallows in its own blood. (RAH to T. B. Buell, 10/03/74; Patterson, vol. 2, p. 103)

There is simply no awareness in this of the ongoing violence that has been a constant feature of American domestic and overseas policies. Although Heinlein is often clear on his hatred of slavery and colour prejudice (a term I have chosen deliberately for its limitations) he seemed as the years went on to have taken the position that it was a problem of the past, and one predominantly of the South.[11]

From here on we have to be careful with Patterson's biography for his commentary is frequently couched in language that seems rather stronger than Heinlein's and sets out a much more libertarian and hard conservatism than I would argue is reflective of Heinlein's actual positions until quite late in the 1970s. But the accounting of Heinlein's gradual drift to the right is true enough. Like many economic conservative-liberals he was alienated by the shift to both identity politics and a large government state. By 1954 he had resigned from the Democratic Party. He voted a split ticket for a decade. Partially in response to what he perceived as a failure of the Democrats to respond adequately to the Soviet invasion of Hungary, he voted for Eisenhower who appeared to him a good military man, but he was devastated when later Eisenhower signed a test ban treaty with the Soviet Union – this was not his Patrol or Planetary government, it was more like supping with the Devil and hoping you had a long enough spoon. Heinlein's politics had perhaps too much faith in an absolute good and evil. As the Cold War extended, this aspect of Heinlein's work deepened, so that he had to defend an uncompromising scene in *Have Space Suit—Will Travel* (1958) in which Kip stamps on a Wormface skull to obliterate it completely. His editor, Alice Dalgliesh, felt this inappropriate; Heinlein saw it as a demonstration of the absolute intolerance of evil that he felt should be inculcated (RAH to Alice Dalgliesh, 12/4/57; Patterson, vol. 2, p. 147).

This principled absolutism motivated one of the great disasters of Heinlein's political life, his creation of The Heirs of Patrick Henry

---

11   This is a very common position. See James W. Loewen's *Sundown Towns: A Hidden Dimension of American Racism* (New York: The New Press, 2005) for an account of the geography of housing discrimination in the twentieth century.

Society, which Ginny described as 'dark days'. It destroyed much of his faith in his fellow Americans. He chose the name because of Henry's 'Give me liberty, or give me death!' war cry.[12] In April 1958, SANE (National Committee for a Sane Nuclear Policy) organised in order to campaign for unilateral suspension of American nuclear testing. To the Heinleins this was appeasement and betrayal. Like many, Heinlein understood the world in terms that may now seem odd to us. 'Can't they figure out that if warfare is limited to old-fashioned "humane" weapons then 170,000,000 are certain to lose against a combination of over a billion?' (RAH to Lurton Blassingame 04/05/58; Patterson, vol. 2, p. 152). I quote this directly to demonstrate one of the odd moments in Heinlein's analysis. Whatever one thinks of nuclear weapons, the history of warfare from the late nineteenth century onwards has been a continual refutation of that assertion, but it does sum up the yellow peril stories of Heinlein's own youth, notably in his early novel *Sixth Column* (1941).

Heinlein decided to use his political experience to launch his campaign group, The Heirs of Patrick Henry, to coalesce protest and push back. The timing was wrong. Many of the Heinleins' friends, even while making encouraging noises, refused to sign the letter they composed. They could not get local newspapers to pick it up. The Heinleins were dropped by some people and others they dropped themselves. The end result was bitterness and a certain political isolation. Foreign policy was never really a subject matter in Heinlein's fiction, but his experience with the Patrick Henry campaign fed into his growing sense that the America he loved was changing.

---

12   The choice of this name is an example of Heinlein's not untypically partial response to history. It is mystifying why Heinlein admired a man who purchased up to seventy-eight slaves and probably owned many others. The same is true regarding his admiration for Jefferson's declarations of liberty, in the face of the man's slave holding. In neither case does Heinlein ever even consider the juxtaposition.

One aspect of Heinlein's growing discomfort with late 1950s America, which would only grow more pronounced, was its education system. Judging the US education system is always tricky because it is a patchwork of authorities with some states having one school board, others having many; some areas having a rigidly defined curriculum, and some having none. The nearest there has ever been to a uniform system is the Scholastic Aptitude Test (SAT), introduced in 1926, followed by the No Child Left Behind Act of 2001, and now Common Core. In 1965, the far-reaching Elementary and Secondary Education Act (ESEA), passed as a part of President Lyndon B. Johnson's War on Poverty, explicitly forbade the establishment of a national curriculum.

The history of the SAT is complex in that in its early years, until it was gamed by Stanley Kaplan in 1936, it was intended to judge aptitude and inherent intelligence, but in reality seems predominantly to have judged acculturation or the degree to which the candidate was Jewish or otherwise undesirable. The test has since been revised to test college readiness, but it remains one of the few college entrance exams in the world that is not aligned to the school curriculum. Standardised testing has been pitched at so low a level as to be a better indication of extreme poverty than of a child's achievement and is a tool used more to judge schools. This means we have relatively few ways to truly judge what American teens were learning until after 1957, when the successful launch of Sputnik led to a mass panic about US education, with a particular emphasis on the poor standards of science teaching. But what we do know is that the US education system over the past fifty years has tended to emphasise breadth over depth when compared to European systems (and even more so when compared to the Japanese). The rise of esteem education, associated with the left but really a much wider part of American high school social culture from John Dewey onwards, and of American self-help culture as propounded by Dale Carnegie, did nothing to help emphasise the actual knowledge base.

Heinlein's concern started a little earlier: a neighbour child had failed to learn to read in school (there could be many reasons for this but the Heinleins blamed the school); in his local town library *Scientific American* was notable by its absence but there were twenty astrology magazines. Perhaps the oddity here is that Heinlein was surprised: he had noted the strong thread of hostility to science and to rationality in a number of his books, from *Revolt in 2100* through 'Gulf', and he had seen his friends succumb to Dianetics. But Heinlein had lived in a bubble for a while: his close friends were science-fiction writers or military people. He did not, and never really would, spend much time with that other strand of American thought. Furthermore, like most American liberals, he presumably thought that the Scopes trial (in 1925, when a teacher was prosecuted for teaching pupils about evolution) had done for a certain kind of religious anti-science. The rise of the fundamentalist churches, steady throughout the 1950s,[13] would be invisible to much of the left (and in these terms Heinlein was very solidly still on the left and always would be) until the mid-1970s.

Heinlein's juvenile novel *Have Space Suit—Will Travel* – perhaps the most quintessential Heinlein juvenile – was both a protest novel and a rescue manifesto for children isolated in a superficial or inadequate school system. *Podkayne of Mars* was a similar counterblast against irrational education. *Starship Troopers*, with its depiction of a soldier rising through the ranks through self-education and determination (and already old-fashioned in being based on his brother's career), also fits this pattern. Increasingly, complaints

---

13 See Joel A. Carpenter, *Revive Us Again: The Reawakening of American Fundamentalism* (New York: Oxford UP, 1997).

about poor education would underpin all Heinlein's near-future novels – they are perhaps most extreme in *I Will Fear No Evil*, which is positively dystopian in a number of ways, but not least in the depiction of a post-literate society. Yet the post-literate character in this novel, whose school did not teach reading, is a highly talented and productive artist.[14] The education issue is also significant because it pushed Heinlein further to the right, towards the Republicans, who for the next forty years would gain a moral high ground advocating 'old-fashioned' education as a cure for all of society's evils.

For the record: by the standard of many liberals I am a rather *illiberal* educationist, being suspicious of modern pedagogy with its 'flipped classrooms' and 'esteem' education and I tend towards behaviourist rather than constructivist approaches. In plain speech, I like 'chalk and talk'. I am even a fan of rote learning in its place. But I cannot but help notice that many 'traditionalists' have little idea of the very high rates of illiteracy produced by 'traditional' modes of teaching – or lack of access to education – in the past (illiteracy in the USA was around 10 per cent in 1900 and 0.6 per cent in 1979).[15] Heinlein tended to make assumptions about the quality of teaching in the first half of the twentieth century that are unfounded, but did not fall into the other traps, so far as I can see.

The writing of *Starship Troopers* was to trigger the break with Scribner and Alice Dalgliesh. Dalgliesh liked the book; it was the board

---

14 I am reminded of Somerset Maugham's 'The Verger' (1936), sacked for being illiterate, who starts a successful line of tobacconists. When his bank manager wonders, 'Where would you be if you could read and write?' the man responds, 'A verger'.

15 National Centre for Education Statistics: https://nces.ed.gov/naal/lit_history.asp. The politicians who represent this wing are often reluctant to commit additional resources to educationally disadvantaged students they already see as having failed, and are even more reluctant to accept the very clear scientific evidence that improved nutrition has a bigger impact on test scores than does teaching styles. Katie Adolphus, Clare L. Lawton, and Louise Dye, 'The effects of breakfast on behavior and academic performance in children and adolescents', *Frontiers in Human Neuroscience* (2013) 7: 425.

that rejected it, and Dalgliesh left Scribner shortly after. It has never been clear why, but something about the tone of the book was clearly askew in relation to the contemporary publishing scene. It may be significant that a letter from Alfred Bester compares the book to the work of Kipling and speaks of the dangers of jingoism (Patterson, vol. 2, p. 167). The relevant Kipling text here might well be *Stalky & Co*, which is a revelation if one assumes Kipling's patriotism to be 'jingoistic'. In the book the boys are all at a school where the majority of them are the sons of officers and civil servants (as Heinlein was himself). All expect *to serve the empire*. When confronted with a jingoistic politician they are alienated and disgusted. Their commitment is quiet, understated, taken for granted. This is the model that Heinlein uses in *Space Cadet* and again in *Starship Troopers*. At the beginning of the decade, when service to most meant the war against the Japanese and the Germans, this worked. By the end of the decade, as America moved into an imperialist and aggressive phase, precisely fuelled by jingoism, it was out of step with those – Heinlein's traditional friends and publishers – who opposed this from the left. Other aspects of the story, rooted in 1930s socialist ideals, also rang false, the irony, of course, being that Heinlein himself would no longer have used the term 'socialist' to describe himself. In the end it didn't matter: the story was picked up by Putnam, Heinlein added the candidate school section, to bring Johnny Rico up in age, and the book was cross-marketed to children and adults.

Writing the story of *Starship Troopers* as above, however, misses an important point: finding himself out of step with publishing friends did not put Heinlein out of step with readers per se. Reviews were mixed; reception was mixed. *Kirkus* magazine liked it. The *San Francisco Chronicle* did not. Poul Anderson disagreed with it. *Starship Troopers* began to create multiple audiences for Heinlein's work: those who liked the military and swashbuckler stories, and those who would prefer Heinlein's near-future exercises in socio-economics, with Heinlein as what one observer at the first meeting of the John Birch Society called a 'writer of philosophical fiction' (Patterson, vol. 2, p. 174). Increasingly – and mirroring what was happening in American politics – Heinlein would attract single-issue or single-novel admirers. *Starship Troopers* was just the first inkling of this. It would work for Heinlein as a writer precisely because he wasn't a single-issue writer, so that rather than catering to the expectations of a single readership, his later works would increasingly upset at least one section of it at any given time.

In terms of the development of Heinlein as a person and a writer, the reaction to *Starship Troopers* may have been the first time Heinlein registered that the military (rather than military activities) had become part of the political debate and that part of the country had become hostile to the idea of military service, an idea he would pick up again in *Glory Road*. More worrying for Heinlein's own open-mindedness is that there is growing evidence of an intolerance of political criticism. When the responses to *Starship Troopers* came in, he dismissed much of the criticism as essentially 'conservative . . . spineless, boneless, suffocating . . . do-goodish, and quasi-socialist' (RAH to Theodore Sturgeon, 03/05/62; Patterson, vol. 2, p. 185). What we start to see is a closing of Heinlein's receptivity to alternative viewpoints, which creates much of the didacticism in his later books and which, by the time of *The Cat Who Walks Through Walls* (1985), is overwhelming in the fiction itself. In another author this might have been disastrous, but Heinlein's inner self was sufficiently cranky, awkward and complex that there was plenty of material to mine. The same person who disliked what he increasingly would see as a misplaced pacifism, and anti-patriotism on the left, also disliked the shibboleths of the right: 'I'm going to write what I please – about sex or love or duty, or marriage or politics or epistemology or God' (letter to Theodore Sturgeon, 03/05/62; Patterson, vol. 2, p. 186).

Which is why the next book to come along was *Stranger in a Strange Land* (1961). *Stranger in a Strange Land* was Heinlein's breakthrough book, changing his audience completely. But before it came out there was the trip to Russia.

The Heinleins' trip to Russia in 1960 went much as one might expect. They hated the food. They found byzantine ways of paying for provisions. They managed to be in Moscow for May Day and to hear of the Soviet capture of the US spy pilot Francis Gary Powers. Ginny got into a fight about the existence of gulags in Russia, which was then being denied, and they almost lost their visas and found the friendly locals had turned frosty. This is where my comment about the Heinlein's use of 'facts' comes in. Accurate as their comments are, they did not consider that few tourists to the US would be likely to be shown around the prisons or slums, though any Russian visitor to the US around 1960 could have found some very brutal practices in the South. Chain gangs had not long been phased out. Such comparisons simply did not occur to the Heinleins.

They left Moscow, travelled to Tashkent and Samarkand, to Tbilisi, Kiev and then to Vilnius, where they discovered the official line that Lithuania had *always* been part of the Soviet Union. On Sunday 15 May they saw people celebrating the launch of a manned spacecraft, only to hear it denied when the spacecraft was lost. They travelled on to Riga where they were hosted by the Soviet Writers' union – but were unable to recover royalties – and then to Leningrad, arriving on 16 May 1960, the day the Paris Summit between Eisenhower and Khrushchev began. They were still there the day it collapsed over Eisenhower's refusal to apologise for the spy-plane incident. The next day the Heinleins curtailed their vacation and left by train to Helsinki. By contrast they loved Finland, Norway and Sweden, where they travelled next, and they flew back by Anchorage, Alaska.

It is probably an understatement that the Heinleins were not natural visitors to the Soviet Union. They travelled there suspicious and became hostile. Heinlein's essay 'Pravda Means Truth' is essentially about the regime of mistrust and propaganda he saw. But he seems to have been oblivious to his own abuse of his hosts: when he reached Wiesbaden he was taken by a friend to US Intelligence and was debriefed. In effect, the Heinleins had spied for the USA, exactly what they feared they might be deported for while understanding themselves as tourists. It was not honourable but it *was* consistent: while Heinlein easily found the mote in the Soviet eye, he was less inclined to examine his own. He was debriefed at least twice more, once by the CIA, and to his credit refused to sign a secrecy order although this may have been more because this was marketable material than because he recognised the hypocrisy involved.

Heinlein arrived back in time to receive an urgent message to get himself to the World Science Fiction Convention in Pittsburgh, because he had won a Hugo for *Starship Troopers*. The critics might not have liked it, but the fans very definitely did. Modern voting systems mean that early warnings no longer occur in this award, but this was another time and Heinlein was to acquire an unfortunate though not wholly false reputation for turning up at Worldcons only when he had won. He was also invited to be a charter member of the Playboy Club (at the time *Playboy* magazine was an excellent market for SF stories by male and female writers). He was also asked to cut 150,000 words from *The Man From Mars*, aka *Stranger in a Strange Land*. The mind boggles. The restored version however is only 60,000 words longer than the first edition.[16]

In the 1960 election Heinlein voted for Nixon but did not actually care for either candidate. He was rapidly becoming a very typical, disaffected, white, male, leftish-leaning voter: he disliked the

---

16   I blame Heinlein for the word length of this book. Clearly he is haunting it.

internationalist, anti-war trends on the left, and he equally disliked the internationalist Realpolitik of the right. In 1964, he became attracted to Barry Goldwater, an ex-FDR liberal, because he saw both parties as moving to the left, by which he seems to have meant becoming statist (Patterson, vol. 2, p. 249). Heinlein declared that he and Ginny were libertarians, absolutely committed to individual liberty. This attitude he continued to express in all his social satires. He could reconcile it with his collectivism, as we shall see in Chapter 5, because he believed in educating people in a civic virtue that he believed would see individual liberty serve the whole. His willingness to overlook Goldwater's links to right-wing racists was characteristic of a shift among the demographic to which he belonged, which saw civil rights as a done deal, and saw federal intervention in institutional and particular state structures as illiberal. This is why Patterson thinks Heinlein was later able to accept Goldwater voting against the 1964 Civil Rights Act (Patterson, vol. 2, p. 252 – an odd decision for Heinlein), because he saw it as a disagreement over tactics, not aim (Patterson's suggestion that he saw it as a federal versus state issue is, given Heinlein's political heritage, ridiculous). This coincided with the publication of *Farnham's Freehold* (1964), and underpins both the racism and antiracism of that book.

Heinlein became involved in the Goldwater campaign but if he thought the accusations of racism mere smears he was disillusioned when his local campaign manager proposed to refuse an offer of help from an African American woman. He stuck by Goldwater, because he truly disliked Johnson (almost certainly because Johnson was using conscription to fight the Vietnam war, perhaps the thing Heinlein felt most deeply about), and because he objected to Johnson telegraphing the enemy about this intention to attack, but it was not a happy experience. At one point the local party even seems to have tried to impeach Heinlein.

Heinlein understood his own politics as pragmatic. He had believed in the New Deal when he thought it answered to the circumstances. As circumstances had changed, he no longer believed in that set of solutions. Crucially, like many who made the traverse from left to right in this period Heinlein felt that the issues had changed. 'The central problem of today is no longer individual exploitation but national survival' (RAH to Rex Heinlein, 12/08/60; Patterson, vol. 2, p. 206). The threat of nuclear war overrode all other threats. This, remember, is written in *1960*. The civil rights movement is in full swing, women's demands for basics such as equal pay and access to abortion are just around the corner. Why would Heinlein so comprehensively ignore these issues in defining his political position? There is no easy answer, and I do not find it helpful simply to point to Ginny's influence – but I would tentatively suggest that by settling in Colorado Springs, Heinlein had moved away from the very areas, both geographically and politically, that had fuelled his earlier beliefs. He was a self-employed man, who communicated primarily with others who were self-employed, or in the services or publishing. He was no longer involved in block politics, and he did not spend time with people employed in large businesses. In effect, Heinlein was chronically long-sighted: he could see the problems abroad with great clarity, but those close to home were blurred to inconsequence.

Stranger in a Strange Land came out in 1961 and was picked up for the Doubleday Science Fiction Book Club (US book clubs sent out automatic selections; to be picked up by a book club was to ensure automatic success in sales, if not reception). The pre-release reviews were strong although the *New York Times* did not like it: 'A disastrous mishmash of science fiction, laborious humor, dreary, social satire and cheap eroticism' (quoted Patterson, vol. 2, p. 210). Fan response, however, was excellent. *Stranger in a Strange Land* won the Hugo in

1962, giving Heinlein Hugos for two successive books. This response had to last him a while because neither *Podkayne of Mars*, a book which feels rather retrograde in comparison, nor *Glory Road* (both 1963) would appeal anything like as much to his fans. *Glory Road* did pick up a Hugo nomination in 1964, but it was beaten in the voting by Clifford Simak's *Way Station*.

Meanwhile the North American Air Defense Command (NORAD) had decided to construct the Cheyenne Mountain Combat Operations Centre to coordinate telemetry and the missiles and aircraft defence for the entire country. Heinlein gave his 'Pravda is Truth' speech as guest of honour at the 1961 World Science Fiction Convention, and then went home to put his money where his mouth was: he built a fallout shelter. Having done so, he turned the effort into research and used his experience, and the experience of living through the Cuban missile crisis in 1962, to write *Farnham's Freehold* (1964). One element of the novel is its exhortation to the population to prepare for Armageddon.[17] Patterson notes that removal of the missiles was verified the same day as Executive Order 11063 banned segregation in federally funded housing (vol. 2, p. 232). This coincidence *may* lie behind the premise of the novel in which a future post-nuclear-war world is a racially divided world in which blacks rule. Heinlein believed that he was writing an 'if this goes on': without a change in racial attitudes, things would one day be turned forcibly around. The book did well enough, but it did not deliver Heinlein's usual success. In addition, the critical response was such that it utterly wrecked his anti-racist reputation: I will discuss it in detail in

---

17 See Alice L. George, *Awaiting Armageddon: How Americans Faced the Cuban Missile Crisis* (Chapel Hill, NC: University of North Carolina Press, 2004) for just how typical Heinlein was of a response which paid little attention to the realities of life for many Americans. Heinlein's earlier nuclear story, 'The Year of the Jackpot', at least acknowledged that there would be no shelters for people in the cities.

Chapter 6. Heinlein's next real breakthrough would be *The Moon is a Harsh Mistress* in 1966.

Meanwhile both he and Ginny were in poor health. Heinlein had cataracts. Ginny had variously amoebic dysentery, kidney stones, and evidence of problems left from childhood TB, and eventually they realised she had altitude sickness, a miserable and incurable condition. They were going to have to move. When Heinlein had gone through his second divorce he had been oppressed by the need for publicly conservative behaviour. Isolated in Colorado Springs with relatively few local friends, the impression is given, by Patterson at least, that this continued. Not shocking the neighbours may have kept much of Heinlein's imagination in check. The Heinleins now set out on a states-wide tour (or at least the shortlist of states they could imagine living in) to look for a new place to live, and put the house in Colorado Springs on the market at the same time. They settled first on Watsonville, about thirty miles north of San Francisco, and then when that didn't work out, Bonny Doon, about thirteen miles from Santa Cruz. In terms of the turn Heinlein's work was taking, with a growing emphasis on social and sexual radicalism, this area was probably a good choice. Santa Cruz had plenty of liberals and conservatives, colonies of hippies and a branch of the John Birch Society. Heinlein was enamoured of the bookshops of both, even while he had little patience for hippies whom he saw less as a movement than a social consequence.

Again the Heinleins built a house, this time without a bomb shelter. Instead they went for luxury, with bathrooms with outside entrances, and a swimming pool, and a cat-free cottage for the allergic. This was paid for by the delivery of *The Moon is a Harsh Mistress* and the sale of foreign rights for a number of books. Heinlein's international reputation was growing. *Stranger in a Strange Land* was rapidly turning into a cult book with sales of 10,000 copies a year, although Putnam refused to acknowledge this and the book went out of print in hardback in 1966. At the same time Heinlein's critical reputation was beginning to coalesce.

Science-fiction criticism was in its infancy in the 1960s. The most solid work, if not the most insightful, came from Sam Moskowitz, who had appointed himself as chronicler of both science fiction fandom and the development of science fiction literature. He was a neophile, and he approached science fiction with a strong belief that what mattered was who got to an idea first. This meant that he was strongly attracted to the work of Heinlein but tended to see his work in terms of the scientific ideas Heinlein came up with.

Moskowitz valued at least some of what Heinlein valued. The fanzines, proving grounds for SF criticism, were not always so friendly, often suspicious of Heinlein's work. Heinlein himself dismissed this, noting 'I was awarded three of my four Hugos for "best novel" *after* the fanzines started panning me' (Patterson, vol. 2, p. 351) but it must have been frustrating, and Heinlein was not sufficiently embedded in fan culture to realise that criticism and admiration often went hand in hand.

Heinlein was a great deal more suspicious of growing academic interest: his experience of 'literature' was that of most science-fiction writers of the period – disparagement – but the approach by the University of California, Santa Cruz, to host his papers was welcome. You would think that this would mean he was happy when Alexei Panshin started to show interest in the contents, but Heinlein disliked Panshin's *Heinlein in Dimension* (which does often read as editorial critique), and resented an 'anticipatory' review in 1973 of an unpublished book, *Time Enough for Love*, that Panshin had not read (Patterson, vol. 2, p. 351). A long-term problem, however, is that with the exception of George Slusser and Leon Stover, all the *substantial* academic engagement with Heinlein – the book-length monographs –

has come from the left. This book is, of course, no exception. Heinlein disliked the work of H. Bruce Franklin (although he seems to have liked him personally) and does not even seem to have been very keen on the work of George Slusser, although Slusser and Heinlein shared relatively close political views, if Patterson is to be believed (vol. 2, p. 402). I am afraid I do not think Patterson *is* to be believed in all respects when he narrates Heinlein's relationship with Franklin. Most dubious is the allegation that Stover's paper on Heinlein was dropped from the Modern Language Association (MLA) conference programme thanks to Franklin's machinations. As an organiser of conferences I was sceptical. A call to Franklin resulted in laughter and an account of meeting Heinlein, and of being approved of by Heinlein's cat. The story may have resulted from an attempt by Stover to explain why the MLA rejected a paper proposal; in reality the MLA is generally oversubscribed and rejects many proposals.

Heinlein would turn down an invitation to the MLA from Thomas Clareson in 1975, because it was to be chaired by Dr David Samuelson, who had written an article Heinlein did not like, and he also resented the unpaid nature of the gig. This is a frequent source of contention: academics tend to think 'I'm doing this for free, why won't s/he?', forgetting that even if they are paying their own way – not all academics are supported by their departments – they are paid with rising critical esteem and, hopefully, promotion. The guest author on the other hand is unlikely to build new audiences in this way and is to a degree being presented as 'the text' (see Patterson, vol. 2, p. 369 for a link to the article).

Much of Heinlein's response to criticism over the next twenty years was shaped by his annoyance over being admired for what he felt were the wrong reasons. Although Heinlein felt he was moving away from science fiction, his readers saw him rather as extending the form. He also started to rethink his own sense of what he was trying to achieve, and as his novels began to consistently break out from the science-fiction community, Heinlein's admiration for Mark Twain began to mutate into an ambition to be regarded in a similar light. Winning a fourth Hugo Award for *The Moon is a Harsh Mistress* (the most Best Novel awards won by any writer to that date) was no longer enough. To his credit he had no interest in the kind of admiration that both his friends Campbell and Hubbard had sought. He was repulsed when people turned up on his doorstep wanting spiritual advice. He was actively alarmed to hear that he was listed alongside J. D. Salinger and Lawrence Ferlinghetti as a 'personal guru' in a class at UCLA. Heinlein was always adamant, at all times in his life, that he wanted to teach people to *think*. For all his grumbling about hippies and weak-minded liberals, Heinlein was not interested in followers: he wanted critical thinkers for his readers. And, of course like all authors, he had little patience with people (not all of them children) who wanted him to do their homework for them.

However when Heinlein did respond to fan letters he often said rather interesting things that flesh out aspects of his work. A young woman writing because her boyfriend was trying to pressure her into sex (something that had always been anathema to Heinlein) because he argued sex engendered love, was told firmly, 'it is *your* viewpoint which is being expounded [in *Stranger*] ... the sharing of sex takes place after and only after the two persons already share love' (RAH letter to Marie Browne, 12/18/68; Patterson, vol. 2, p. 294).

The Moon is a Harsh Mistress changed the public's approach to Heinlein. He found himself the focus of attention from both anarchists and libertarians, and it is in response to this that we get one of the clearest statements of Heinlein's position:

> I miss being an utter anarchist only by a very narrow margin – i.e.
> a misgiving about the possibility of maintaining a complex society

> capable of mass production without a certain amount of sheer force,
> both internal and external. (RAH to Poul and Karen Anderson,
> 06/22/62; Patterson, vol. 2, p. 302)

We should not over-interpret the word 'force' but this does make sense for a man trained in the navy, where force always lies behind teamwork and collaboration.

One truly delightful consequence of Heinlein's growing fame was an invitation to watch the launch of Apollo 11 as the personal guest of Lee Atwood, Chief Executive Officer of North American Aviation, who led the design of the Apollo command and service modules, and the engine. This was then capped by being invited by CBS to act as one of the live commentators. For a writer who felt an intense *sensibility* about space travel, reflected in those classic stories such as 'The Long Watch' and 'Requiem', the experience was ecstatic (Patterson, vol. 2, p. 308).

I Will Fear No Evil (1970) is perhaps the first coming together of a myriad of Heinlein's concerns and interests. Patterson ascribes the origins of the novel to stories about transplants, but as we will see in Chapter 4, the story builds on persistent strands around social decay, identity issues, and on a new strand that will become very important, but which lay back in the mists of time, with *For Us, the Living*: the active construction of family. It is a complex novel, big and baggy, with an almost classic later Heinlein motif of intimate events set against a collapsing and chaotic world. It owes something to the style of the popular culture novels of the period in that it focuses on the elite of society, much as had *Stranger in a Strange Land* and much as all of the later novels would, except *Friday* and *Job* (novels which have certain parallels).

At the very start of January 1970 Heinlein's world was rocked by the news that the Tate-LaBianca murderers were claimed to be inspired by *Stranger in a Strange Land.* Heinlein himself was too ill to respond: after he had been misdiagnosed by two doctors in a row Ginny had had him transferred to Stanford medical centre where he was discovered to have peritonitis from a perforated diverticulum. It was to be a genuine brush with death, and as Patterson notes, Heinlein was saved in part by donations from the National Rare Blood Club, which he had researched for *I Will Fear No Evil.* The peritonitis led to a series of operations, resulting in the discovery of a gallstone; then during Heinlein's convalescence to an attack of shingles accompanied by a *staphylococcus* infection. The only good thing was the acquisition of a waterbed which a manufacturer had based on the one in *Stranger in a Strange Land* – that kind of guru he was happy to be.

The responses to *I Will Fear No Evil* were very mixed, some reading it as SF, some as Heinlein intended, as a trance/delusion novel, some complaining about the lack of sex which was indicated, but not graphic; on the other hand, a weird melange of libertarians, hippies and feminists loved it. It is with the novels of this period that the feminist response to Heinlein becomes very complex and as bound in with shifting waves of feminism as with changes in Heinlein himself. The sales however were excellent, and the book sold out the first three impressions and spent several weeks on the *New York Times* bestseller list.

After Heinlein's operation, and one on Ginny who was having trouble with her feet, he turned to the next novel, *Time Enough for Love* (1973), a picaresque and a scheherazade, which saw the return of Lazarus Long and, whatever Heinlein may have said, provided a channel for some of Heinlein's wit and wisdom. It is a compound novel – becoming fashionable at the time – but also mimics the framed fix-ups that heralded science-fiction paperback publishing, when authors were rushing to make use of their linked story collections.

Heinlein continued to accept speaking engagements but he was more and more out of step with the youth he thought of as his natural allies – a recording of a speech at Annapolis in 1973 has audible heckling in the audience as someone questions the value of patriotism. One of the ironies for Heinlein in this later period would be that the natural audience of his youth disappeared, while many of his new fans would love his work but question his politics or use it in ways he would not approve of. During this period both his health and Ginny's health were failing. Ginny had extensive dental troubles – Patterson does not say this but a crumbling jaw (*osteonecrosis*) is sufficiently rare that given Ginny's wartime work there is probably good reason to suggest an environmental cause. She had to have bone transplants and dental implants. Meanwhile Heinlein had to go on a very strict diet to control his blood pressure and numerous other indicators. Neither of them was ever really well again, and one factor in Heinlein's continuing to write up to the end was almost certainly the pressure illness put on their finances.

Finances were relieved when the success of *Time Enough for Love* and the ripple effect on other books pushed them into a higher tax bracket and into a position where they could invest in dividends. *Time Enough for Love* was nominated for the Nebula, but lost to *Rendevous with Rama*, which Heinlein accepted on behalf of his long-time friend Arthur C. Clarke. Heinlein found himself an honoured guest at the National Rare Blood Club banquet in the same year, celebrated for the effect that the appeal cards in *I Will Fear No Evil* had had on blood donation rates. For the next few years the Heinleins would be engaged in organising blood drives at US conventions, and in researching blood donor systems – coming in the process to admire the more collectivist approaches of Canada, the UK and the Commonwealth countries, a small rebalancing perhaps for earlier cultural disappointment. Whatever Heinlein's avowed belief in privatised health care, the evidence presented in Patterson is of continual horror at poor hospital provision and medical support, and near bankruptcy as a result of necessary medical care. (Heinlein went on to undertake a great deal of research on blood, and eventually wrote the entry concerning it for the *Encyclopaedia Britannica*.)

Heinlein's organisation of blood drives among fans and authors led him to two realisations. First, that he really was genuinely liked and admired. People would turn out for him. An essentially solitary man, he had never been sure of this. From the mid-1970s he could relax. Like many an expressive introvert he loved a role and as Patterson puts it, he 'found that working the blood drive didn't seem to take as much out of him as plain convention work' (Patterson, vol. 2, p. 385). The other aspect is that the sheer size of turnout – he was assured that Science Fiction Writers of American (SFWA) blood drives were returning response rates fourteen times higher than at non-SF events – may have changed the way he felt about the civic-mindedness of his fellows. For much of the late 1960s and early 1970s he had been railing about the decline of American patriotism in both his fiction and non-fiction, and had felt that much of it had fallen on deaf ears. In the success of his blood drives Heinlein rediscovered the civic-mindedness of his fellow citizens that he had once expressed in the broadcast 'This I Believe . . .' (1952) and which the last part of this book will argue was such an essential part of his writing.

In 1975 Jerry Pournelle created the Grand Master position within the Science Fiction Writers of America; Patterson believes this was essentially to give Heinlein an award (vol. 2, p. 367). At a time when the New Wave was dominating the Nebulas, Robert James thinks that Heinlein not winning awards bothered Pournelle (pers. comm.). Heinlein demonstrated no tendency to appreciate such gymnastics but he most definitely appreciated the ovation the banquet gave him. He was moving into a new phase. Few of his original peers were still writing and the dominant forces in the field in the early 1970s had almost all read Heinlein's work from their first encounters with science fiction. In 1977 Heinlein accepted a Doctorate of Humane Letters from Eastern Michigan University, but his health was becoming a worry and some people were noticing slurring in his speech. While working on *'The Number of the Beast'*, he gave a speech at a small convention in Utah. His performance there seems to be the source of the rumour that his later books were his 'senile' period. As we shall see, it might be better to say they are his near-posthumous books. He completed the manuscript, but for the first time Ginny said 'no'; the book was a mess. Heinlein considered that he might follow his father in developing Alzheimer's. They left the book and went on holiday to Tahiti. On January 3rd his vision failed and he experienced partial paralysis.

Heinlein had had a Transient Ischemic Attack (TIA), similar to a stroke. The incident left Ginny and his friends worrying for his life, and led to a lengthy convalescence. While recovering Heinlein sorted out the book that was to be *'The Number of the Beast'* (called initially *Panki-Barsoom*, showing that however miraculous his recovery, his tin ear for titles was not transformed). His generosity remained characteristic. When a chance came to reprint *The Worlds of Robert Heinlein* with Tom Doherty at Ace, Heinlein suggested to SFWA that they use it as a test case for the SFWA model contract that was being touted.

By 1978, when *'The Number of the Beast'* was delivered, Heinlein was suffering from polycythemia, which affected his balance and his mobility. The treatment was bloodletting and that helped but Heinlein increasingly found travel burdensome. He was experiencing mixed emotions. The book sold at auction for half a million dollars and for $43,000 for the New English Library British rights but the space programme was faltering and Heinlein no longer saw the future he had dreamed of. Much of that ambivalence emerges in

Friday (1983), where a chaotic world is the background for a story of personal success and family-building. In Heinlein's own politics he was one of many New Deal Democrats to switch his allegiance firmly to the Republican party in 1980 for the election of Reagan.

'*The Number of the Beast*' was a critical failure and a sales success, which was becoming par for the course. Increasingly the Heinleins felt, with some justification, that his market was so large, mixed reactions were inevitable. Heinlein then found himself among thirty people from the science, military and elsewhere convened as what later became known as think tanks, in this case the Citizens Advisory Council. This was the group that produced plans for High Defence or what was later known as the Space Defence Initiative, SDI (or more derisively, Star Wars). It may have appealed to Heinlein precisely because it was defensive and non-interventionist; he saw it as a 'bullet-proof vest on our bare chest' (RAH in a letter to *Survive! Magazine*, September–October 1982; Patterson, vol. 2, p. 427) but also, as Patterson notes (p. 435) because it was a way to get the US back into space.

Friday continued a trick that Heinlein had begun in '*The Number of the Beast*' of reviving old characters; he would carry this into his final two novels. Here it was less metatextual and was simply a return to the world of 'Gulf' and the recovery of the patriarch, Kettle Belly Baldwin. It's easy to dismiss this character as another Jubal Harshaw or Lazarus Long, but *Friday* begins with the death of Baldwin and is essentially about his heir apparent and the different future she will choose, one he cannot contemplate. In that it is a reflection perhaps of how Heinlein had always seen his books, creators of *those who would make* the future. Although *Friday* carries much of Heinlein's fear for contemporary America – for a now-avowed Republican it contains a very sharp attack on international corporations – it also, as I will explore elsewhere, carried much of his feminism, not always up to date, but stronger in this novel than anywhere except perhaps *To Sail Beyond the Sunset*

(1987). But *Friday* is the more notable here for its dedication page. Heinlein was paying his dues to some of his closest female friends, fans, authors, an agent, a nurse, and just women he admired, as Heinlein had always admired women. The novel is dedicated to a number of women, identified only by their first names, who equate to:[18]

> Ann Nourse; Anne Passovoy; Barbara Stine; Betsy Curtis; Mildred (Bubbles) Broxon; Carolyn Ayer; Catherine Sprague de Camp; Dian Crayne; Diane Russell; Eleanor Wood; Elinor Busby; Gay Haldeman; Jeanne Robinson; Joan D. Vinge; Judy-Lynn Benjamin Del Rey; Karen Anderson; Kathleen Heinlein; Marilyn Niven; Nichelle Nichols; Pat Cadigan; Polly Freas; Roberta Pournelle; 'Rebel' (Mrs Albert Trottier); Tamea Dula; Ursula K. Le Guin; Verna Trestrail Smith; Vivian Markham; Vonda McIntyre; Testu Yumiko and Virginia Heinlein.

The reviews, when they came out, were divided, but as an individual he was now intensely popular, receiving an ovation at the American Bookseller's conference in Anaheim in May 1982. At seventy-five, Heinlein had places to go and things he wanted to see so the Heinleins set off for Antarctica via Japan and also visited China. Much of the Antarctic scenery ended up in *Job: A Comedy of Justice* (1984) and in China – which they liked – Heinlein was invited to speak with local writers.

Under Reagan the space race was on again and Heinlein found himself as a guest at the Los Angeles Space Development Conference and in demand for pieces on the space race and the defence agenda. The space shuttle programme proved unsatisfactory to Heinlein and

---

18   The list here is compiled by Jane Davitt and Tim Morgan at RAH: Robert A. Heinlein, nitrosyncretic.com. See Davitt and Morgan, 'Heinlein's Dedications', 2002 for details of research and speculation.

many others – it did little to expand the distance we could travel – and he became involved in fundraising to support NASA's telemetry for the Viking probes on Mars and campaigns to support tax-exempt equatorial spaceports. Heinlein's lack of faith in government-backed space travel seemed supported by the stagnation of the 1980s.

Job itself however reflected some of Heinlein's unease. Reagan had come to the office of President in part through the mobilisation of the evangelical vote. One aspect of Heinlein's politics that never shifted was a deep dislike of organised religion and a belief in the power of science. The character of Alexander Hergensheimer and the world he lived in was uncomfortably close to that of the growing breed of televangelists, quick to condemn the sins of others, slow to look to their own, and utterly resistant to any science that contradicted what they believed to be the revealed word of God. The book gained a welcome boost when televangelist Jerry Falwell condemned it (Patterson, vol. 2, p. 444).

Heinlein was slowing down. He had always been a smoker, had had a brush with TB, and had probably worked with some very unhealthy chemicals during the war. He developed Chronic Obstructive Pulmonary Disease. He would take a final trip through the Northwest Passage with Lars-Eric Lindblad to the Arctic, and then on to Japan, but life was circling in on itself: *The Cat Who Walks Through Walls* looked back to the background story in "'All You Zombies—'" and with links to '*The Number of the Beast*' created a Time Corps who would travel to rescue.

In 1984 Heinlein met Leon Stover. Patterson describes this meeting and notes Stover 'did something that must have impressed Heinlein: he accepted what Heinlein told him at face value and integrated the new information into his mental picture' (Patterson, vol. 2, p. 440). For Heinlein this demonstrated that Stover could accept new *facts*; for most critics however, it also reinforces his insistence that his *intentionality* superseded reader response. This as much as anything was the core of his frustrations over the years with both fans and critics.

Heinlein wasn't too happy either about the people he met through the L5 Society (a group that aimed to promote the idea of orbital space colonies): too many were anti-militarists. He regarded SDI as a reasonable response to nuclear threat. However he was also, in his own way, still an isolationist pacifist: he saw SDI in a way that would have been far more familiar to 1930s politicians, as an ultimate weapon, one that would end war for ever (Patterson, vol. 2, p. 446). When Arthur C. Clarke published a collection of anti-SDI essays in spring 1984, he let their friendship cool. In what is a great irony for a man who once thought in terms of a universal government, he also told Clarke off for interfering in the politics of another country, and the defence of the USA. Heinlein, never very familiar with international diplomacy, could not make the stretch to see that US defence politics was being played out throughout the world.

In 1982 the family cat, Pixel (of a long line of Pixels) became ill and Heinlein immortalised him and his antecedents in *The Cat Who Walks Through Walls*, a picaresque time-travel story with a strong streak of sentiment. As in *'The Number of the Beast'* adventurers set out to save beloved characters from time and space. The target this time was Mike, the computer from *The Moon is a Harsh Mistress*, but Hazel Stone came along for the ride, and so did Lazarus Long. The book also drew attention – as Ginny noted – to the intense sentimentality both Heinlein and science-fiction fans had for cats. All the fans wanted to know (including this one) was whether the kitten survived. At the end of March 1986, Heinlein was able to finish *To Sail Beyond the Sunset*, which expanded on the time patrol, revisited Lazarus Long's childhood and rescued the kitten.

In 1986, Heinlein experienced a nasal haemorrhage which led to the need for blood transfusions. It took three operations to get him out of hospital and it was December before he was active again, though he never really recovered. When the proofs of *To Sail Beyond the Sunset* came out, he had to be persuaded to read them. The Heinleins decided to move to be nearer hospitals and they began tidying up the literary estate, saying what could and could not be accessed. In conversations with Stover he tried to ensure that his reputation would be safeguarded as an American writer rather than as a genre writer. When *Robert A. Heinlein*, Stover's book, was released it sold 759 copies in the first two months, a respectable number for an academic book.

In January 1988 Heinlein decided to take a risk with a new operation for emphysema but recovery was very slow – not helped by Ginny's own increasing frailty. After three weeks he was still bedridden. He was transferred back to hospital and into intensive care for a week. When he returned home it was to hospital-style nursing. There were three more hospitalisations in response to medical incidents but eventually it was decided to send him home permanently. Robert Heinlein died in his sleep on 8 May 1988.

The Heinlein story does not end there of course. There was the posthumous *Grumbles from the Grave* and other unpublished material, including *How to Be a Politician* and *Tramp Royale*. Virginia Heinlein proved a ferocious guardian of both the literary and the historical estate: the papers are at Santa Cruz, and the books have been re-edited to Heinlein's preferred editions (typos removed), in the Virginia Edition (which I will not be using). The Heinleins left a foundation to support space travel. There was the influence on many other writers, and a reaction against Heinlein, discussed in the introduction. There was more academic interest in the form of theses, and the establishment in 1997 of *The Heinlein*

Journal. Late in 1994 there was a new movie of *The Puppet Masters*, and in 1997 a very strange version of *Starship Troopers*, directed by Paul Verhoeven. Most recently the Spierig brothers directed a very faithful version of "'All You Zombies—'", releasing it as *Predestination* (2014). After Virginia's death *For Us, the Living*, based on a surviving photocopy, was released by the estate and against the wishes of both Heinleins. It is not a wonderful book but its ideas are fundamental to many of the arguments made later in this book. *For Us, the Living* offers us a map of Heinlein that contains all his idiosyncrasies and renders much of what was once seen as a changeable arc as rather more consistent. Perhaps crucially it demonstrates that the Future History was not imposed on the short stories but was fundamental to them.

2

Heinlein's Narrative Arc

For many years there has been an understanding that Heinlein's output should be seen as divided into roughly into three sections: his short stories, the juveniles and his adult novels. This chapter will stick with that division.

Heinlein's career as a short-story writer runs from 1938 to 1959 (from 'Life-Line' to "All You Zombies—"'). His first juvenile novel was published in 1947 (*Rocket Ship Galileo*) and his last in 1963 (*Podkayne of Mars*, although the fix-up of *Orphans of the Sky* in the same year can be understood as a juvenile). His first novel (we will discount *For Us the Living* for a moment) was serialised in *Astounding* magazine in 1941 (*Methuselah's Children*), and his last published in 1987 (*To Sail Beyond the Sunset*). A visual representation of Heinlein's career can be found in Appendix 1.

As we will see in this chapter, you can pick up intertextual references moving from the juveniles to the adult novels to the short stories and back again. This is not simply a reflection of the extended

Future History, published in 1941.[1] If an idea or character worked well, Heinlein never had any hesitation about picking it up again, turning it around a bit, polishing it and reconfiguring it. Often he would write stories that took opposing sides in an argument.

Short Stories

Heinlein's short-story output follows a number of threads and has a number of phases. Many of the threads are obviously mined from *For Us, the Living*. In his letters and interviews Heinlein was very clear about this and it explains the sense of uniformity we often feel from otherwise very different stories. At times, it feels as if Heinlein is giving us a glimpse of the same world in different times and places. Eventually he would frame this as his worked-out Future History clearly laid out in *For Us, the Living*. The Future History shaped the short stories and the backgrounds of the Lazarus Long novels, and forms the world of Maureen Smith Long as it is narrated in *To Sail Beyond the Sunset*.

From 1939 to 1942, a mere three years, Heinlein was overwhelmingly an *Astounding* writer; of twenty-nine published stories, only three were *not* published in either *Astounding* or its stablemate, *Unknown Stories*. Not all of these were under the Heinlein byline. Of twenty-one stories for *Astounding* and three for *Unknown*, nine are published under pseudonyms. The conventional reason given for pseudonymous bylines is that it enabled an editor to display more variety than would otherwise be the case in a still immature genre, and Robert James is insistent that this is the case, but it is noticeable that the stories from the last half of 1941 and all

---

1   *Astounding Science Fiction*, May 1941. Heinlein began his Future History chart, on the back of one of his political campaign posters, in August 1939. See Gifford, *Robert A. Heinlein*, pp. 14–16 and 216–17.

the 1942 stories are under the byline of Anson MacDonald (with the exception of 'The Unpleasant Profession of Jonathan Hoag', which was published in *Unknown*, under the byline of John Riverside). As there is no indication that the different bylines fronted different types of story, then taken at face value, I would argue that this is a *downward* trajectory, in which a writer is trying to capture a market with a new identity or, as is the case with the Lyle Munroe stories, often trying to bury failures. Early Heinlein was not the super-successful science-fiction short-story writer that memory has rendered him.

During 1939–1940 all of Heinlein's stories for *Astounding* were published under his own byline. The first, 'Life-Line', is the most conventional of them all, a classic 1930s model invention story in which an invention that could threaten the livelihood of an industry – in this case a method to predict an individual's death which would render life insurance pointless – would disappear on the death of its inventor. Later invention stories make the characteristic shift that has been identified as Heinlein's contribution to the genre: they move us to *after* the invention has been rolled out and consider the changes in the world this has created. Thus, in 'The Roads Must Roll' we find ourselves in a complex technological future in which the world has become intrinsically dependent on its infrastructure and thus on those that maintain it. This is not a story about inventing rolling roads, but about how one manages them: the story ends up providing a psychometric/human resources answer to an engineering context.

However, Heinlein was not wedded to particular solutions. In 'The Roads Must Roll' a manager breaks a strike and aims to resolve it by creating a different type of worker (the new cadets, loyal to the company). The psychology of the workers, the use and abuse of technocracy as a philosophy and the best way to educate management trainees, is of far greater interest to Heinlein than is the engineering of the roads, which may engender a sense of wonder but is not front and centre. In direct contrast to this, in 'Blowups Happen' the psychometric problem of the tension and instability involved in running a dangerous power plant is resolved with an engineering solution: send the power plant off-planet. Of the two stories, published within two months of each other, 'The Roads Must Roll' is fundamentally the more interesting story: for all that Heinlein always consciously wanted to inspire through the engineering story, it is less the engineering – the invention – that he finds inspiring than the individual's engagement with the future.

That focus on *people* and how people experience the future is the key to the Heinlein 'voice' and mode and it emerges early: in 'Misfit' (1939), Andrew Jackson Libby is an awkward, gawky (and we learn many books later, transgender) kid stuck in the Cosmic Construction Corps as a way of rescuing him from his family's dissenter background. He experiences space sickness, learns to clean up, but never gets along with his peers; for him all the *new* is just so much noise and confusion. Unlike the reader, he is not caught up in the sense of wonder. Instead, we see a lost kid discover his genius for mathematical calculation, in the moment when he just knows that blast material has been incorrectly laid. 'Misfit' generates some of Heinlein's classic themes: the hidden genius, the need for education to complement genius (genius knows things, education helps genius understand why things must be so); the role of self study, the challenge of new environments, and a firm belief that a healthy society can find a place for *everyone* that will be evident in *Starship Troopers*, and which cracks only in *The Cat Who Walks Through Walls*.

In 'Coventry' (1940), a young man is reminded that it is not just that society needs him but that he needs society. Heinlein's argument (drawn from *For Us, the Living*) is that we are only fully human when we create the machine of society for ourselves. The hero of 'Coventry' chooses Hobbesian libertarianism, only to find that even the 'most free' societies have systems and consensus agreements; that he prefers the consensus agreement, the Lockean social contract, and recognises, crucially, that it is a contract that is continuously being remade by its participants. This point is also central to "'If This Goes On—'" in which Heinlein creates a future in which people are seduced into a false contract – with the prophet – by the denial of the basic right of education in the possibilities of the world. An intensely complex tale published over two months, February and March 1940, this story of a coup against a totalitarian religious regime is also a classic bildungsroman in which a young man grows out of childish beliefs and into the ways of the world. I will consider the story in greater depth later on but the key point here is that John Lyle *experiences* the change and the consequences of the change. He is not an adventurer, he is a sidekick, and it is through him that we feel the breaking open of the confined religious worldview, and through him that we see that what is taken for granted is often uncertain, unstable or untrue. In Lyle, Heinlein shows us what it's like living through revolution.

The same is true of 'Requiem', although in a very different way. The first story of 1940, this concerns Delos D. Harriman, a businessman whose entire life has been spent yearning for the Moon. Harriman persuades a couple of rocket-ship barnstormers (Heinlein would have been familiar with their aerial ancestors) to take him to the Moon. He recalls the childhood spent watching the stars, the loss of college, the business plans, the uncomprehending wife, and eventually the health condition that kept him from the Moon. This is a story of a man who became a cog that made a machine turn to put other people in the place his heart desired. Harriman has lived through a technological revolution and seen others reap the emotional rewards. After a law case, he succeeds in his desire: they take off for the Moon, his heart gives out and he dies there. It is in his view of Earth that he finds the sublime.

The last story of 1940 was Heinlein's 'The Devil Makes the Law', for *Unknown*. In May 1940 Heinlein (as Lyle Monroe) had published "'Let There Be Light'" in *Super Science Stories*. Overlong for what it is, the story is still of interest for its style – discussed in Chapter 3 – and as an insight into the social driver behind traditional trajectories for the invention story. When the engineer and scientist (male and female respectively) discover a new form of power, they keep it secret because patent law is so weak (even now an individual working for a company is not automatically entitled to a share in their invention), only to change their minds and go for what we'd now call Open Access and trust their invention to look after itself. 'The Devil Makes the Law' fits into the same category as a story about restraint of trade and how to deal with it. In this case, however, the story turns into – appropriately for *Unknown* – a tale about a hidden world of devils and magical creatures. This sense of the hidden is doubled in the story: hidden politics becomes hidden magic. Heinlein's unease with secretiveness, which he brought to all his politics – the intrinsic nature of democracy for Heinlein was that it was a magic performed in public – is made manifest.

"'—And He Built a Crooked House—'" (February) and 'By His Bootstraps' (October and bylined as Anson MacDonald) were the first of Heinlein's three time-travel stories. "'—And He Built a Crooked House—'" is not usually listed this way but I am including it here because all of Heinlein's time-travel work, up to and including *To Sail Beyond the Sunset*, makes use of the Klein-bottle theory of time; all dimensions and times are the same dimension and time and thus one can move along, back and through time without fundamentally changing anything because all time is the same. In "'—And He Built a Crooked House—'" the tesseract house that collapses in on itself is a microcosm of a universe in which all surfaces become the same surface (an idea used again when Valentine Michael Smith makes things disappear in *Stranger in a Strange Land*, Chapter 13). 'By His Bootstraps' is the quintessential time-travel story in which a man discovers that he is chasing his own tail as both tyrant and revolutionary. Heinlein uses the same structure much more effectively in '"All You Zombies—"' in 1959, but it is here that he first nails the trajectory of the story.

It is in 'Logic of Empire' (March 1941) that we first see Heinlein's concern with slavery; it links to both *Between Planets* and *Citizen of the Galaxy*. In 'Logic of Empire' an ordinary citizen, convinced that transports and volunteers for Venus have it easy, gets into a fight with a friend. Both get drunk and before he knows it he has woken up as a bonded labourer on Venus, if not a slave then certainly trapped in debt peonage. 'Logic of Empire' is in part a criticism of poor education and the ignorance of the average citizen. 'Universe' (May 1941) and 'Common Sense' (October 1941) extend the idea to the extreme and interestingly critique ideas that Heinlein expresses elsewhere. In these stories a generation ship has lost its collective memory. The very training school and officer caste that Heinlein advocates for in 'The Roads Must Roll' and so movingly in 'Solution Unsatisfactory' (also May) here contains and, through containment, swallows knowledge. The two stories together generated a new subgenre, one which has proved particularly popular in children's science fiction, in which younger people challenge the knowledge base of their elders. The stories are also noticeable for something that is unusual in a Heinlein story: they denigrate women. No world in which women are treated as bond slaves is a good world in a Heinlein story.[2]

Three 'squibs' – short satirical pieces – were published under the byline Lyle Monroe in 1941: 'Beyond Doubt', an Atlantean story

---

2   Diane Parkin-Speer argues in 'Almost a Feminist' (1995) that there is a consistent attempt to portray marriages as egalitarian. In Chapter 9 I will explore the ways Heinlein often gives women status advantages in marriage.

intended to 'explain' the Easter Island statues, in *Astounding*; 'My Object All Sublime', a slick invention story in which a man makes himself invisible and turns superhero, for *Future*; and 'Lost Legion' for *Super Science Stories*. 'Lost Legion' is not a good story but it has moments of interest. A surgeon (Ben) accidentally wipes out a man's telepathy during brain-surgery experiments with his psychologist friend (Phil) and with Joan who seems to be their joint girlfriend right through the story – a leftover of the sexual radicalism in *For Us, the Living*. They are 'called' to a mountain where they meet an Asian guide, Mr Ling, who inducts them into an order of wonder-workers who follow Jove and seek social equality. After a disastrous trip home, they return, Phil takes over and they decide to organise 'boys' camps' to tempt and train young people. Joan decides to get married but Heinlein does not say to whom ...

Another byline Heinlein used for *Astounding* in this period was Caleb Saunders, a name used just once, for a curiously old-fashioned story, 'Elsewhere' (later republished as 'Elsewhen'). The story does link to 'Lost Legion' in being concerned with parapsychology, and has clear elements of the mysticism that shows up again in *Stranger in a Strange Land*. A doctor experiments with four students to travel through time. Instead they travel through dimensions into their 'perfect' worlds: pure spirit for one, a war zone for another.

By 1941 the Anson MacDonald byline was asserting itself. The three-part serial *Sixth Column* appeared in *Astounding* at the beginning of the year, a reworking of a Campbell story about an Asian invasion of the USA. The second MacDonald story is a contrast. 'Goldfish Bowl' is notable because it is an 'aliens are superior to us' story, initially rejected by Campbell in 1941, probably because he was notoriously 'humans first'. In this story humans who set out to explore a strange phenomenon are captured and kept as pets. One escapes and is washed up dead with a warning tattooed on his skin, but no one can understand it. Campbell agreed to take the story, with changes, perhaps in order to keep Heinlein in his stable, and published it in 1942.

The third MacDonald story, 'Solution Unsatisfactory', has gone on to be a Heinlein classic. The story is set in period: it is 1940 and Dr Estelle Karst and Colonel Clyde Manning discover a radioactive dust. This is demonstrated on Berlin; Hitler surrenders and other countries are persuaded to sign a Pax Americana on the basis of films of the effects. The pilots who take the film die. Dr Karst commits suicide, horrified by the outcome. Manning sets up a patrol and, when a new president seeks to take it under American control, Manning refuses and creates the independent force that we later see in *Space Patrol*. Heinlein was still a convinced fan of the corporatism expressed in 'The Roads Must Roll', so we hear that 'The long-distance plan included the schools for the indoctrination of cadet patrolmen, schools that were to be open to youths of any race, any color, or nationality and which they would go forth to guard the peace *of every country but their own*.' It also reflects the legalistic peace tradition that emerged in the inter-war years in both America and Europe, and of which Heinlein was firmly a part.[3]

'Solution Unsatisfactory' shows what would become a trademark sentimentalism in Heinlein's stories, but the last four Anson MacDonald stories are all in their way much more hard-headed social commentary. In '"—We Also Walk Dogs"', Heinlein explored the business methods of a small company of 'fixers' as they seek to match supplier to need through a series of complex business exchanges. In 'Waldo', Heinlein looked at the effects on an individual of being very smart and very disabled, and incidentally popularised (not invented,

---

3   Akira Iriye, *The Globalizing of America, 1913–1945* (*The Cambridge History of American Foreign Relations, 3*) (Cambridge: Cambridge UP, 1993), p. 23.

since he had taken the idea from a magazine report about a man with myasthenia gravis) the idea of remote manipulators that could, like a pantograph, increase the size (or force) of movements.

Two pre-war stories are left, both for *Unknown*: 'They', in which a doctor becomes convinced that his world is peopled with artificial constructs, and 'The Unpleasant Profession of Jonathan Hoag' published as by John Riverside in 1942, in which two investigators discover that their world has been painted on a faulty canvas, and that the original 'painting' is breaking through. Both stories are paranoid fantasies that posit a real world and a hidden world where real decisions are taken; both are rather prescient for wartime.

The war brought a halt to Heinlein's publications, allowing us to pause and consider what themes were mapped out. The engineering stories are there, but they are either squibs or far more interested in the people who work the machines than in the machines themselves. There is a very strong element of social commentary which, for all it advocates openness and faith in the American people, also displays an unnerving *lack* of confidence in both rulers and ruled, as demonstrated in the idea that the young should be indoctrinated in new and distinctly corporatist values, the ease of indoctrination by the forces of good, and a concern that minorities are always at risk. This is compounded by a belief that there are hidden decision-makers everywhere. These tensions will be vivid in Heinlein's post-war publications.

Although Heinlein's career was on hiatus during the war, his move to Philadelphia, however much he disliked the area, seems to have cemented both his networks and his literary reputation. He was now near enough to New York to be engaged with the publishing industry in a wider sense, was receiving invitations to speak, and was working with congenial people, some of them science-fiction people. By the end of the war, 'Heinlein' was a commodity. There would be few pseudonymous publications after this (though he did use 'Simon York' for his mysteries) and he was about to enter into his most prolific period, with a four-track career: prestigious short-story publications, essays, juvenile novels of the frontier and adult novels of political and social concerns. However, Heinlein did not at first realise this. There was a spate of unpublished essays as he experimented. 'How to be a Politician', a rather good description of how to campaign in a block, found no takers, and nor did the fictional version, 'A Bathroom of Her Own', a simple story of a post-war election campaign. Neither did 'Free Men', which reads like an outtake of *Sixth Column*, nor did the essays, 'How to be a Survivor' or 'The Last Days of the United States', in which Heinlein argues for depopulation of the cities in the event of nuclear attack – almost certainly too much too soon. (He later reused the material in the stories 'Water is for Washing' (1947) and 'The Year of the Jackpot' (1952).) 'Sky Lift' (1953), in the minor magazine *Imagination*, is a story about a man realising his family is more important than glamour. This was the era of 'togetherness', when *McCall's* magazine could write 'the most impressive and the most heartening feature of this change is that men, women and children are achieving it together ... not as women alone or men alone, isolated from one another, but as a family sharing a common experience'(1954). It is worth noting because later Heinlein will become ever more family-centred. Heinlein began to worry that his work would no longer sell. It didn't help that he was determined to change markets, to move into the slicks and to end his dependency on one market.

When Heinlein did break through, it was in the prestigious *Saturday Evening Post*, and with one of his best stories, 'The Green Hills of Earth' (1947). He sold three more stories to the *Saturday Evening Post*: 'It's Great to Be Back!', 'Space Jockey' and 'The Black Pits of Luna'. 'The Green Hills of Earth' encapsulates Heinlein's understanding of heroism, and has that strong streak of sentiment that was to become so characteristic. 'It's Great to Be Back!' is very American: in the story emigration is understood to filter out the population to ensure a higher standard of intelligence (an idea Heinlein seems to have held simultaneously with his belief, which only grew stronger, that Americans were suckers for religious fraud). 'The Black Pits of Luna' was a juvenile and I will deal with it later in the chapter, along with 'Nothing Ever Happens on the Moon' (*Boy's Life*, 1949) and 'Tenderfoot in Space' (1958).

After four stories the *Saturday Evening Post* decided it did not want more science fiction and ended the run. From here on, Heinlein published in a range of what can only be called secondary markets. The year 1947 was particularly poor, with sales to *Startling Stories*, *Thrilling Wonder* and *Vertex*. Between 1948 and 1959 the only repeat sales were to *Boy's Life* and *Magazine of Fantasy and Science Fiction* (two each). Only seven were sold to respected SF markets: *Amazing Stories, Argosy, Galaxy, Magazine of Fantasy and Science Fiction* and *Weird Tales*. This does not of course mean that the stories were poor, but by the time Heinlein – at Ginny's suggestion – made the shift decisively to novels, his record of sales was rather spotty and he could not regard himself as a guaranteed short-story writer. The stories are very varied. The four he wrote for the girls' market will be dealt with as juveniles. 'Jerry is a Man' was a rather moving but in some ways problematic analogy story in which a woman goes to court to defend the right of an enhanced ape to be regarded as a man, with rights in his own life. The story is probably more interesting for its insistence on *women's* property rights. 'No Bands Playing, No Flags Flying' is not a science-fiction story but a simple tale of what heroism is, to which I will return in Chapter 4 because it is so crucial to the socialisation of the Heinlein reader. 'Gentlemen, Be Seated', in which a man blocks an air breach in a moon tunnel with his backside, works with the same theme, as does 'Ordeal in Space'.

'Ordeal in Space', published in *Town and Country*, 1948, has the signal honour of being the first of Heinlein's sentimental cat stories and tells the tale of a spaceman who gets over his trauma-triggered agoraphobia when he needs to rescue a kitten from the ledge of a skyscraper. His second cat story is 'Our Fair City', in which a whirlwind (called Kitty) is tamed by a hobo and dances with rubbish, helping to expose government corruption. It's not a subtle story but it is rather lovely and demonstrates Heinlein's more playful side, which was to become stronger with time, and which also shows up in 'Delilah and the Space Rigger'. This story is probably most significant for being the first time Ginny Heinlein aka Hazel Stone shows up in Heinlein's work. Heinlein was very clear that this story was based on Ginny's own experiences during the war. When a new radio engineer shows up on an asteroid and she is female, the foreman is worried she will distract the men, and tries to harass her out of her job. She gains the support of the psychologist and the men and the eventual decision is to open up positions to women to create both a gender balance and the 'incentive' for men that working around women is now perceived to create. We'll turn to this story when we consider the complexity of Heinlein's feminism in Chapter 5.

'Gulf' (1949), serialised over two months, is the one unequivocally bad piece of writing in this period. But the story is important because it creates a character, Harley 'Kettle Belly' Baldwin, who is vital to the much later *Friday*, and because *The Cat Who Walks Through Walls* is essential a rewrite of this story. In 'Gulf', Joe Green is recruited by Baldwin to join a group of supermen who can use a compact language invented by Alfred Korzybski to speed talk. They have to stop someone using a super-weapon to blow up Earth: it's a suicide mission, though this is never really conveyed. More interesting is the way in which the weapon is described. Baldwin argues, 'It's not a weapon. It's a means of destroying a planet and everything on it completely. If that's a weapon, military or political, then I'm Samson and you're Delilah.' As we discussed in the previous chapter, Heinlein was essentially a military man first and a politician second, and super-weapons make nonsense of army, navy, air force and the political process. We also see Heinlein's sentimentality becoming stronger in the late 1940s. 'The Elephant Circuit' (1948) aka 'The Man Who Travelled in Elephants' is a slight whimsy, a story of a couple who 'travel in elephants' to give their life meaning and who extend this into the afterlife. In 'The Long Watch' (1949) a patrol man gives up his life, making his choices step by step, buying time to prevent a coup.

In the 1950s, Heinlein produced some of his best stories, including 'The Man Who Sold the Moon' (1950), in which D. D. Harriman, who makes the Moon landings possible, is left behind, too old to fly, too important to be spared from his business; and 'Sky Lift' (1953), in which a young man sacrifices his health to rush a vaccine at very high G-force to another planet. In 'Project Nightmare' (1953), the assembled telekinetics set out to defuse super-weapons/nuclear bombs planted by Russia; the military are powerless to do anything other than wait for the psychokinetics to find the planted bombs to defuse, and eventually to find the Russian arsenal so that it might be destroyed. Heinlein's final story came a few years later: '"All You Zombies—"' (1959), an intense exploration of time travel, transgender/intersex alignment and loneliness. The ending of the story is heart-wrenching. If there had to be a last Heinlein short story, this was his most perfect: sixty years later it remains one of the great classics of the field.

By the end of the short-story period, all the key elements of Heinlein are in place: sentiment, family first, a clear idea of bravery and duty, women matter, slavery is wrong, and the traces of sexual radicalism evident in *For Us, the Living* showing through in stories such as 'The Year of the Jackpot' (1952), 'The Menace from Earth' (1957) and '"All You Zombies—"'.

The Juvenile Novels

The Heinlein juvenile novels run from 1947 to 1963. Too often *Starship Troopers* is remembered as the last of the sequence but this is actually *Podkayne of Mars*. There are fifteen novels and eight short stories, four of which were written for boys (the first is 'Misfit' which we have already discussed) and four for girls (although one was unpublished); and the stories for girls are not science fiction. They are nonetheless important because without them it is unlikely that *Podkayne of Mars* would exist, and without them we can misunderstand what Heinlein was trying to do in that novel.

Heinlein's first juvenile novel was *Rocket Ship Galileo* (1947). It is not a particularly good book, and probably owes too much to a very successful series of the time, *Radio Boys*. Heinlein never mentions this as an influence but the connections between radio and science fiction, via the editorship of Hugo Gernsback and the back pages of several magazines, were strong, and the structures of the books – a group of early teen boys mentored by an older man in what looks a lot like a 'take your kid to work' plot – are very similar. The book is very much about the boys' rocket club and about how this will prepare them for the making of the rocket (an idea picked up later in *Have Space Suit—Will Travel*). In *Rocket Ship Galileo* there is also the unnerving sense of a fantasy game: the rocket seems oddly fragile, and the adventure, in which they catch Nazis, is straight out of the Hardy Boys. It also has great qualities: it is multi-ethnic and multi-religious and in this way sets the tone for the other juveniles, as we shall see. At a time when Jews (and blacks and Irish) were generally sidekicks in film, radio and books, it is Morrie Abrams from a large Jewish family who, although not the main protagonist of the book, is the pilot of the rocket ship.

Heinlein found a surer footing with his first juvenile short story and his second juvenile novel. 'The Black Pits of Luna' (*Saturday Evening Post*, January 1948) is a neat story in which a boy takes a trip to the Moon with his parents and younger brother. The parents are demanding tourists who give into everything the younger boy asks for, and when the boy goes missing, they panic. The elder manages to track him down, and in doing so 'proves' (in the terms set in 'It's Great to Be Back!') that he is good migrant material. It is a very nicely centred story. It's a scouting tale and unlike *Rocket Ship Galileo* it takes the crucial step for the juvenile of leaving the adults behind. Perhaps more important for Heinlein's ideas of childhood, discussed in Chapter 5, it makes leaving the parents behind a crucial step out of childhood. The idea is repeated in 'Tenderfoot in Space' (1958), in which a Boy Scout sets out to win his Eagle Scout badge on the Moon, to become the first triplanetary Scout. (Heinlein never seems to be too bothered about the planetary status of moons: the landing 'planet' in 'Common Sense' is a moon.)

Building on ideas he had used in 'The Roads Must Roll' and would use again in 'The Long Watch' (the chances are they were written more or less together given the often longer lead time in magazines) Heinlein sets up *Space Cadet* (1948) so that not only must a child leave its parents, it must transfer its loyalty to something greater: to comrade and to institution. That process of transference becomes a key element in all of the juveniles. In *Red Planet* (1949) the purpose of the school is to create cohort loyalty among people who will work very far apart across the planet; in *Farmer in the Sky* (1950), serialised as 'Satellite Scout' in *Boy's Life*, the scout troop becomes a way of creating the same kind of communal loyalty, which is then reinforced, as in *Space Cadet*, by vertical strands of loyalty through apprenticeship structures.

In these first three juveniles Heinlein set out to create something he believed in fiercely, society as weave and weft, where to be a simple thread was an honourable position. He also, as we see over and over again, regards adulthood as a process of knowledge acquisition. These are the novels in which readers *learn* things about the world: astrogation in *Space Cadet*, the creation of soil in *Farmer in the Sky*, international politics in *Between Planets*, *The Star Beast* and *Citizen of the Galaxy*. All of these books are career books, a subgenre of the juvenile market that was highly popular in the 1950s, at a time when most children left school much earlier than they do today. The clear aim of these books was to show children what opportunities were out there. Heinlein simply lifted the conceit wholesale. If we skip over *Between Planets* (1951) for a moment, a book that fits better with the later-model juveniles, we can see the same thing in the second 'set', the four juveniles that Heinlein produced consecutively between 1952 and 1955, and a short story.

The Rolling Stones (1952) is a loose tale of a family travelling between settlements, motivated equally by the older boys' desire to trade and their father's desire for a *wanderjahr*. In *Starman Jones* (1952) Max Jones is dispossessed of his farm by his mother's second marriage, and discovers that his uncle forgot to bequeath his place in the astrogators' guild to him. He secures a place on a ship through trickery, and through his eidetic memory makes himself invaluable when the ship gets lost and one of the officers destroys the log tables in a fit of madness. Unlike the case of Libby in 'Misfit', this is not presented as genius. By this time presumably Heinlein, after the war and working in an engineering shop, was clear on the difference. Finally, there are *The Star Beast* (1954), in which the boy discovers that the pet his great-grandfather brought back from space is actually an alien space princess who thinks she is breeding humans (like any child might breed guinea pigs), and *Tunnel in the Sky* (1955), in which Rod sets out on a school trip to win his off-planet licence, is stranded, discovers the strengths of communalism and helps to build a new society, until the party is rescued and he has to rethink his options.

Each of these books pushes the career-book model a little further. Not one of the characters in any of these books is 'self-made'. All are helped by either family or friends; all have their business interests underwritten or their education supported, or their houses erected by the others. The Stones boys are clearly setting out to begin their entrepreneurial careers early, as Heinlein and his friends had done on the streets of Kansas City. In *Starman Jones* there is both an argument against hereditary career practices but also an argument about seizing the day, not allowing such practices to keep you out. In *The Star Beast* we are taught all about the civil service and, incidentally, how to be a politician's wife. In *Tunnel in the Sky*, we learn that being a lawyer can take you to really interesting places, but also that careers aren't always planned, and that in many ways our future is determined by the doors we decide to walk through and what we choose to do on the other side. In the short story, 'The Menace From Earth' (1957), a young woman discovers that marriage and career are compatible.

The second set of stories, the ones that turn away from the career-book model and towards something much more consciously political, begins with *Between Planets* (1951), includes *The Star Beast*, and from the second half of the 1950s, *Time for the Stars* (1956), *Citizen of the Galaxy* (1958) and *Have Space Suit—Will Travel* (1958). These books could even be seen as deliberately intended to induct teens *into* the body politic, and if understood that way mean that we can frame *Starship Troopers* as far less of an outlier than collective memory would have it.

With *Between Planets*, a story that owes something to 'Logic of Empire', Heinlein took a different turn. Here Don is precisely ripped from the cloth in which he thought he was bound and discovers, as he loses his identity as a man with inter-planetary citizenship, that if he ever wants to be part of a cloth again he must weave it himself. Don starts off in school, like the characters in *Red Planet*, but the adults in his life prove unreliable (even his parents seem to be willing to see him used as a courier). He finds himself displaced to Venus, a refugee, and when Earth takes over he is recruited into the local guerrillas. When he does find a place for himself it is because he has made friends/is in love with a young woman who is part of established Venusian society and it is clear that she will eventually pull him back in. Heinlein prescribes a clear parabola for the move from childhood to adolescence and into adulthood which he will repeat in *The Star Beast* (1954) and *Citizen of the Galaxy* (1958), and which will be picked up in *Time Enough for Love*. For Heinlein the family was central to his construction of adulthood from a very early period.

Between Planets is an essentially optimistic book: Don may feel betrayed by his schoolmaster and rejected by his schoolmates as his own sense of interplanetary neutrality is increasingly framed by others as enmity, but his experiences on Venus introduce him to a new settler mindset, and give him comrades-in-arms and a new loyalty. The book is framed in the American understanding of revolution as inherently natural and explicitly parallels the breaking away of a child from his peers and his parents with the breaking away of a colony from its motherland. But it does so still by positing Don (and Venus) as the 'good' child chafing at the reins (which raises parallels with the protagonist of 'Coventry' who is positioned as the result of poor parenting). This narrative will be extended into the adult novel, *The Moon is a Harsh Mistress* (1966) and then formalised as a political process that should be recognised in *Time Enough for Love*, when the collective protagonists leave for Tertius.

Good parenting and good political parenting begin to emerge as a very strong narrative in the late 1950s in Heinlein's work.

This is the point at which it becomes problematic to separate the juveniles from the adult novels. There are poor fathers and mothers in *Starman Jones* (1954), *The Star Beast* (1955), *Double Star* (1956), *The Door Into Summer* (1957), *Starship Troopers* (1961), *Podkayne of Mars* (1963) and *Farnham's Freehold* (1964). In each book substitute parents are found, often in politicised mentors: Sam the hobo steward's mate in *Starman Jones*, the career civil servant in *The Star Beast*, the metaphysical legacy of a politician in *Double Star*, or the Moral Philosophy teachers and sergeants in *Starship Troopers*. In *Podkayne of Mars*, the one book where no such mentor is really found (her uncle is rarely on stage), and to which I will return, the result is disastrous both personally and politically. The one example of good parenting comes in *Have Space Suit—Will Travel* (1958), in which well-parented children are able to convince parental galactic guardians that they represent a childish race that can also benefit from good parenting. For an essentially positive book its conclusion is rather humbling.

The juveniles of this period also become increasingly pessimistic. By 1956 Heinlein's faith in a new world order was crumbling. The American monopoly of nuclear weapons had not lasted long and its impact had been squandered. The presence of nuclear weapons was doing nothing to prevent Soviet expansionism. The suppression of the Hungarian uprising, with little protest from the USA, contributed to Heinlein's belief that the USA had lost its leadership role and this, combined with the testing agreements, led to disillusion. Heinlein began looking outwards. *The Star Beast* is a novel in which humans are relatively insignificant in the grand scheme of things. The best we can hope is to negotiate ourselves a place in the galaxy as tolerated amusements. The outcome of *Have Space Suit—Will Travel* is not much better but where John Thomas IV is a somewhat hapless hero who is pushed in the direction that his planet needs him to go (see also Johnny Rico in *Starship Troopers*) and his girlfriend would like to go, Kip, in *Have Space Suit—Will Travel*, is more representative of the typical SF adventurer and thus perhaps of the direction Heinlein hopes for the human race. The book version of *Methuselah's Children* was published the year after *Have Space Suit—Will Travel* and it shares with that book the same outward-bound trajectory and the same narrative of a species growing up.

The standout among the juvenile novels, the one which least fits any overarching narrative, is *Citizen of the Galaxy* (1957). Although we see the same mentorship structure between Thorby Baslim and his Colonel, the Beggar, the trajectory is more like that in *The Star Beast*: Thorby, for all his wealth, is less a cog in the wheel than a pawn in others' plots. Usually presented as a book about the iniquities of slavery, it also demonstrates Heinlein's distrust of big corporations, raised in *For Us, the Living* way back in 1938, and which will extend into *Friday* in 1982. For a capitalist, Heinlein in 1958 was deeply distrustful of mega-capitalism and the political arguments in this book encourage his juvenile readers to share this distrust.

The final two juveniles were *Starship Troopers* (1959) and *Podkayne of Mars* (1964). Much has been written about the final version of *Starship Troopers* but for a moment I want to concentrate on the actual juvenile novel, which is the first two-thirds of the book: the last third, in which Johnny Rico goes through officer training school, was added to turn the juvenile into a bildungsroman for the adult market. *Starship Troopers* is a cousin to *Space Cadet* and to the later *Glory Road* (1963): its basic theme is how to inculcate corporate identity into the young. Johnny Rico is a follower, someone who wants to be shaped by his environment and to find a wider meaning within a cohort. What Heinlein does, which I think caused so much offence, is to make that explicit. Johnny Rico is another result of poor parenting – not bad, but certainly not much engaged. Johnny Rico willingly gives up his mind, heart and conscience to the military. He is not brainwashed into lack of conscience; he chooses a loyalty to his mates. At no point does he ever really become politicised. Beyond a belief that civic responsibility is something to be earned, and that there are aliens about to destroy Earth that need to be prevented from doing so, Johnny never has a political idea in his life. So this is a political novel with an apolitical protagonist, a really unusual move to make, and one that was quite deliberate: Heinlein the politician was increasingly concerned, after 1958 and the failure of his Patrick Henry movement, with how to motivate the apolitical.

Starship Troopers however is also about opening up opportunities and supporting individual development. The set-up from the start is that of the classic scenario known to many working-class children (although Johnny himself is not working class) in which limited opportunities at home are replaced with widening opportunities in the world, through the institutions one can join. Rico is rescued from poor parenting by positive institutional parenting. No such good result is available to Podkayne.

Podkayne of Mars has a poor reputation. It is a novel of disappointment and loss and prefigures both *Friday* and Heinlein's general loss of faith in American education and opportunity. It seems a let-down after the other novels, and in its depiction of a young woman, it seems to renege on the evidence (there in 'The Menace from Earth') that Heinlein was supportive of women's ambitions. But if we read it as a juvenile, and as part of his trilogy of non-science-fictional girls' stories, then the book is much more in line with Heinleinian ideas about parenting and society and education that are expressed elsewhere.

Between 1949 and 1951 Heinlein wrote three short non-SF stories for girls about Maureen or 'Pudding', for Alice Dalgliesh: 'Poor Daddy', 'Cliff and the Calories' and 'The Bulletin Board'. The first two were published, the last was not and may actually be the middle story in terms of when it was written. They are all delightful. In 'Poor Daddy', Daddy is an ordinary chap who sets out to prove himself to his very smart wife; in 'Cliff and the Calories' Maureen goes on a diet to keep her boyfriend; and in 'The Bulletin Board' she sets out to improve the popularity of a rather isolated young woman. The second story is endearing: the entire family ends up on a range of diets, they all fail and Maureen discovers her boyfriend has a penchant for Rubens paintings. But it is that first story that is the key to *Podkayne* (Puddin') *of Mars*. In the story Mother is constantly distracted by new ideas, and Daddy is often chasing after her. Maureen is in some ways benignly neglected. They do not, for example, notice her cramping her ambitions to match those of her boyfriend in an effort not to be her mother. Combined with 'The Bulletin Board', the three stories taken together are in part about the pressures on being female in 1950s America. It is this which Heinlein transfers over to *Podkayne of Mars*, writing a juvenile about a young woman who does not have parental support – whose parents barely know her and still insist on seeing her as a child – and who gradually learns that she will not be admitted into the peer groups and mentorship structures that both her boyfriend and her brother can expect to access.

Before leaving the conventionally identified juveniles, I want to add one more novel to the group, *Glory Road* (1963). Published contemporaneously with *Podkayne of Mars* but by Putnam, and not written for the adolescent market, I nonetheless think it is far better understood in this category. Rather than an adult behaving rather childishly, this is a novel about one last throw of the adolescent dice. E. C. Gordon is the classic delayed adolescent. His late teens and early twenties taken up with the army, he is convinced that the army has prepared him for adulthood, only to realise that it has kept him from integrating with society. In this he has the same realisations as Matt Dodson and Johnny Rico; he no longer *fits*; but whereas for them it is a source of pride, for him it brings bitterness. He has been trained and conditioned to want adventure, to enjoy the highs and lows of risking his life. Some of this is from the army, but Heinlein is also nodding in the direction of all the great adventure writers he ever read, who led him and others down the garden path to glory: Hemingway, Burroughs, Leiber and Dumas, among others. This is not, in Heinlein's terms, adulthood. Adulthood, as we shall see over and over again, is about creating family and E. C., or Oscar as Star will call him, rejects that path. Bored and fed up when Star finds him, he willingly accepts the offer to become an adventurer, champion and playmate in what at times feels like a Live Action Role Play. Even the discovery that Star is far older than Oscar, with a family already and no real intention of starting another, reinforces this perception. Oscar will get to play at being a toy boy for the rest of his life if he wishes, with no responsibilities other than to come when called and have another adventure. He is locked into adolescence.

The Adult Novels

Those novels which are listed as Heinlein's 'adult' novels mostly coincide with what he understood as his novels of social satire, and also some experiments with form in which he was clearly emulating known texts. Knowing this helps a great deal when we get to *Farnham's Freehold* (1964) and *'The Number of the Beast'* (1979), the two novels which are generally regarded as Heinlein's worst (*To Sail Beyond the Sunset* is usually regarded as weak, rather than actively bad). The last of the thirteen juveniles Heinlein wrote for Scribner was *Starship Troopers*, which they rejected. The book was placed with Putnam, and with the exception of *'The Number of the Beast'* (Fawcett, 1979), *Friday* (Holt, Rinehart, 1982) and *Job: A Comedy of Justice* (Ballantine, 1984), his later novels were all published by Putnam.

Astounding published two of Heinlein's novels in serialised form in 1941. The first was *Sixth Column*, as by 'Anson MacDonald', about the resistance to an Asian invasion of the USA. 'Sixth Column', the story of a Pan-Asian [sic] invasion of America and the guerrilla resistance, was serialised in *Astounding* from January to March. Based on an unpublished Campbell novella (collected in Campbell's *The Space Beyond*, 1976), the story fits clearly into the yellow peril tradition, but also reflects the Japanese expansion of the period. The serial was slight, a piece of patriotic propaganda, but it relied on similar ideas to "'If This Goes On—'" in that once more Heinlein created a false religion, the Sixth Column of the story. Although he uses the fake religion to cover a political conspiracy, it once more pointed to Heinlein's belief in the vulnerability of Americans to religious fervour and fakery, a trope which runs from the Future History sketched out in *For Us, the Living*, through *Stranger in a Strange Land*, and *Job: A Comedy of Justice* into *To Sail Beyond the Sunset*.

The second serialised novel was *Methuselah's Children*. Superficially this is a story rooted in the eugenics movements so dominant in early twentieth-century America. In the nineteenth century the Howard Foundation has been set up to research longevity and has opted to breed long-lived humans. That it is not strictly a eugenics story is reflected in the 'large number of defectives' to which we are directed, the results of inbreeding. The plot is basic: a group of people with a hidden genetic trait are discovered and forced to run, led by the unexpected arrival of the oldest of their generation, Lazarus Long, a name certainly chosen to encapsulate the myth of the Wandering Jew. It is the first time we begin to see the figure of the picaro that will dominate Heinlein's later work.

In the following year, *Astounding* serialised Heinlein's third novel,

Beyond This Horizon (April–May 1942), under the byline Anson McDonald. This is essentially a rewrite of the then unpublished *For Us, the Living*. It eschewed the classic utopian form of the stranger as point of view; instead it is a fantasy of someone happy yet uneasy in a utopia. It also raised the question of how you deal with ennui (brought up again in *Time Enough For Love*) and explored the possibilities and limitations of eugenics. These first three novels appeared in book form after the war: *Beyond This Horizon* in 1948, *Sixth Column* in 1949 (subsequently retitled *The Day After Tomorrow*), and *Methuselah's Children*, in rewritten form, in 1957.

The Puppet Masters (1951) is a cold-war thriller in which invading slugs became a projection of Heinlein's and America's fears about communism. It reflects what Warren I. Cohen identifies as a growth of rhetorical hostility in contemporary culture, traceable to the inflammatory language of Truman. This language, Cohen argues, allowed Truman to ensure that the executive dominated the legislature as it did in a time of war, keeping America on a military footing with clear consequences for the management of civilian life.[4] We see this clearly expressed in *The Puppet Masters*. As Joseph Brown notes in 'Heinlein and the Cold War', 'the effort to conform and lose autonomy is done precisely to differentiate oneself from a Soviet society that demands conformity and loss of autonomy. Heinlein . . . recognized the dilemma and packaged his response as a kind of gesturing at the loss of some trivial personal liberties . . . [but] . . . attached this gesture to his frequent trope of personal choice and responsibility' (p. 118). But the novel also expresses Heinlein's dislike of sexual oppression and sexual dissimulation, and his preference for

---

4   Warren I. Cohen, *America in the Age of Soviet Power, 1945–1991* (*The Cambridge History of American Foreign Relations* 4) (Cambridge: Cambridge UP, 1991), pp. 39–40.

a nudity culture; all of which put him sharply at variance with the sexual culture of the 1950s.

Double Star (1956) is trickier. It is one of the novels which has lasted well perhaps because, for all its satirising of America Firsters and Isolationists, it is not actually a satirical novel: quite clearly a version of Twain's *The Prince and the Pauper*, it is a fundamentally democratic book which argues that anyone can become anything, but also mourns the loss of self that this might entail. With some stretching it can be considered as a sequel to *Stranger in a Strange Land*, written in the future of that book when our relations with the Martians and the Nests have expanded, and humans are resisting the consequences of that. I have not listed it among the juveniles although it follows the same trajectory: Lorenzo Smith is brought in from an unsettled adolescent existence of play-acting, into a constructed political 'family' where he is inducted into the institution of government as if it were a collective such as the military. Here he must learn to care not just for humanity but for the inhabitants of the galaxy as his wider family, abandoning the Us/Other dichotomy he has learned. His trajectory as the faux Bonforte becomes the trajectory of Earth, growing out of its temperamental and self-centred childhood. The *figure* of Bonforte is in a sense Kip from *Have Space Suit—Will Travel*. Having survived his day in court, Bonforte must practise that experience every day in the Galactic Arena.

The Door Into Summer (1957) is written on a much smaller scale, a story about a man who travels back in time to alter his future, and another novel of conspiracy, double-cross and betrayal, that ends with the (re)construction of family. It is written on a domestic canvas, makes use of some of the tropes in *For Us, the Living*, and figures as a time-loop romance that in some ways has more in common with the later World as Myth novels than with the social satires of this period.

Glory Road is a medieval romance in which much of the sexual activity in that book is framed around, and concluded by, a critique of American sexual mores that we saw first in *For Us, the Living*, and will see later in *Job: A Comedy of Justice* (1984). It is one of Heinlein's great themes: the immorality of jealousy and possessiveness, and the appalling behaviour that creates the 'moral code' that permits destructive illicit unions and condemns open sharing.

Farnham's Freehold (1964) is clearly channelling Twain's *A Connecticut Yankee in King Arthur's Court*, as Hugh Farnham goes into a future and discovers a seeming primitivism masking far higher technology. The novel's satire is surely intended to be modelled on Swift's *A Modest Proposal* and Heinlein clearly thought his track record as an anti-racist would support this. He was one of the very few writers to regularly use non-white characters and protagonists and integrated scenarios, and he had already built challenges to racial politics into his juveniles, such as *Space Cadet*, *The Star Beast* and *Podkayne of Mars*, and his adult novels, *Beyond This Horizon* and *Double Star*. But he failed to register that the novel had to stand alone and that he did not understand the structures of racism and the perpetuation of racism. The book's racism and anti-racism will be discussed extensively in Chapter 7.

The Moon is a Harsh Mistress (1966) has its own ambiguities, enough that it has been a darling of both the left and the right, who see a successful anarchy/libertarian utopia. It is a classic Heinlein revolutionary novel with many of the same ideas about colonial expansion, the inevitable breakdown of empire and how to organise a revolution. The novel is rich with sexual radicalism – Heinlein's rock-solid belief in *consent* comes to the fore – and scathing comments on racial prejudice. The main character is, like all third-generation Loonies, a person of colour; the love of his life is white (there is an excruciating 'blacking-up' scene) and all are involved in a complex line marriage. The novel also introduces the concept of TANSTAAFL – *there ain't no such thing as a free lunch* – into science fiction, a phrase that does not actually mean what countless libertarians think it does. The reference is to hidden costs ('free' lunches for drinkers in 1920s saloons), not to free riders. It is also short, sharp and punchy, the very last of Heinlein's novels to be so.

To go back in time to 1961, we are in at the beginning on Heinlein's expansionist period, a time in which his novels regularly ballooned to, and were cut back from, 250,000 words. We are also at the beginning of his more intimate, Rabelaisian books. *Double Star, Starship Troopers* and *The Moon is a Harsh Mistress* had fairly clear messages and Heinlein was reasonably comfortable with their reception. Those who did not like the books were generally not expected to. And those who did like them shared Heinlein's mind-set.

Stranger in a Strange Land is Heinlein's big attempt at an American satire and owes a great deal to Sinclair Lewis's *Elmer Gantry* (1926), and also to the inversion of the utopian tradition in which, instead of us commenting on them, the representative of utopia comes here and comments on our weird habits. Heinlein uses it to criticise sexual expectation (and predation), politics and religion. *Stranger in a Strange Land* set Heinlein on a different course. Inspired by Kipling's *Jungle Book* and probably also Edgar Rice Burroughs' *Tarzan* stories, this began life as the story of an abandoned child on Mars raised by aliens, who thinks he is an alien and imports that mentality when he is brought home. The first third of the book sticks roughly to that model, but Part Two, in which Michael Valentine Smith traverses the land as a fact finder for the Martian Nests as well as himself, and Part Three, in which he starts a new religion and destroys an old one, head in a different direction altogether, instead becoming an exploration of religious ecstasy. The novel, constructed in five parts, also makes use of the Pentateuch, as Smith is the Adam evicted from Eden, then serves as Moses bringing the children of Israel away from the false gods of the Fosterites, and eventually the New Testament (see Part Five) as Smith emerges – driven from a theological seminary – as a saviour genuinely reborn. In using the Old Martians as the source of all wisdom Heinlein also made use of two science fiction-rooted religious stories, the Shaver mysteries and of course the mythos of Scientology, which by this time was gaining traction.

Remembering Heinlein's Future History there is a touch of what Heinlein himself called 'the Crazy Years'. The book, as is well known, was immensely successful, becoming a sleeper and cult hit. Heinlein discovered there were college courses on the book's spirituality, received letters from distressed young women whose boyfriends were using it to coerce them into sex, and eventually of course there was the murder of Sharon Tate, in the name of a cult based loosely on the book. It is probably no surprise that Heinlein backed off from this line of storytelling and returned to the much more conscious political satire. A decade after *Stranger in a Strange Land* and four years after *The Moon is a Harsh Mistress*, Heinlein released *I Will Fear No Evil* (1970). As with *Stranger* there is a real sense of mining the sexual radicalism that was so much a part of Heinlein's youth, but here we begin also to see the strong economic and economic-social conservatism that defined his later works.

In *I Will Fear No Evil* a very rich man has his brain transferred into the first compatible body that comes along. There isn't much choice because he has a rare blood group. This turns out to be the body of his much-loved secretary who has been attacked and killed on her way home. In this persona he learns to perform as a female, has several sexual adventures, discovers that people treat women differently and finally falls in love with and marries his lawyer. The story is set against a declining America in which literacy is becoming a minority skill and where the streets are too dangerous to move around in. The image of inner-city America peddled by many news outlets in the 1970s is reflected in the work of science-fiction writers as disparate as Philip K. Dick and Samuel R. Delany, and is not, *ipso facto*, a right-wing vision. The book is radical in its depiction of a transgender character (although we will discuss in another chapter what this does and doesn't mean in terms of Heinlein's understanding of transgender and intersex) and of a love that can cross gender, sex and sexual preference, in the love of the lawyer for Johann Sebastian Bach Smith and his later persona, Joan Eunice.

Before discussing the Lazarus Long series with which Heinlein concluded his career, I will deviate to consider 'The Number of the Beast' (1979), *Friday* (1984) and *Job: A Comedy of Justice* (1984). 'The Number of the Beast' and *Job* are both interdimensional romps: the first is optimistic, for all that the characters are fleeing a threat; the second more pessimistic even though the main character is moving steadily towards a kinder, more caring world view. In 'The Number of the Beast' four characters intentionally drawn from the work of E. E. 'Doc' Smith and Edgar Rice Burroughs move through metatextual universes and find many of their ideas about the world reinforced. It is in *Time Enough for Love* (1973) that Heinlein begins to resolve the difficulty of having constructed a future history with which the present has caught up, and he does this by hinting that Lazarus Long has been on a different timeline from us. This is clarified and becomes the basis of the complex romp 'The Number of the Beast' while in *Job*, the protagonist is the plaything of the gods and his character is slowly stripped bare. Both books bear Heinlein's trademark scorn about the world's sexual morality and in *Job*, as in the stand-alone novel *Friday*, the female protagonist is held up to the interested reader as a far healthier model of sexual behaviour and interaction. *Friday*, of course, is also one of Heinlein's anti-slavery novels, demonstrating what he asserts in *Citizen of the Galaxy*, that humans will keep finding ways of reinventing and renaming slavery in an attempt to render it palatable.

Time Enough for Love was the first in the Lazarus Long sequence (*Methuselah's Children* can be regarded as a prequel). Told as a scheherazade, it is simultaneously one of the weakest yet the sweetest of Heinlein's later books. It begins with the rescue of Lazarus Long (against his wishes) from a flophouse and proceeds as an attempt to keep him entertained while he is being rejuvenated. It contains inset stories about Long's life which pick up on old Heinlein themes, with lots of friendly sex and family building, and finally a trip back in time so that Heinlein/Lazarus Long can meet his mother and fall in love with her. *Time Enough for Love* is continued in *The Cat Who Walks Through Walls* (1985) in which Hazel Meade Stone becomes the latest Heinlein character to be revived, and travels in time in order to find a hero (Richard this time, not Oscar) who turns out to be a direct descendant of Lazarus Long. It is this novel that shows Heinlein's really decisive socio-economic shift to the right but, as ever, it maintains its sexual radicalism. The sequence was completed (at least to the degree that Heinlein died with only intentions of a next book, not a proposal) with *To Sail Beyond the Sunset* (1987) in which the rescued Maureen Smith has her own adventures in time and space and Heinlein provides a fascinating trip through the twentieth century as he understands it.

Conclusions

For an author with a career that spanned almost fifty years, and who wrote no true series, there are a remarkable number of clusters within Heinlein's work. Some of the repetitions are superficial. There are many redheads: his first redhead is Delilah in 'Delilah and the Space Rigger' but once redheads appear, they appear regularly, as Castor and Pollux in *The Rolling Stones*, as Vicky in *Time for the Stars*, Lapis Lazuli and Lorelei Lee Long and of course Lazarus and Maureen

Smith. Some repetitions are thematic: the hands-off fathers of *Rocket Ship Galileo, Have Space Suit—Will Travel,* and the problematic mothers of *Starman Jones* and *Farnham's Freehold.* Both have their opposites as well; Heinlein's poor fathers are controlling, his good mothers supportive. Jane in "'All You Zombies—'" is re-outfitted to be Friday, in the novel of that name. But there are also characters who repeat. Andrew Libby (who is also Max in *Starman Jones*) appears as himself in *Methuselah's Children, Time Enough for Love* and *The Cat Who Walks Through Walls.* Hazel Meade Stone comes up in *The Rolling Stones, The Moon is a Harsh Mistress, 'The Number of the Beast', The Cat Who Walks Through Walls* and may also be the Hazel in 'Logic of Empire' and, as Hazel Hayakawa, appears on the monument in 'The Black Pits of Luna'. It is just possible that she and Richard Ames are also the Mr and Mrs Joseph Green of 'Gulf', who also have a bit part in *The Moon is a Harsh Mistress,* although I cannot prove this.

The Boy Scout/Patrol/Soldier stories show a clear set of values arranged around a cohesive civic identity that I will be arguing later was core to Heinlein's writing. In addition we can trace a Patrol trilogy, formed of *Space Cadet,* 'The Long Watch' and 'Solution Unsatisfactory', that cuts across the juvenile/adult/short story/novel divide. *Space Cadet, Farmer in the Sky, Between Planets, Double Star* and *The Moon is a Harsh Mistress* also create an imperial quintet in which we see the Earth expand its empire and then contract and learn to get along with a diverse galaxy.

There is a constant anti-slavery theme running from 'Logic of Empire' and 'Jerry was a Man' through *Citizen of the Galaxy, Farnham's Freehold, Friday* and *Time Enough for Love.* There is a clear tendency to mine his own ideas: *For Us, the Living* keeps Heinlein going after its novelisation in *Beyond This Horizon* and we see flashes of it in almost every novel he writes for adult readers. There is a series of survivalist stories ('How to be a Survivor', 'The Last Days of the United States', 'Water is for Washing' and 'The Year of the Jackpot') that link together to create attitudes towards preparedness and bravery that crop up again and again, most memorably in *Farnham's Freehold* and *Friday*. And at the gentler end are the family dynamic novels, from *The Rolling Stones* to *Time Enough for Love*. In *To Sail Beyond the Sunset*, perhaps aware of his mortality, Heinlein linked many of his Harriman stories into the bildungsroman he created for Maureen Smith. Lazarus Long, it turns out, had his life-line measured by Dr Pinero (in Heinlein's first published story) and was given his money back.

3

Technique

The conventional categorisation of Heinlein's work, which I outlined in Chapter 2 – short stories, juveniles, novels – elides the degree to which Heinlein was an experimental writer who worked with a range of genres. In this chapter and the following, I want to make the case that we can understand his work better if we understand Heinlein as exploring a number of modes and rhetorical techniques. There are two core narrative strategies, the didactic and the sentimental (Hugo Gernsback commonly described it as the fact and the romance). The intertwining of these two is a core element of what I believe science fiction to be: when harnessed they are precisely what critics have dubbed 'the sense of wonder' and it is this that Heinlein mastered and perhaps championed as the heart of science fiction. Chapter 3 deals predominantly with the didactic, and explores the roles of cinematic techniques, the use of the sidekick, the ways in which Heinlein wrote engineering stories and the construction of his time tales.

The sections of this chapter and the next do not represent an even or ordered mapping. Heinlein's work followed a spiral path, and elements that I wish to identify turn up, are discarded, and then returned to again in later work. But there are three clear divisions in terms of the rhetorical techniques Heinlein uses: the cinematic, the didactic and the picaresque.

NB: I have used the re-edited versions of *The Puppet Masters* and of *Stranger in a Strange Land* as both, as Heinlein believed, provide a smoother read than the originals.

The Cinematic

The strongest intimate influence on Heinlein's earliest writings was his second wife, Leslyn MacDonald. MacDonald was a noted script editor and, as Patterson has observed, was Heinlein's writing coach for his earliest stories. In his Denver speech he cites her as co-writer. The result is a recognisably cinematic quality to all of the earliest, pre-war stories, expressed in the sweep of the *mise en scène* that opens many of them.

In many of the early stories, the narrative 'camera' sweeps in from above or a distance. Take the opening of the very first published Heinlein story, 'Life-Line':

> The chairman rapped loudly for order. Gradually the catcalls and boos died away as several self-appointed serjeants-at-arms persuaded a few hot-headed individuals to sit down. The speaker on the rostrum by the chairman seemed unaware of the disturbance. His bland, faintly insolent face was impassive. The chairman turned to the speaker and addressed him [. . .]

The camera pans the room in a broad focus until it settles and zooms in on the two who will begin the story. A similar pan takes place at the opening of 'The Roads Must Roll': 'The speaker stood still on the rostrum and waited for his audience to answer him.' In this story it is almost three pages before the *observation* of a large audience switches to a more intimate relationship with a protagonist.

In '"Let There Be Light"', although the story begins in the protagonist's head, it also begins with him reading a telegram. The second paragraph, which is his internal dialogue, could as easily be filmed as he mutters to himself, 'He was, was he? He did, did he? What did he think this lab was; an hotel?' 'Requiem' begins with an overview of the fair, moves to the view of the chauffeur and only slowly positions itself to watch the protagonist; the camera is clearly on a dolly representing an ever-closer move towards the person of interest. Of the early stories, it is only '"If This Goes On—"', written in the first person and what we now call a novella, that opens with a retrospective narrative that could not be filmed without wrenching the story out of its trajectory, familiar perhaps from the movie *It's a Wonderful Life*.

The trajectory of the narrative moves towards intimacy. 'Misfit' begins with a mustering-in parade in which the object of the main story, Andrew Jackson Libby, is at the end of the opening sweep. The camera spends much of its time on the general action. Libby attracts its attention only at odd moments, in his locker or when he is trying on his suit, or during the first reveal when he calculates the distance to the horizon. We are halfway through before any indication that he is the object of the story coalesces in a scene in which Libby prevents the detonation of a charge and finds himself the focus of both the camera and the captain's gaze. The 'film' reaches the high point of the arc where Libby, in close-up 'Four hours later . . . was still droning out firing data, his face grey, his eyes closed. Once he had fainted but when they revived him he was still muttering figures': a scene remarkably similar to one in the Frank Capra movie, *Mr Smith Goes to Washington* (1939). 'Requiem' begins with the visit to the fairground, details Harriman's business and ends with the cramped and confined voyage to the Moon. The story has a structure remarkably like that of Orson Welles's *Citizen Kane* which came out two years later: it consists of reminiscences, of wrong turns, wrong choices taken, and threaded through it all is a consistent desire that drives him to go to the Moon. It takes place in fairgrounds and law courts, all very public places, but ends, quietly, with Harriman 'rubbing his hands against the soil of the Moon [...] He *was* where he had longed to be – he had followed his need.' Of the sequel, 'The Man Who Sold the Moon', Stephen Baxter has noted that it is 'very screenplay in structure. It is an elemental tale of a man with a well-defined and appealing surface structure, given a simple goal, whose deeper character is revealed as he makes choices under pressure.' ('Moon Believers', 1998, pp. 27–8).

As Heinlein developed, this approach fell by the wayside and he moved towards a more intimate position. In '"—We Also Walk Dogs"' the opening scene is a simple interaction between two people. Heinlein uses it to establish the wider compass in which the story as a whole will be set. The *mise en scène* is more intimate but the sense of 'here is where we are' before the story commences remains palpable. This technique reaches its apex in 'The Green Hills of Earth' in 1947 and in Heinlein's final short story, '"All You Zombies—"' in 1959.

The two stories are positioned very differently. In 'The Green Hills of Earth' we are in the hands of a covert narrator, as befits a story about a storyteller. 'This is the story of Rhysling, the Blind Singer of the Spaceways – but not the official version...' the tale begins. It is a construction of legend through the retelling of a secret history and the voice of the story aims to draw us into a conspiracy of hidden knowledge. Yet even the 'us' is doubled, for this story is 'told' in 'a family magazine' of the future, a descendant perhaps of the *Saturday Evening Post*. The story is embedded in three layers of public narrative, and construction of legend is then further embedded in a narrative of expansion and colonialism. Where Harriman stands for the business of expansion, Rhysling stands for the process and the people: a victim of the rush for the planets, although he would never understand himself that way. The narrator then uses him to create a double vision in which what we see and what the blind poet Rhysling 'sees' are juxtaposed.

> [On Mars] The capital was well into its boom; the processing plants lined the Grand Canal on both sides and roiled the ancient waters with the filth of the run-off [. . .] half the slender, fairylike towers had been torn down and the others were disfigured to adapt them as pressurized buildings for Earthmen.
>
> Now Rhysling had never seen any of these changes and no one described them to him. When he 'saw' Marsopolis again, he visualized it as it had been, before it was rationalized for trade [. . .] [the] ice blue plain of water untouched by tide, untouched by breeze, and reflecting serenely the sharp, bright stars of the Martian sky, and beyond the water the lacy buttresses and flying towers of an architecture too delicate for our rumbling, heavy planet.

Filmed, this would involve two *mises en scène*, one fading into another. Rhysling the blind becomes the camera. The story circles in, getting ever closer to Rhysling, until the story ends in the same way as 'Misfit' and 'The Long Watch', with one man counting down. The technique is repeated, memorably, years later, at the very end of *The Cat Who Walks Through Walls*, in a story that begins with open-spaced picaresque adventure and ends, as all these stories do, with just one person (or in this case two people and a kitten) locked in a room, waiting to die.

'The Long Watch' is a much more solitary tale from the beginning, an example of one long dolly shot, the unities preserved throughout. The story links in both theme and that same continuous long shot with the final short story I want to consider here, "'All You Zombies—'", a tale told in the modernist, continuous stream of consciousness. At the end of 'The Long Watch', Johnny Dahlquist thinks of himself as dead: 'He was dead – he knew that he was dead; yet for a time he was able to walk and breathe and see, and feel.'

By 1949, Leslyn MacDonald was no longer influencing Heinlein's writing. Heinlein worried over his ability to write, but never actually *said* 'without Leslyn's editing'. We might surmise that it was part of his concern, particularly because although Virginia Gerstenfeld was later to read and comment on every piece, their initial relationship was based far more on their war-work than on his writing. It is noticeable that when Heinlein returned to the field his stories were more conventional third-person narratives and, if anything, 'Delilah and the Space Rigger', 'Poor Daddy', 'The Year of the Jackpot' and 'Skylift' show the influence of TV, in which Heinlein was to demonstrate an interest: they are stageable.

Most of the juveniles are also filmable, particularly *Space Cadet*, *Red Planet*, *Farmer in the Sky* and *Tunnel in the Sky*, but they are much more attuned to adventure serials than to the Capraesque techniques we saw in the short stories. *Starship Troopers*, however, does open with the classic *mise en scène*, and the eventual novel closes with the intimacy of reflection that I have outlined. It may be the last novel to do so: after this Heinlein will turn to a different technique, in which a potted history of the situation is recounted as in the opening of *Stranger in a Strange Land*, or an overview of the political situation in the opening of *I Will Fear No Evil* (there is a particularly good example in the opening of Chapter 12), but these are written rather than narrated accounts: the narrative voice has slipped out of view, or, as more than one critic has commented, been embodied in Jubal Harshaw, Kettle Belly Baldwin, Lazarus Long, Friday or Maureen Smith Long. A few stories will use a more conversational and Socratic technique, as in the dinner-time or classroom-framed economics and politics of *The Rolling Stones, Have Space Suit—Will Travel, Starship Troopers* and *Farnham's Freehold*.

The cinematic techniques that are so striking in Heinlein's early work are not restricted to the *mise en scène*. Also notable are the three-act structures and the slick repartee. Movies of the period had three acts: the Set Up, the Confrontation and the Resolution, and given both Heinlein's tendency to autodidactism and Leslyn MacDonald's influence, it is not unreasonable to assume that he was aware of this. There would have been at least two texts available, William Archer's *Playmaking* (1912) and Kenneth Rowe's *Write that Play* (1933), and Leslyn brought to the partnership her MA in Theatre from the University of Southern California and a season at the Pasadena Playhouse.

We can see this structure in the earliest short stories. 'Misfit' is perhaps one of the clearest examples, in that act one is the establishment of the environment; act two is the identification of the boy; act three is the boy's rescue of the project. But it is there in all the early short stories and also in the longer pieces: in 'Coventry' (disillusion, recruitment, revolution), in *Methuselah's Children* (escape, adventure, return and reconciliation) and into the later work, *Space Cadet, Double Star* and *Starship Troopers*, which, although also bildungsromane, help establish the classic SF/fantasy three-part trope of recruitment, training, graduation/ascendance that came eventually to typify the three-volume epic (see *Star Wars* Parts IV, V and VI). By *Stranger in a Strange Land* Heinlein has begun to experiment and repurpose, using five acts to shift narrative positions, focal characters and even, it could be argued, genre as the novel shifts from satire, through adventure, through picaresque and, by the end, into eschatology. This structure is retained into the 1970s: we can see it in *I Will Fear No Evil*, and in *Friday* in fairly conventional forms – in

Friday it helps move the titular character across landscapes and ideologies – and only gives way as Heinlein discovers, with *Glory Road*, the delights of the picaresque.

But we are not yet finished with the cinematic influence. Heinlein's dialogue has been criticised by many as studied and false. In *The Issue at Hand*, James Blish argues that 'Heinlein sometimes tries to prove his characters wits and sophisticated by transcribing page after page of the painful travelling-salesman banter which passes back and forth over real drawing boards and spec sheets' (p. 71). I am not about to argue with this, but rather to place it in context. There are two aspects to Heinlein's dialogue: one aspect is the didactic that I will discuss later, and the other is the exchange. Here I want to consider the pattern of exchange, and specifically that between men and women.

Heinlein's dialogic style is drawn from the cinema of the 1930s and 1940s, in particular the screwball comedies. It is the classic repartee of these genres. The stories in which this is most evident are '"Let There Be Light"' and *Beyond This Horizon* but the legacy remains right the way through Heinlein's work – the lack of heterosexual romance in all but a couple of his juveniles may help explain their survival – and results in some of the more excruciating dialogue of *I Will Fear No Evil* and *'The Number of the Beast'*, not because the dialogue is bad but because this mode encodes certain assumptions of heterosexual flirtation that are being challenged by the 1970s coming, and that, to the eyes of many modern readers, present as abusive.

'"Let There Be Light"' (1940) is the first indication we have of Heinlein's clear alignment with contemporary feminism. When Archibald Douglas receives a telegram from Dr M. L. Martin, he assumes it is a man. When he goes to a restaurant and eyes a young woman he likes the look of his thoughts are 'Pretty fancy! Figure like a strip dancer, lots of corn-colored hair, nice complexion, and great big soft blue eyes. Rather dumb pan, but what could you expect?' The tables are turned: meeting Douglas, Dr Martin protests, 'You! I don't believe it. You look more like a – a gangster.'

You need to hold the contrasting images of the main characters in your mind when reading the story. They are fundamental to the interactions. The dialogue is quick and sharp. In the first pages there is a great deal of exchange of scientific information, but after they sort out the common problem they settle into the domestic harmony familiar to anyone who has watched Cary Grant and Katherine Hepburn or Rosalind Russell in action. Three weeks after the first discussion Mary Lou Martin is cooking eggs over a Bunsen burner, wearing her apron over shorts and a sweater, and 'The expanse of shapely leg made her look like something out of a cheesecake magazine.' The interaction of science and domesticity forms the conversation. 'Listen, Ape, the percolator seems to have burnt out. Shall I make the coffee in the fractional distillator?' 'Ape' is matched with 'kid' and when Douglas comes up with a good idea, Mary Lou 'cluck-clucked admiringly. "Mama's *good* boy. Mama knew he could do it, if he would only *try*".' When they discover politics will wreck their source of funding (Douglas's father's factory will be charged discriminatory rates for power) they seal the deal to challenge it. The story concludes with Archie grabbing Mary Lou by the arm.

'What the hell, Archie! Let go my wrist.'

'Not likely. You see that building over there? That's the court-house. Right next to the window where they issue dog licenses there's one where we can get a wedding permit.'

'I'm not going to marry you!'

'The hell you aren't. You've stayed all night in my laboratory a dozen times. I'm compromised. You've got to make an honest man of me – or I'll start to scream right here in the street.'

In *Beyond This Horizon*, this repartee is much more domestic and sexist. Hamilton Felix meets Longcourt Phyllis in Chapter 4. Phyllis makes the running, turning up on his doorstep, and they enter into the classic repartee. Phyllis, 'in defiance of usual custom for her sex', is armed.

'Why, damn your impudence! What the devil do you mean by invading my privacy like this?'

'Tut! Tut! Tut! Mamma spank. Is that any way to talk to the future mother of your children?'

'Mother of my fiddlesticks! If I needed anything to convince me that I want to have nothing to do with the scheme, you have given it to me. If I ever do have children, it won't be by you!' [. . .]

'What's wrong with me?' she said slowly.

'Hunh! What's wrong with you! What isn't wrong with you? I know your type. You're one of these "independent" women, anxious to claim all the privileges of men but none of the responsibilities. I can just see you, swaggering around town with that little spit gun at your side, demanding all the rights of an armed citizen, picking fights in the serene knowledge that no brave will call your bluff.' (Chapter 4)

As this is Heinlein, Phyllis calls Felix's bluff and pulls a gun on him. Felix instantly shows respect until she drops the gun, when he physically overpowers her. This isn't necessarily playing fair by Heinlein's *own* code. In his rants about women politicians in the pre-war 'The Devil Makes the Law' and the contemporaneous *How to Be a Politician* and 'A Bathroom of Her Own', he is deeply respectful of women whom he sees as playing the man's game and giving no quarter. The rest of the scene veers into the typical 'mock' coercion, 'light-hearted' BDSM of 1940s cinema. Hamilton forces her to the floor, disarms her, puts her on his lap, slaps her in return for a defensive bite, and then kisses her, holding her arms to her side; he accuses her of never being kissed before because 'Men seldom make passes at girls that wear guns.'[5] And despite calling him 'a dirty heel' she acquiesces and accepts a drink, a dinner date and his attentions. That interchange continues in their later encounters and is encoded in their relationship.

When we move into the 1970s the reliance on banter and provocation and often explicit but playful sexual threats becomes uncomfortable. The 'light-hearted' BDSM carries perhaps a little too much genuine threat. In *I Will Fear No Evil* the performativity of such an exchange, in which, ironically, Joan Eunice is asking for sex and Jake is refusing (he doesn't want sex in the back of a car) does not obscure the fact that again the male is very clearly framed as properly taking over the senior role from someone who, as a male, has given him orders.

> He picked her up; she stopped crying and looked suddenly happy.
>
> The expression did not last. He turned her over in his arms as he sat down on a straight chair, got a firm grip on her, and walloped her right buttock . . .
>
> He got her more firmly, placing his right leg over both of hers, and applied his hand smartly to her left cheek. Then he alternated sides, stopping with ten. (Chapter 14)

Much of the verbal negotiation in the whole of *I Will Fear No Evil* is a similar dominance game. In Chapter 22, when Joan and Jake are dating, her wishes are entirely overridden. When she notes she's booked a table Jake says to her nurse, 'Winnie, you haven't been coaching her enough. [Joan] Eunice, you're not supposed to

---

5   A take on the Dorothy Parker epigram: '**News Item** Men seldom make passes/At girls who wear glasses.' First printed in *New York World*, 16 August 1925.

be making such a decision.' And although he takes her there, their date becomes a show of deference: he seeks out a comfortable chair when she dislikes the seating, she asks him to buy the place when she decides she wants to refurbish it, although she has more than enough wherewithal to buy it. And her poor choice is confirmed when one of the bodyguards is killed in a card game.

Eunice counsels Joan in becoming a woman in ways that teach Joan constantly to hide her intelligence and be lesser. Eunice recounts to Joan many incidents of 'friendly groping' and many incidents of talking men into friendly sex rather than hostile sex, using one to defuse the other (this is the book that tries to render gang-rape happy). It never seems to occur to either of them that Eunice is coaching Joan to be secretary instead of boss, to acquiesce rather than control. It may well have occurred to Heinlein later however as he gives Maureen in *To Sail Beyond the Sunset* a post-divorce emergence into independence both sexual and economic.

However, this show of deference and repartee also allows Heinlein to place analysis in the mouths of women. In *I Will Fear No Evil* he gives Joan Eunice a set of conversations about sexuality which are revealing of Heinlein's understanding of the complexity of male–female relations in a world he is depicting as sexually unequal but gender diverse, a world in which young people claim to have six sexes (Chapter 14). This reader may not like the conclusions Joan takes from her lessons with Eunice but the bantering tone constructs an illusion of control in a context where Eunice's very death, and later that of Joan, suggests an absence of such.

The character who really benefits from this structure is Betty Sorenson in *The Star Beast*. The character relationships in this novel are very much that of the not terribly bright male being distracted and directed by his much smarter female companion, which turns out to be a metaphor for another female's control (the whole novel is a version of *Bringing Up Baby*, only the leopard is an alien space princess and she is holding the leash). John Thomas Stuart XI calls Betty 'Slugger'. A very typical conversation takes place on the way to the court to deal with the damage the alien Lummox has caused. Betty stops to check her make up:

> 'Hi, Slugger.'
>
> 'Hi, Knothead.'
>
> 'I didn't know you knew the Chief.'
>
> 'I know everybody. Now shut up. I've gotten here, with all speed and much inconvenience as soon as I heard the newscast. You and Lummox between you could not manage to think your way out of this, even with Lummox doing most of the work – so I rallied around. Now give me the grisly details. Don't hold anything back from mama.' (Chapter 1)

In Chapter 3 Betty tells John Thomas what to do, educating him on homestead law which allows a person to keep the tools of their trade (Lummox as a potential exhibit) and at the end of Chapter 10 it is Betty who reminds John Thomas that, having developed hands, Lummox is now protected by law. The interchange which leads to that takes the better part of a chapter and is constructed in the usual way, in which Betty intervenes, John Thomas tries to keep her out of it, and through sheer force she convinces him that her ideas are better. As she notes when he comes up with a good idea, 'You're usually right, Johnny – two or three weeks late' (Chapter 10).

Heinlein, for all his vision in constructing Betty as an independent minor (a real thing in California at the time), sets her up as the power behind the throne. If she is bullying at times it is because the best outcome she can hope for is to be in charge of Johnny's career. By the time we get to *'The Number of the Beast'*, many women are getting rather sick of this and Heinlein puts their feelings squarely in the mouth of Dejah Thoris 'D. T.' Burroughs, cast as the mad scientist's beautiful and brilliant daughter. The initial badinage is very similar to that in '"Let There Be Light"' and is often cited as an example of really embarrassing writing, as the protagonist, Zeb, admires her 'cantilevering', and Deety, as she is known, notes that his response is 'rude, crude, unrefined and designed to change the subject'. They then exchange qualifications and initially Deety thinks she is outranked because although her Ph.D is in computing (as we find out later) his, she thinks, is in mathematics. As it turns out that is his cousin: but we have the interesting scenario in which each participant thinks they are courting someone smarter than themselves. As they set off to get married, in the company of Deety's father and his girlfriend, soon to be wife, Hilda, they get shot at, discover that each has a link to Edgar Rice Burroughs through their names (Zeb is Captain Zebediah John Carter), head off in an inter-dimensional camper van, and each party takes turns to captain.

It is in this book that the exchanges in '"Let There Be Light"' are clarified as grounded in mutual respect for one another's abilities, for they are contrasted quite sharply with more 'gentlemanly' concerns. Both Hilda's and Deety's tenure as captain is plagued by Professor Carter's back-seat driving. Hilda, accustomed to humouring men, snaps, and Deety gets to explain the kind of man her father is; the kind who assumes female competence only to a point and only in certain ways. She notes, 'Pop is one of those men who sincerely believe in Women's Lib, always support it – but so deep down that they aren't aware of it, their emotions tell them that women never get over being children' (Chapter 25). One way this is portrayed is precisely in the *absence* between Hilda and Jake of the challenging, locking horns, cinematic repartee Heinlein uses for Zeb and Deety. If we now track that through a range of books we can see that the pattern repeats steadily. Where there is mutual respect between the sexes – *Starman Jones, Glory Road, Friday* between Friday and Georges, Jubal Harshaw and his women, Maureen and Brian in *To Sail Beyond the Sunset* among others – we see this jousting. Where there is not, for whatever reason – Friday and Baldwin for example, Michael Valentine Smith and his friends, or between Lazarus Long and the women around him, there is an absence of respect. Long loves and *thinks* he respects women, but he teaches the women around him to defend themselves because he regards them as weaker and slightly inferior. He admires women, but that is not quite the same thing as respecting them, and I'd argue that this is demonstrated in *'The Number of the Beast.'* The dialogue is purposeful, and is there to tell us about character relations.

One aspect to this issue however is that it is not just the dialogue that Heinlein lifted from a particular section of cinema, but also the characterisation of men. In particular, what one can only call at best the 'ordinary chump' or at worst, 'the doofus male', embodied in cinema and TV in every man from the Mr Smith who goes to Washington to Homer Simpson. Both John Thomas Stuart XI and Zebediah John Carter fit this model (even if Zeb is very smart, he isn't anything like as smart as his wife). The doofus male may be smart in his own right, but he has to be courted with a metaphorical club and/or dragged in his destined direction by a metaphorical tug of the hair. The doofus male – interestingly – has never taken his rightful place alongside Heinlein's competent man as a key Heinlein character. Both club and tug are usually operated by the highly competent Heinlein female.

These doofus males are oddly strong in the juveniles. Max Jones of *Starman Jones* is both courted by Ellie and abandoned by him when he is no longer her best option. John Thomas XI has no idea Betty has groomed him or that she is planning his career. He is, like many a screwball comedy hero, fixated on something else. In the adult fiction the same pattern is there in 'A Bathroom of Her Own' and 'Delilah and the Space Rigger' although in both cases it is not love that is at stake but a job. In *Double Star*, you can still see the traces of the form as Lorenzo Smith is wooed and tempted into a role and eventually into a life. Oscar, likewise, in *Glory Road*, is a man remade into the image desired by the woman who 'courts' him. The structure holds in *The Cat Who Walks Through Walls* but is beginning to creak: the effect in this book is to render Richard rather weak, which might be why Heinlein has to conjure up the sudden stubbornness (about receiving the unsolicited gift of a leg graft, from a man who might well be his absentee father). Without this, Richard is far too much follower for his description and for Gwen/Hazel's needs, yet as follower he positions us to admire Gwen and to see the world through her eyes. They are, in effect, cameras.

The Sidekick

This model starts much earlier in the fiction and is tied to a choice Heinlein makes which is rarely commented on: many of Heinlein's novels and almost all of the juveniles are told from the point of view of the solid sidekick.

The classic adventure story, such as Robert Louis Stevenson's *Kidnapped* or J. K. Rowling's *Harry Potter and the Philosopher's Stone*, is a fantasy of visceral experience; the point of the story is that we share the fear and the elation, the highs and the lows. In that sense classic adventure (for any age, in any genre) is on the same genre arc as the horror narrative. *Discovery* is a process of revelation and it is the thrill of revelation that is the pay-off. In that scenario you need your protagonist to be the object of the action.

In contrast, in fantasies of knowledge, where the trajectory is a growing awareness of the world and an accumulation of knowledge, where the point is to learn more, not feel more, it is more useful to focalise on the Companion. In this context it is actually better if your protagonist can be situated slightly back from the scene to observe and to learn, preferably from someone who knows what they are doing, rather than necessarily taking part in the action. The most notable version of this is probably the role of John Watson in the narration of the adventures of Sherlock Holmes.

The companion or sidekick focalisation functions to centre another character as a deuteragonist, an active role model for the reader, in a context in which the reader is expected to learn rather than simply experience. The Watson figure retains the centre of the adventure, and serves as the agonist (the champion around which the conflict revolves), and the companion he admires becomes the deuteragonist. In the world of science fiction, as we will see when we look at Heinlein's construction of didacticism, the role of companion (see *Dr Who*) exploits this Watsonian role of *learner*. Although there is some formal teaching in Heinlein's work, much of what he depicts as learning is a combination of private study (in both *Space Cadet* and *Starship Troopers*, for example) and observation and emulation of those who are more advanced in knowledge and career – mostly to emulate, occasionally as in *Starman Jones* or in 'Universe' and even at times in '*The Number of the Beast*', to learn how not to act or behave. But Heinlein intensifies the focalisation, so that the Watson figure genuinely becomes the centre of interest.

You can see this in Heinlein's earliest work, in "'If This Goes On—'", in *Space Cadet, Starman Jones* and others, even in *Starship Troopers*, which is most often represented as a classic adventure. In "'If This Goes On—'" John Lyle's main purpose is to listen to his friend Zeb: it is Zeb who tells us about the state of the world (although Heinlein does send Lyle into the world – primed – to confirm Zeb's assertions). Furthermore, over and over again we are told and shown that Lyle just isn't as bright as his friend. The three-act structure of the novella as it was published in 1953 reinforces this. At the beginning Lyle is positioned as the ingénu, the centre of the story: it will be his role to rescue the princess. By part two this has become merely the motivating factor that catapults him into a revolution of which he is simply a cog. By part three, he is simply even that, sidelined, and effectively chosen to be the third act in someone else's romantic drama as he is 'chosen' by Sister Maggie.

Space Cadet lays out the structure clearly: Matt Dodson listens to his elders, his officers and his friends. First he bonds with Tex who he thinks is smarter than he is but who he gradually realises is at best his equal. He looks up to and admires an older cadet, Bill Arensa, without really registering that Bill is taking a long time to graduate. When Arensa decides to leave the patrol, it becomes part of Matt's (temporary) disaffection. He is momentarily seduced by the attraction of the marines, looking up to an older man *because* he seems more mature. It is only when he finds good role models – Lieutenant Wong first, then his own peer Oscar Jensen – that he begins to settle in and eventually he and his friends are able to rescue themselves, their captain and a cadet school 'problem' from a marsh on Venus. But the key thing to note is that although Matt is the focal character he is simply not the hero. The hero/protagonist is Oscar Jensen, who is far smarter, speaks fluent Venerian and is clearly heading for a career in diplomacy. In the far future one can imagine Matt being interviewed about his schoolboy friend the Commander (as Heinlein was interviewed about his).

The adventure told through the sidekick is repeated in a number of the juveniles. In *Farmer in the Sky*, Bill meets Hank, whom he originally dislikes for 'being a politician', but over and over again Hank will prove his worth as the smart protagonist to Bill's stalwart companion role. It will be Hank who organises things after the earthquake and pushes on to find the crystals. Bill is not stupid of course – it is he who shoves his Scout uniform into the breach when the ship is holed – but Bill is a quick thinker, not a planner. The role of planner always goes to the deuteragonist. Jo Walton noted that in *Have Space Suit—Will Travel*, 'The oddest thing about Have Spacesuit is that the protagonists, Kip and the little girl genius Peewee, are mostly passengers in the plot' ('Ever Outward', 2010). The adventure actually belongs to the Mother Thing.

Heinlein's technique is clearest in *The Star Beast*, where John Thomas XI is pushed around by not one but four people, all rather smarter, stronger or more powerful than he is, all of whom believe they have his best interests at heart and all of whom teach us, the reader, something about the world. There is John Thomas's mother (who is at least a skilled manipulator); his girlfriend; his 'pet'; and eventually Mr Henry Gladstone Kiku, OBE, the Permanent Under Secretary for Spatial Affairs. The story is absolutely John Thomas's, but he is not the one making it happen; rather, he is a random pawn of fate (like Alexander Hergensheimer in *Job*). Nor is he the protagonist, for that is Lummox, the kidnapped alien princess, who at times serves as a focaliser. It is the deuteragonist, Betty, who controls much of the outcome of the adventure. It is with her that Mr Kiku negotiates. Betty of course is absolutely the protagonist in her own story, of which we see only a glimpse. That this is an intensely cinematic structure we can see by homing in on one of the most successful science-fiction movies of all time, *Star Wars*: it is not hard to swap Lummox for R2D2, John Thomas for Luke Skywalker, Mr Kiku for Obi-Wan Kenobi, and Betty for Princess Leia (if the sympathetic policeman had a larger role he'd make a decent Han Solo). For all Luke thinks he is in charge, he is being shepherded in the right direction by every other character. The form allows the 'reader' to accompany great men, to serve as cabin boys on the good ship *Story*.

The structure is extended into the adult novels. The first plan for *The Moon is a Harsh Mistress* envisaged Wyoming as the central character. Instead Heinlein went with Mannie, an 'ordinary Joe' who services the central computer, Mike. Mannie is positioned as the sensible, practical one, while the imagination and the brains are left with Mike and Wyoming. His role in many ways is to connect people within the revolution and to observe it for us, and at the end to be the apostle who tells us of the passing of the prophet. Whether we use the identification with or emulative model of reading, the relationship between ourselves and the protagonist is on a reasonably easy level: we like Mannie, and we too are being caught up in great events.

Although I do believe this companionate structure is deliberate, it is hard also to avoid the issue that Heinlein did not actually write smart people terribly well from the inside. 'Gulf' is unconvincing in part because the super-smart protagonist does not feel particularly smart. In later novels, it is hard to believe that Jill or Ben in *Stranger in a Strange Land*, or Oscar in *Glory Road*, or Richard in *The Cat Who Walks Through Walls* are all that intelligent. If Heinlein is writing from the self, as many writers cannot avoid doing, then there are at least two factors that contribute to this. The first is that Heinlein was a younger brother who worshipped and competed with his older brothers; the emulative mode may be a reflection of his own internal monologue at least when he was younger. The second issue is that for all his massive success and for all the arrogance that can come through in his letters, there is also an anxiety that Heinlein is not that clever. We see it neatly encapsulated in Alexander Hergensheimer in *Job*: Alex is clever enough to be a theologian, not clever enough to be an engineer. For Heinlein it is a matter of being clever enough to be an engineer, but never quite clever or successful enough when it came to politics, which he truly cared about, and never quite clever or confident enough to make some major leaps – his decision to get married when it wrecked his chances for a Rhodes scholarship suggests a tendency to self-sabotage that he may well have been aware of. This seems to have been intensified because Heinlein admired a certain type of intelligence that both Leslyn and Virginia Heinlein seem to have had – a ferocious and analytical intelligence. This he gives to his female characters: Hazel Meade Stone, Deety and Hilda, Maureen (and after her immersive training in synthesis, Friday); but never to male protagonists, only to male agonists. In many of his novels, *Glory Road*, *The Cat Who Walks Through Walls*, *The Star Beast*, even *Starship Troopers*, the men are sidekicks or enablers of a clever female's adventures (in *Starship Troopers* Carmen is off-stage but she is having adventures all of her own).

The companionate structure is what many critics have (mis-) identified as the strong authorial mouthpiece. In *Starship Troopers* Johnny is – as both fans and critics of the novel have pointed out – less a mouthpiece for the author than an earpiece for the reader; his role is to channel the voices of wisdom. Throughout the novel, in fact, Johnny is positioned as a follower and subject to the *rhetoric of convincement*. Dad thinks Johnny is a follower as well. His school friend thinks he is a follower and persuades Johnny to follow him into the military. So that when the recruiting sergeant is giving all that guff – a reworking of the talk Matt receives in *Space Cadet* from the marine he *almost* follows – he is actually daring Johnny in the kind of game of chicken that Johnny has been following all his life. His teacher thinks Johnny is a follower – it is why he asks Johnny a question when he wants a demonstration answer. He is 'Bob' in the classic construction 'as you know, Bob'. The scene in which this is clearest is when a colleague persuades Johnny to go career: he is actually told he is the right kind of stupid for the task (as John Lyle has been informed before him).

None of this is to deny that Heinlein had a strong authorial voice, but it is not necessarily vested in the figures of authority. Usually identified as authorial mouthpieces are Kettle Belly Baldwin ('Gulf' and *Friday*), Lazarus Long (*Time Enough for Love, To Sail Beyond the Sunset*) and Jubal Harshaw (*Stranger in a Strange Land*) but less often noted is that all of these authorial mouthpieces receive pushback: Baldwin may dominate in 'Gulf', but he is the father figure to grow beyond in *Friday*, and one who has clearly screwed up in the past; Lazarus dominates the tales he tells in *Time Enough for Love*, but by the end of the novel he is relegated to the role of indulged patriarch who thinks he is making all the decisions but really is not.

The Engineering Effect

Heinlein's engineering stories are told almost entirely in the paratactic voice: one plain sentence then another plain sentence. They are straightforward, focus on problems and on solutions. But there are far fewer engineering short stories than an impressionistic history of Heinlein's work would suggest. In the first period to 1942 only "'Let There Be Light'", 'Misfit', 'Blowups Happen', "'—And He Built a Crooked House—'" and 'Waldo' are truly 'engineering' stories in the sense that they discuss physical problems. Of the post-1942 stories, only 'Gentlemen, Be Seated', 'Delilah and the Space Rigger', 'Destination Moon' and 'The Long Watch' fit the category.

"'Let There Be Light'" is receiving more than its fair share of attention because this story, although in many ways one of Heinlein's weakest (it shows every sign of having been incentivised by cent-per-word payment), contains many of the markers to be explored later, and this is just as true with the paratactic language and didacticism. In this story it is linked to the cinematic repartee, but the paratactic style which supports this mode also supports a story

128

which is striving to convince the readership of both an engineering and a political truth – power drives the economy, and the release of power changes the political structures of the economy. The narrative construct which John Huntington (*Rationalizing Genius*, 1989) has described as the 'rationalising genius' of science fiction supports a cinematic screwball structure: both forms tend to like a convergent narrative in which ideas and events draw together to an *inevitable* conclusion . . . (Mendlesohn, 'The SF Short Story', 2017). Two scientists of course create an invention; a man and woman of course become a couple.

In 'Blowups Happen' a nuclear power station is monitored by psychiatrists, who watch the pile engineers for signs of breakdown. It is only the pile engineers who are watched: the combination of an understanding of nuclear theory and (as it turns out rightful) scepticism of the theory of a self-limiting reaction, a clear sense of social responsibility, and the awareness that they are being watched, brings them to the edge from which they cannot be reclaimed. The decision is taken to bring in a new psychiatrist, a catalytic character, Dr Lentz, a physicist and psychologist who argues that both are branches of mathematics (following the theories of Korzybski). However, notably, and unlike in 'The Roads Must Roll', Dr Lentz fails. His role as catalyst turns out to be practical: he distracts two experimenters, leading them to combine two isotopes in testing, and thus create the atomic rocket fuel that will allow them to place the pile in space and thus make it safe. The attempt to engineer people fails but the attempt to engineer the pile succeeds.

It is, however, the telling of the story that is of interest here. Heinlein places in the mind of Dr Silard, the in-house head of psychiatry, a monologue about his responsibilities and those of the men he watches: unlikely as it seems, in a sleight-of-hand Heinlein positions him as the third-person narrator who can describe the scenario. And the descriptions are detailed and scientific; they take no quarter.

> The tortured beryllium yielded up neutrons, which shot out in all directions through the uranium mass. Some of these neutrons struck uranium atoms squarely on their nuclei and split them in two. The fragments were new elements: barium, xenon, rubidium – depending on the proportions in which each atom split.

This mode of description continues for around 500 words and sums up the current state of knowledge about the consequences of a meltdown. It is essentially an engineering description, in which this happens and this happens and then this happens, but it is precisely the possibility of the chain of events *not* working which spooks the engineers. The role of Dr Lentz is to be the interested enquirer. The people he is interrogating do not know he is a physicist so he 'plays' the companion role. This allows Heinlein to create a controlled conversation in which the focalisation plays a double game: people who explain things to Dr Lentz are explaining them to the audience.

Heinlein is clearly more interested in the psychiatry, and it is this he wants the reader to learn. So when Lentz trades places and becomes the explicator, he takes King step by step along the line of engineer-like reasoning that leads him to exclude a psychiatric solution. I have split the quotation into bullet points:

- You don't dare entrust control to less sensitive, less socially conscious men.
- To situational psychoneurosis there are but two cures. The first obtains when the psychosis results from the misevaluation of environment. That calls for semantic readjustment. One assists

the patient to evaluate correctly his environment. The worry disappears because there never was a real reason for worry. . .

- The second case is when the patient has correctly evaluated the situation and rightly finds in it cause for extreme worry. . . The only possible cure is to change the situation.

- The only possible solution is to dump the pile – and leave it dumped.

There is no true logic here, but the didactic delivery helps to convince us that there is, when actually the last line should be the more generic 'The only possible solution is to change the situation.' Which it turns out is the solution: a new interpretation of physics combined with the engineered psychiatric argument reflects the engineered practical solution, which leaves the engineers only the problem that they have to convince the company, which is not operating with the same engineering logic. King the engineer offers the Harper-Erickson discovery that will allow the pile to be taken off Earth, discovers that money trumps everything, and that by corporate logic risk is more acceptable than financial loss. Only when Lentz presents them with a different *kind* of logic, the logic of bad publicity and the psychiatry of public relations and advertising, do they cede the point: they are *engineered* and accept the psychological engineering that will produce the outcome that the real engineers need.

'Waldo' has a similar outcome in that Waldo is asked to seek an engineering solution to the problem that the power source is proving unreliable (and incidentally, probably poisonous) but the actual change that will take place in the end is a singularity, not a solution: a new source of power will be found that simply undercuts the engineering problem. And it is particularly unnerving that in a story in which much of the *mise en scène* and context is precisely the wonders of an engineering solution to a medical problem (remote manipulators for the weak), the actual *resolution* is the discovery of magic.

Engineering stories, stories where engineering provides the solution, are rare in Heinlein's oeuvre. The two clearest are 'Gentlemen, Be Seated' and 'Destination Moon'. In 'Gentlemen, Be Seated' a journalist on vacation takes a trip to the Observatory to find a story. Jack Arnold manages to wheedle a trip into the construction tunnels that will eventually form the slidewalks which will connect the colony buildings. When the dangers of the Moon are explained to him it is in neat paratactic language that carries both force and a certain weariness:

> 'Every engineering job has its own hazards,' he insisted, 'and its advantages, too. Our men don't get malaria and they don't have to watch out for rattlesnakes . . . we rarely have any broken bones in the Moon; the gravity is so low – while that Des Moines file clerk takes his life in his hands every time he steps in or out of his bath.'

The engineering problem that is explained is that because the chemicals in rubber that keep it flexible boil away in the vacuum, they have to work the seals to the tunnels in layers. Arnold is then given a trip to see how it works, only for an explosion to hit, the power to go out and for a leak to open. With the other side of the airlock depressurised they find themselves trapped and unable to reach the sealant (which does of course beg the question why each person is not carrying an emergency kit). They use a suit but when 'Fatso' Konski realises it can be used to get someone out to fetch help he takes the suit's place by sitting on the leak. When he faints, Arnold takes his place. Although clearly told *as* an engineering tale, with the rhetoric of an engineering tale and the paratactic voice of an engineering tale, the 'engineering' solution is no such thing: it is a personal sacrifice of a kind that crops up in many of Heinlein's stories.

'Destination Moon' was a novelisation of the movie, and was sent to the non-SF market of *Short Stories Magazine*. It is very heavy on exposition, and was in part repurposed from Heinlein's first juvenile, *Rocket Ship Galileo* – the 5,000 words at the start argue for safety with politicians instead of parents and it is the Soviets who are the enemy instead of the Nazis. It is a much clearer engineering story in that the problem is caused by an engineering mistake – shedding water to get rid of people trying to stop the rocket take-off – and it is understood with mathematics and resolved with skill. The decisions of *how* to land on the Moon are spelled out in detail:

> Two principal styles of landing were possible – Type A, in which a ship heads in vertically, braking on her jets to a landing in one maneuver, and Type B, in which a ship is first slowed to a circular orbit, then stopped dead, then backed to a landing when she drops from the point of rest.

The story is less engineering fiction than it is rather leaden space action. The engineering lies in figuring out how they are going to get back with not enough fuel. They have to find a place to take off, calculate their route, then discover that they are misaligned and thus are unable to get a radio message to the United States, and finally they strip the rocket to keep its weight as low as possible. All of this is discussed in meticulous detail.

The decision in the story to shed weight is, technically, an engineering response. The story pre-dates Tom Godwin's 'The Cold Equations' by four years but the basic storyline seems to have its roots in traditional riddles. But once more the potential solution is a personal response, to give the mission a chance, to head back even though they think they may die, in order to tell people what they have found (pressure domes on the Moon). Heinlein's interest is in how humans respond when it is their life or someone else's: engineering, for Heinlein, is a facilitator rather than protagonist. We can even see this in a story such as 'Space Jockey'.

'Space Jockey' is full of the sense of wonder of space. But it is the description of the *engineering economics* of space travel that captures the imagination:

> The Commerce Commission has set the charges for the present three-stage lift from here to the Moon at thirty dollars a pound . . . a ship designed to blast off from Earth, make an airless landing on the Moon, return and make an atmospheric landing, would be so cluttered up with heavy special equipment used only once in the trip that it could not show a profit at a thousand dollars a pound! [. . .]
>
> So Trans-Lunar uses rockets braced for catapulting and winged for landing on return to Earth [. . .] The long middle lap, from there to where Space Terminal circles the Moon, calls for comfort – but no landing gear [. . .]
>
> The *Moonbat* and the *Gremlin* are good only for the jump from Space Terminal down to Luna . . . no wings, cocoon-like acceleration-and-crash hammocks, fractional controls on their enormous jets.

In the centre of the story, when the rocket is thrown off course by a child in the cockpit, we settle into two pages of site checks and calculation. Eventually, the pilot calls home and gets support from the computer (a person, not a machine) on Earth who gets him to start from scratch: 'Forget about the orbit on your tape. . . Pick a new groove.' And helps him calculate it.

But for all the narrative romance of a moment in space travel in which everyone is still dependent on naval-style astrogation, the actual storyline is of a man who has set his job against his wife. When Jake left his home that morning he left behind a distressed woman and a marriage under strain. The story is told in point and counterpoint as Jake prepares for the flight and thinks about his own boredom with his job and how much he misses his wife, and as each of them writes letters they regret (but luckily don't send). The story is summed up with this thought. "'The Romance of Inter-Planetary Travel" – it looked well in print, but he knew what it was: A job. Monotony. No scenery. Bursts of work, tedious waits. No home life.' At the end Jake's reward is a steady job on the Moon, where his wife can join him in Luna City. The emphasis is less on the romance of engineering than on romance itself.

That leaves us 'Delilah and the Space Rigger', in which Heinlein is upfront about the matter. The narrator's opening lines read: 'Sure, we had trouble building Space Station One – but the trouble was people', and the story continues with a constant list of the people problems on the ship. And although there is much admiration for engineering, and a pause for a close-up shot of the space station – 'Mighty pretty . . . a great network of shiny struts and ties against black sky and stars' – the closest thing to an engineering problem successfully tackled in this story is the ship-fitter who figures out how to build a heatless still, and is busted for it. The problem to be fixed in the end is one man's unreasoning sexism that leads him to try and sack a woman for refusing orders that the narrator notes he wouldn't have given to a man.

Time after time Heinlein presents engineering stories in which the problem and the solution are both human. We particularly see this in his juveniles, from 'Misfit' which, despite the emphasis on the work to be done, is truly about the creation of camaraderie and family, through *Space Cadet*, *Tunnel in the Sky*, *Farmer in the Sky* and *Red Planet*. What confuses the issue is that in each of these juveniles – less so in the later ones, perhaps – there is scientific and engineering material for the child reader to pick up. *Farmer in the Sky* and *Have Spacesuit—Will Travel* are the most upfront of these, and it is these two that I will consider before we move on, not to engineering stories but *engineered* stories.

The engineering in *Have Space Suit—Will Travel* is confined mainly to the beginning of the book, in Chapter 3, in which Heinlein has Kip lovingly lay out the process of restoring the second-hand space suit he has won. But there is relatively little technical material in the rest of the novel. It is essentially a political novel concerned, like many of Heinlein's books, with interspecies and intergender relationships. More focused perhaps is *Farmer in the Sky*. This novel is *'Little House on the Prairie* in space' (the description of food in Chapter 10, 'The Promised Land', is straight out of a mid-western colonist fantasy) and it shares with that novel the determination to teach readers something. Chapter 6, 'E=MC²', is devoted almost entirely to describing the functioning of the ship as one of Bill's lessons on board the migration ship. Here we have the clear engineering descriptions of hydroponics and mass conservation, and the inability to reach light speed, that we expect of a Heinlein juvenile. Later, on the planet, Kip is persuaded by his friend Hank to switch to a Ganymede-based Scout troop specifically so he will learn something (Chapter 12, 'Bees and Zeroes') – that something proving to be *four full pages* on planetary ecology and agronomy. Yet, even in this book, the trajectory is less towards the victory of planetary conquests than to the sacrifices – Bill's stepsister, Peggy, and many of the homesteaders – which are made along the way.

Time Tales

If the engineering stories turn out to be less driven by engineering than we sometimes think, and some of the fantasy stories are rationalised (see Chapter 4), there is at least one set of stories that are *engineered*; the stories of knotted dimensions and time.

Heinlein wrote relatively few time travel stories: "'—And He Built a Crooked House—'", 'Elsewhere', 'By His Bootstraps', *Time for the Stars*, *The Door Into Summer*, "'All You Zombies—'", *Have Space Suit—Will Travel*, *The Cat Who Walks Through Walls*, and *To Sail Beyond the Sunset*.

Time for the Stars is a straightforward exposition of relativity and contains time travel only in the sense that time dilation returns the protagonist to an Earth in which many more years have passed than he has experienced. *Have Space Suit—Will Travel* contains time travel only in the sense that the two children are returned to the same starting position in time. At the end of *The Cat Who Walks Through Walls*, Gwen and Richard head back through time to rescue the computer, Mike, who had led the Luna revolution, but we don't see them return until *To Sail Beyond the Sunset*, and for Heinlein it is a remarkably conventional piece of change-the-past time interference. As in *To Sail Beyond the Sunset*, time travel becomes a means to collect family. They are exercises in time-archaeology and they consistently move along a linear notion of time in which there is a past and a present, and the traveller's own future is inaccessible. I include them here for the sake of completeness but there is little to say about any of them in this context. I am excluding 'The Number of the Beast' because that is not travel through time but travel through dimension.

However, there are four stories in which Heinlein experiments with time. The time-loop stories are "'—And He Built a Crooked House—'", 'By His Bootstraps', *The Door Into Summer* and "'All You Zombies—'". The choice of "'—And He Built a Crooked House—'" over 'Elsewhere' in this section is *entirely* structural: although 'Elsewhere' sends people along a space-time continuum, it is more concerned with alternate realities and also a theme that Heinlein explored far more in the picaresque: the finding of the right universe for each individual personality. 'Elsewhere' is in this sense part of a trilogy with *Job* and *'The Number of the Beast'*, a story about finding somewhere to be yourself. Its structure is outward-bound. Heinlein's time-travel stories are otherwise almost all *inward-bound* and construct a time loop.

Although '"—And He Built a Crooked House—"' is not a time-travel story per se it is Heinlein's first outing with the loop. It is a clever story about a man who uses a model of a tesseract to build a house. When an earthquake hits, the building collapses and the people inside are trapped. While from the outside the house appears to be a cube, inside the house has become an Escher object, a description that is deliberate, as it is quite possible that Heinlein had already seen some of Escher's earliest work (*Still Life and Street* was printed in March 1937). The story is a classic micro-exploration story in which first one route and then another is tried until the logic of the space-loop is traced and it can be collapsed. The tracing is important, as the story is also a labyrinth story: follow the thread and you can find the path to the outdoors or to the past or the future. The classic explication of this, a causal loop, is of course Heinlein's 'By His Bootstraps'.

In 'By His Bootstraps' Bob Wilson is writing a thesis on time travel when a man surprises him from behind and tells him it is rubbish. The man tries to get Bob to go through a time circle but he refuses. They fight, and he is pushed through. On the other side an older man, perhaps forty-five years old, who identifies himself as Diktor, tends Bob's wounds and then sends him back to collect a person. Bob does so and realises he has collected himself. Diktor then introduces Bob to the world around him, and asks him to return to Earth to collect things Diktor needs. Bob agrees, goes back, finds his two selves fighting and sends both back, then goes off to find the stuff. On his way he calls in on his girlfriend, which explains why she had called the apartment, and makes a call to the apartment himself to confirm what's happening. He then returns but can't see Diktor. Using the tools he has collected and a dictionary he has found Bob establishes himself as dictator over the sheep-like people, until the day that a bruised man lands in his courtyard and the loop plays out again to create, as the story would have it, 'a perpetual motion fur farm'.

In one sense this story is fanfic; it is Heinlein among the Eloi. Our hero is sociopathic in his behaviour, using his girlfriend Genevieve as a disposable doll (although this is 1941 and *Astounding Science Fiction*, it is pretty clear they have just had sex). In a move that is common to Heinlein, the adventure reveals the hero rather than making him. The protagonist's treatment of Genevieve – fucking, proposing, abandoning – is the same pattern as his treatment of the domesticated people he meets in the future. Thus the loop is not only physical: Bob is not merely travelling in his own time, but along a thread of his own character. He does not become Diktor, he is not predestined to be Diktor, he is Diktor. Heinlein uses two time memes: one is the time loop, the other is time as a physical, metaphysical and social construct and there are overlaps between the two. This is repeated in the other three stories. The structure is a loop, but not a particularly tangled one.

In *The Door Into Summer*, Heinlein took a time loop and ran it so that it crossed over a number of times. Dan is cheated out of his business by his crooked girlfriend, Belle, and his weak best friend, Miles, a lawyer. He decides to go into cold sleep with his cat, Pete, but is grabbed first and bundled into cold sleep alone. His last sight of Pete is the cat fleeing out of the door to escape Miles and Belle. In his cold-sleep dreams he keeps imagining Pete out in the cold dying, and he dreams of Ricky, Belle's little girl, to whom he has become close. A great deal of this book is about love and responsibility and the pain of not being able to look after someone you love.

By accident Dan discovers that a scientist has developed time travel and he talks the man into sending him back in time as a guinea pig. He goes back in time to three years before his world collapsed and with the help of some friendly nudists, John and Jenny, two of his karmic heroes, he recreates much of his work and patents it. Then when the time comes, Dan stands outside his own house, waits until Pete comes barrelling out of the house in fright and scoops him up. With Pete in hand he goes to find Ricky, who is living with her grandmother, and signs over all his stock, persuading Ricky to get her grandmother to take custody of her. Then he and Pete go into cold sleep with a different firm and he dreams of Pete trying to find the 'Door Into Summer', as he had in real life. When he wakes, he heads for where he knows Ricky to have gone into cold sleep, and he and the now twenty-one-year-old Ricky marry and settle down.[6] The book ends with Ricky pregnant and Pete getting old.

Once one reaches the end of the book, it becomes clear that Dan had stolen Belle's patents; he is the man who had always rescued Pete, which was why no one knew what had happened to him. Although Dan speculates at the end about an alternate universe in which Petronius the Arbiter (to give the cat his full name) wanders lonely and starved, it is an impossible speculation. The loop is unbreakable, the pathway is into a time that already exists and existed and will exist. Which takes us to Heinlein's masterpiece, "'All You Zombies—'".

---

6   Jo Walton recoiled from this ending on rereading, noting the age gap and arguing that Ricky grows up knowing that she will marry Dan. But first, the age gap is less than that between myself and my partner, and second, Ricky does *not* know she is going to marry Dan. She makes a child's proposal and could easily forget it by the time she is twenty-one. Had Dan told Ricky that they *would* marry that would be different. Dan cannot be sure the time loop is closed (*What Makes This Book So Great*, 2014, p. 328).

"'All You Zombies—'" is Heinlein's last short story. It is the classic Möbius strip of the science-fiction story; it manipulates the position of the tightly focalised narrator to create a spiral in which a character is situated in a story within a story and yet is still within one, singular circular narrative. Mary Ellen Ryder offers a very acute analysis of this story, exploring the ways in which clues delay the knowledge that there is only one character, 'allowing a condensing of all the enactors into one character through frame overlay only at the very end of the story' ('I Met Myself Coming and Going', p. 230).

The use of the first-person narrative in "'All You Zombies—'" mirrors the human desire to impose a solipsistic story upon the universe, whether it is the me/I of narrative, or the we/us on a wider scale. It was far from the first story to deploy the grandfather paradox, but – as with 'By His Bootstraps' and *The Door Into Summer* – the story is about the paradox itself and a way to resolve it.

In "'All You Zombies—'", a barkeeper greets the man who walks into his bar as 'the Unmarried Mother'. The young man – who is very bitter – makes a living writing confessionals and this is just one of his pseudonyms. Invited to unburden himself he reveals himself as a foundling, but the story takes a turn for the unusual when the barkeeper gives him a nudge to explain why – 'You have an amazingly sure touch with the woman's angle' – and he responds, 'When I was a little girl—'.

The Unmarried Mother grew up as a girl in an orphanage, too plain to be adopted. Fighting off boys (Heinlein, a sexual radical, is clear that the issue is abuse) she preserved her virginity and planned to enter the space hospitality corps as a 'Space Angel', actually a sex worker, a highly respected profession whose members frequently married one of the men they served. Unfortunately one night she meets a slick young man in a park, they court for some weeks, and after she finally sleeps with him she discovers that she is pregnant.

Disastrous as this is, the real problems start when the baby is born. During an emergency caesarean the surgeon finds two full sets of organs, one male, one female, both immature, although the female set is developed enough to carry a baby once. The surgeon has removed these 'and rearranged things so that you can develop properly as a man'. The news is delivered callously and with a certain assumption that the patient will be delighted, and will naturally have her child adopted. She declines, but four days later her baby is stolen from the ward. The protagonist is left bereft of baby, femaleness and profession.

The barkeeper offers her a chance to meet the man who seduced her and a job with 'high pay, steady work, unlimited expense account, your own boss on the job, and lots of variety and adventure' which seems about as implausible as the offer to meet the man. And so, to the tune of 'I'm My Own Grandpaw!' (Dwight Latham, 1947) blaring from the jukebox, they depart. And from here I will switch to using the male pronoun for our Unmarried Mother (UM).

The barkeeper takes him into a storeroom, throws a net over both of them and takes them back into the past. He leaves the UM there, moves forward nine months, takes the baby, returns, collects the UM who has by this time seduced himself, and asks him, 'Now you know who he is – and after you think it over you'll know who you are . . . and if you think hard enough, you'll figure out who the baby is . . . and who I am.' The rest of the story is a summary of how recruitment works, what the Temporal Bureau is doing, and a last contemplation.

I glanced down at the ring on my finger.

The Snake That Eats Its Own Tail, Forever and Ever . . . I *know* where I come from – *but where did all you zombies come from?*

I felt a headache coming on, but a headache powder is one thing I do not take. I did once – and you all went away.

So I crawled into bed and whistled out the light.

You aren't really there at all. There isn't anybody but me – Jane – here alone in the dark.

I miss you dreadfully!

The hints, clues and foreshadowing have been there throughout. The first person is the only legitimate way to tell this story. There is no omniscient external narrator because there is nothing external. Jane is object, subject; she is actor and actant; she is both God and God's people. The story has nowhere to go but the next turn of the spiral in which the Unmarried Mother will become the barkeeper who will snatch baby Jane who will grow up to become the Unmarried Mother who . . . And on. Jane travels not only along her own timeline but, in effect, *the only timeline there can ever be*. The story can only end when the universe ends.

It is ironic that this, the most engineered story, the one in which the precision of the language builds the precision of the time loop, is one of Heinlein's most sentimental tales. It leads us into the next chapter.

4

Rhetoric

Heinlein is strongly associated with the hard SF wing of the field, but this is problematic on two grounds: first, because what Heinlein is truly interested in is how people respond to the future; second, because he has a sentimental streak that inflects almost everything he writes. In this chapter I will explore the construction of his sentimental rhetoric, because this is a key element that Heinlein gifted to science fiction. The chapter will also take us in the direction of exploring another aspect of Heinlein's writing, his rationalised fantasy and his use of the picaresque mode, that otherwise might sit outside his science fiction. Understanding the role of the sentimental in his work helps us to link these. It is the intertwining of the didactic and the sentimental rhetorics that shapes Heinlein's work so distinctively.

The Sentimental

Only those outside science fiction think it is an unsentimental mode: without the sentiment there can be no sublime. Sentiment is a handmaiden to the sense of wonder. Arthur C. Clarke's short story 'The

Star', for example, relies on the moment when physics collides with theology and collides again with an acquired admiration for the species wiped out so that a star could shine over Bethlehem on a particular night in a particular year. Sentiment is what makes the rhetorical logic of science fiction *matter*. Without it, science-fiction stories have the emotional impact of unwinding clockwork – which does of course have its own appeal (see the work of K. J. Parker or Ted Chiang).

David Nye argues that there is such a thing as the technological sublime, in which 'technological objects were assumed to be active forces working for democracy' and in which 'the sublime was inseparable from a peculiar double action of the imagination by which the land was appropriated as a natural symbol of the nation while, at the same time, it was being transformed into a man-made landscape'.[1] It is in this tradition that Heinlein finds both his sublime and his sentiment.

Heinlein has few big-picture moments of the sublime, and those he has are often deliberately quiet. Harriman at the end of 'Requiem' sits on the Moon, battered and broken:

> He *was* where he had longed to be – he had followed his need. Over the western horizon hung the Earth at last-quarter, a green-blue giant moon. Over-head the Sun shone down from a black and starry sky. And underneath the Moon, the soil of the Moon itself. He was on the Moon!

The sublime in this is less in the image itself, than in the man's reaction to the image. This interchange is the core of Heinlein's work.

Many of Heinlein's short stories insist that we recall that on the end of every neat and world-shattering invention, there is a person;

1 David E. Nye, *American Technological Sublime* (Cambridge, MA: MIT Press, 1994), pp. 33, 37.

that in the prosaic is the sense of wonder. In 'Life-Line' (1939) a young couple expecting a baby are lied to by Dr Pinero, for he does not wish to ruin their joy. He knows they will die young and in an accident. In 'Requiem' a man who fought and lived to make the Moon a possibility for others fights one last personal battle for the right to die on the Moon. And it is with this story we will begin.

'Requiem' (1940) may be one of Heinlein's most prescient stories, in ways he would not have anticipated. As Homer Hickam Jr. explores at the end of his astonishingly Heinleinian autobiography, *Rocket Boys* (1998, reissued in 1999 as its anagram, *October Sky*), the unspoken tragedy of the conquest of space is that, so far, it has not been those who cared most about space – the engineers, the designers, the technicians – who have flown.

'Requiem' begins with a pause, a Robert Louis Stevenson poem, 'Requiem' found '*scrawled on a shipping tag torn from a compressed-air container, and pinned to the ground with a knife*' [italics original]. We are tantalised by this lone (and very cinematic) image, then dragged swiftly into the setting of a run-down fairground, its condition a metaphor for the man. We feel sorry for the 'not much of a fair, as fairs go' where we might not feel sorry for the man in the chauffeur-driven car. But our sympathy is dragged to Harriman, when he spots a boy, 'nine or ten years old [who] hung around the entrance and stared at the posters' advertising a rocket flight. He pays for them both to go in; 'the kid's eyes shone.' At that moment a link is made from Harriman to the boy. We see the boy in Harriman, and that boy stays with us throughout the rather mundane chit-chat between Harriman and the rocket pilots. He is still the boy that 'set my heart on being one of the men to walk on the surface of the Moon, to see her other side, and to look back on the face of the Earth, hanging in the sky.' He is still the kind of boy 'who thought there was more romance in one issue of *The Electrical Experimenter* than in all the books Dumas ever wrote.'

And thus, it is once Harriman is in space that we see its sublime qualities, and we see it not in the abstract, as Clarke might have written it, but through the eyes of Delos Harriman, the man who lost the chance of an astronomy degree when his father died, who sat on a back porch and realised his eyesight was going and he could no longer see the Mare Crisium, who realised that his dream of spaceflight had come true but he was too important, and then too old, to go.

> The Moon swung majestically past the view port, wider than he had ever seen it before [. . .] the Earth itself as he had envisioned her, appearing like a noble moon, many times as wide as the Moon appears to the Earth-bound, and more luscious [. . .] He savoured the mellow blue of the Pacific Ocean, felt the texture of the soft green and brown of the continents.

This quotation gets us to the heart of what sentimental rhetoric *is*. It is what is felt, what is understood in the viscera: it can be grounded in hard facts but it is the personal response that creates the moment of the sublime. But Heinlein does not leave the story there. In 1950 he returned to it with 'The Man Who Sold the Moon', where he tells how Harriman funded the first moonshot, lying, cheating and tempting, and in the end selling what he didn't own: rights to the Moon. Yet this hard-headed story is powered by passion and sentiment. Stephen Baxter has noted that it shares with '"All You Zombies—"' an intense solipsism: 'his younger self as the cherished son he never had' ('Moon Believers', p. 28). The conclusion is that kicker, at the end, when he cannot go to the Moon, because if he does, the business acumen that powered the moonshot collapses. Someone comments, 'He looks as Moses must have looked when he gazed out over the Promised Land.'

The power of the Harriman stories, and of the old invention stories of Heinlein's early years, lingered, not just in their regular anthologisation but in their role in the Heinlein canon. When, in his final books, Heinlein began to mine his own work for World as Myth it is to these he turned. In the final part of *'The Number of the Beast'* many of the characters from these stories and others are gathered together and Heinlein's sentimentality is exhibited in his determination to 'rescue' from within the plots and the world he builds, all the characters and stories of which he is most fond. In Chapter 20 of *To Sail Beyond the Sunset*, when Maureen talks about her investment profile, it is a roll-call of all the old invention stories, while in Chapter 23 she turns out to be one of the investors in the Harriman Foundation that gets this timeline to the Moon. If we recognise it the heart cannot but miss a beat.

There are many stories in which Heinlein constructs the visceral sentiment, as in the courtroom scene in 'Jerry is a Man', in the discovery of the hobo, dead trying to save two children in 'Water is for Washing', and in the celebration of a marriage and of the ordinary in 'The Man Who Travelled in Elephants'. Each of these stories relies very heavily on the response to someone or something overcoming the facts as they exist (or in the case of 'The Man Who Travelled in Elephants' don't exist) on the ground.

The two stories in which Heinlein wrote this visceral response most successfully are two of his justifiably most acclaimed: 'The Green Hills of Earth' and 'The Long Watch'. 'The Green Hills of Earth' is great, grand opera, beautifully paced, slow and cumulative; it depends on the contrast of sublime poetry and imagery with scandalous verse for at least part of its sentimental effect. Rhysling the Blind Poet is, to a degree, the tart with the heart of gold. But the real movement is the sense that while Rhysling has been thrown away by the company, he himself has remained loyal to the company's *task*, to take people safely across the stars. As he sings and works, the importance of his role as both engineer and poet are enmeshed.

As with 'Requiem' the story begins with a poem, but this time it is the words of the poet himself:

I pray for one last landing
On the globe that gave me birth;
Let me rest my eyes on the fleecy skies
And the cool, green hills of Earth.[2]

The story is told through intimacy between author and reader – let me tell you the *real* story – a story of unmasking, in that the poetry of the famous singer is to be removed, in order to relate the warts and all; in that the painting of Rhysling, done for the company, is shown to be hagiography:

[it] shows a figure of high tragedy, a solemn mouth, sightless eyes concealed by black silk bandage. He was never solemn! His mouth was always open, singing, grinning, drinking, or eating. The bandage was any rag, usually dirty. After he lost his sight he was less neat about his person.

Yet the purpose of the author is to draw attention not only to the gap between the 'true' story and the hagiography but also to something far more interesting: the contrast between the job done and the job felt. The romance of the spaceways is in reality the hard and dangerous life of the sailor: 'Half the ships that went further than Luna never came back.' 'The others trusted the skills of the captain to get them down safely; jetmen knew that skill was useless against the blind and fitful

---

2   The first iteration of this poem is actually hummed by Northwest Smith in C. L. Moore's 'Shambleau'. Heinlein took it on and added several stanzas. https://en.wikipedia.org/wiki/The_Green_Hills_of_Earth.

devils chained inside their rocket motors'. Captains have an analytical, unromantic relationship to their job. Jetmen dig beneath the viscera to find the hidden, the unpredictable and the intimate. 'Jetmen don't wait; that's why they are jetmen'. When an emergency happens, Rhysling reacts to the thing felt and Heinlein uses very physical imagery to depict this: 'A jetman had to know his power room the way your tongue knows the inside of your mouth'. But Rhysling is left blind by an event depicted prosaically: 'There was light – the emergency circuit – but not for him. The blue radio-active glow was the last thing his optic nerve ever responded to.' In the prosaic is the sentiment.

Once blind, the narrator author introduces a new element: the poetry of contrast between what the singer poet *knew* and what was true. The change in perception affects Rhysling's life and increasingly places the emphasis on the audible, whether the sound of a woman's voice or the sound of the jets, so that the sound of words drives the songs in the way music once did and the assonance of the *Jet Song* reflects their sound (and produces what is effectively a shanty):

Hear the jets!
Hear them snarl at your back
When you're stretched on the rack;
Feel your ribs clamp your chest,
Feel your neck grind its rest.
Feel the pain in your ship.
Feel her strain in their grip,
Feel her rise! Feel her drive!
Straining steel, come alive,
On her jets!

Not quite synaesthesia, the doggerel is *visceral*, linking the bones and blood of the jetman to the steel bones and fuel of the rockets.

The final song is dictated across the intercom as Rhysling tries to find the links to reinstall the blown damping plates and is a version of a song he has been working on before.

> *Let me breathe unrationed air again*
> *Where there's no lack or dearth*
> *Let the sweet fresh breezes heal me*
> *As they rove around the girth*
> *Of our lovely mother planet,*
> *Of the cool green hills of Earth [. . .]*
> *We rot in the molds of Venus,*
> *We retch at her tainted breath.*
> *Foul are her flooded jungles,*
> *Crawling with unclean death.*
> *We've tried each spinning space mote*
> *And reckoned its true worth:*
> *Take us back again to the homes of men*
> *On the cool, green hills of Earth.*

In the ellipsis Rhysling has catalogued the Solar System: 'harsh bright light of Luna', 'Saturn's rainbow rings', 'the frozen night of Titan'. The entirety is an exercise in antithesis; the joy and sublime in the solar system is undercut by the aching ring of homesickness. The story ends with one last piece of mundane romance that locates the sentiment where Heinlein ultimately believes it belongs, in a man just doing his job. Or in this case, two jobs.

> The ship was safe now and ready to limp home shy one jet. As for himself, Rhysling was not so sure. That 'sunburn' seemed sharp, he thought [. . .] He went on with the business of flushing the air out through the valve [. . .] While he did this he sent one more last chorus.

The insistence that the most moving thing a man or woman can do is to do their job when it is most essential and demands most sacrifice will run through Heinlein's work, but its most intense execution is in 'The Long Watch'.

'The Long Watch' is Heinlein's *tour de force*. I cannot speak for anyone else but I have never been able to read the story without weeping. Its origin is in a roll-call of names in *Space Cadet*. Lieutenant Dahlquist is a member of the Patrol, serving on the Moon, when a coup takes control of the nuclear weapons that circle the Earth. He asks for time to think and is given until lunchtime. He heads for the bomb storage areas, and once in there sets out to put the bombs beyond use. He begins by dismantling the 'brains'. When the commander gets wind of what is happening and heads out to talk with him, Dahlquist realises they can still get in and reconstruct the bombs. He considers setting off the bombs, but he does not want to die. Finally he realises that the only way to truly render the bombs dysfunctional is to destroy the perfect surfaces of the plutonium hemispheres. In the process of doing this, he spreads so much radioactive material that he realises he *is* going to die. He sits down, and smokes a cigarette. His body is found by the arriving Patrol and flown home in state.

In 'The Long Watch' Heinlein uses three threads to slow time and transform the pace of a thriller into the slow march of an elegy. The first is the conversation between Colonel Towers and Lieutenant Johnny Dahlquist; the second is Dahlquist's conversation with himself; and the third is the narrative direction that segues from the didactic to the sentimental, flawlessly.

In the first of these elements, Heinlein uses cinematic banter to create an interrupted conversation that each side thinks they are controlling. In the first exchange Colonel Towers explains his position while Johnny listens. In the second, the Colonel calls to ask what

Johnny is doing, and Johnny plays dumb, requesting that the Colonel come out to him. In the third, with the Colonel outside, Johnny threatens him first with a bluff, the effect of explosive decompression on the bombs, and then with a dead-man switch. Quite deliberately, Johnny has mirrored the conversation the Colonel intends to have with Earth.

One interesting aspect is that it is Towers who acts with what he believes to be logic – he thinks the UN will fail, someone must take charge, and that war can be prevented by 'a psychological demonstration, an unimportant town or two. A little bloodletting to save an all out war.' Johnny from the beginning acts through sentiment. This takes us to the second element – Dahlquist's conversation with himself. These are the steps Johnny goes through on his way to becoming a hero.

> Johnny had followed a blind urge not to let the bombs – *his* bombs!
> – be used for 'demonstrations on unimportant towns'.
>
> He decided to stay in his space suit; explosive decompression didn't appeal to him. Come to think about it, death from old age was his choice.
>
> He wondered if he had the courage. He did not want to funk – and hoped that he would.
>
> 'Pal, better break this deadlock or you are going to shine like a watch dial.'

Johnny never intends to die. His Colonel even knows this but makes the mistake of giving Johnny time to set up a dead-man switch. But there are two trajectories at work in Dahlquist. Lieutenant Dahlquist is sensibly and logically putting the bombs beyond use; Johnny Dahlquist is propelled by that blind urge that whatever happens, they *must not* be used. The two together lead to the inevitable ending, in that Johnny finishes his task, walks past the Geiger counter and discovers that he is a dead man already.

The third thread in this story is the narrative direction. The story begins with a didactic political lecture, ironically of a kind Heinlein will later put into the mouths of his good guys, and did so in fact in the precursor story, 'Solution Unsatisfactory', but it is not uncommon for Heinlein to use a political argument twice, once in the service of right, once in the service of wrong. It takes up the pace of a thriller for a short period – 'The rocket car flung itself at the hills, dived through and came out on a plain studded with projectile rockets [...] it dived into a tunnel through more hills.' Dahlquist fights his way into the armoury, but then, despite the emphasis on speed – 'In fifteen minutes he must make the bombs unusable' – Heinlein sets out to describe where we are, and the mechanism of an atom bomb to his readers. This is classic thriller mode in that the absolute time of the story – the flow of events against a ticking clock – is subsumed in the relative time of the story and, unusually, is deliberately slowed down to take in the step-by-step thoughts that might otherwise be mere flashes in the narrative.

> The only tools at hand were simple ones used in handling the bombs. Aside from a Geiger counter, the speaker on the walkie-talkie circuit, a television rig to the base, and the bombs themselves, the room was bare. A bomb to be worked on was taken elsewhere – not through fear of explosion, but to reduce radiation exposure for personnel.

The description of the room continues for another twelve lines, and throughout the narrative Heinlein uses these interventions to slow thought and time. But he also uses them to segue into the sentimental, for a number of these descriptions seek to express the dangerous wonder of science.

The Geiger counter clicked off the 'background' radiation, cosmic rays, the trace of radioactivity in the Moon's crust, and secondary radioactivity set up all through the room by neutrons. Free neutrons have a nasty trait of infecting what they strike, making it radioactive.

All these threads come together in the final thousand words of the story. Johnny is dead. He knows this. 'Plutonium taken into the body moves quickly to bone marrow. Nothing can be done; the victim is finished [...] He accepted, without surprise, the fact that he was not unhappy. There was a sweetness about having no further worries of any sort.' He is no longer in conversation with the Colonel but with others who had stood the watch alone, 'the boy with the finger in the dike, Colonel Bowie, too ill to move [...] the dying Captain of the *Chesapeake* [...] Rodger Young peering into the gloom.' When he is found, the comment is prosaic: 'Better get some handling equipment – uh, and a lead coffin, too.' But the final description of his cortege is elegiac.

The decisions Dahlquist makes are taken step by step, each one taking him further in a direction that leads him away from a mindless institutional loyalty to one rooted in something deeper, that understands what this loyalty is *for.* Patriotism here sees the entire world as one's patria. 'The Long Watch' owed part of its history to 'Solution Unsatisfactory' but also to the roll-call of four names recounted in *Space Cadet,* each time a unit of the patrol musters: Dahlquist, Martin, Rivera and Wheeler. We know nothing about Martin and Wheeler but learn that Rivera was sent to his native city to negotiate with belligerents. He left orders that were he to be taken hostage, there should be an attack. This was duly carried out and he died. Duty to others – to one's institution but also to a wider notion of humanity – was core to Heinlein's construction of sentiment. All his sentimental stories share this element (even 'Ordeal in Space' where the wider community includes a kitten).

The names recited at muster of the Patrol become both a way of honouring the dead and reassuring the living. When, in a ship fuelled with a synthesis brewed up by the Venusians, the four young men take off, they call the roll, there is a moment's hesitation and then... 'I answer for Dahlquist...' and only the hardest-hearted of readers can fail to respond. When the crew is told that they have acted in 'the fine tradition of the Patrol', their hearts swell *because* this ritual has stitched them into the fabric of the institution. Later, in *Red Planet* Scout troops, in 'The Black Pits of Luna' the craters, and in *Starship Troopers* (1959) bases, ships and other installations are named for people who are not only important but are significant in the sentiments for which they argue. In a novel in which anyone, with any handicaps, has the right to serve, it is probably deliberate that the unit is named after Rodger Young, an almost completely deaf infantryman, and the 'Ballad of Rodger Young' is its call sign.

Heinlein locates sentiment in both background and foreground. In the background is his selection of names: over and over again Heinlein characters, and particularly walk-on characters, are equipped with names that indicate *where they belong*. Andrew Jackson Libby's name ('Misfit') indicates that he is an outsider. Franklin Mitsui Roosevelt's name, in *The Day after Tomorrow*, is a clear indication of his Americanness. Podkayne's name identifies her as a child of Mars patriots before ever she opens her mouth. Tom and Pat, in *Time for the Stars*, indicate very different takes on Americanness. Friday's name in the novel of the same title, taken from the old fortune-telling rhyme, indicates her role in life. Names are meaningful.

Institutional identity was an immensely important sentiment to Heinlein. Its first outing was in the short story 'The Roads Must Roll' in that the managerial corps of the rolling roads is inculcated into loyalty to the company and to the roads: a mode of corporatism that would be very familiar to 1950s employees. It is handled in a very heavy-handed fashion, with a corps of management militia wading in to break up a strike, singing company songs as they go. As his writing developed, Heinlein was able to look below the surface of the thing to the integrity that should underpin institutional identity (even if in *Orphans of the Sky* he shows how it can go wrong).

In *Starship Troopers* integrity was stitched into a system of sentimental mentorship; the names of bases and ships create a mentorial paradigm of who and what the army wants people to become. The structure of leadership, in that officers are selected from volunteers who have 'gone career', ensures that the leadership is built from the ground up with bonds of sentiment between officers and men. Who trained whom becomes a familial structure: Johnny Rico meets people he has trained with, and served with, or who have trained with and served with his sergeant or officers. When he himself is training as an officer he and his comrades are stitched into the lineage with the assignment of their third lieutenant's pips, each set of which has once belonged to someone else who has served with honour. When he cannot be given his old class teacher's pips – they were lost with a later holder – he is given the privilege of taking the pips once worn by the head of the academy, and asked to break the bad luck that has dogged them. The chapter ends with hearing that another set of pips, a set that carried much honour but also much grief, has come back; his friend Birdie 'was commissioned two weeks later and his pips came back with their eighteenth decoration – the Wounded Lion, posthumous' (Chapter 12).

Sentiment is not a weakness for Heinlein but a fundamental part of identity, the thing that structures who and what a person is. Much of Heinlein's sentiment focused on the issue of belonging and on what humans will do for other humans. In three stories, 'Water is for Washing', 'The Long Watch' and 'Sky Lift', the greatest act, that a person should give his or her life for others, provides the viscera of the story. 'Water is for Washing' is not a science-fiction story, although it is an illustration of Heinlein's much later essay, 'No Bands Playing, No Flags Flying'. In the essay Heinlein considers the nature of true bravery, in this case of a man who continued with a medical procedure, having watched others die before him. In 'Water is for Washing', a man who almost drowned as a child finds himself caught up in a flood: yet in fleeing he still picks up a child by the roadside and the child's Japanese friend, despite his loathing of 'Japs' (this is 1947). During the night he and a tramp (who had stolen from him at the gas station) hold the children to keep their heads above water. During the night the tramp slips and is drowned, and the final scene is of him burying the tramp. The bravery and the sentiment lie in a man confronting his terror, and in two men seeing only people. Some of the story's sentiment is grounded in the unlikelihood of the protagonists, a hobo and a man scared of drowning, and some in the decision to rescue a Japanese-American child. It is a story about the true meaning of neighbourliness.

Belonging may be one of the most powerful motivators in Heinlein's work, for all he is frequently presented as a highly individualistic writer. His juveniles are, without exception, about growing up to becoming a cog in the machinery of humanity. But for Heinlein cogs have individual shape and finding one's place is deeply satisfying, an enormously moving and emotional trajectory. Heinlein's notion of society is constructed in participatory individualism, not through cutting down the tall poppies: the trick is to find the right-shaped hole for the weirdly shaped piece. In the moments when this happens is located much of Heinlein's sentiment. In 'Misfit' the fitting of the boy into the corps is paralleled by the manoeuvring into place of an asteroid. As they complete the task they hear over the radio: 'Helio from Flagship: "Well done, Eighty-eight".' The message is then cancelled.

A look of surprise and worry sprang into Doyle's face – then the audio continued: 'Helio from Flagship: "Well done, E-M3".' And there is the sentimental moment of a job well done, in both cases.

The Rationalised Fantasy

Although we term Heinlein a science-fiction writer, he also has a small body of fantasy to his credit. Frequently this is subsumed within the science fiction under the rubric of 'science fantasy', a term that was very popular in the 1950s and 1960s to describe a rationalised fantasy which was often immersive (a fully built world) but remained recognisably 'our' world. The striking feature of the rationalised fantasy, however, is not so much its trappings – which vary, as we shall see – but the rhetoric. In the rationalised fantasy the rational is *in* the rhetoric; it is precisely the use of demotic and paratactic syntax that constructs an intimation of the rational in this mode of fiction (the best example may be Charles Stross's 'A Boy and His God', 1998). As a form it tends to combine noir tropes with horror and with the old *slick* style. This mode of fantasy, although not solely the purview of Americans in the 1940s, dominated the American magazines, whereas a more courtly style predominated in the British market. The stories are included here because of the degree to which as slicks, they were both cinematic and relied on the paratactic voice. Each of them has an element of engineering, a sense of a story that works through resolute logic applied to the fantastic.

'The Unpleasant Profession of Jonathan Hoag' was published in John W. Campbell's *Unknown*, a companion magazine for *Astounding*, specifically intended to draw off the fantasy, and offer a kind of fantasy perhaps that would appeal to science-fiction readers. 'Our Fair City' was published in *Weird Tales*, but it may have been written for *Unknown*, as this quirky fantasy would have suited *Unknown* much better. *Unknown* folded in late 1943; perhaps Heinlein had submitted this story too late.

'The Devil Makes the Law' is written almost in the mode of an Ed McBain police procedural although there are no policemen involved. The protagonist, Archie, is a building-supplies merchant who uses magic in his business, and who finds himself at the receiving end of a protection racket which is seeking to go legitimate through the use of training and licensing legislation (not dissimilar to the use of this in the US to control hairdressers – a predominantly female and often black business area), the control of professional practice and other monopolistic strategies. The language reflects Archie's position. As Mark Forsythe notes in *The Elements of Eloquence* (Chapter 11) the paratactic is the language of the ordinary man.

The story follows the classic crime trajectory, an outward-moving spiral as each level of conspiracy uncovered leads to another, larger conspiracy so that the small-town protection racket is directly linked to state-wide legislation. At each stage – as is not uncommon in fantasy – a new Companion is recruited to aid the effort, in this case escalating the number of magic users and the amount of magic. The magic and the magic users are key to the characterisation of this as both *slick* and *rationalised*: although Archie feels awe at their efforts, it is the awe for expert professionals, not for magic per se. So his first experience, with a Mr Biddle, is rendered in the casual language reserved for the plumber: even the argument over the call-out fee is reminiscent of an argument with this kind of tradesman. His second and third experiences are quite different when, with his friend Jedson (who plays the Heinleinian smarter friend), he contacts first Mrs Jennings, who is a very powerful witch, and then an academic, Dr Worthington.

Mrs Jennings becomes an object of reverence for Archie, Dr Worthington of awe, but both are understood as professionals, and the rhetorical interaction with them is no more magical than one would have with one's doctor. Mrs Jennings' discovery that they are dealing with the 'half world' is expressed as a diagnosis: once established the next step is the prescription and then the surgery, and although the final outcome is given as a kind of war mission, the language remains demotic and paratactic.

The choice of paratactic language is even more obvious in 'Our Fair City', a squib of a story, but a delightful squib, and one of Heinlein's election stories. The discovery of a live whirlwind which collects oddments from the streets is treated as magical but not surprising (a trick most often associated with the author Joan Aiken). The hobo who has found the whirlwind treats her as a pet, and the story unravels as a journalist finds a way to use 'Kitty' to expose a crooked machine politician. The story is essentially cinematic, a narrative voice over the events, which combines the sense of wonder of *Twilight Zone* with the mundane step-by-step processes of the investigative reporter who wants 'just the facts' and a 'human' interest story.

The demotic and matter-of-fact tone of these two stories is carried through in two 'wainscot' stories (see Clute and Grant, *Encyclopedia of Fantasy*, 1997): 'They' and 'The Unpleasant Profession of Jonathan Hoag', both written for Campbell's *Unknown* magazine. In 'They' a professor insists that he has always known that the people around him were scenery, or there to keep him from worrying about the scenery. He makes concerted efforts to lift himself from what he believes is an illusion. The doctor brings the professor's wife to see him, and the professor, bitter, accuses her of always distracting him from the moments when he is about to remember or break through. There is one particular moment when his wife tries to stop him going upstairs. When he does, he realises that it is raining at the front of the house but not the back. The story reveals that he really is in containment, really in a virtual reality; a fantasy and horror story resolves as science fiction. This has a horror of its own, but it means that the satisfaction is in the rational reveal, not the on-going horror of the professor's situation. Similarly 'The Unpleasant Profession of Jonathan Hoag' ought to be a horror story, and it has its moments. The tale begins and is told as a crime narrative: a detective team – a man and his wife – are asked by Jonathan Hoag to follow him, as he has no idea what he does during the day. In doing so they discover that their own world is merely a work of art, and Hoag is an 'art critic' who has uncovered another 'world' beneath theirs which is leaking through. Once again this is essentially a cinematic treatment (and was optioned a decade later); the demotic narrative of the detectives however cuts across the more Gothic presentation of Hoag so that the result is rationalised gothic rather than horror.

The Picaresque

Over and above institutional loyalties, Heinlein believed *in people* and was frankly sentimental about his belief. In a 1952 radio broadcast he declared, 'I believe in my whole race. Yellow, white, black, red, brown, in the honesty, courage, intelligence, durability and *goodness* of the overwhelming majority of my brothers and sisters everywhere on this planet.' In *Glory Road, Time Enough for Love* and *Friday*, these beliefs come to the fore, and they are enabled by Heinlein's choice of the picaresque for these texts.

Thrall and Hibbard, writing in 1935 in *A Handbook to Literature*, identified seven characteristics of the picaresque: it is usually written in the first person, the protagonist is of low character or class, relies on wit, frequently stopping only just short of illegal activity, and rarely undertakes permanent employment although he or she may take on tasks. There is relatively little character development – this is a protagonist who moves through the world, changing others – and the protagonist is positioned as an outsider, who moves through a world whose rules somehow do not apply to him or her. There is no plot as such: the picaresque tale is a series of loosely connected links; it is usually but not always told in the demotic voice and is usually but not always a tale of realism. When it is not mimetic, it adopts a tone that you are dared to disbelieve and it is in this inversion of mimesis that it usually encodes its satire or parody.

Science fiction and fantasy have long made use of the picaresque: early English language proponents included Margaret Cavendish's *The Blazing World* (1666) (although it is unlikely Heinlein would have known of this), Jonathan Swift (to whom Heinlein was indebted in a number of ways), Mark Twain in *A Connecticut Yankee in King Arthur's Court*, H. G. Wells (whose *The Time Machine* is a very stuffy, Victorian version of the form), and within the emerging American science-fiction field, Robert E. Howard and L. Sprague de Camp's *Conan* stories.

Slusser, in *The Classic Years of Robert A. Heinlein* argues that 'Heinlein's novellas often contain numerous episodes. These are organised, however, not in a linear series, but in concentric layers around a single center. In each novella, "action" is restricted to one pivotal problem or adventure. This is rapidly set forth and circumscribed; ensuing events tend to gloss it, building upon this center in analytical fashion [. . .] [W]e do not find linear movement toward a point, but pulsatory movement away from it. The "action" will expand into various satellite realms, and then suddenly contract upon the point in order that the story may end.' (*The Classic Years of Robert A. Heinlein*, pp. 24–5)

Heinlein's use of the form is unusual, in that while his picaros do leave the requisite chaos and upturned worlds in their wake, the process of their movement around their world is one of discovering the truth of what Heinlein argues, that the world is full of the overwhelmingly *good*. Heinlein first indicates his interest in the form in *Methuselah's Children*. Lazarus Long arrives at a meeting of the Howard Families, establishes his credentials and takes over, without ever truly accepting authority. In modern gaming terms he is a chaotic neutral or catalyst who moves others to action. The novel itself is three linked adventures and unusually for a purported science-fiction novel, it has very little consequence, in that the truly interesting science-fictional problem – how to extend long life – has been worked on and solved while Lazarus has been off leading his Israelites in their forty years in the wilderness. The novel is of interest in terms of the picaresque however, less because of Lazarus – to whom we will shortly return – but because in this novel Heinlein effectively establishes the human race as the roguish, unruly protagonist in the stable picture of the universe. When the humans meet the Jockaira's gods, they are given the option to become a domesticated species; they decline and flee, but they remain less actors than catalysts in another's (the Jockaira's) story. The humans as a group become the picaro, a disruptive element in the Jockaira's universe, and while they reject the kindness of the Jockaira, it is clear that the Jockaira are 'good neighbours', willing to clothe and feed the refugees.

Although it may seem a strange segue, the second Heinlein novel to use this form is the juvenile, *The Rolling Stones* (1952). Castor and Pollux discover through their grandma, Hazel Stone – later to emerge as a rogue picara in her own right in *The Cat Who Walks Through Walls* – social rules that are negotiable, economic rules that are manipulable, and hard physical rules that will get you killed if you act (in modern parlance) like a special snowflake. In the end however the 'learn better' trajectory of the classic juvenile prevents the novel from ever being truly a picaresque. Yet it still encodes the sentiment that structures Heinlein's work and the notion of being a good neighbour. The two most moving scenes in the book are where Dr Edith Stone steps aboard a ship with a deadly infectious disease, because that's what doctors do (Chapter 8), and one where the two boys, selling off Martian flat cats, gift one to the small child of a needy miner (Chapter 17). They even throw in the last of the candy bars. Afterwards, their grandma declares 'In thirty, forty, fifty more years you may be ready to join the human race.' It is a flippant comment but it links us back to Heinlein's core beliefs about what humans *are*, and emphasises that these picaros are not untouched by the lives they meet on their travels.

At least in the early years, it is clearly the picaresque protagonist rather than the picaresque structure of the tale that attracts Heinlein. Lazarus Long, although fitting the generic description, is too interventionist in *Methuselah's Children* to prove a truly picaresque protagonist. The Stone twins are in the end too conformist (as we see when they are paired against the far more Rabelaisian twins Lapis Lazuli and Lorelei Lee in *'The Number of the Beast'* and *To Sail Beyond the Sunset*). Their future is as hustlers, not quite the same thing. While Rhysling is, as a result of his accident, a drifter, he remains a man who lives in the interstices of the world he loves, not outside it, and his tale is of a man who finds one last (fatal) opportunity to perform a service to it.

Valentine Michael Smith is an interesting version of the picaro. *Stranger in a Strange Land* consists of five books, presumably to mimic the Pentateuch, although in theme it is closer to the New than to the Old Testament. The five chapters trace Smith's origin, then his education first as a Martian, then as a Man, then his time in the wilderness in that 'His Scandalous Career' mimics the temptation of Christ but reverses it as Smith accepts temptation, and sanctifies it through justification (presumably Heinlein had read James Hogg's *Memoirs of a Justified Sinner*). Thus in the first book of the novel Smith is entirely passive. He motivates movement through his passivity.

Those who rescue him from the bulrushes of the military medical establishment (Ben and Gillian) are however profoundly affected by his innocence. As the book goes on Smith becomes more active until by the end he is wandering with purpose, with an Errand in the Wilderness (a seventeenth-century term), but for much of the middle part of the book he is just wandering. *Stranger in a Strange Land* is written in the third person but it is focalised very strictly through the characters around Michael Valentine Smith. This is the picaro observed, who can be defined by the space they make in the world.

Thus the first true picaresque is *Glory Road* (1963). It opens when E. C. Gordon, later called Oscar, finds himself at a loose end. He is classically one of Heinlein's abandoned juveniles (something that may link to Heinlein's own feeling that, as a third boy in a large family, he was left to raise himself). Oscar's mother has joined a new husband overseas, leaving him to finish his high school, living with a disinterested aunt and uncle; as a bereaved dependant rather than a war orphan (a distinction specific to this period) there is no money for college unless he takes a football scholarship. When the team is closed, he runs out of money and signs up for the army to avoid the draft (volunteers got better choice of assignments and a better chance of promotion). When he is demobbed in Europe where he hopes to find his family, he discovers they have returned to the USA. He finds himself at a loose end, hanging out at a nudist colony, reading and drinking, when he sees an advert for an adventurer. He responds, meets the woman he has been admiring and conversing with on the beach, and finds himself recruited. Together they have four adventures, which can be loosely described:

- Beowulf: he meets the monster and forces it to eat itself.
- The Pastoral Hero: the adventure of the generous host, in which Oscar (as he becomes) turns down the hospitality of his host's

women and gets them booted out. They have to return so he can do his duty and spread his Hero's genes.

- The Medieval Knight: the adventure with the dragon in which he kills a dinosaur-like creature and leaves its baby weeping.
- The Sword-and-Sorcery Thief: he secures the egg of the phoenix, which turns out to be the memory spools of lost Emperors.

In each of these episodes, Oscar is the champion, sent to perform on behalf of his companion, Star, but in the process he changes the worlds he moves through and is himself changed. Although Heinlein uses the slick screwball language of sexual play in many of the intimate moments, for much of the novel he abandons his preference for realist language. The style has far more in common with the rhetorical techniques used in his fantasies and is probably why this novel is often understood as a science fantasy. It is deliberately studied and slow, elaborate, courtly and hypotactic, told in the language of Malory and the romance poets. The decision to reduce the impact of much of the adventure, and to foreground the conversation, a clear fault in an adventure, can be understood as the narratable form of the epic and the picaresque.

Clearly in the sword-and-sorcery tradition, the novel draws on the wandering champion novels of Edgar Rice Burroughs and Fritz Leiber (with more than a little of Hemingway's masculinist fantasy thrown in, although this is sufficiently performative to suggest irony); the focus of the tale is not on the adventures, often related somewhat cursorily, but on the social consequence of the adventures: the true focus is Oscar's rise in status with both his companion, Star (who turns out to be a meritocratically selected Politician Princess), and with the communities through which he moves.

The conversations between Star and Oscar about their relationship are extensive and could be seen as antithetical to the picaresque structure, if it were not that frequently they act as an education in how to be a picaresque hero. The result is a performance of the picaresque, rather than the thing itself. In Chapter 4, the game begins with Oscar choosing his hero name. In Chapter 5, when Oscar awakes into the pastoral, a great deal of time is spent on clothing (Heinlein's attention to and playfulness with male clothing is in itself a source of fascination). Oscar notes, in one of the first indications that a marker of the Heinlein picaresque will be its intertextuality, that he feels 'like Captain John Carter, Jeddak of Jeddaks, and the Gascon and his three friends all at once'[3] (Chapter 4) and considers that the medievalist garb of buckskins *et al* is French couture.

The tales turn out to be teaching moments. In Chapter 7, where Oscar kills the monster by forcing it to eat itself and disappear into another universe, he learns that the physical rules are different in this world; in Chapters 7 through 9 where he offends his host by declining a bed-mate from the host's family – and the opportunity for the host to acquire the genes of a hero for his family line – he learns that social codes are different. In Chapter 10 he gets a lecture on the deficiencies of American sex culture, and in Chapters 15 through 18 he discovers that a hero is not much use to anyone in a modern bureaucratic state such as the one Star rules and the one he comes from. He returns from his travels a fully finished picaro and one who has learned that the world is full of neighbours.

Oscar is a first working-out of the Lazarus Long whom Heinlein constructs in *Time Enough for Love*. But where Oscar must learn to be the picaresque hero, Lazarus is, as we discover, born one. Having realised in *Glory Road* that the first person is a key element to the narratology, in *Time Enough for Love* Heinlein also returns to the paratactic and the demotic.

---

3   From *Warlord of Mars* by Edgar Rice Burroughs, 1914 and *The Three Musketeers* by Alexandre Dumas, 1844, respectively.

At the start of *Time Enough for Love* (1973), Lazarus Long has been found, dying, in a flophouse. He is rescued by the head of the Howard families and – in a clear and stated violation of contemporary right-to-die ethics – he is rejuvenated against his will. While his nurses Ishtar and Galahad restore his body to life they also look for the means to restore his will to live, and as an interim measure he is persuaded to fill in the Howard family records with the story of his life, a scheherazade tale, though instead of persuading someone to keep you alive so you can tell them one more tale, Lazarus is persuaded to stay alive so *he* can tell one more tale.

The result is a book that is grounded in the picaresque but that, as it develops, becomes part of the craving for family sequence that I discuss in Chapters 5 and 8. The two sections, the family sections and the scheherazade sections, are told very differently but both emphasise, over and over again, the relationships between people.

The familial sequences are third-person, focalised through Long's carers, and mostly told in the demotic voice. They include discussions of medical treatment, sexual transactions, arrangements for cloning and other rather unromantic moments. Crucially they are observational: they are about Long, even when he is not the direct subject of the conversation.

The scheherazade sequences are told tales in which a Lazarus-Long-like figure moves through the world, an itinerant catalyst, the wandering Jew. Not all the tales are ostensibly about Long. The first of them, 'The Man Who Was Too Lazy to Fail', is a classic tale told in a marketplace, of David the boy who would work quite hard if it meant he didn't have to plough a field, who worked out shortcuts in the name of laziness that developed his intellect, and who figured out how to play the system in the navy. David is too directed to be a true picaresque hero but his trademark lazy-but-clever take on the world is firmly in this camp and sets up the character of Lazarus Long for 'The

Tale of the Twins Who Weren't', which is far less about the genetic interest of the twins but is a sequel to *Citizen of the Galaxy*. That book presented Thorby Baslim as a natural resister of slavery. This story is about teaching people to be free – and in that sense is also paired with *Methuselah's Children*. Where 'The Man Who Was Too Lazy to Fail' was told in a rather dreamy third-person voice, here we have the true first-person demotic of the picaresque, crucially combined with the same lack of intentionality. Long never means to acquire slaves – an intense abhorrence of slavery runs through Heinlein's work – but once he has, he sees them as a responsibility that cannot be abandoned and he pauses in his travels to change their lives through education and through establishing them in careers. The same structure and tone is evident in 'The Tale of the Adopted Daughter'. Although Lazarus acquires Dora when he catches her as she is thrown from a burning building, the interaction is the same: Long cannot move on until he has done his duty by her, raised her (with the aid of a foster mother), trained her and married her off, even if it is to himself.

The Dora section is in many ways the most sentimental, and once again it relies on the philosophy of neighbourliness that Heinlein declared in his radio speech. Long's actions in the rescue are those of a neighbour, and his relationship with the older woman in the town is that of a neighbour. When he repels the raiders who try to destroy his home it is because they are incapable of being neighbours, and he regards the homestead as a success *when it acquires neighbours.*

Despite his determination on transience, Long as a picaresque hero becomes engaged with the scenery – by which I mean people – he passes through. Although Long emerges fundamentally unchanged each time, it is not a clear escape. As the Notebooks interspersed between the two major forms of the novel indicate, from each encounter Long takes a kernel of something; from Dora for example, a sense of integrity to oneself.

In the final section, when Long returns to Earth, the picaro is brought low: Dora had given him pause, but when Long returns to his family he discovers the disinterest of the picaro is impossible to sustain and, eschewing the picaro's principal motive – to preserve his own skin – he becomes involved in decisions whose sole purpose is to re-engage with the living thread of humanity (he goes to war). By the end of the book and, as we later witness in *The Cat Who Walks Through Walls* (a novel that might have been named *The Reluctant Knight*), and *To Sail Beyond the Sunset*, this picaro has retired to grass, accepting reabsorption into family life and passing his mantle to his clone twins.

'*The Number of the Beast*' is the novel that introduces us to inter-dimensional travel in Heinlein's world. In many ways it is the most cinematic of Heinlein's later novels, a sex comedy and a road movie. The book is, without doubt, a shambles: Heinlein just isn't interested in the adventure but is interested in the family-building that I will discuss in Chapter 8. Nonetheless, the novel is a homage to E. E. 'Doc' Smith's *Galaxy Primes* in both its premise and its set-up (two couples in love, lots of sexual repartee). The first two-thirds is structured as an ensemble picaresque (or even, at least at the start, as a road movie). Had the blurb for the novel run 'family goes on a camping holiday pursued by villains and in search of fanciful places' it could have been sold as a romp. Had it been made by the British movie Carry On team (*Carry On World-Hopping*?) it might even have made sense. The novel's role as a picaresque is established when one realises the real irrelevance of the 'black hats' who are apparently chasing the family: Part Three of the novel for example is a long shopping trip for a world with competent obstetricians,[4] and

---

4   The need for obstetricians is noted by Jubal Harshaw in the last chapter of *Stranger in a Strange Land*, by Hugh Farnham and by Friday. Heinlein had no illusions about the romance of childbirth, for all that the depiction of it in *Farnham's Freehold* and *Time Enough for Love* has attracted derision.

Part Four resolves into a decision that mothers may have picaresque adventures too.

The basic premise is rather lovely: brilliant egghead mathematician with a passion for Burroughs' Barsoom novels goes looking for brilliant Grey Lensman-type ('Doc' Smith) to help him with his inter-dimensional maths. The snag is, by the time he realises he has found the cousin of the brilliant Grey Lensman-type (that is, Zeb was not the man they were actually looking for) his daughter is in love and wants to marry this chap who makes her nipples crinkle. The daughter, by the way, looks not so much like Dejah Thoris but the wife of Kimball Kinnison, the Grey Lensman: Clarissa MacDougal. This is of course deliberate. The Mathematician is Jacob (Jake) Burroughs and the Lensman-type is Zebediah John Carter. This is both a running joke and our first indication of what is going on, for when Deety spots the coincidence she announces 'We don't have to get married – we already *are* – for years. More than a century.' Jake responds, 'Logical' (Chapter 3). He, if not the others at this stage, thinks they may be fictional.

On the way home Jake's car blows up. Zeb scoops up Jake, Deety and their host, Hilda, and they flee to the Carter hideaway in the hills, with an inter-dimensional space hopper in the basement. Zeb marries Deety, Hilda marries Jake. They realise they are being attacked by aliens and set about hyper-dimension jumping in order first to escape and later to confront the aliens. Their initial hypothesis is that they are creating worlds along the axis of the Number of the Beast – 6 to the power of 6 to the power of 6 dimensions – and their first adventure is to an alternate Mars occupied by Imperial Russians and Imperial British. After trying several Earth worlds and realising they have very little control they leave it to Gay Deceiver, the computer, who takes them to Oz, and then they construct a short list of worlds they all like. This leads to a traverse, in quick succession, through Lilliput, Wonderland (where mysteriously Charles Dodgson is present) and Camelot. By this time they have concluded that they are moving through metafictions.

Although the crew dismiss the work of Heinlein, and only list *Stranger in a Strange Land*, they finally meet Lazarus Long and his family and discover that Deety and Elizabeth 'Libby' Long are universe twins (that both have super mathematical ability links it to their femaleness rather than to Libby's original maleness). They discover also that they have been kidnapped and brought into the Long universe in order to rescue Lazarus Long's mother, Maureen, who appears to have disappeared from the records (and in *The Cat Who Walks Through Walls* their technologies are used to rescue Adam Selene from a fictional past).

The book concludes with a party (Chapter 48) to which Heinlein – revealing that the authorial voice is the true character here – invites all his favourite authors, and corrals the critics in a room with typewriters without ribbons, a bar with no liquor and a dining room but no kitchen. His favourite characters include Hazel Meade Stone, an elderly lady who will be offered rejuvenation to a comfortable and sexy middle age, Castor and Pollux, Star and Oscar, and Jubal Harshaw and his team. This reader was delighted to discover that Holly Hardesty of 'The Menace from Earth' became a 'design engineer, ship's architect type' and that Podkayne gave up on the idea of child-care and opted instead to become an empath counsellor. Interestingly, with the exception of Castor and Pollux, whose sole role is to be married off to Laz and Lor later, none of the male characters from the juveniles turn up. For added sentiment, the Venerian dragon Sir Isaac Newton, from *Between Planets*, arrives at the very end. It is in effect a posthumous fantasy: perhaps they really did die when the car blew up and all their adventures are in their imagination. This is not as preposterous a theory as it sounds.

Perhaps the most sentimental of Heinlein's stories is 'The Man Who Travelled in Elephants', a very sweet story of a man who misses his deceased wife dreadfully. After a lifetime as a travelling salesman, in retirement he has struggled to find a meaning in life: his wife had suggested they 'travel in elephants', scoping out the zoos and circuses across the USA. This is, of course, a wild elephant chase, a reason to travel without ever getting there. But when he is caught in a bus crash he enters the world of his happiest moments, meeting first a dog 'just like' Bindlestiff, sees a woman who looks like his wife, and chases after her until he finally finds her at the head of a circus parade, with many different breeds of elephants. That parade of people crops up in *Glory Road*, *'The Number of the Beast'*, *Time Enough for Love* and *To Sail Beyond the Sunset*. *Job* ends with a very clear posthumous fantasy in which Satan sets Alec and Margrethe up in a personal heaven. *I Will Fear No Evil* is a reworking of '"All You Zombies—"' but in this version isolation and desolation is replaced with an afterlife in which all the people most important to the protagonist are gathered in to the most intimate space possible. The gathering-in of friends and neighbours in an afterlife is the ultimate in community.

The figures we meet towards the end of *'The Number of the Beast'* connect to the characters in *The Cat Who Walks Through Walls* and *To Sail Beyond the Sunset*. The twins, Lapis Lazuli and Lorelei Lee, have all the hallmarks of picaros, even if their progenitor has settled down. They have a rambunctious, Rabelaisian approach to life and to love, and they cut a swathe through the world, but Heinlein did not live long enough to write their story. *The Cat Who Walks Through Walls* also has a claim to be a picaresque. Hazel Meade Stone, aka Gwen, has the characteristics of the picaro, while poor Richard — who turns out to be descended from Lazarus — is another Oscar, an old soldier who she picks up, trains and points in the right direction. And the truest picaro figure is Pixel, the cat who walks through walls, who turns up in *To Sail Beyond the Sunset* as a Loki figure, bringer of chaos and rescue.

The coupling of nostalgia, intertextuality and the picaresque also produces the sentimental structure of *To Sail Beyond the Sunset* in that Heinlein revisits his favourite timeline and uses his picaro to stitch the stories together. Although much of the life Maureen tells is of the domestic, the novel is told in the first person, in the paratactic, demotic voice, and with a sense of the world moving by as Maureen moves through it. Although much of the novel is taken up by Maureen's youth, during that period she can have little effect on those around her; by the middle of the novel we can see how she has altered the lives of friends, and then of neighbourhoods, and eventually major businesses. Heinlein creates a female picaro by contrasting the very ordinary rule-bound life with an essentially amoral character, and the discussion of her amorality is central to the story.

The plot of *To Sail Beyond the Sunset* is flimsy. Maureen Smith is trying to find her father, who has been lost in time. Maureen's incestuous love for her father is part of the amoral construction of the novel. In pursuit of her father she wakes to find a dead body in her bed and herself on a planet she doesn't know. Then for much of the novel she is in prison, visited by Pixel, *The Cat Who Walks Through Walls*, until eventually she is rescued by the World as Myth, then whisked back to Boondock on Tertius. In between we have a version of *Moll Flanders/The Roaring Girl/Fanny Hill/Time Enough for Love* as Maureen thinks back on her days as a wicked but saintly young girl, and even more wicked married woman while maintaining the perfect front.

The second half of the novel is more interesting because when Maureen finds herself divorced she becomes a sharp, pissy older lady – not unlike Hazel Stone of blessed memory. She turns out to have been paying a lot more attention to money than her husband realised, and is a lot more educated even if she has no qualifications. She takes herself off to college, earns several degrees, lectures us on women's rights, hangs out in the community and parlays her investment tips from 'Ted Bronson' into a fortune for both her, the Howard Foundation and Harriman Holdings. All of the tips are linked to Heinlein's very early invention stories: Maureen becomes the link between tales, a classic picaro role. She gets old, she reminds us older people have sex too, she discovers that being too far in age from your kids can make it impossible to understand them, and then she accidentally steps in front of a truck, and wakes up looking into the faces of her descendants. And has to deal with the issue that she slept with her son ...

Maureen is the happiest, most easygoing of the picaros Heinlein creates. Lazarus Long has a residual sense of responsibility, first to the Howards (in *Methuselah's Children*), then to the children he acquires (the Twins and Dora) and eventually to his constructed family. Maureen shucks those off with her divorce and her final, disastrous experience of parenting. Her trajectory throughout the novel is towards ever greater freedom and as it begins with her wandering from her new family, we can assume that family life has not constrained her. She is in many ways the least neighbourly of the picaros, but her travels, like those of others, demonstrate Heinlein's sentiment that the world is full of nice people.

There are two picaros however who are deeply unhappy with their role. Maureen chooses her role; Friday and Alexander Hergensheimer have it thrust upon them. *Friday* is an anti-picaresque. It is also incredibly sentimental. Although Friday moves through the world superficially as a picaro, in an episodic narrative that lacks the conventional structures of plot, she is not strictly speaking a protagonist. Much happens to Friday, but Friday is a trauma victim – this we will consider in Chapter 5 – and it takes her a long time to realise that she can become something or someone (a distinction important in this book) who happens to someone else. The anti-picaro structure is indicated even in her name. Friday's child is loving and giving: Friday gives and never expects to have given to her. 'Friday' is a name common to slaves in the Anglo-American colonies. 'Friday' was Robinson Crusoe's 'man', a person held in slavery in part through the bonds of gratitude as Friday, although well paid, is also held.

When we first meet Friday, she is a courier. She moves with purpose through the world, but it is not *her* purpose. Similarly, if she is amoral, it is because she has been told morality is not for her – as a made person she is neither expected to understand it (as in her failure to 'get' racism) nor be encompassed by it. If she takes life as it comes, then that is because she has had, historically, very little control over her life: as an Artificial Person (AP) and crèche baby and an indentured servant, long-term planning belonged to someone else, and only the short term was in her hands. This training, ironically, is what makes her a good courier: she accepts the world as something she can't control, and whereas in the classic picaresque the picaro is the one who makes the impact on the world, in *Friday*, the world makes an impact on the titular character.

Once one stops seeing this as an adventure novel and sees it instead as a picaresque, and also as a search for home, the story drops into place. The narrative structure is such that each time Friday is heading 'home' (to the company, to her line marriage) something intervenes. On her way home to the company she is attacked and kidnapped. Having returned home to the line marriage (or group marriage) she discovers it is breaking down, may never have been the source of safety she hoped for, and finally interrupts it/sabotages it herself by revealing her origins. As she begins to settle with Ian and Janet and Georges that idyll is interrupted by the collapse of the world economy. Friday is a picaro in order to survive, not from choice. The role gives her distance, even a way to disassociate herself. She only begins to realise this after she flirts with and is then abandoned by Andrew, the closeted AP (Chapter 20), and thus sees how she is understood from the other side, less as a free spirit than as someone who leaves an emptiness in her wake.

Friday's lack of comprehension of her discomfort with the role she has adopted shapes most of her really bad decisions. Friday's involvement with the line marriage, the very attraction to that kind of long-term, ever-regenerating structure, is an attempt to escape the picaresque of her life, even as itself it recreates such a picaresque within it, and as she herself takes the role of the picaro in the family (something she later realises that Anita has actively encouraged).

Eventually when sorting out how she feels about her line family she realises, 'I had paid for the happy privilege of belonging. To a family – especially the homely delights of changing wet nappies and washing dishes and petting kittens' (Chapter 7). Yet the experience of rejection even from this bought family scars Friday, and when she flees from Ian's family it is in part in fear of a permanent place in the story. Friday's attachment to the company, and to her boss, Kettle Belly Baldwin, is a signifier of this also. When the company breaks down and Friday finds herself on her travels, it is noticeable how often this picaro sets out to construct a facsimile of domesticity; most tellingly perhaps in her relationship with Goldie.

Friday is told throughout as a romance. The delivery is light, and frothy at times, not far from the mood of *Glory Road*, and this has proven problematic because it appears on the surface to make light of the very real trauma that Friday – an abuse survivor – has experienced. But Friday is told in the first person, and the picaresque mode is precisely a means to allow Heinlein to deal with some very difficult issues indeed. Its conclusion is intensely sentimental, about belonging and humanity, and once again it is no coincidence that it ends with a list of who Friday's neighbours are on the new planet.

Job is a very different kind of book. Alexander (Alec) Hergensheimer is a righteous man: a minister, a married man, a godly man in his own eyes. It later emerges that he became a minister because he flunked engineering – a highly unusual hero for a Heinlein novel were it not hinted that engineering in his world is undermined by rigid religious doctrine around the nature of the world. While on a cruise, and in a moment of madness, he accepts a dare to take a fire-walk. He comes round from a faint, to find himself in another world where the comely stewardess, Margrethe, is in love with him. However, just as he accepts the possibility of an affair the ship hits an iceberg and they are thrown into another world, beginning a round of adventures, travelling in what Diana Wynne Jones, in *Homeward Bounders*, would later describe as a sequential ring of related worlds.

As they travel, each time stripped of any accumulated property, Alec shucks his morals (although not at first his prudery), and his belief in the efficacy of long-term planning. As the world changes around him and it begins to seem increasingly deliberate, he also becomes ever more paranoid, and in attempting to cope with this becomes the picaro through lack of any alternative. In order to survive he must lose his faith in the possibility of returning home, must become the wandering Jew. In this role he becomes absolutely dependent on the kindness of others. For all that Alec and Margrethe work hard, Heinlein does not show them as individuals and utterly self-reliant: at each stop they are given a helping hand by *someone*. The kindness and neighbourliness is as much an undermining of Alec's earlier ideas as is his experience of other sexual moralities. At the end of the tale, he too is rewarded with the recreation of domesticity and of a neighbourhood. For Heinlein, the freedom and loneliness of the picaro is, it seems, ultimately tragic.

5

Heinlein and Civic Society

Although many of Heinlein's political opinions changed over his forty-year writing career, it is important to understand that his underlying beliefs did not. This core sense of what was *right* and what was *wrong* is behind his enormous generosity to fellow writers, his advocacy of the philosophy of *passing forward* as a civic duty, his engagement in blood drives, his intense protectiveness of those around him – and his inability to cope when that protection was abused – and his more vituperative statements from the 1950s onwards.

Neil Easterbrook argues very convincingly that 'Heinlein provides a good example of a writer deeply concerned with interrogating conventional moral reasoning, but who consistently establishes a moral rather than ethical environment' ('Ethics and Alterity', in *The Routledge Companion to Science Fiction*, p. 387). Easterbrook argues, fairly I think, that this is why readers come unstuck with *Starship Troopers*, in that the argument for an ethical system is actually centred on the *moral* imperative to survive, and why the arguments in *The Moon is a Harsh Mistress* can feel manipulated (ibid., p. 387).

As John Clute has argued, 'Heinlein always had to believe he was acting according to principle' and he 'walked a tightrope between patriotic gallantry and transgression' (*Stay*, p. 80).

For our purposes however what matters is the degree to which Heinlein's sense of right and wrong shaped his writing. We can divide Heinlein's expression of his beliefs into big-picture approaches – the right ordering of society and how to make it a purposeful society – and the small picture – the right ordering of self. This chapter focuses on the right ordering of society.

The Structure of Society

For Heinlein, the right ordering of society was in itself a civic duty. In a letter to Frank Robinson dated 18 September 1969, he writes that when writing *Starship Troopers* and *Stranger in a Strange Land*, essentially alongside each other, there was never any conflict because both 'are based on the twin concepts of love and duty'.[1] His own family had been engaged in the abolition movement, his mother was a birth-control advocate. To advocate for the less fortunate was the responsibility of the individual. To contribute to society was, for Heinlein, a political act, an act of civilitas. We can see this in the templates he created for civic societies in a number of his works: *For Us, the Living, Beyond This Horizon, Red Planet, Tunnel in the Sky, Starship Troopers* and *The Moon is a Harsh Mistress*, and in the anti-templates, such as 'Coventry', 'Universe', and the glimpses we get in the later novels of an America 'gone wrong'.

Heinlein's first foray into considering the right ordering of society was the long-unpublished *For Us, the Living*. Comments on the much later *Starship Troopers* confirm that Heinlein was familiar with

---

1   Letters courtesy of Henry Wessels.

Edward Bellamy's *Looking Backward* (1888) and there is a clear sense in this book of the communitarianism still current in American life in the 1930s. In *For Us, the Living*, civic duty is focused on contribution, and respect for the individual's social liberty; privacy is absolute, childrearing is no longer solely an occupation for women – Diana has shuttled between parents as a child – and sexual jealousy is a mystifying illness. *For Us, the Living* is two books: the intimate story of Diana and Perry, and a long series of lectures. In this it presages the structure of many of the later books, suggesting that this was always what Heinlein wanted his books to be and do. In the intimacy, we see a notion of civic duty that is very family-oriented, a duty to care for those for whom one has taken responsibility, and a notion that there is civic duty in sexual morality even though it is not contemporary morality.

In *For Us, the Living*, society becomes the family and health care is free, because it is seen as in the interests of a wider society: 'any government official would know that it is dangerous to everybody to let people be hungry and sick. Why, from the most selfish standpoint possible, if people are sick they can be the centre of an epidemic, and anybody knows that a hungry man is not responsible for his actions and may do something dangerous' (Chapter 3). We also see the first indications of an idea that will come to fruition in *Starship Troopers*, that people have a responsibility for the politicians they choose and for the wars those politicians approve. This was almost certainly a reaction, common to Europeans as well as Americans, to the events of the First World War: the war left a legacy of distrust in Heinlein of government warmongering that the events of Korea and Vietnam – despite Heinlein's support for the wars themselves – hardly alleviated.

The imagined twenty-seventh amendment to the constitution reads: 'except in case of invasion of the United States, Congress shall not have the power to declare war without submitting the matter to a referendum' (Chapter 4). Further, 'Only those eligible for service may vote' and 'Those who voted to declare war automatically enlisted for the duration of the war . . . Those who didn't vote were the next draft, and those who voted no the last draft' (Chapter 4). (Heinlein may have got the idea from Mark Twain's 'The Curious Republic of Gondour'.) But everyone in the America of *For Us, the Living* has to take a civics class, and voting is compulsory. And despite the civics class there is no examination. In a clear reference to Jim Crow: 'If there were, the party in power might use it to disenfranchise the opposition. We just make sure that the citizen has been thoroughly instructed in the machinery of government' (Chapter 12). This strategy is used again in *Starship Troopers* where civics class is compulsory and similarly cannot be failed. Only in the event of an invasion were all citizens at risk of the draft. In all other circumstances Heinlein believed in 1939, and continued to believe into the 1980s, the draft was abhorrent. This is a point that is frequently lost in the discussion of *Starship Troopers*.

For Us, the Living is the proactive version of Heinlein's ideal. It is not a utopia ('In spite of everything we get a certain percentage of stupid, or unqualified, or small-souled men in office. This isn't Utopia, you know. This is just the United States of America in 2086'; Chapter 12). But it is a consensual society and one that values everyone. Heinlein demonstrates his early belief in the importance of this consensus in two stories, 'Coventry' and 'The Roads Must Roll'. In 'The Roads Must Roll' the argument against the philosophy of 'Functionalism' is that it fails to understand society as an organisation. Functionalism is dangerous; it is a denial of the interlocked state of society. In 'Coventry' the offence for which the protagonist chooses Coventry is essentially a denial of the consensus – not what the consensus is about but that a consensus is key to the right operating of society. In this short story, and in *Tunnel in the Sky*, individualist survivalism is severely criticised. Although by the end of his career Heinlein moves over to a more individualist position – as represented by Lazarus Long, and perhaps influenced by his move to live a rather isolated life in Colorado – the idea that the right society is a collaborative and co-operative society never quite goes away. In the later books, quite often a small group of people, whether the collective identity of Joan Eunice, or Lazarus Long's family, becomes a collective facing an atomised society.

Clute has written, 'The secret is that Robert A. Heinlein thought that drawing a true plan about the future of America would make America adhere to the Truth' (*Stay*, p. 82), and seeing his secret plan is revealing. *For Us, the Living* was never published in Heinlein's lifetime, and we have to turn to *Beyond This Horizon* (1942) for a fictional, and already shifting, account of what civic duty might look like in a large society. This book is almost a classic example of Istvan Csicsery-Ronay's narratology of SF: 'SF writers usually construct these vivid object-worlds with two inter-locking kinds of historical narrative: megahistories of the human species as a single great collective actor, and the personal histories of protagonists in a critical moment of that covering megahistory' (*Seven Beauties of Science Fiction*, 2008 p. 82).

Beyond This Horizon is the tale of two men's experience of a future world and their places within it. In this world, famously, everyone who wishes to be considered a full citizen goes armed. They are expected to be willing to defend both their actions and their words. But it is a society supported in part by wealth distribution – on the same model adopted by Alaska, where a society surplus is redistributed as a regular income. And it is also a society with huge social and individual incentives for what we might call right breeding; not precisely eugenics but what anthropologists call intensive child-rearing, selecting for the best and brightest from each couple. The focus of the plot is around two civic duties, the duty to have children and support the improvement of society's genetic stock, and the duty to contribute purposefully. At the start of the story Hamilton Felix has no desire at all to do either, something that may reflect 1930s concerns about the prevalence of 'companionate' childless marriages among the middle classes, and the delay in childbearing caused by the Depression.[2] It also indicates the pronatalism that was about to sweep the United States.

One form of 'right ordering' that Heinlein played with was the corporate state: we see it in the cadet managers in 'The Roads Must Roll', who have almost supra-national powers – there is no attempt to consult the government in the story's crisis – and in the setting up of the Patrol in 'Solution Unsatisfactory' (1941) and its depiction in *Space Cadet* (1948), where national governments are forced to cede power to an international and unelected military. The Patrol is very American – although Matthew Dodson makes it clear that this does not mean American interests will be prioritised. It is also essentially aristocratic and relies on a feeling of separateness: Matt's visit home creates in him the realisation that civilians do not have the same sense of civic duty that Patrol cadets have. That Heinlein had doubts about this separation however is evident early on in 'Universe', where we see what a corporate state, unchecked or criticised by any 'fourth estate', can become – not merely corrupt but *ignorant*, a far greater sin in Heinlein's eyes. Later, in *Starship Troopers*, the military government is on the French model of a citizenry militia, and thus while civilians and military are disconnected, the route from one to the other, from service to the economy to service to the community, is much stronger.

All of this of course underlies Heinlein's ideas of patriotism. Patriotism to Heinlein is not merely love of country: it is absolutely

---

2   See Elaine Tyler May, *Barren in the Promised Land: Childless Americans and the Pursuit of Happiness* (Cambridge: Harvard University Press, 1997).

tied to a belief in the systems of the country and to a willingness to defend it. The country Heinlein wishes to defend is fundamentally communalist (not to be confused with communist). In 'This I Believe' he declared:

> I believe in my townspeople. You can knock on any door in our town saying, 'I'm hungry' and you will be fed. Our town is no exception. I've found the same ready charity everywhere. But for the one who says, 'To heck with you – I've got mine', there are a hundred, a thousand, who will say, 'Sure, pal, sit down.'

This manifesto is played out in his settler novels, whether the communitarian *Farmer in the Sky* and *Tunnel in the Sky* or the more individualistic but still communalist *Red Planet* and *The Moon is a Harsh Mistress*.

Heinlein, his settler novels and his juvenile novels more generally, were all products of an ideology called 'boyology', coined by H. W. Gibson in 1922 (see Kenneth Kidd, *Making American Boys?*, 2004, p. 1). This ideology saw boys as little 'savages' who could be tamed and who emerged as 'characterful' men, by which was meant, men, who could take their place in a wider community as contributing citizens. It was very strongly linked to both the movement to keep boys on the farm and to organisations such as the American Scouts.

Farmer in the Sky is a comprehensive debunking of the idea of individualistic survival, while nevertheless valuing the individual, and it follows the strategies advocated by the boyology movement. It is structured in three 'acts' and can be understood as three acts of community organisation. The first act is the creation of the key unit of society, the family (Heinlein is not arguing for a norm, but accepting that his emigrant society demands this). George and his son, Bill, have been alone for a while, but when George decides to emigrate he understands that he needs to be part of a family to be accepted for the trip and marries his co-worker Molly, who has a young daughter. In the second act, aboard ship, Bill is part of a group of boys who form a Scout troop: again, a community organisation that supports the infrastructure. Then in act three, when they arrive, farms are established. Although there is a high level of individualism, in that each farms their own land eventually, there is also a clear sense of communal infrastructure; the heavy-digging machinery is held communally, and while waiting for it to become available Bill works for Schultz, a more established farmer, apprenticing in the art of farming on Ganymede. When he eventually takes on his own land we also see Schultz give him garbage to make his soil and help with planting; eventually the Scout troop turns up to raise his house. We are told firmly, 'pioneers need good neighbours', and when disaster comes, while individuals do survive they are, with only one exception (the Schultz family), those who live near enough to the civic centre to get help in time.

We can see the insistence on what we might call 'the individual in community' in *Tunnel in the Sky*. The plot is one of Heinlein's best. Rod needs to take a survival course to qualify for Outland (work on other planets), although this will probably be as a lawyer. He could wait until college but his school offers the credit and he decides it will free up possibilities later. His tutor tries to talk him out of it because Rod is a romantic, but in the end, his romantic drive will be an asset – one of the issues Heinlein is clearly trying to demonstrate is that the practical man without romance will lack vision. Once through the wormhole, the first dead person he sees is the boy who had insisted on his ability to survive on his own, with only the company of a vicious dog and a gun. The dog is dead. Rod is then hit on the head and robbed, but days later he is managing to survive. He teams up with Jack, who is living in a cave, and they find Jimmy, who is sick. Jack nurses Jimmy while Rod hunts, and it is Jimmy who realises Jack is female. The three of them start advertising for others, and attract Bob and Carmen (who are, interestingly, Quakers).[3] The group grows under Rod's leadership, which is essentially both practical and romantic: he has a vision for the community and houses are built for couples pairing off, plans are made for crops. One night an older student and his university coterie launch a very civilised coup in which Rod's leadership is replaced by committees and constitutions and being sensible. Rod and his friends are sidelined, and brought back in only when necessary. Eventually this leads to a wrong decision – to stay in the path of a fauna migration. The colony is almost wiped out when the 'dopey joes' turn into nasty killing machines. Rod takes over again (but keeps the colony where it is as a point of principle).

The community functions. By the time of rescue there are children, and a small school. It is being a community that has made survival possible. Learning about the capacities of individuals rather than classes has proven essential: when Rod arrives on the planet he is sceptical about the abilities of both Jack and Caroline and in both cases has to (rather publicly) eat his words. In *Tunnel in the Sky* there is a great deal of discussion about modes of civic organisation and responsibility to each other: strong leadership does not preclude democracy, democracy is not actually a mode of project management, and collectivism requires the full activity and contribution of the individual. The formula 'From each according to his ability, to each according to his need' demands that both elements of the equation are fulfilled. This is even more evident in *Starship Troopers*: the

---

3   There is a division in US Quakerism and it is quite possible that Heinlein's primary experience was of the non-pacifist Western Quakers. See Thomas D. Hamm, *The Transformation of American Quakerism* (Bloomington: Indiana UP, 1988).

Federal Service is not permitted to turn away any volunteer. 'From each according to his ability' is an absolute.

Red Planet and *The Moon is a Harsh Mistress* are the two novels of revolution, and although very different, are each in their way fundamentally communitarian. In *Red Planet*, the entire social structure relies on co-operation. On Mars there is only one school, a boarding school, run by the company, but the experience of school creates a community identity among isolated colonists: those you go to school with are likely to be your friends for life. The result is that the company tries to isolate the children from their parents (a tactic Heinlein may have been familiar with by reading about both Soviet and Fascist youth organisations and possibly also the Native American boarding-school scandal) and to isolate the parents from each other by preventing the annual migration. It is the connections between people that allow them to fight back.

The Moon is a Harsh Mistress is, of course, the book that is always cited as Heinlein's libertarian book, and this is, broadly, true: but Heinlein's libertarianism is communal, not individualist and in some ways extremely punitive. This is a community where if norms are not followed retaliation is quick; the objections to taxation by Earth relate to the lack of service in return, not opposition to taxation per se, and people are expected to make provision for themselves but do so through collective services (health care is managed by taking out a bet with a bookie). Women work and have power in their marriages because they can walk away (although both Neil Easterbrook in 'State, Heterotopia', 1997 and Robin Anne Reid in 'Reading the Man in the Moon', 2015 think it rather more complex and problematic than that). TANSTAAFL (There ain't no such thing as a free lunch) is a mere fact of life: on the Moon if you don't contribute there is no facility for living in the interstices. The colony is dependent on 'from each according to his abilities'. Lack the abilities and you are likely to get yourself and others killed. On the Moon, individuals are connected in networks of work, honour, debt and family. Family is essential: family is your back-up and families need to be flexible, hence the line marriage and the willingness to adopt. The individualist (and Mannie, the central character, is presented as a bit of a loner) needs back-up. It also means debt is serious. An unpaid debt might leave the creditor stranded.

The Moon is a Harsh Mistress represents both the degree to which Heinlein believed in the community, and the degree to which he was beginning to despair of the ability of Americans as individuals to understand their role in creating that community. In 1958, furious and deeply distressed at the negotiations with the Soviet Union, Heinlein tried to launch a campaign to oppose it. Heinlein was devastated by his failure to rouse people's passions: for him, people who could not be bothered to defend their own liberty probably didn't deserve to keep it (see his newspaper article, 'Who are the Heirs of Patrick Henry?').

Heinlein's beliefs about reciprocity between state and individual hardened: he retained his 'no conscription' stance, and his stance in *For Us, the Living*, that those who vote for war should be the ones to fight it, acquires the corollary that only those who have served should be able to vote. Other ideas begin to emerge: that 'the people' of all classes are too willing to vote themselves bread and circuses; he considers that people might purchase their votes – and with what I have come to believe is a characteristic naivety argues 'Rich people would take over the government? Would they now? Is a wealthy man going to impoverish himself for the privilege of casting a couple of hundred votes?' Given the attempted corporate coup in *Friday*, he had realised by the 1980s that the answer was 'yes'. Heinlein also suggests an algebra test, which might make sense if there were equal access to education, but Heinlein in 1958 must have been aware that there was not (see *Have Space Suit—Will Travel*).

Heinlein was determined to espouse the 'right ordering' of society, and one aspect of this was to teach his readers about society. These stories almost all derive from the ideas and from a future history first sketched in *For Us, the Living*. Inherited from this book are not only the ideas but the desire to influence. This desire is there from the earliest of his stories. Heinlein is a teacher.

Many of Heinlein's texts and the knowledge he wished to purvey are rooted in predictions that no longer seem valid. Written before the green revolution, the invention of the pill and widespread distribution of other modes of contraception, or the adoption of birth control policies in China and India, *Tunnel in the Sky*, *Time for the Stars* and *Methuselah's Children* are all part of a world that saw overpopulation as a real and looming problem. Interestingly, Heinlein never advocates population control (unlike many of his colleagues): his own solution for overpopulation is mass migration, and the role of eugenics is to breed people sufficiently long-lived to engage in star travel.

In the 1940s Heinlein was still decidedly of the American left, a wing of politics profoundly influenced by populism, and less anti-capitalist than anti-big business and against the concentration of power in any one set of hands. His own family had experienced the effect of big-business buyout and the increasing difficulty for the American small businessman to engage in the capitalist economy. So, in *For Us, the Living* we are taught about the financial services and the way in which big business, against which Heinlein remained resolute (see the events in *Friday*) needs to be controlled. 'In another place in the constitution, corporate persons were defined and declared to have no rights of any sort except wherein they represented rights of real persons. Corporate persons could not be damaged. An act committed against a corporate person must be shown to have damaged a real person in order to constitute an offense' (Chapter 4; see also Chapter 9).

This is expressed in his earliest short stories. In 'Life-Line', Dr Pinero is up against the scientific academy and the insurance companies: the first demands a monopoly of knowledge, the second a monopoly of the industrial spinoff. Both resent a 'foreigner' entering their fields. Heinlein very cleverly acknowledges the racism that could be behind monopoly practices when he focalises the description of Pinero from the point of view of the academics: 'we may not be familiar with the university that bestowed his degree' the President notes, and 'if the eminent doctor's manner appears a trifle inurbane for our tastes, that the doctor may be from a place, or a stratum, not so meticulous in these matters'; or to be blunt, Pinero is of the wrong class, probably a foreigner and maybe even Jewish. Heinlein was also well aware that this kind of prejudice was not unique to the upper classes; his wariness of union monopolies had its origins in part in the prejudice he saw there.

In 'The Roads Must Roll' another kind of monopoly is being challenged, a dual monopoly of unionism – controlling who does the jobs – and of the industry itself. The purpose of the strike is to demonstrate that the society cannot function without this particular industry, and that therefore the workers of this particular industry should receive preferential treatment. That this is not simply anti-unionism is displayed through a range of other stories. *Starman Jones* is a story that, while in the end it reaffirms the status quo, is predicated on the existence of problematic restrictive practices that prevent Max Jones enlisting in the guild on merit. The fear of a dominating industry is also enlisted in 'The Devil Makes the Law', in that there is an attempt to monopolise magic precisely to ensure that the magic industry can gain political dominance, and in 'Logic of Empire', where Humphrey Wingate, a prosperous lawyer, discovers the monopolistic practices of the Venus settlement company when he signs indentures for bonded service on Venus.

Company monopolies could be most threatening on the frontier, where the American narrative argues that independence is highly valued. It is there in *Between Planets* and *Red Planet*, but the latter offers the most clearly worked out of the stories: the company hopes to control the settlement by making the colonists dependent on them for insulation, food and fuel. Although Heinlein drops the issue for some time – it emerges in *The Moon is a Harsh Mistress* as colonial control – it is crucial to the events in *Friday*: Friday is trapped with Ian, Georges and Janet because the corporations, no longer based in any one country, are at war. We don't hear very much about it, but it is clear that Heinlein, by this time a libertarian-leaning conservative, is no more amused by corporate monopolies in the 1980s than he was as a leftish radical liberal in the 1940s. It is also (at least until the aliens appear) implied as the motivation behind the attack on Jake in *'The Number of the Beast'*. By this point it can make Heinlein seem curiously old-fashioned, as we have come to live with monopolistic behaviour. Much of the supposed monopoly busting of the 1980s led to ever more unchallenged mega-firms, but Heinlein remained determined to challenge this control.

Some of Heinlein's anti-statism, exhibited in particular in *Time Enough for Love* and in *'The Number of the Beast'*, can be understood through this lens. Heinlein recognises that where there is a single supplier or single customer, that party has control of the market. Thus the argument against nationalising a bank in the Dora section of *Time Enough for Love* is an argument both against expropriating private property, and against trusting an economy to one bank. This is repeated with the discussion of the Chairman Pro Tem's role on Secundus in *Time Enough for Love*: the intention is for the role to be hands-off. When Secundus becomes over-controlled by a monopoly, the government, Lazarus Long wants to be gone.

Heinlein's opposition to monopolies of any kind may underpin the shift in his apparent attitude to state medical support. In *For Us, the Living* health is a community enterprise: 'The community can't afford to let anyone be sick for fear of contagion and unsocial maladjustment... Medical men are public servants' (Chapter 10). This impression lasts long enough that when Dr Edith Stone, in *The Rolling Stones*, both mother and doctor of the family, volunteers to enter a ship with plague it is framed as her duty. There is also the simple fact that in any closed system – a moon colony or a space ship – the health of one is the health of all. It is noticeable that the Howard families of *Methuselah's Children* maintain a collective system of health care for their disabled children. As late as 1961, Heinlein saw health care as at the very least a collaborative effort. In his 1961 guest of honour speech for Seattle (the 19th World Science Fiction Convention) he declared that he still believed in a world government, 'guaranteeing permanent peace and civil liberty to all, even to those nations that choose to remain socialistic, a concerted effort by all nations to control population and raise living standards for all' (*Requiem*, p. 170).

For a society to use people effectively, Heinlein argues, that society has to be egalitarian, and one of the strengths of Heinlein was the degree to which he argued that on behalf of women.

For the past sixty years they [women] have voted ... but we have not see the enormous improvement in government that the suffragettes promised us.

Perhaps we did not go far enough. Perhaps men are still corrupting government ... so let's try the next century and a half with men disenfranchised. (Fair is fair. My mother was past forty before she was permitted to vote.) But let's not stop there; at present men outnumber women in elective offices, on the bench, and in the legal profession by a proportion that is scandalous.

> Make males ineligible to hold elective office or to serve in the judiciary, elective or appointed, and also reserve the profession of the law for women. (*Expanded Universe*, p. 328)

Heinlein is explicit about the role of women in the right ordering of a capitalist society from some of his earliest stories. '"Let There Be Light"' begins when a scientist is misgendered, and proceeds with the assumption that women can and should be scientists.

The idea that women should be integral to policy-making is there in 'A Bathroom of Her Own', a non-science-fiction story from 1946, and in 'Jerry was a Man', where Heinlein reminds us that women were at the forefront of the anti-slavery movement. In 'Delilah and the Space Rigger' Heinlein counters the idea that women are a distraction in industry by suggesting that their integration will raise standards. In 'The Menace from Earth' and *The Rolling Stones* he argues for married women's rights to work and intellectual life.

Heinlein was both concerned and fascinated with gendered behaviour in a range of ways, and he had a strong, explicit and activist engagement with gender. Issues of gender are not accidental in his work; they are fundamental to his understanding of both the right ordering of society and of the individual. One of the things that makes Heinlein stand out is that he exists as a writer in a co-educational society. Very few of his novels have the kind of absolute male atmosphere common to those of his contemporaries. Much of this is simply age: many of his authorial contemporaries went from school to the army and then into male work environments. Heinlein was slightly older, grew up in a large family with sisters as well as brothers, had a working life in California in the interwar period, and, because he took related civilian service during the war, he worked alongside women.

With the exception of the short stories, which tend to be less diverse in a number of ways, the degree to which the world of a novel and the worldview of a protagonist admits of a gendered society and treats women as bearing a significant role in that society frequently acts as a marker of the level of civilisation of a given society or individual. Thus in 'Common Sense' and 'Universe' the treatment of women as chattels is a very real indicator that this is a broken society. Similarly, in *Revolt in 2100* the exploitation of women and the disregarding of their personal integrity condemns the prophet, and we know we are on the right side because Sister Maggie is integral to the revolution. In *Beyond This Horizon*, although gendered games are played and Heinlein does not truly play fair over the issue of guns, there are a number of women in power in this society. The same is true in *Methuselah's Children*, where the focus on the issue of persecution can disguise the role which women play. Similarly we should notice women's political roles in *Stranger in a Strange Land*, in *Glory Road*, in *Friday* and eventually in *To Sail Beyond the Sunset*, where one woman actually experiences the whole shift of gender politics in the twentieth century while young enough to enjoy it.

Even in the juveniles, individuals such as Max Jones in *Starman Jones* and Kip in *Have Space Suit—Will Travel* indicate their maturity with female friendships; John Thomas Stuart XI might not be smart but he's smart enough to let his girlfriend lead, and Mr Kiku is smart enough to respect her; similarly in *Between Planets*, where Don's only good decision is to trust Isobel. In contrast in *Red Planet* at least some of Jim's poor understanding is expressed in his treatment of his sister, although this is the most patriarchal of the novels – no adult woman in this book is anything other than a wife.

Heinlein is explicit also with the role of sex and sexuality in the right ordering of society: character after character condemns moral prudery and hypocrisy, from Zeb in *Revolt in 2100*, through Jubal

Harshaw in an extended commentary on the iniquities of the Old Testament in Chapter 24 in *Stranger in a Strange Land*, and on to Lazarus Long, who lives in a long-lived society where long-term is intolerable, and the easy sexuality of Maureen in *To Sail Beyond the Sunset* (1987). One of the reasons the Fosterite church in *Stranger in a Strange Land* survives, we are told, is precisely because Foster avoids the sin of possessiveness (Chapter 27). His church is one that gifts to all sexual permissiveness.

And in case we have any doubts, Alexander Hergensheimer in *Job* (1984) epitomises an extreme of everything Heinlein ever hated about early twentieth-century mid-western society, and the rise of the late twentieth-century 'moral majority'. His list of 'accomplishments' in Chapter 11 is a modern evangelical wish-list: 'A federal law making abortion a capital offence; a federal law making the manufacture, sale, possession, importation, transportation, and/or use of any contraceptive drug or device a felony', the abolition of gambling, tobacco a prescription drug (although that is as much a dig at the liberal left), and a court ruling that the 'community standards' of a 'typical or median-population' applied to all cities, thus ensuring that cities could no longer serve as refuges within rural states.

In both *The Moon is a Harsh Mistress* and in *Time Enough for Love*, prostitution is legal and in the latter book prostitution is a highly regarded profession. Heinlein is also astonishingly open – even by today's standards – about female bodily functions. Hugh packs sanitary equipment in his bomb shelter. Johann Sebastian Bach Smith begins to think he is a woman because he correctly suspects he is experiencing a period.

Heinlein's hatred of sexual coercion is sharp: he was explicit about it in his own private notes and he extended this into his writing. It is hinted at in *Podkayne of Mars* first, where Podkayne is uneasy with the 'fatherly pats', and explicit in the contemporaneous *The Moon is a Harsh Mistress* where, as is well known, sexual autonomy lies entirely with the female and there are two clearly described assaults: the first is what we would now call an attempted date rape, where a tourist refuses to take 'no' for an answer and tries to push a flirtation further than the young woman is willing to go; and the second where a woman who may or may not be a prostitute, or just a girl out for a good time, is assaulted and killed by guards. It is made clear that both are grievous sins: the tourist escapes with his life due to the kindness of his arrestees because he is ignorant. It is not a 'lesser' crime than street rape. Perhaps almost more shocking in its radical nature is Heinlein's understanding of rape in *To Sail Beyond the Sunset* for it most clearly espouses the rallying cry of the Reclaim the Night movement: 'however we dress, wherever we go, yes must be yes and no must be no.'[4] Although it is very unlikely Heinlein was aware of this slogan (it seems to have reached the US only with the spread of 'slutwalks') he would have espoused its intent, and, more, he goes beyond it. 'Rape' argues Maureen as Heinlein, 'is not intercourse; it is murderous aggression' and 'In any century rape is the favourite sport of large numbers of men when they can get away with it.' This is 1987 and Heinlein has placed into the mouth of his heterosexual 'round-heels' (sexually promiscuous) heroine the kind of comment that gets women labelled as radical feminist man-haters.

But the issue here is not just sexual autonomy of the yes/no kind, but that family structures are defined by women in *The Moon is a Harsh Mistress*, and also in *Friday* (for good and ill). In the former, Mannie must ask his senior wife for permission to bring Wyoming home, and it is the women in the family who negotiate the marriage. This is not egalitarianism, but more a system of checks and balances that recognises a systemic problem: it undercuts the exploitation

4   See the *Guardian*, 9 December 1980, p. 3.

199

of women in a society where women have in the past been in short supply (although presumably once it stops being an immigrant society the balance would be restored: Mannie's family is already moving to a turn-and-turn-about set of marriages). In *Citizen of the Galaxy* Heinlein is explicit that female control of mating undercuts the explicitly patriarchal structure of the work environment by gifting to women control over the general and also familial alliances (the author Lois McMaster Bujold will emulate this and be perhaps more explicit in exploring its limitations). In *The Puppet Masters* Sam offers Mary a wide choice of possible contracts, some permanent, some temporary, some exclusive and some inclusive. The choice is hers. In the final novel, *To Sail Beyond the Sunset*, Heinlein will tackle directly the degree to which without some mode of control – in this case community property laws and Maureen's own financial acuity – a complacent man will happily regard it as 'just' to retain a disproportionate share of property accrued within a marriage.

All of this is entwined with his firm belief that women in pioneer societies should have many children – but this in turn leads us into Heinlein's understanding of family as a civic institution, to which both men and women should contribute. Heinlein may think children are a societal good – in *The Moon is a Harsh Mistress* contributing babies to a family is a gift – but he does not regard women's work as outside the capitalist framework and he formalises this in the policies of the Howard Foundation. It is worth noting that the women in his heavily populated societies are rarely reproductively active, or they delay such activity; and that in societies where women's alternate work is valuable, childrearing is regarded as a gendered burden. In *Podkayne of Mars*, for example, although Mars uses crèches for the early years (attachment disorder and the need for babies to attach to a parent very early was yet to be discovered), Podkayne's mother, and eventually Podkayne herself, are heavily recompensed for the accidental release and activation of stored triplets. In this Heinlein is rather ahead of both conventional economists and the Marxists of his period.

Family and Childrearing

Heinlein's materialist take on the family is consequent on his belief – one ironically rooted in traditionalist cultures – that the family is the key unit of society.

The family as the place to which you return is central to *The Moon is a Harsh Mistress*. Mannie both does and does not live with his family, effectively commuting in and out, using them in part as dormitory but far more as emotional centre to his life. It is in *The Moon is a Harsh Mistress* that we first see the working out of the family structures for which Heinlein has become best known, but only half of the family structure has been popularised. For Heinlein the purpose of the family was to raise children. This is expressed over and over again in later novels. This is not a statement about when sex or romance is appropriate, but a statement about the civic role of families: families (not individuals) are reproductive units. In *Time Enough for Love* ('The Tale of the Twins Who Weren't', 'Valhalla to Landfall'), Lazarus Long argues, 'Marriage is an economic contract to provide for children and to take care of mothers while they bear kids and bring them up – but it is much more than that. It is the means this animal, Homo sap., has evolved – quite unconsciously – for performing this indispensable function and be happy while doing so.'

The evidence is there from the beginning. Like many radicals of his period, Heinlein was fascinated by the nature/nurture debate, and by extension the proper education of children. In *For Us, the Living*, childcare, in imitation of many of the ideas in circulation in the 1920s, is a communal effort and crucially is the duty of the state as civic entity. Heinlein complains that society is all too quick to ask 'what about the children?'

> Many of the things which were believed to be bad for children were bad only in the unventilated minds of the religious moralists. For example, we now realise that it is not bad for children to be used to naked human bodies – on the contrary it is very *un*healthy for them not to be. We know that knowledge of the objective fact of bisexual procreation is not harmful to children – on the contrary if we satisfy their natural curiosity by telling them lies, we are building trouble for the future. (*For Us, the Living*, Chapter 12)

But much the same argument can be seen in 'Gulf', in *Stranger in a Strange Land* (inevitably) and in almost every other novel where one of the characters is given the opportunity to embrace new social standards: each time, we are enjoined to construct a society in which children can grow up without oppressive moral constraints.

Heinlein frequently makes the argument that raising a child is a complex business best left to professionals. Diana, the heroine of *For Us, the Living*, has grown up with her father and mother in turn, but spends two years in a development centre between the ages of fourteen and sixteen, in order that her own mental health develops and that she learns to be part of a community. Although most of Heinlein's juveniles have conventional American family arrangements, crèches crop up again later, favourably, in *The Moon is a Harsh Mistress* and *Podkayne of Mars*, and unfavourably in *Friday*, where it is arguable that the issue is not the crèche per se but the prejudice and bigotry of the crèche workers. Even in his more conventional novels where children are raised in the family home, it is often the organisation they join later that completes their education and inducts them into a civic family.

It is in *The Moon is a Harsh Mistress* that we first see the line marriage, whose purpose is explicit in these terms: the line marriage accumulates, people are added as they come along and the marriage continues, never ending. It turns the marriage from a one-generation business into a multi-generation business, and its business is threefold: parenting security, sexual security and financial security. I have deliberately put them in that order because if we compare the line marriage in *The Moon is a Harsh Mistress* to the one in *Friday* we can quickly see that the order of those priorities is crucial. Mannie's family place the well-being of the (shared) children first, talk about sex and barely discuss the money. *Friday*'s New Zealand family begin by discussing money, make sex a very formal business (and the decision of men, always a big warning sign in a Heinlein novel) and don't discuss the well-being of the children until it goes wrong. This is how we can tell that this is a bad marriage. The other rule of thumb is that the more formal the line marriage, the less likely it is to be healthy; the formality loses sight of what it is for. The purposeful family in a later Heinlein novel has as its intrinsic purpose the care and raising of children. Everything else – sex and money – is a way to reinforce the bonds that render the family secure for that purpose.

If the key role of families in a Heinleinian society is to produce children, then the consequent role is to produce fit citizens. In *Have Space Suit—Will Travel* the homework assignment that causes Kip's father to check his curriculum is a discussion of family structures, which is ironic given that Heinlein is obsessed with family structure. Heinlein sees family as the bedrock of society – it's a very French/US Republican ideal which is a little different from the monarchist European idea of the King as 'father' of the country. The latter is strictly hierarchical and punitive; the former is far more about setting an example and creating a holistic environment, and tends to be more woman-centred. But in both, the 'right ordering' of the family is the same thing as the right ordering of society. The cultivation of civic duty within the family enhances civic duty to the nation. Hence in *Starship Troopers*, that Johnny's father has no sense of civic duty is a fundamental part of the structure of his trajectory towards both military family and a sense of civic obligation: the two are linked, and this is not coincidental.

Heinlein is firmly on the nurture-over-nature side of the debate. In the 1930s this placed him rather firmly on the left, but American society has, for reasons of its own, always leaned towards the nurture argument, so that overall this is not a left/right argument. Because he regarded raising a child as the job of society, and society comprised each doing their civic duty, Heinlein regarded his own writing – perhaps both the juveniles and his adult writing – as an essential part of a child's complete breakfast cereal . . . to steal a much-derided phrase. The juvenile novels were his clear contribution to child-rearing (and one which readers have recognised).

Heinlein's juveniles fit solidly within a genre of fiction that is lost to us now, the career book. At the end of the Second World War, the school-leaving age of American children began to rise. Unlike in the UK, where there is a clear legal framework which extends to all children, in the US it was a combination of state legislatures, federal rules on child labour introduced in the New Deal years that lowered its value, and changing workplaces that caused the rise in school-leaving age. I am not clear how visible the change was at the time but you can see it in the street scenes in US movies. In the 1930s the streets are packed with working children – small children collect things to sell (see the *Our Gang* and *Little Rascals* movies), twelve-year-olds are working as messenger boys and newspaper salesmen. By the 1940s they are more likely to be portrayed at home studying. In *It's a Wonderful Life* (Frank Capra, 1946) there is a contrast, unremarked on, between George Bailey's own childhood in which he heads to work at the pharmacy after school every day, although barely fourteen, and that of his children, which seems to involve no such thing. Children by the 1940s, and even more so by the 1950s, were expected to be in school (although, as is often the case, the children of the very poor, and particularly poor black Americans, were not necessarily in this favoured position).

Graduating from high school slowly began to be the norm, and although it would be well into the 1960s before college became the norm for most middle-class Americans, for many readers the gap between leaving childhood and entering the workforce was ever-elongating. Furthermore, as Olivier Zunz noted, as career choice became less and less about inherited businesses or even inherited roles (many factories in the 1950s still employed staff via kinship networks) anxieties about entry routes and training came to the fore and marched parallel with widening opportunities in new industries and service sectors.[5] The career book was tailored to assuage both of these anxieties: it showed teenagers new opportunities and it showed them what the route to those opportunities – routes their parents often could not trace for them – might look like.

Heinlein's classic career books include his first juvenile, *Rocket Ship Galileo*, *The Rolling Stones*, *Space Cadet*, *Farmer in the Sky*, *Citizen of the Galaxy* (in a very strange way), *Have Space Suit—Will Travel*, *Starman Jones*, *Podkayne of Mars* and eventually of course *Starship Troopers*.

First of all, to reinforce my point about the growing length of childhood, compare the ages of the children in *Rocket Ship Galileo* to those in *Podkayne* or *Starship Troopers*. The children in the 1947 novel are barely teenagers, yet they are already considering careers. Podkayne and Johnny Rico are both eighteen (I think) and yet they are

5   Olivier Zunz, *Making America Corporate, 1870–1920* (Chicago: U. of Chicago Press, 1990), pp. 125–31.

only just making those lifetime choices. The world they exist in has stretched childhood for them, and it is fair to argue that Heinlein is not enthusiastic about this. Many of his later books stress the competence of the child as actor (think of the twins Laz and Lor in *Time Enough for Love*) and reflect his own experiences as an outdoor, free-roaming boy-child. *Have Spacesuit—Will Travel* begins with the father expressing disgust at the pointlessness of much of Kip's education.

Rocket Ship Galileo is almost the classic 'take your child to work' story, where three boys are released by their parents to be apprenticed to a rocket scientist. In this novel formal learning is barely acknowledged. In contrast *Space Cadet* is all formal learning, even if much of it is undertaken on one's own: this book, the one most closely based on Heinlein's own experiences, is a clear pathway to the skies or seas. *Starship Troopers*, for which Heinlein researched Marine training, is similar: this is a career book entirely about learning and applying formal knowledge in a high-stakes environment and going from someone who takes orders to being someone who gives orders.

Starship Troopers, ironically the book that Scribner rejected, is almost the classic career book, in that it begins with Johnny about to embark on a mission, flashes back to the choices he made that started him on his path, has ups, downs, moments of doubt, and eventually a realisation that he has made the right choice. Although the book has its subtleties, its trajectory is not subtle. Had it been published in its intended market it might not have aroused the puzzled hostility that it did, for it shares with its juvenile subgenre the uncritical passion for the profession explored.

Max Jones, in *Starman Jones*, would love to be able to take the routes that Matt and Johnny find open to them, but life has conspired against him, and in an unusual exploration of institutionalised discrimination, we see that his access to a supposedly meritocratic career is curtailed by traditional and exclusivist hiring practices. Yet the eventual path is the same: Max's reward for being a useful loose part is to be recruited into the machine. In this, *Starman Jones* is a novel-length version of 'Misfit', and part of Heinlein's belief that society needs cracks in its systems through which the renegade can be rescued (see also 'Coventry').

Heinlein himself was not actually very good at being part of the machine once he left the navy. His family background was in business, and he had a strong practical bent. He used this sense of self in *The Rolling Stones*, where we see Castor and Pollux engaged in the kind of street trading that was common for American children, the emphasis on entrepreneurship and handiness reflecting a world in which a great deal could be made, made-over and resold: for all their parents' portrayal as professionals (father is an engineer, mother a doctor) the two boys are apprenticed in a different world, that of the lower-middle-class male. That this is not depicted as downwardly mobile is in itself fascinating. For Heinlein and many other Americans of all classes, the self-sufficiency of this lifestyle gave it cachet. Similarly, in *Farmer in the Sky*, another culture might understand Bill's translation from potential professional on Earth to farmer-settler on Ganymede as a downgrade, but while Heinlein is by instinct a Jeffersonian – we see his love of the homesteading ideal in *Farnham's Freehold* and in *Time Enough for Love* – he is not a romantic, so that when Bill is apprenticed to Farmer Schultz it is a demonstration of how a city boy learns to be a farmer. Bill, Castor and Pollux are all self-motivated, and this thread is picked up on in *Have Spacesuit—Will Travel* and 'The Menace from Earth'. Neither of these is technically a career book in the usual sense of the word, but what each emphasises is that careers are to be prepared for in advance: what you do now opens doors for you later.

Citizen of the Galaxy is perhaps the strangest of the apprenticeship/training books: inspired at least in part by Rudyard

Kipling's *Kim*,[6] Thorby Baslim is a slave, and when he leaves his master/father Major Baslim he is taken in by the Free Traders, a people who travel the space-ways and who have a very rigid training and inheritance system. Thorby discovers first that he has in effect been apprenticed to Baslim as a spy rather than a beggar, then that he has a new apprenticeship to work with the Free Traders, then as a Space Guard in the cruiser Hydra, and finally that he will have to do it all again in the company he proves to have inherited. In all these capacities he begins with no power, no authority and very little sense of what is going on. What renders the book effective in career-book terms is that Heinlein manages to communicate just how awful being a junior is, but that it is part of the process, an experience also depicted in *Starship Troopers*. At each stage, Thorby learns from below how an entire business ecosystem works.

Podkayne of Mars is both the last of the juveniles and the last of the career books. It is a problematic book because Podkayne doesn't succeed in her career plans. If read in isolation this is an anti-feminist book in which Podkayne is patted on the head and told that she is too sweet a little girl to compete in a big man's world. But *Podkayne of Mars* was not written in isolation. It is part of a matrix of stories in which educated, professional women appear as background, as important side characters and as protagonists. What then is happening in this book? To begin with Podkayne is another Max Jones. Although unlike Max she is loved and cherished, like him she is not respected: her parents have not nurtured her intelligence or in any way encouraged her. She is forced to seek knowledge in scraps, here and there. As Podkayne does not have an eidetic memory like Max, and is not a super-calculator like Andrew Jackson Libby – a reflection as much of

6   Introduction to *Citizen Of The Galaxy*, Virginia Heinlein edition, by Robert James, Ph.D. and William H. Patterson, Jr.

Heinlein's increasing abandonment of super-hero characters generally (*Friday* is another case entirely: she wants not to be a super-hero) – she is consistently disadvantaged, and comes to realise this, in the competition for the plum job she wants, even before she has to deal with the sexism of hiring practices (which we know Heinlein thinks is silly because he favours women pilots in *Starship Troopers* and elsewhere). *Podkayne of Mars* is an anti-career book, not a warning to children, but a reminder to parents that careers don't just happen.[7]

Heinlein's work is obsessed with family and with the construction of non-traditional (if heterosexual) families. His boys' families – shown at the beginning of novels as something to leave – are rarely very healthy. One of the worst examples is the off-stage father in 'Coventry':

Dave's father was one of the nastiest little tyrants that ever dominated a household under the guise of loving-kindness. He was of the more-in-sorrow-than-in-anger, this-hurts-me-more-than-it-hurts-you school, and all his life had invariably been able to find an altruistic rationalisation for always having his own way. Convinced of his own infallible righteousness, he had never valued his son's point of view on anything, but had dominated him in everything – always from the highest moralistic motives . . .

John Thomas's mother in *The Star Beast* fits the same mould and adds controlling to the list. In *Starship Troopers* there are several discussions of versions of poor parenting – the parent who doesn't discipline, the parent who indulges. *Podkayne of Mars* concludes with a searing attack on parents who don't take responsibility for their children's education. But perhaps the most trenchant indictment

---

7   This interpretation is indebted to conversations with Kari Sperring who, like me, did
     not feel the conventional reading to be correct.

of bad parenting is in *Farnham's Freehold*, a novel which – because it is told from Hugh Farnham's point of view – is often seen as being self-justification. This is the only time that Heinlein turns his full attention to the nuclear family, and he does it to show it as a depressing, confining, dysfunctional institution misshapen by both external and internal expectation.

Hugh Farnham is a solid businessman and father. He loves his wife and his two children, a boy and a girl, but he is not actually good at being either a husband or a father. His wife is a lush, and he regards his son as a brat, well-meaning but poorly trained, ascribing this to his wife protecting the boy from corporal punishment. His daughter shows every sign of becoming her mother, Grace: finding a meal ticket and then descending into alcohol-fuelled boredom.

Hugh is an Eisenhower man: he has a high sense of justice and injustice but very little sense that he can change the world. Instead, he has tried all his life to make changes at the micro level – his family is his kingdom – and watched his attempts swamped by the world in which he lives; he attempts to protect by surrounding people with walls, whether literal (the bomb shelter) or metaphorical, protecting someone from the outside world. Take Grace, his wife, who is apparently another avatar of the nagging wife who appears in a number of Heinlein's short stories and books. Grace was once a well-born young woman who married down, worked hard at her marriage and crucially supported Hugh in his business. Once he no longer needed her input he 'gave' her leisure and she descended into a maelstrom of boredom, prescribed tranquillisers including Meprobamate (known as Miltown), launched in 1955 and a blockbuster of a drug. By 1967 it was on the list of highly addictive drugs. *Farnham's Freehold* is late enough that Heinlein now understands – and gives to Hugh his own understanding – that enforced idleness is a cruel way to treat a bright young woman. It is too early for him to be aware that force-feeding her Miltown is neither cure nor salvation. But it is not too early for Hugh to be aware that his 'protection' has created or exacerbated Grace's (and perhaps in retrospect Leslyn's) alcoholism.

Hugh's guilt over Grace messes up his relationship with his son Duke. Hugh frames it as poor parenting and continually laments the lack of corporal punishment, but there is also an element that we are shown in that what is clearer is that Hugh has forced his son to take sides, and his son, like many children in an abusive marriage, has taken the side of the abused. Hugh does not want to be an abuser but – as his comments on his inability to force Grace to be well, and his reluctance to become her prison guard betray – that is the role he has taken up in shaping her life in the conventional way he has. Hugh wants to be a good father, but his insistence on the paterfamilias role takes him down the path of humiliating his son, and by the end of the book, when Hugh has experienced the whip himself, he comes to understand that acquiescence to corporal punishment has very little to do with discipline.

Good parenting is also included in Heinlein's work, and it is noticeable how hands-off it is. Presenteeism is not what Heinlein is mourning, but common sense and engagement. This is parenting of the free-range child. Roger Stone in *The Rolling Stones* has more or less given up on parenting his older twins. He warns them when they are assuming he is stupid, he lets them make predictable but relatively safe mistakes and creates merry hell when they do something really dangerous. He is a proportionate parent. He also – an idea Heinlein reuses in the Grandfather/Woodie relationship in *Time Enough for Love* – reminds us of the important role of good grandparents: experienced enough to be wise, distanced enough to be trustworthy to a young person stretching their minds and bodies.

Perhaps the best parent, the one we tend to remember, is Kip's father in *Have Space Suit—Will Travel*, the man who takes one look at Kip's school books, checks his ambitions and notes that, if he wants to be what he wants to be, then he needs a completely different set of subjects to do it; who explains to Kip what honour looks like; and who believes Kip when he explains what has happened. *Stranger in a Strange Land*, although not to my knowledge usually seen this way, could be understood as a handbook to good parenting, as Jubal Harshaw leads Michael Valentine Smith through toddlerhood (feel free to explore, kid, but don't be surprised when the lamp falls on you), adolescence (experiment but do so safely and courteously) to late teens (off you go, call home occasionally and you know where I am when you need me).

This idea that a family is a purposeful rather than a natural unit is worked out in *Citizen of the Galaxy*, in which the least supportive family Thorby Baslim will meet is his natal family. His first true family – his birth family – is lost, and never even recovered narratively. His second, of course, involves the parenting of Colonel/ Beggar Baslim, but it is always clear to Baslim, if not to Thorby, that this is a temporary arrangement. Baslim craves family on Thorby's behalf and it is Baslim who posthumously sends Thorby to the Free Traders with a geas that they should search for his own family. The Free Traders offer a different look at family: extended, loose in some ways but rather rigid in others. The moiety system (adapted from the work of Margaret Mead who receives a nod in a key character) creates a dual family in which the primary taboo is marrying within one's own moiety, a system designed to prevent inbreeding in a ship where distant but multiply inter-related cousins socialise freely. Furthermore, Heinlein gave to the moiety a rigid system of descent: oddly like the structures in 'Universe' the free traders make use of a semi-hereditary structure only partially mediated by a need for a meritocratic sifting process between the potential heirs. Heinlein, a moral relativist, argues through the resident anthropologist (a genuine authorial mouthpiece) that the system is acceptable because it serves the purpose of the family.

The purposeful family in *Citizen of the Galaxy*, however unusual its form, is the meme that shapes the later books. In *Glory Road*, Oscar's family is noticeable by its lack of purpose. It fails the immediate test by simply not being there for E. C. Gordon. He is orphaned thanks to military action (but not an official war, a sleight-of-hand that impoverished many US and UK military widows), his mother remarries and leaves him with his aunt and uncle, and after he serves time in the draft and gets demobbed in Europe, he discovers this is just in time for his mother and her new family to have been sent back Stateside. As a rule of thumb, where E. C. Gordon's family is, he is not. The driving force behind E. C. Gordon/Oscar's actions is essentially loneliness and a craving to belong (he has tried both football and the military and neither have given him that sense of belonging – not least, as he notes, because the patriotism was beaten out of him at school). In his companionship with Star he finds a new kind of family, one much looser that allows him the freedom to come and go, but *that* is always there and will always be there, a solid core to return to.

Along with arguments about parenting come arguments about education. In his juveniles a visible part of Heinlein's agenda was to discuss what a child should learn to do. *Rocket Ship Galileo* is all about the making of things and how to do the making of things. For all the technical details which Heinlein is keen to get right, the lesson is less the content than the process: the boys make notes, record their experiments and make small changes in process accordingly. The language is solid and descriptive and the Nazi adventure is only a small part and possibly the least interesting element of the tale. We need to note this because it's easy to miss how often – including even in *Starship Troopers* – adventure takes place almost as an afterthought in these novels. The interest is in the preparation for the adventure.

Teaching a child to be a scientist, and the importance of this, has already been flagged. In 'Universe', the thing that has gone wrong is the replacing of science with theology (a point repeated in *Job*). In 'Universe', in an anticipation of 'science studies' (a rather controversial discipline), Hugh Hoyland's interest in science is squashed by having to treat science texts as literature or religion and subjecting them to higher criticism. One of the things he has to learn is that lack of understanding on the part of the student does not invalidate information, and that to replace an attempt to understand with an attempt to interpret is a route to obfuscation. It is perhaps Heinlein's first argument not just in the paratactic voice but for it. 'None of you has tried believing clear words the way they were written and then tried to understand them on that basis.' This was to be his complaint about reactions to a number of his books and might of course turn out to be his posthumous complaint about this one.

The other point that Hugh has to learn, which is embedded in *Rocket Ship Galileo* and is argued over and over again in later juveniles, is that successful transmission of knowledge within cultures is vertical, not horizontal. In 'Universe', science training and the role of the crew has been undermined by peer affiliation and horizontal loyalties. 'It was impressed in him that he was expected to maintain a primary loyalty to the bloc of younger men among the scientists.' This overtakes everything. In the short story 'The Roads Must Roll' and the novella 'Coventry' this type of horizontal loyalty is used to control people, in the first story for the good – but it gives the story more than a whiff of fascism – and in 'Coventry' for the bad. Vertical education in Heinlein's view is the way to introduce new ideas, and if we pay close attention to alliances in 'Coventry' we can see that while John Lyle is friends only with his peer group, the 'corrupted' Zeb has friends of all ages.

This idea is most evident in *Space Cadet*. It is consciously modelled on the naval school he himself experienced, and which itself used the traditions of self-education of the British navy, where midshipmen studied on their own, grabbing tuition where they could, and submitting themselves for examination when they felt ready. The organisation of learning is a combination of individual effort, peer collaboration and hierarchical dissemination of knowledge through demonstration. The textbook material is taught by reading textbooks, the problem-solving by witnesses and taking part in problem-solving (sometimes as exercises, sometimes for real). For all it feels superficially conservative, it is actually rather radical.

For Heinlein Scouting was one way to combine a natural affinity for peer groups with the creation of vertical learning structures. In the short story 'Nothing Ever Happens on the Moon' (1949), written for *Boy's Life Magazine*, the role of Scoutmaster, the experience of the Moon Scouts and the initiative of the Earth Scout all play a part. The pooling of knowledge is part of the process of developing both knowledge and skills. This is even clearer in *Farmer in the Sky*. While on the ship Bill helps form a troop of Boy Scouts, and as a peer group they develop the mutual loyalty to each other that will enable them to establish a community on Ganymede, and learn to collaborate to get things done. But Bill learns his trade (farming) through apprenticeship to another farmer, Schultz, just as Matt in *Space Cadet* was effectively apprenticed within a ship.

The idea that learning skills is often horizontal and communal, but knowledge is disseminated vertically, is repeated in *Between Planets*, in *Space Family Stone* and in *Starman Jones*. In *Between Planets*, Dom always turns to a older person he trusts (even his girlfriend is a little older than he is) for advice and information, but the skills he does acquire he learns in the restaurant from watching, and as a soldier from the people he fights with. This may explain why

John Thomas Stuart XI in *The Star Beast* comes over as being not so very bright. He is quite isolated compared to the average Heinlein hero: no friends apart from Betty – who is far smarter than he is – and Lummox, even smarter though John Thomas doesn't yet realise it. So that this novel, unlike the other juveniles, is dedicated to telling a young man he should let his elders and betters push him around.

The Rolling Stones and *Starman Jones* couldn't be more different. Castor and Pollux are in constant tension between their father's and grandmother's good advice and their own ambitions. They are rather too used to manipulating their father, and get him to buy a spaceship in part on their behalf. Both adults resolve this by adopting the Socratic method of making sardonic comments about the twins' plans and leaving them to either figure it out, or go ahead and try to kill themselves. Only when they almost kill their baby brother do they really learn that adult rules exist for real reasons.

The absence of that good father is Max Jones's problem in *Starman Jones*. His uncle was meant to step into the breach but was killed and Jones finds himself flailing. He has neither peer group to learn with nor reliable adult to learn from. *Starman Jones* is a fairy tale. Max is a simple farm lad displaced by a wicked step-mother and step-father; he inherits only a set of astrogators' books and sets out in search of his fortune. When he meets a beggar (con man Sam), he is trusting, kind and shares his food. In return, the man steals his astrogation tables. In traditional fairy-tale tradition Max will have two other encounters, the truck driver who feeds him and Ellie, a pretty girl who is of course the magic witch or fairy complete with familiar, Mr Chipsie. Max is honest, brave and true and much of the time he is hopelessly lost. Yet the vertical teaching structure is in place: when Max is rejected by the guild he meets up again with Sam, who fakes papers for him and gets him a place on a starship. But Max learns very little in this novel: although Max performs as captain when the ship runs into trouble, he is doing so without training and without peer group. Sam dies rescuing them from the indigenes, and Max is an orphan again. To be fully educated Max needs a family with both peers and parents (or perhaps older brothers) and he is relieved when his final reward is to be absorbed into the Guild family.

I have concentrated so far on how people should be educated (not just children, as Heinlein believed education to be a continuous process) but Heinlein is perhaps better known for what he believed education should consist of. In his juveniles and later in *Stranger in a Strange Land* he made a pitch for mathematics as the basis of all education. Matt has to work hard to pass the astrogation exams. Holly in 'The Menace from Earth', whose mother is a mathematical chemist for General Synthetics, sees maths as essential to her future as a starship designer; and Podkayne understands she needs it to fly starships. But over and above that, what Heinlein is best known for is the assertion of a practical competence, an ability to take one's knowledge, think through a problem, work out what one wants to know, go away and learn it, apply it, discover there are things you didn't expect, go away and start the process again: the practical version of the scientific method that is these days called action research. We see Rod in *Tunnel in the Sky* as the finest proponent, with Kip in *Have Space Suit—Will Travel* as a junior apprentice. Podkayne is important because she has not been taught these things; she is a demonstration though absence (and in her uncle's diatribe at the end) of the essential importance of parental support.

There are several crucial scenes in *Tunnel in the Sky*. First, perhaps, there is Rod's packing. It is carefully considered, discussed with his sister, pared down to essentials and promptly lost when he is attacked on the planet. Others include Rod's realisation that just as he has been told much of his equipment is useless against that most dangerous of animals, man, so man – or his peers, including women – are far more valuable to him than are any specific tools or weapons. One of the indications that Cowper, the older man who pitches for the leadership of the colony, is a waste of space is that he does not respect the abilities of the women, downgrading their roles and sending them away from a fight.

What Rod learns – and teaches us – is that practical people can create tools, settlements and societies. We also learn that impractical people can fail to do any of those but will enjoy taking credit for 'managing' them, not a bad lesson to learn. There are also basic lessons about how to build a fort, how to defend one without escalating hostilities (the tunnels to allow wildlife to run under the village) and other practicalities. This is maker fiction, as is *Have Space Suit—Will Travel*, in which Kip takes us through how to maintain a space suit. Most people take away from the book the lesson to 'be prepared' and 'be methodical': to do the apparently unnecessary.

Podkayne has learned all of this, but she has had to learn it by sneaking around: no survival classes for her. Unlike Caroline or Rod's sister in *Tunnel in the Sky*, her father doesn't want his little girl to grow up to be able to defend herself. No real maths class: as Podkayne is self-taught and to get extra training – used as she is to being unsupported by those around her – she dissimulates rather than asks: 'The second officer, Mr. Savvonavong thinks it is simply amazing how fast I pick up mathematics' (Chapter 9). But of course, she has studied it before on a supplementary course. Later she hides her desire to be a captain from the young man who is courting her, Dexter.

Podkayne's mother is overcompensating for her own success, and in the process has set for her daughter a model which emphasises the social and disparages her own education and achievements. You can hear this in Podkayne's description of her, where Podkayne has absorbed what is really important:

Mother is twice as good-looking as I am. She holds a system-wide license as a Master Engineer, Heavy Construction, Surface or Free Fall, and it entitled her to wear both the Hoover medal with cluster and the Christian Order, Knight Commander, for bossing the rebuilding of Deimos and Phobos. But she's more than just the traditional hairy engineer; she has a social presence which she can switch from warmly charming to frostily intimidating at will. (Chapter 1)

And Podkayne's mother has done nothing to contradict this, paying little attention to her daughter's intellectual development, channelling Podkayne – who is beautiful – into being merely decorative. Worse, Podkayne has been educated to assume that there are limits, and without anyone to confound this, she follows the trajectory of many a post-pubertal girl, bit by bit giving up her unsupported ambitions and 'settling' for what she will be able to find support for. It's easy to read this as Heinlein downgrading Podkayne as a person, but Podkayne gets to say this:

My education has encompassed cooking, sewing, quite a lot of math and history and science, and such useful tidbits as freehand drawing and how to dip candles and make soap. But hand-to-hand combat I have learned sketchily if at all from occasional border clashes with Clark. I know Mother feels that this is a lack (she is skilled in both karate and kill-quick, and can shoot as well as Daddy does) but Daddy has put off sending me to classes – I've gathered the impression that he does not want his 'baby girl' to know such things. (Chapter 13)

And given Uncle Tom's (off-stage) chastising of her parents for their failure to educate her properly, and given what we know of Heinlein's attitudes to education, this is not the right reading. Podkayne is a demonstration – as Max is to a degree – of the sense of lostness that a child without either an educative parent or peer group will experience. Education does not, Heinlein argues, take place in a vacuum. It is unfortunate that in his family novels Heinlein never wrote a story about a girl inducted into a cohort, although we see hints of this in the back story of Rod's sister in *Tunnel in the Sky*, in the Pudding stories, and in Holly's story in 'The Menace from Earth', for it means that there is nothing with which to contrast Podkayne to determine to what degree it really is her parenting and peer isolation that Heinlein is critiquing.

At some point during the period in which he was writing juveniles, Heinlein became emotionally attached to the Boy Scouts of America. Was the first story a commission? He himself was never a Scout, but a number of things about the movement quite clearly appealed to him: its attempt to bring very different kinds of boys together, its emphasis on resilience and competence, its emphasis on preparation for exploration, and perhaps most of all, its emphasis on collaboration – the heroes of Heinlein's work are never lone heroes (not even Oscar, of *Glory Road*) but are always part of a team.

The Boy Scout stories, published between 1948 and 1958, are 'The Black Pits of Luna', 'Nothing Ever Happens on the Moon', *Farmer in the Sky* and 'Tenderfoot in Space' (1958, *Boy's Life*), but Heinlein's interest first appears in an article, 'How to be a Survivor', that he wrote in 1946 but that remained unpublished until 1980. In this article, which assumes that the US may fall to an invader at some point and which is linked to the novel *The Day after Tomorrow* and an unpublished short story 'Free Men', Heinlein sets out some basic tenets for escaping what he sees as America's doom.

Don't be there; get out of the cities, decentralise.

Carry salt, but not canned goods because they make you a target.

Hunt with a knife or trap, keep bullets for men and deer.

Make sure you have a medical kit and a home medicine book.

Be a boy scout and learn to live off the land.

In this list is everything Heinlein will reiterate in all his post-survival books for the next twenty years (*Farnham's Freehold* is the most conspicuous example) and to an extent lived his life by, hence his move with Ginny to a rather isolated area of Colorado. But for now the key thing is that sense that the Boy Scout movement was the best means for boys, and particularly city boys, to learn these skills. As a movement, it was also a place for boys to prove themselves, to embark on the trajectory away from childhood, and away from home; away from dependence and towards independence in a structured, managed fashion.

The very first story in this loose sequence, 'The Black Pits of Luna', also positions the Scouts as in some way a compensation for bad parenting. So when the protagonist finds himself on the Moon it is with a father who thinks he can buy anything, and a mother who expects the world to revolve around her. They are the quintessential self-absorbed couple and they are bringing up their younger boy to feel the same way – that the older boy is not the same is due entirely, it is implied, to his enrolment in the Scouts. This story offers the argument – used several times by Heinlein – that separation from the parents is a crucial part of growing up, and that taking on new values appropriate to the environment is the mark of an adult.

In 'Nothing Ever Happens on the Moon' an Earth Boy Scout comes to the Moon to try and add Moon Eagle Scout status to his badges from Earth and Venus – to become the first triple Eagle Scout. This is a very short bildungsroman in which the boy goes from the arrogance of a boy, assuming that what he has learned in his home environment will be adequate, to realising – even though he has survived a disaster and rescued himself and his Moon Scout guide – that he has a great deal more to learn, and he is rewarded with the chance of intensive coaching to pass the tests. This idea that there is always more to learn, that a reward for excellent performance is to be given the chance to learn more, is picked up in the non-Scout stories *Space Cadet* and *Starman Jones*. Matt Dodson and Max Jones both think that outstanding performance will bring confirmation of status and both learn to be happy with the idea that outstanding performance brings a shot at access to that status.

Collaboration, sometimes not even with a human, is essential for Heinlein. In the rather sentimental 'Tenderfoot in Space', a much younger boy, Charlie, is emigrating to Venus. He manages to get his father to agree to take his dog with him in cold sleep – Heinlein is always consistent that animals should not be abandoned and indicates Johnny Rico's weakness of character in that he had allowed his dog to be sent outside. Charlie joins the Scouts on Venus, and when he and another Scout are lost and injured it is the dog Nixie who goes for help and wins his own Scout life-saving badge. Charlie saved Nixie, Nixie saved Charlie. From each according to his abilities . . .

The trajectory of all the Scout stories is away from home and into an adult cohort. The Scouts take boys who are individuals, and turn them into a cohort, both loyal to each other and recognising the support from each other. Whereas in some of the early stories this produces a rather sinister corporate loyalty (see 'The Roads Must Roll', 'Blowups Happen' and 'Universe' or 'Common Sense'), in the Scout stories and those stories that use similar sets of values, it is framed far more in terms of living up to an ideal of manhood established by those gone before. This is clearest in the sentiment of 'The Long Watch', repeated in *Space Cadet*, and expressed visually in the roll-call of names of those people who prevented a fatal accident in 'Nothing Ever Happens on the Moon'. It reaches its apotheosis in *Starship Troopers*, which is, at its heart, a Boy Scout novel expressing much the same values. When we consider the kind of education that Heinlein approves of we need to understand that any rhetoric of individualism is overwhelmed by a more pervasive and older ideology of manhood as a growing sense of fitting in.

Where Heinlein begins to emerge on the right on this issue is in his growing conviction – expressed first in *Space Cadet* in action, but more forcefully in *Starship Troopers* in Johnny's reaction to the hanging of a deserter and rapist – that once raised, a human being cannot be fundamentally changed: that society can only intervene in childhood. This has a range of quite distinct and (for this reader) disquieting consequences. Because Heinlein believed in nurture over nature, he also believed in the slave mentality. This is discussed obliquely and displayed in *Farnham's Freehold*. It is also there in the – to modern eyes – deeply uncomfortable analogy story, 'Jerry was a Man', where the confirmation of humanity does not confer equal rights, because those, the implication suggests, have to be earned through education and uplift. I will return to this in Chapter 6.

The Making of Society

For Heinlein society is not made once, but continually, through and in its political processes. Heinlein's belief in the importance of electoral engagement was ferocious. His loss of faith in voluntary engagement, which occurred when he tried to mobilise the Patrick Henry movement, was even before then shaping the arguments lurking in *Space Cadet*, hinted at in *Time for the Stars* in the names of his protagonists, and made explicit in *Starship Troopers* and in the mouth of Jubal Harshaw (in both *Stranger in a Strange Land* and 'The Number of the Beast'), that the right to vote should be earned, not

223

because Heinlein believed it should be earned, but because he believed it would then be valued more greatly. Before he took this turn however, he first tried exhortation in the form of two stories and a handbook.

Before writing the electoral stories, Heinlein might have been seen to side with corporatism and technocracy. In 'Blowups Happen' and 'The Roads Must Roll' the problems of the politician as a species and the partisan nature of politics is swept away by the rule of experts, in very direct and forceful terms. Given the discussion in *How to Win an Election*, however, it seems unlikely that Heinlein, although regarding expertise highly (see his reprimand to Campbell for undermining the war effort by peddling ignorance), was truly convinced by this argument. Although he could become splenetic about the need for 'facts' he understood politics as the art of interpretation, and the application of interest, as in the story 'A Bathroom of Her Own'. Furthermore, he was deeply concerned about party machines (see 'The Devil Makes the Law') and the undue influence of big business (see 'Lifeline', '"Let There Be Light"', 'The Devil Makes the Law'). For Heinlein therefore the best elections were those involving active, engaged citizens, armed with the 'facts' and arguing the interpretation. In three stories he made serious attempts to activate his readership, and in particular, despite some rather odd rhetoric, his female readership.

In 'The Devil Makes the Law', a builder's merchant finds his ability to employ magic undermined by the emergence first of a protection racket ('sign up or have bad luck') and then the creation of a large agency employing restrictive contracts (of a kind Heinlein was to protest against himself at Scribner's). Although they call in Dr Worthington, a black South African professor and witch smeller (portrayed with very great respect) and the local white witch, Mrs Jennings (an elderly lady, also portrayed with great respect), this is in part a story about controlling local politics and for that, the resisters need a senator. Their choice is Sally, who is unfortunately complimented for the degree to which she is *not* 'a woman politician': 'she is simply a politician, and asks no special consideration because of her sex. She can stand up and trade punches with the toughest manipulators on the hill.' Sally helps them oppose a licensing bill which – like many of the food safety acts of the period with which Heinlein would have been familiar – is a subtle way of closing down small competitors, but ultimately they lose and go back to using witchcraft.

More interesting is the story 'A Bathroom of Her Own' and its intersection with *How to Win an Election*, both 1946. In the latter, Heinlein provides a strikingly good handbook about how to engage in from-the-ground-up politics, including how to build a neighbourhood block or constituency, how to both mobilise and assess volunteers, the arts of negotiation and how to build influence. Particularly worth noting is hostility to two types: the first is the paid campaigner who is not only not worth as much in energy as the unpaid, but can, Heinlein insists, eviscerate a campaign. The second is the club woman whose involvement in politics is peculiarly apolitical.

> Most women in the United States have a short-sighted, peasant individualism resulting from the male-created romantic traditions of the last century. They were told they were superior creatures, a little nearer to the angels than their menfolks. They were not encouraged to think, nor to assume social responsibility. It takes a strong mind to break out of that sort of conditioning, and most minds simply aren't up to it, male or female. ('The Devil Makes the Law')

This a rhetorical bait and switch. Very quickly Heinlein shows how a different kind of woman can be incredibly invaluable to a campaign and in politics. The short story 'A Bathroom of Her Own' is essentially about the creation of a politician of this kind. In this story, once again Heinlein asserts that a male candidate cannot use the ordinary rough-and-tumble against a female candidate for fear of being considered ungentlemanly (it's a nice idea but a study of the campaigns against Eleanor Roosevelt, Sarah Palin and Hillary Clinton quickly renders it nonsense: if anything women arouse huge hostility from sections of the electorate on both the left and the right). But in the context of the story, it leads a prospective male candidate against the machine to resign in the face of a female machine candidate – a female veteran, itself a nice touch – who has a good story to tell about the crisis in the housing market (US elections are very much swayed by the good story), that all she wants is a bathroom of her own. (Presumably this is a desire expressed to Heinlein by Ginny early in their relationship as she later executed it in their Colorado house: see Patterson, vol. 2, p. 58). The story then runs as a coaching session, a fictional version of *How to Win an Election*: Frances X. Nelson turns into a good senator, the narrator into a field councillor or what the British would call a special advisor. The lesson is that citizen engagement can defeat an entrenched machine.

This is the mentality behind 'Who are the Heirs of Patrick Henry?' By this point Heinlein's suspicion of communism, honed in the inter-war years when the left was genuinely split by the role of communism and communists ('infiltration' suggests that the communist presence was secretive but this is not the case) had rendered him suspicious of all attempts at rapprochement with the Soviet Union. It is whenever Heinlein gets on to the subject of communism that his rhetoric becomes intemperate and interestingly, most reasoned, if we understand reason as being the engagement in a closed circle of logical philosophy. What Heinlein is aiming for – and this extends throughout his post-1958 writing – is to generate a commitment as strong as that shown by communists. While the polemical outrage itself seems to be a break with Heinlein's previous style, this concept of the committed citizenry is a constant.

The rhetoric of the Patrick Henry letter is stentorian. It is a voice that Heinlein never uses in his fiction – in his juveniles patriotism is more muted, and of the Kiplingesque variety approved in *Stalky & Co.* It misfired in the SF community precisely because it was too directive. The model of political rhetoric which had come to dominate the SF community of the time – ironically because Heinlein had helped develop it – was of the show, don't tell, or 'if this goes on' unravelling: demonstrating the failure of a political model by projection.

The result of Heinlein's disillusion, not with his ideas of society, but with the people who made up America – reinforced by the very complex responses to *Starship Troopers* – was a series of novels in which the context for each is an America in crisis. In the background for *Have Space Suit—Will Travel, Glory Road, Farnham's Freehold* and *I Will Fear No Evil*, is an America that is going to hell in a handbasket. This is not simply about the epidemic of urban violence but about Heinlein's conviction that there was a decline in education and honour. Crucially, Heinlein understands it as a decline in patriotism. E. C. Gordon/Oscar notes, 'After you've spent years and years trying to knock the patriotism out of a boy, don't expect him to cheer when he gets a notice reading: GREETING: you are hereby ordered into the Armed Forces of the United States' (*Glory Road*, Chapter 1). Heinlein is knocking not the lack of patriotism per se, but the messed-up system that educates people out of communal responsibilities and a sense of reciprocity and yet demands what he always regarded as indentured servitude (that is, conscription) to compensate for the lack of connection to the commonweal.

Much of this fed into the political design of *Starship Troopers* and *The Moon is a Harsh Mistress* and into the polemics of Lazarus Long,

Johann Sebastian Bach Smith, Jubal Harshaw and Maureen Smith, and helps to explain Heinlein's drift away from electoral politics as the future of America and back towards the kind of Taylorism/ scientific management that he advocates in 'The Roads Must Roll', with the difference that as he also remained suspicious of monopoly, he increasingly – in the figures of Delos D. Harriman, Jubal Harshaw and Maureen Smith – looked to individual business people and magnates to drive innovation. But Heinlein also had a long track record as a literary revolutionary.

6

Heinlein and the Civic Revolution

There is a strong sense running through Heinlein's work that, in the right circumstances, rebellion and revolution is a civic duty. After twenty years of Michigan Militia and Tea Party rhetoric this may seem more provocative than it did when Heinlein was writing, rather than less. It bears serious consideration as part of the construction of Heinlein's worldview, because it balances the sense in other work (particularly his juveniles) that Heinlein requires young people to sign up to corporate or patriotic ideals without much critical thinking.

Revolution

The first half of Heinlein's writing career is pro-revolution (see 'Violent Revolution in American Science Fiction', Edward James, 1990). In *For Us, the Living* a number of revolutions have occurred in the past of the book, between Perry's sleep and his awakening. Each of these revolutions had a different cause and a different mission.

But in each case – with the exception of the Prophet Nehemiah Scudder's rise – they are portrayed as popular revolutions. It is thus interesting that in "'If This Goes On—'" and *Sixth Column* and, later, *The Moon is a Harsh Mistress*, Heinlein – ferociously anti-communist and disliking intensely the communist method of infiltrating organisations – makes use of precisely Bolshevik modes of organisation and Bolshevik arguments. This is true even though the Brotherhood in "'If This Goes On—'" is only one revolutionary group in the theocracy; the existence of Mormon, Jewish and other organisations is a reflection of the communist, socialist and ethnic American union chapters in the first half of the twentieth century. Franklin sees this as an ongoing flaw in Heinlein's work:

> [H]e will continue to see essentially just two alternatives: either the elite (the *good* elite) saves the day, which obviously contradicts the democratic principles he sometimes espouses, or society succumbs to the ignorance and folly of the masses of common people. His concept of revolutionary social change imagines something created *by* an elite *for* the benefit of the people, usually quite temporarily. He seems incapable of believing that progressive social change could come through the development of the productive forces and consequence action by the exploited classes themselves. (*Robert A. Heinlein*, p. 34).

I think this misses the point that most successful social movements in American history have been constructed in the way Heinlein, not Franklin, imagines. Even the mass civil rights movement was structured this way with the ideas of the 'talented tenth' and training camps as major elements of the struggle. And almost every successful change Heinlein would have seen was a movement in which an elite led a mass.

"'If This Goes On—'" is as much a revolutionary's manual as *How to Be a Politician* is a democrat's manual, and they share some basic assumptions: that you are less trying to engage the electorate in a conversation to change their opinions and desires than you are attempting to convince them that their self-interest is best served by swinging behind a new leadership/ruling group or class. This is not hypocrisy: Heinlein's account of his own voting practices, as recorded in letters cited by Bill Patterson, suggests that he chose his own electoral preferences in the same way, although his definition of 'self-interest' was wider, and encompassed his sense of 'America's interest'. The role of "'If This Goes On—'" as a revolutionary manual explains why it is focalised through an agonist, not a protagonist. This is a teaching book. It leads the innocent to unstitch their world and consider how to organise a resistance.

In "'If This Goes On—'", the revolution is being led by a minority trying to actively create the conditions for revolution in direct opposition to the will of the people. There is, for example, an agreement in place that when all the odds are at least 2:1 in favour of the revolution then the Brotherhood will rise. However, at the point this happens, evidence suggests that 62 per cent of the population are still 'genuinely devout', and 'We can win the revolution but it will be followed by a long and bloody civil war – which we will lose'. The revolution is wholly undemocratic and illegitimate, a palace coup: all the people we meet began as insiders in the regime.

The revolution in "'If This Goes On—'" is pulled back from the cusp of tyranny by a rejection of outright psychosocial conditioning. Despite the use of general semantics to feed propaganda to the population, the novella distinguishes between developing a vanguard whose role it is to convince and lead free men and developing a cadre who will control them. 'Free men aren't "conditioned"! Free men are free because they are ornery and cussed and prefer to arrive at their own prejudices in their own way – not have them spoon-fed by a self appointed mind tinkerer!' Along the way one of the ideas rejected is that democracy is the equivalent of turning explosives over to children: 'They passed two resolutions: that no citizen should be subjected to hypnosis or other psychosomatic technique without his written consent, and that no religious or political test should be used for franchise in the first elections.' The revolution proceeds, but while we see the uprising, we do not see the outcome, in the sense of the society emplaced in the post-Scudder world.

There is a trilogy of revolution stories in the juveniles: *Space Cadet*, *Red Planet* and *Between Planets*. *Space Cadet* is not itself a book about revolution but it is a book about a post-revolutionary settlement. Its revolution is the failed coup of 'Requiem' and the establishment of world government in 'Solution Unsatisfactory'. Its post-revolutionary settlement is the cadet corps outlined in 'The Roads Must Roll', which is modelled on the American Scouting movement (the influence of which is discussed elsewhere). Interesting is the insistence on creating a rather rigid society within which free thought is encouraged, presumably modelled in part on the naval academy, and which adheres entirely to meritocratic selection (Heinlein had been the recipient of patronage but he consistently opposes this in his boys' books – see also *Starman Jones*). As is promised in 'The Roads Must Roll' this is a revolution that is creating a loyal cadre by skimming off the best and brightest and channelling their loyalty to a central authority that is utterly unrepresentative and unaccountable – unlike the government in *Starship Troopers*.[1]

---

1 In *Starship Troopers* the requirement that the governing classes should have served in the military is a corollary to Heinlein's opposition to conscription, rather than a contradiction. Heinlein had during his lifetime seen the rate of military service among congressmen decline. See the Pew research here: http://www.pewresearch.org/fact-tank/2013/09/04/members-of-congress-have-little-direct-military-experience/

In *Red Planet* the revolution is far more a war of independence, a rejection of external control.[2] In this novel the revolution is created not by the colonists but by the company, through a series of decisions that pressure them into rebellion. Furthermore, the very decision to delay the migration means that when the colonists realise what is happening they are concentrated and in a position to respond. In this book Heinlein seems to be saying 'this is how not to create a revolution.' Given that Heinlein was an anti-imperialist (hence the title as well as the story of 'Logic of Empire') this is a take on revolution quite consistent with his beliefs: empires are *ipso facto* bad, because it is not possible to rule justly from a distance. So *Between Planets*, the most revolutionary of the juveniles, rehearses many of the arguments that will appear in *The Moon is a Harsh Mistress*.

Between Planets seems to have brought together the material Heinlein used in three distinct places: in *The Day After Tomorrow*, 'Free Men' and 'Logic of Empire'. That last story lurks in the background of *Between Planets*, in that the opening up of Empire is itself dependent on exploitation: Don finds himself a contract labourer and discovers just how unfree 'free' labour can be when there is a monopoly employer backed by the government, or nowhere else to go. He also discovers that there is somewhere to go: Venus, like America, is a large place. In both *The Day After Tomorrow* and 'Free Men' Heinlein has a turn at organising guerrilla warfare and gives clear instructions for a cell structure, for sabotage and how to deal with traitors. *The Day After Tomorrow* is essentially an 'if this goes on' story in the tradition of Katharine Burdekin's novel *Swastika Night*. It has been derided as being merely a yellow-peril novel, and

2   There is some discussion of the role of the War of American Independence in Heinlein's thought in Edward James, 'Violent Revolution in American Science Fiction.' In *Science Fiction, Social Conflict and War*, edited by Philip John Davies (Manchester: Manchester UP, 1990), pp. 98–112.

it is, but it is hard, reading the novel in the cold light of day, not to realise that, if anything, Heinlein underplayed Japanese retaliations and punishments in mainland Asia.[3] However, he very deliberately makes an American of Japanese ancestry the most heroic individual in the book; it is worth noting that the serialisation of the novel (as *Sixth Column*) was before Pearl Harbor, but Heinlein changed nothing about the Pan-Asiatics for the book publication in 1949.

In this novel, Heinlein understands the threat to civilians represented by a guerrilla resistance: 'their hands were bound by the greater certainty of brutal multiple retaliation against their own kind. As with the Jews in Germany before the final blackout in Europe, bravery was not enough, for one act of violence against their tyrants would be paid for by other men, women and children at unspeakable compound interest' (Chapter 2). Furthermore, as in '"If This Goes On—"', in both *The Day After Tomorrow* and 'Free Men' it is not clear that everyone wants to be free; there are plenty of collaborators. Nor is there any guarantee of success. The revolutionaries in the unpublished 'Free Men' (possibly told from within the world of *The Day After Tomorrow*) have to deal with deserters who see the invasion as purifying and freedom as illusory. You could be pushed around by the cops, a 'free press' didn't mean you could own a newspaper, and the resistance merely have 'Freedom to starve, freedom to sleep on the cold ground, freedom to be hunted' (*Expanded Universe*, p. 185). There is a fear that no country has ever liberated itself without external help so that the movement is pretty much pointless. In the end the cell is wiped out and has to start over again with a new leader. This may be why the story remained unpublished: it lacks the

---

3 More of which comes to light each year: see, most recently, Jeanne Guillemin, *Hidden Atrocities: Japanese Germ Warfare and American Obstruction of Justice at the Tokyo Trial* (New York: Columbia UP, 2017).

assumed American victory of mid-century American science fiction.

In contrast to *Red Planet*, *The Day After Tomorrow* or *The Moon is a Harsh Mistress*, most of the organisation of the revolution in *Between Planets* is actually taking place off-stage. In a very neat trick Heinlein makes Don the protagonist only of his own adventure. Within the revolution he is less than a pawn, for a pawn makes moves that are actively contributing to the war on the ground. Instead, Don is a mule, an unwitting courier of information. Don is swept up in the revolution like many before him. He has none of the choices of a conventional hero. He also finds himself on a planet with uneven development (itself a common sign of imperial power where development tends to be focused on the centre of control) and where the revolution is being carried on in guerrilla warfare that is essentially without honour and in which he may die unmourned. It is a juvenile, so Don of course survives (although his survival is bought by another captive in the concentration camp), but even though he has served as a guerrilla fighter, Don is chagrined to learn that this has had far less influence on events than the conversation he had with the Venusian dragon Sir Isaac Newton, or the gift of the ring to Isobel, the bank manager's daughter who took pity on him. What Don and the reader learn is that the revolution is ruthless and depends on most of the people involved not actually knowing what they are involved in. They also learn that revolutions do not happen in a day: it is in *Between Planets*, written in 1951, that Heinlein shows his clearest awareness that an anti-imperialist revolution is a long-term project but one that the imperialists cannot defeat, since Heinlein believes both colonies and empires to be inherently and structurally impossible.

The trilogy is a quartet if we add in *Podkayne of Mars*, where we have a rare glimpse of a post-revolutionary society, still plagued by attempts from the mother planet to undermine it, and also dealing with the cultural and political disparagement of Terrans. Although

I will tackle this in full later, Heinlein neatly ties the racism of Earth into the prejudice against colonials – it takes Podkayne a while to recognise the racism in the anti-colonial prejudice she has expected.

The classic revolutionary novel is, of course, *The Moon is a Harsh Mistress* (1966). As Neil Easterbrook has noted in 'Ethics and Alterity', it has no indigenous population to deal with, it is genuinely a barren land, and it is a prison planet which imprisons the children of prisoners; it is clearly unjust. The population of the Moon does not have a mission, but finds one – as America has found one – in the revolution itself.

The notion that to rebel is a civic duty is clearest in this novel. The uprising in *The Moon is a Harsh Mistress* is rooted in Benjamin Franklin's arguments that revolution is inevitable as the needs of the colony diverge from the needs of the parent state, and in what emerges as one of the strongest elements of the revolution, that rule without representation is unjust, that absentee rentiers and landlords cannot possibly rule in the best interests of the colony. Thus, in this novel, to rebel becomes patriotism: we can see this in the way the rebellion seeks to ally workers with traders and different ethnic blocks with each other. The revolutionaries in *The Moon is a Harsh Mistress* are setting out to build a nation and do so in the choices they make. One of the issues in the book is that if it is to succeed, it needs to change from a movement led by a few to one supported by the many. Mike (the computer, and a Benjamin Franklin figure in his deviousness) decides that one way to do this is a direct approach to Earth.

If we accept the idea that the family is a microcosm of the society, or its smallest units, then the type of marriage is an ideological statement about the entire culture that the revolution is fighting for. Mannie is chosen to go to Earth: he is dark-skinned like most Loonies, not 'well spoken' and with a family structure (the radical line marriage) that itself is a statement of Luna values. It is the choice of

Mannie as ambassador that changes this from a financially motivated rebellion to a genuine revolution that seeks to win hearts and minds at home as well as on Luna. The treatment of Mannie gives Luna something to fight for as well as against.

Sadly, we only see the post-revolutionary Luna colony of *The Moon is a Harsh Mistress* at a distance, through the behaviour of Hazel in *The Rolling Stones*, written well before *The Moon is a Harsh Mistress*, and in her behaviour and that of Richard in *The Cat Who Walks Through Walls*. This will be the last true revolution in Heinlein's work. The 'revolution' in *Friday* is an attempted coup, and it remains mostly off-stage.

Guns: An Aside

One aspect of Heinlein's beliefs about civic society was that the citizen had a right to carry arms and that this was a fundamental element of individual responsibility. Rafeeq McGiveron notes succinctly, 'Heinlein rarely says that might makes right; he is correct, however, in reminding us that might may be necessary to *preserve* right' ('He just plain liked guns', p. 67).

However, although Heinlein was a ferocious supporter of the Second Amendment, regarding licensing as a 'violation of civil liberty' (letter to Alice Dalgliesh, 19 April 1949; *Grumbles from the Grave*), it is very hard indeed to find evidence that he considered guns to be an effective weapon of defence. In novel after novel guns fail to be useful: individuals are overpowered when they attempt to defend themselves; attackers (even government attackers) are overwhelmed by the angry and determined unarmed (a position possible to hold in the days before mass shooters went in with AR-15s). They aren't even terribly useful in single-person attacks: more than one attacker is disarmed.

One clue to this might be in the letter to Alice Dalgliesh in 1949 mentioned above and so often cited. First, the letter was written in 1949. We still need later evidence as to his opinions. Second, he writes 'I am not inexperienced with guns. I have coached rifle and pistol teams and conducted the firing of millions of rounds from pistols to turrets. I am aware of the dangers of guns, but I do not agree that those dangers can be eliminated or even ameliorated by coercive legislation.' We tend to focus on the support for guns in this statement. What is rarely noticed is its revelation: Heinlein never fired a shot in combat or was ever shot at in combat. Heinlein's primary use of armaments would have been the large guns of a ship. His use of firearms was carefully controlled. In this section I intend to argue that Heinlein's work reflects this, from his use of the code duello, through his restriction of where guns are appropriate, and on to his tendency to undermine, in his narrative trajectories, any rhetoric or argument about guns as a weapon of defence.

One of the most oft-quoted lines from Heinlein is this one: 'an armed society is a polite society.' It continues, 'Manners are good when one may have to back up his acts with his life . . .' Very few people, if any, however take a look at the context of this quotation. Most people do not even notice that the quotation comes near the end of *Beyond This Horizon* (Chapter 15 of 18), a novel that is all about on what basis supremacy and hierarchy in a society should be organised, and what should happen to those at the bottom of, or outside, the hierarchy. The paragraph from which the quotation is taken continues: 'gun-fighting has a strong biological use. We do not have enough things to kill off the weak and the stupid these days. But to stay alive as an armed citizen an man has to be either quick with his wits or with his hands, or preferably both' (Chapter 15). As Martin Albright has noted, implicit in this statement is that 'the whole reason an armed society is a polite society is that in an armed society, the penalty for "impoliteness" might be summary execution' ('Is An Armed Society Really a "Polite" Society?', 2010), which is polite only in countries with a tendentious relationship to the rule of law.

While I have no intention of questioning Heinlein's commitment to the right to bear arms, I do question the lack of contextualisation of this quotation; at least one part of this contextualisation would be as music to the ears of the survivalist strand of the pro-gun community, even while another strand would horrify them. The World of *Beyond This Horizon* is not our world. It is a post-scarcity utopia, a society with a minimum income, a planned economy and a reinvestment of resources to generate wealth (Chapter 1). Not socialist certainly, but on the 'socialistic' spectrum. As the time traveller John Darlington Smith (the protagonist in *For Us, the Living*, a mere sideshow here) discovers, there is no such thing as profit, only resources (Chapter 6). There is no such thing as a fixed currency, only the abstract symbology of flow. It is, therefore, a world with relatively little income inequality and no actual poverty: Heinlein might have offered a correlation, '*a comfortable society is a polite society*'.

The world of *Beyond This Horizon* is not our world. It is a post-post-post-eugenicist society, where extreme eugenics have been rejected, and where in a later iteration the pacifists bred to end war succumbed to the more warlike (Chapter 2). It is a world where parents are encouraged to engineer their children to produce the best they can, but not to go beyond the basic human (Chapters 2 and 3); but it is also a world in which human beings have been bred for stability, for 'cool self interest'. Mordan asks Hamilton, 'Why didn't you shoot it out with me last night?' and receives the response, 'Because there was nothing worth fighting for' (Chapter 2).

This is not our world. When Heinlein says everyone he really doesn't mean everyone. Women in this world may carry a gun, but over and over it is indicated that no one assumes that they will, and when we see Longcourt Phyllis wearing one it quickly becomes clear we are not to take it seriously. Hamilton is outraged when he sees Longcourt is carrying a gun.

> I know your type. You're one of these 'independent' women, anxious to claim all the privileges of men but none of the responsibilities. I can just see you, swaggering around town with that damned little spit gun at your side, demanding the rights of an armed citizen, picking fights in the serene knowledge that no brave will call your bluff? (Chapter 4)

Longcourt is furious, points out that she hasn't drawn in years and 'Is there anything wrong with a woman preferring the dignity of an armed citizen?'

Apparently there is. She challenges Hamilton to strap on his gun and instead he moves towards her to disarm her. She draws, he steps back to parley and when she relaxes he goes for her and disarms her and sexually assaults her (one of two clear sexual assaults leading to love that Heinlein has in his work: a theme common in contemporary rom-coms). It stops at a forced kiss and spanking and is turned into play, but it is a clear denial of Longcourt's adulthood and full citizenry. Hamilton compounds the insult by claiming a man would never have asked for his gun back, but he would also not have insulted a man in this way. Hamilton has broken the rules of his society: he has been neither polite nor respectful to an armed citizen. Thus *an armed society makes decisions about who it feels is rightfully armed and is less than polite to those it thinks improperly armed.* There is also one more issue relating to this: when Monroe-Alpha tries to set fire to his lady-love for the sin of being a Control, she 'brought her hand down sharply near the wrist joint of his right hand. At the same instant her right fist made a painful surprise in his stomach. He dropped his gun' (Chapter 8). Twice someone has drawn a gun. Twice someone is disarmed.

The first scene in which we see the much-vaunted politeness is when Hamilton Felix is challenged in the restaurant. It is actually two incidents, not one. In the first part of the scene Monroe-Alpha struggles with a crab leg, and it goes over the balcony, drops into a wine glass and splashes a woman's dress. Of the men there, two respond. The older man has 'coldly dangerous eyes'; the younger 'was clearly annoyed and reluctant to comply' when his elder takes the role of challenger. Hamilton leans over the balcony and offers a formal stiff apology: 'my clumsiness has disturbed the pleasure of your meal and invaded your privacy. I am deeply sorry' (Chapter 1). The older man demands assurance it was an accident and the incident is over quickly, but what strikes this reader is that far from being 'polite' this is a huge over-reaction. It is only because courtesies are exchanged that there is no duel, but what kind of society fights over a splashed dress? If this is a polite society, it is not a comfortable one. The second half of the scene follows quickly. An onlooker from across the room deliberately (as we are later shown) provokes Hamilton to a duel by insulting him. Hamilton issues a formal insult and draws. His new Colt 45 sends a ballistic bullet through the young man before he can chop downward with his ray (Chapter 1).

Anyone paying attention ought to note – but rarely does – that there is nothing in this scene whatsoever that supports the argument that an armed society is a polite society. Courteous, yes, but the existence of courtesy is often a ritual of violence. This is brought to a head at the end of the book, in Chapter 14, when John Darlington Smith gets himself into a mess. Smith is a racist who, on at least two occasions, brandishes his whiteness as a flag, once by telling Hamilton that his offer of help is 'mighty white' and second, when declaring he's no 'nigger'. He is a brassarded man, wearing the arm-band that indicates that someone is not armed and cannot accept a challenge. He is forced to give way on a pavement (ritual and discriminatory courtesy, not politeness) and when he is lectured for his refusal, he strikes the citizen. The citizen's friend sends a challenge and Smith refuses to apologise: 'what do you think I am, a nigger?' Hamilton is bemused at the relevance of this and after some time Hamilton suggests that he offer a fist fight and accept the drubbing that he does receive.

If we have any doubt whatsoever by this point that the role of guns in this society is to create a hierarchy to which not all can be admitted, and a set of rituals of courtesy that rob many of full agency, it is clarified by Mordan's comment to Felix that he should not take on the brassard: 'The brassard is an admission of defeat, an acknowledgement of inferiority' (Chapter 15). Laying guns down, as many older men do in the culture, is an abdication of full citizenship.

Politeness or courtesy, whichever you will, is essentially a transaction between equals: lurking in the small incidents of the book is a strong indication that for those who are brassarded and at the bottom of the heap, the world would look very different. The only effective use of guns in this book is to keep rebels at bay, and even then, Hamilton and Mordan are overcome by gas used by their own side.

Beyond This Horizon contains a very clear statement about guns, and the role of guns in society, and it is this statement that those who believe in unrestricted access to guns tend to cite. Far less observed is Heinlein's wider attitude to guns, to what guns are for, and to the responsibilities that go with them. I will explore that next, while never pretending that Heinlein was anything but a literalist second-amendment supporter.

In 1949 Heinlein published his third juvenile for Scribner: *Red Planet*. It is a juvenile in the full sense in that the protagonists, Jim and Frank, are in their early rather than late teens. We know this because they are heading off to high school for the first time and only just settling into the idea of careers. We have always known that this juvenile was heavily edited for two things: first, Heinlein's editor, Alice Dalgliesh, removed the scene in which Willis lays eggs in Jim's bed, and second, she asked Heinlein to pull back on the presence of guns in the novel. This will be the one occasion when I consider the 'author's cut'.

First, let's take that 'egg' issue (forgive the innuendo), because it helps to frame the editing. It might help the modern reader to know that Jim has just woken from sleep, and is lying in 'tumbled silks' in a Martian room, and that the eggs are not described as such but as 'a dozen small, white spheroids, looking like so many golf balls' (Chapter 8, p. 189 2006 edition). It is Frank (Jim's best friend) who asserts that they are eggs and thus that Willis is female (about which he teases Jim). When asked if s/he has laid eggs, Willis 'shrugged his shoulders and washed his hands of the whole matter . . . His manner seemed to say that if Jim chose to make a fuss over some eggs or whatever just happened to show up in the bed, well, that was Jim's business' (Chapter 8). Far from Alice Dalgliesh exhibiting unwonted prudery, it rather looks as if Heinlein tried to slip a description of a wet dream into the book, particularly given that Heinlein opts for gender indeterminism for Willis at the end. I have tackled this incident solely to establish that the opinion of Alice Dalgliesh, an award-winning writer herself, and a close confidante of the librarians to whom she hoped to sell, is not to be lightly dismissed.

In 'Red Planet, Blue Pencil', Jane Davitt has discussed the changes in great detail. I have taken a different approach, and simply read the 'author's cut' of Red Planet (published in 2006), comparing crucial scenes, and asking: 'what does this version say about gun ownership?' Ironically, I would argue the book sounds a little less like Heinlein's juveniles, which have a rollicking turn of speech. Instead, in the person of Dr MacRae, it has rather more of the tendentious tone of the mid-period books such as *Starship Troopers* or *Farnham's Freehold*. Almost all of the lectures on gun ownership and the right to unimpeded gun ownership come from Dr MacRae (see Chapter 2, 2006 edition). It should also be noted that MacRae is a sexist old coot who believes they are living in a frontier society where 'any man old enough to fight is a man and must be treated as such – and any girl old enough to cook and tend babies is an adult too' (2006 edition, p. 184). I am not arguing that this is not the genuine voice of Heinlein, it has the right ring, but this frontier society is highly technological and needs rather more than men who can fight and women who can tend babies. MacRae is not just pro-gun ownership, he is an early Lazarus Long who is keeping one step ahead of civilisation/bureaucracy.

> 'Sir, it is not the natural limitations of this globe that I object to; it is the pantywaist nincompoops who rule it – These ridiculous regulations offend me. That a free citizen should have to go before a committee, hat in hand, and pray for permission to bear arms – fantastic! Arm your daughter, sir, and pay no attention to petty bureaucrats'. (2006 edition, p. 16)

Before we get too excited about this, this has taken place minutes after Jim and his sister Phyllis have had to grab Jim's loaded gun from the hands of their baby brother (p. 15). In the edited version, Jim explains to his father that the gun was uncharged; in the author's cut it was loaded and it is Phyllis who reprimands Jim and tells him to unload it.

The book is focalised through Jim who as a 'just teen' appears to be going through a sexist phase in which he continually dismisses his sister and puts her down as only a girl, implying even that her desire for a gun is unladylike (p. 17). The book is one of the most sexist of Heinlein's juveniles; only *Farmer in the Sky*, the following year, is as bad. By *Starman Jones* (1953) Heinlein has increased the age of his protagonists, given them an awareness of girls and allowed them to notice girls are smart. Heinlein is a good writer: when he focalises through a thirteen-year-old, he has them as dewy-eyed and naive as a thirteen-year-old might be. He might, however, expect rather more of his adult readers, and the following is what an adult reader of the author's preferred version of *Red Planet* might notice.

For the first third of the book, every time Jim goes to draw his gun and either can't or his holster is empty, this turns out to be a very good thing.

He meets a Martian, but because of the way the Martian picks him up, 'Jim was unable to get at his gun, which was just as well' (p. 34).

The headmaster takes Willis away from Jim. Jim has 'tears streaming down his cheeks, sobs of rage and frustration shaking him'. He shakes off the comfort offered by Frank and declares 'I should have burned him. I should have burned him down where he stood.' Frank is the voice of reason: 'Want to spend the rest of your life in an asylum?' (p. 63).

When Jim finally arrives home he reacts to the news of an impending arrest: 'His right hand, almost instinctively, was hovering around the place where his holster ordinarily hung' (p. 149). Once more there is a note of relief that he does not actually have his gun with him.

Whatever Heinlein thinks about the right to own guns, he is not arguing that everyone is ready for one. Jim is a hothead. Without Frank there, or the conventions about guns, the chances are he would not have made it through the book (and his carelessness would have made his baby brother one of America's sadder gun statistics). One wonders if the definition of adulthood might be better expressed as 'boys old enough to be trusted with the baby'.

That the kids in the school have guns does nothing to prevent them being tyrannised, although I find it hard to see being made to tidy your room as tyranny, or for that matter being required to hand in their guns (p. 64). And the reasoning is sound – guns are needed outside the building, not inside it – even if the intent is not. Frank and Jim hide theirs, but they do not, when they take them, turn them on their tyrant. When Frank asks Jim about his escape plans Jim declares, 'I'll wait until daylight and just walk out. If Howe tries to stop me, so help me, I'll blast him' (p. 79). In Chapter 3 I noted that many of Heinlein's protagonists are neither the clever ones nor the decision-makers. In the work of many another author a Heinlein protagonist would figure as a sidekick. So Frank, who is a leader, is sidelined as advisor. He is forever the voice of reason: 'The idea . . . is to get away, not to stir up a gun battle' (p. 79).

Almost all the resistance, and particularly the successful resistance, we see is non-cooperation: refusal to turn in guns, Willis's resistance, the decision of the colonists to migrate in the face of guns. In Chapter 6 they are abandoned in a service station at Cynia by the driver who had given them a ride deliberately leaving them to be picked up by the cops. The agent at the station tells them that 'Clem is a peaceable man and he told me he wasn't a cop. He said he would have no part in trying to arrest two strapping, able-bodied boys, both wearing guns' (p. 93), and then notes that he is not wearing his and that they can take the station apart if they want. We can see this as an indication that the guns have been a threat but being able-bodied seems more to the point. They have still been stranded, and the guns have helped them not one bit. Jim blames the incident on his desire to eat something, but as Frank says, 'Can you imagine us shooting it out with a couple of innocent bystanders and hijacking the scooter? I can't' (p. 94). So what exactly were the guns for? They certainly don't turn them on pursuers although this would clearly be a defensive action. The very first time Jim draws his gun is to kill the water-seeker chasing after the now sick Frank (p. 119).

When the colonists do finally rebel their first action is not violence of any kind (Mr Sutton is deterred from 'taking the place apart with my two hands'). Again guns are put to one side: although the company proctors and the colonists are all armed, Mr Sutton empties his holster and offers to toss them out of the colony bare-handed (pp. 160–1). No gun threat is ever made and the act of equalisation is actually to disarm.

The colony meeting leads to a migration and the colony ends up back at Jim and Frank's school as the halfway point, and a place with beds and food. They station a guard but when a 'cop' does show up Kelly lets him go: 'I couldn't stop him without shooting' (p. 177). Only the belligerent MacRae responds that they should have winged him, and to the query that they aren't yet in a shooting war tells an anecdote in which a citizen shoots a gunslinger in the back and argues 'if you use sportsmanship on a known scamp, you put yourself at a terrible disadvantage' (p. 177). From this point MacRae is openly arguing that they should start a shooting war, capture the company offices and trigger a revolution. For him, it is the 'logic of the actions you've already taken' (p. 178). But before we rush to assume that this is Heinlein's authorial voice, note that within the page Marlow challenges MacRae as to why, if he had such a clear analysis and plan, MacRae had refused the chair when offered. MacRae shuts up. When someone loses an argument in a Heinlein novel (see Jake in 'The Number of the Beast') they lose.

Meanwhile the colony is under siege and when three people decide to surrender we discover what sensible people know: guns are no defence against a government, because governments tend to have bigger guns. Two of the three are shot while attempting to surrender; another is shot and killed later while attempting the same thing (pp. 187, 204).

The final release of the colony is down to several things: Jim sends Willis to find the Martians, MacRae sows discord among the company men, and eventually the colony launches a raid and it is this raid that makes use of guns (pp. 207–12). But even this is a damp squib; the building they are raiding turns out to have already been taken over by hostages who had talked down the guards and disengaged most of the clerks and enforcers from the company. At that point the Martians turn up and 'disappear' the two most culpable humans.

So, to summarise: in two-thirds of the book any action that involves drawing weapons is the wrong one. In the last third colony guns prove fairly useless in the face of company big guns, and the real damage is caused and victories won through sowing dissension (something Heinlein had continually advocated in 'Revolt in 2100', *The Day After Tomorrow* and will later advocate in *The Moon is a Harsh Mistress*). At no point do they ever go up against the company. There is at most one incident in this book that demonstrates guns as a weapon of freedom; elsewhere the main weapon of freedom is civil non-cooperation. In the very final scenes it becomes clear that the human predilection for guns leaves the Martians rather unamused and it is Jim's love of Willis that has stood between the humans and extinction. At the end even the Company's big guns prove irrelevant. By the end of this restored manuscript, one is left wondering how he actually thinks the power of guns can preserve liberty. This question is answered in part in *Tunnel in the Sky* (1955).

People rarely quote the lines from *Tunnel in the Sky* in the way they use *Beyond This Horizon*, *Red Planet* or *Time Enough for Love* to assert Heinlein's attitude to guns, yet *Tunnel in the Sky* is sincerely and profoundly hostile to gun-use in the context in which it is set. Although Rod is heading to a frontier planet – precisely the context in which MacRae argues for guns – everyone around him argues him out of the idea of taking a gun. His sister Helen, old enough to look after babies, cook and serve as an assault captain in the Amazons, is the first to nix the idea: 'On this tour you are the rabbit, trying to escape the fox. You aren't the fox' (Chapter 2). 'Your only purpose is to stay alive. Not to be brave, not to fight, not to dominate the wilds – but just stay breathing. One time in a hundred a gun might save your life; the other ninety-nine it will just tempt you into folly . . . That test area is going to be crawling with trigger-happy young squirts. If one shoots you, it won't matter that you have a gun, too – because you will be dead. But if you carry a gun, it makes you feel cocky; you won't take proper cover' (Chapter 2). The one boy who does take a gun – and an aggressive attack dog – turns into proof of Helen's argument before the end of Chapter 3. Look back to *Red Planet* and realise that the 'ninety-nine [times] it will just tempt you into folly' pretty much describes Jim's behaviour.

The trajectory of *Tunnel in the Sky* throughout is towards communication, collaboration and consensus: the major struggle is diplomatic. Rod loses because he has never paid much attention to politics, and wins long-term because he has proven an effective collaborator. Weapons are used for hunting and for protection against animals and in the event a brute-force fight in which Rod has to prove he is better than the other man, and loses. Rod is rescued by his team, and particularly by Caroline, a girl, specifically the girl he had declined to partner with – on account of her being a girl – at the start of the book.

So that is guns, fisticuffs and sexism routed in one go.

It isn't really fair to judge Heinlein by the material for juveniles because within them he had to meet the demands of the libraries, enforced and policed by the experienced Alice Dalgliesh, even if he did claim them himself as teaching tools, so we need to turn to some of his later books. In many of them it is simply surprising how few guns there actually are, or what happens to those people who try to use them. In *The Puppet Masters*, 'Sam' only carries one gun, and it takes Mary's three to prevent him disarming her completely. Guns are mostly used in the novel to persuade people to undress, or to kill 'carriers'. But perhaps the most startling is the realisation that the use of guns in *Stranger in a Strange Land* is mostly an indicator that someone cannot be trusted. When agent Berquist draws a gun on Jill, Smith magics him and it away (Part 1, Chapter 12). Later in *Friday* someone who draws a gun on Janet ends up very dead indeed (Chapter 3).

But surely there would be guns, and properly used guns in a novel about a revolution, such as *The Moon is a Harsh Mistress*? The answer, surprisingly, is not very many. There are around twenty mentions of guns. Most of them are held until relatively late on by the Warden and his goons (first police, later crack troops). When the revolution comes it doesn't depend on guns; most of the revolutionaries' guns are acquired by overwhelming the guards by sheer force of numbers, when 'They fought professionally and quite fearlessly – and died' (Chapter 24). Guns simply aren't very important in this society, and it would be hard to argue that they contribute either to the revolution or to the manners and mores of Luna.

The absence of guns is in part about controlling the population, but in the end the population learns some crucial things: that they are many, their jailers few; that having guns is possibly less important than taking them away from the other side; and that to win freedom they must sow dissension among their enemies and exhaust their enemies' resources (Heinlein points out that the Americans did not exactly beat the British when they won their independence – they wore them out). Furthermore that far from needing individual arms, they must militarise. If Professor Bernardo de la Paz is wrong in his militant libertarianism, it is because the infrastructure of a state (even an underground illegitimate one) is needed to construct the defensive and offensive weapons that finally win the Loonies their freedom.

However, this is to fixate on guns. What is extended is Heinlein's idea that an armed society is a polite one: it is just that here 'armed' is a combination of knives, the need to collaborate to survive and a pervasive undercurrent of violence.

It makes sense to begin with the last of these points: Luna is colonised predominantly by convicts. Although not all of these have been sentenced for antisocial violence, it is clear that just being 'subversive' is probably not enough. We are given a clear enough hint that Mannie is the descendant of an ANC terrorist ('shipped up from Joburg for armed violence and no work permit' – the lack of work permit coding him firmly as black: Chapter 1); his family is descended from a woman who was a juvenile delinquent and another who was sentenced to 're-education' (Chapter 1). Luna colonists are selected for an orientation to nonconformity of one kind or another. The society they generate depends on collaboration to survive – a man will always share oxygen with someone in need – and a strong belief in repaying debt as that oxygen may keep him from dying at another time (Chapter 11); most of all, over the matter of women, as families are constructed by women and are polyandrous. A man who cannot work and live with other men is not going to stay married.

The society on Luna is in many ways a proto-experiment of the one in *Beyond This Horizon*. The purging is taking place, the politesse is ground into the culture by the need for contrarian individualists to collaborate to survive in a physically hostile environment. The violence becomes contained by a set of customs that admires and rewards those who choose law (as the teenage gang does). There are very few true individuals because the primary unit in this society is the extended family (in a range of forms) and because Heinlein writes novels in which men want to be in families, which creates a huge incentive to politesse. In this context there is a willingness to enforce manners and mores in the absence of laws, in Mannie's words they 'are self-enforcing because are simply way things have to be, conditions being what they are.' But they are supported by an easy belief in 'elimination'. Used seven times, it is so casual that the tourist Stuart does not realise how serious it is. Mannie responds to his disbelief: 'But we figure this way: If a man is killed, either he had it coming and everybody knows it – usual case – or his friends will take care of it by eliminating man who did it. Either way, no problem. Nor many eliminations. Even set duels aren't common' (Chapter 11). And newbies, many of whom die, are dismissed as 'accident-prone'.

So the end point is a novel in which relatively few guns are deployed either in daily life or in an armed revolution: Professor La Paz is revealed as using guns in Chapter 5 in the ineffective raid on Stilyagi Hall, and Mannie kills eight in the laser-gun fight at the end of Chapter 3, but most guns are taken from guards – suggesting that the guns are not wholly useful as weapons of defence – and there is no mass arming of the citizenry. Liberty (and libertarianism) are fought for in this novel by a Bolshevik-style cabal using predominantly the weapons of economic disruption, sedition and propaganda. With Heinlein it's always a case of being a little bit more complicated than it initially seems.

The Moon is a Harsh Mistress can be understood as one of several survivalist novels: the others are *Tunnel in the Sky*, already discussed, *Farnham's Freehold* (1964) and *Time Enough for Love* (1973). *Farnham's Freehold* is the classic novel of survivalism: oft-quoted and highly controversial for its racism (discussed in the next chapter). Here I am just focusing on one element: how important are guns to either Hugh Farnham's plans, or his survival?

The novel opens with a family argument over the imminence or otherwise of a nuclear war and the advisability of preparedness for it.[4] The family guest, Barbara, has a kit in the trunk of her car

---

4 See A. L. George, *Awaiting Armageddon: How Americans Faced the Cuban Missile Crisis* (Chapel Hill, NC: U. of North Carolina Press, 2004) for how rooted Heinlein was in the episteme: although, if anything, *Farnham's Freehold* may be a little out of date in its paranoia.

that contains 'lots of things. Ten gallons of water. Food. A jeep can of gasoline. Medicines. A sleeping bag. A gun—' (Chapter 1) (as well as a shovel, clothes and a radio). But the majority of the discussion between Hugh and his son is about the bomb shelter that Farnham regards as the equivalent of an insurance policy on his car. The chapter ends with the call on the radio to take shelter. Chapter 2 takes place in the shelter and contains the scene in which Duke challenges his father and Hugh gets Joseph to pull a gun on him, 'a Thompson sub-machine gun'. The incident ends with Hugh getting Joseph to stow the tommy gun. Hugh hands his automatic pistol to Duke; 'His son put the pistol in a pocket'. Chapter 3 takes place in the shelter, and concludes with Karen and Barbara heading out first. At the start of Chapter 4 Hugh declares to Joe, 'I'm going out. Get me a forty-five and a belt. I shouldn't have let those girls go out unarmed.'

What they find is a wild paradise. They are all armed except Grace, but Hugh decides the ground is open, there is no fear of bears, and he settles his rifle on the ground while he relaxes and has a smoke. In Chapter 4 Duke raises his rifle to drop a deer. In Chapter 5 Barbara lists the guns: two 'lovely ladies' guns, .22 magnum rimfire with telescopic sights', and Duke's bear rifle.

They spend the rest of the chapter settling in and at the end of the chapter Duke shoots his first deer ... with an arrow. It's an odd switch. Even given the desire to conserve ammunition this immediately reframes the use of guns: if bow and arrow are for hunting, then the purpose of guns can only be for defence. So how well does that work? Well, we have already noted that the gun is used to intimidate Duke: it could be an incident of defence, but Joe could just as easily have brought Duke down from behind physically. Duke wasn't looking in that direction.

In Chapter 8 a gun is used by Barbara to signal that Karen is going into labour – three shots, three wasted bullets. In Chapter 10 the guns and ammo are split by Hugh and Duke when Duke decides to head off with his mother; and the cavalry arrive, in the form of 'a dark shape proportioned like a domino' flying overhead. When four of them are overhead Duke cries out 'Dad! For God's sake, can't you get at your gun?' Hugh is wearing his .45, a gun whose only role is to shoot people, but he responds, 'I shan't try' ... If we hold still, we may live longer'. Within a page the rifle has been taken and although Hugh seems to still have his .45, he does not use it. Duke is furious. 'Aren't you even going to try to fight? Where's the crap you used to spout about how you were a free man and planned to stay free?' Hugh reasonably points out that 'You start anything and you'll get us all killed'. But it does not alter the fact that Duke is correct: Hugh's rhetoric has not held up to the moment, and his guns have provided no redress.

If we fast-forward to the end of the novel, to Chapter 18 and to Hugh's escape, we can see here that guns also play little part. Hugh has a knife to aid in his escape, and when he is attacked with a whip, 'kicked the whip hand so fast that the whip flew aside as he closed. Then this – and that! – and sure enough! The man's neck was broken, just as the book said it would be'. But Hugh is still brought down: 'He never saw the whip that got him' (Chapter 19). The escape attempt fails.

It is thus a great irony that the next time Hugh sees a gun is when his captor decides to send him back into the past and returns to him all his belongings, which includes his .45 automatic pistol (end of Chapter 20). The gun he collects when they return to the past is the gun Barbara carried in her car – too far away to ever have been of any use. Given that there are many ways Duke could have been threatened, no gun in *Farnham's Freehold* is ever truly useful.

The one clear incident that I can find in all of Heinlein's books which demonstrates the use of guns as a weapon of defence is in 'The Tale of the Adopted Daughter', in *Time Enough for Love*. On his frontier world,

Lazarus Long carries his blaster under his kilt, although we never see it used. He does use a needle gun to bring down a 'dragon' that attacks his wagon, and continues to use it all summer in this fashion, although gradually aware of running out of power – it takes seven years to build the mill that will supply it. In Chapter 12 a real threat finally arrives: a wagon, containing a man and his two grown sons. The make-up of the family makes it clear these are not pioneers. 'The mounted two were carrying guns at their belts – reasonable in loper country. I had a needle gun in sight myself, as well as a belt knife.' From the first he feels uneasy: he tells them to come to supper in an hour, ostensibly to give Dora a chance to prepare, but really to make sure they are prepared. When they arrive he demands they drop their guns: 'gentlemen don't wear guns when they dine with a lady. Drop them here or put them in your wagon.' They do and Lazarus starts to think where their second guns would be. He is right to worry. One of the men kicks the dog who is checking him out. Lazarus refuses to send the dog out. After dinner, the threats begin with wrestling banter, then sexual threats. The older man pulls his second gun.

> From the kitchen Dora shot the gun out of his hand just as a knife suddenly grew in Dan's neck. Lazarus shot Montgomery carefully in the leg, then even more carefully shot Darby – as Lady Macbeth was at his throat.

When it is over Long finishes off Montgomery with the knife.

It is an absolutely clear scene of self-defence. Dora shoots to disarm, but Long uses a knife to kill the second man, and the third is essentially killed by the dog. The gun has at best been a means of distracting the men, then of execution; in refusing the men entry to the house while they carry guns, Long has placed a clear paradigm around where guns may or may not be carried. Interestingly, this is not the first time: in that gun-heavy novel *Starship Troopers* a different restraint is suggested. Heinlein creates a clear division between the right time not only to use arms but to have them in one's possession, and the wrong time. Johnny Rico and his comrades learn that they are not being taught to use dangerous weapons, they are being taught to be dangerous (Chapter 5); and as a corollary, in Chapter 8, when the boys are attacked in Seattle and put their attackers in hospital, they realise how much more serious it could all have been had they been armed. There is a time and a place to carry weapons.

Heinlein's belief in the right to bear arms never wavered, but his hopes and fears for society did. In all of the texts considered prior to the 1970s, Heinlein demonstrated his belief that the world and the humans in it were getting better. Heinlein's comfort with gun ownership was strongly linked to his faith in people and in Americans in particular. From the 1970s, Heinlein, like many Americans, lost that faith and although we see flashes of it in all the later books, the kind of Americans he believed in and wanted to see are almost always portrayed as the Remnants, whether the family who save Alex and Margrethe in *Job* (who actually turn out to be Satan and friends) or Janet et al in *Friday*. The key text in which we first see this emerge is *I Will Fear No Evil*, where gun violence as a modern trope first makes its appearance in Heinlein's work.

The sense in the 1970s that Heinlein was moving to the right has been discussed extensively by H. Bruce Franklin who points out what many of us now recognise, that Heinlein represented a realignment of American politics that led to the election of Ronald Reagan and the rise of the 'moral majority'. The first Heinlein supported, the second would have horrified him. Heinlein never stopped being a radical liberal; he just changed his mind about the party that best represented that. But the background story to *I Will Fear No Evil* (and to an extent that also of *Friday*) shows us the world he saw.

I Will Fear No Evil is roughly contemporaneous with Samuel R. Delany's *Dhalgren* and the picture of America it constructs is very similar. I'm noting this because from this distance it is too easy to dismiss the doom and gloom in this novel and in *Friday* as right-wing rhetoric. America in the 1970s was scared. The complacency of the 1950s had been rocked, the promises of the 1960s had ended with the blood and violence of assassination and riot. The collapse of American heavy industry was destroying the corporate utopias of single-industry towns, and ripping the heart out of many cities. Heinlein is not right-wing because he notes this, but because of how he reacted to it. Where Delany recognised the cultural growth within the cities, Heinlein as we shall see locked himself and his characters away from it. The 'donut effect' was well observed: downtown Detroit, New York and Los Angeles were all seen as no-go areas. The novel is studded with interludes about the decline of American society and the collapse of the world order.

I Will Fear No Evil starts at the bedside of Johann Sebastian Bach Smith. It is after this scene that we see the world of the novel, and it is a violent one. Jake Salomon escorts Eunice to his car, 'waved the guards aside ... Shotgun locked them in, got in by the driver-guard and locked that compartment.' We learn her husband doesn't want her riding in public lifts and Salomon offers to send her to the door with a guard. When Salomon discovers that Eunice has cut through an 'Abandoned Area' he is horrified. Eunice is not attacked on that occasion but later, when she goes out on a blood donor call (she is a rare blood group) she is attacked. 'Happened when I came out. This frog tried to hop me between parked cars. Don't know whether he was after my purse. Or me. Didn't wait to find out ...' She hits him with 'A stun bomb in his face with my left hand as I zapped with my right and didn't wait to see if he was dead' (Chapter 2).

But neither Eunice's armaments nor the guards Salomon provides protect her when she uses the passenger elevator to travel nineteen floors to the garage, in a hurry to make a blood donation. The novel has little else to say about guns and the use of guns, but by this point my argument must be evident.

Disability

If Heinlein's actual use of guns in his work does not quite create the societies we might expect, his portrayal of disability reinforces the sense that he is absolutely serious that if society is to provide for people's needs, everyone must contribute. One of the areas where Heinlein's notion of civic society becomes so clear is in the area of disability. Heinlein argues throughout his work that individuals must have a clear sense of themselves as individuated people in order to have a sense of esteem and hence honour. In most of his early writing his disabled characters are clearly understood along this spectrum, and exist within a medicalised model of disability, in which their disability is an individual failing which affects their individual character and in turn affects the worlds they build. In 'The Roads Must Roll', for example, the manager with mental-health problems is a threat to the good ordering of society, which is reduced by forcing him to a mental breakdown. In 'Waldo', Waldo's myasthenia gravis forces him to build a world for himself which then advantages the world he leaves behind but also poisons his character. Crucially, he is the one who generates his own aids; there is little sense of the responsibility of a world to this sick child. In 'Requiem', Harriman is afflicted with that disability known as old age, and the story is very much about his own decision to overcome this barrier to the thing he wants to do. In 'The Green Hills of Earth', Rhysling is barred from space work by his blindness. His society yields no quarter and it is his burden to carry and overcome.

Yet even in these early stories there are some hints of a wider social model. In 'The Green Hills of Earth', although Rhysling is excluded from space, we see his society shift over to make room for him, and in both this story and in 'Waldo' one argument within the stories is that both characters still have much to contribute, and thus are not excluded from Heinlein's understanding of civic society.

The group quite obviously excluded from civic society are the Muties in *Orphans of the Sky* and the 'defectives' in *Methuselah's Children*. The issue of reproduction and contribution to the genes of the species are separated in Heinlein's work from the issue of the utility of the individual and contribution to the societal development of the species. Waldo is thus 'crippled' less by his disease and to a far greater extent by his contempt for humanity. Whether the Muties, who function far better at low gravity than do the unmated humans, are socially disabled is of course a question taken up in the 1990s by Lois McMaster Bujold, whose Quaddies live in an environment in which bipedal humans are socially disabled.

The story in which this notion is clearest is Heinlein's 1939 'Misfit'. Heinlein's Andrew Libby is a misfit because of his education (his gender identity is expressed much later in Heinlein's oeuvre, so we need to be careful not to retrofit) and also when seen through modern eyes, probably because he has at least mild Asperger's. Even without any modern labels however he is also a savant. In this very early story Heinlein has, without presumably realising this, adopted the social model of what a disability is wholesale: a disability is an issue that renders it difficult to participate in society as society is constructed. Hence Andrew Libby is disabled. But the entire direction of the story is that it is the duty of the Civilian Conservation Corps to find space for everyone, and to find a way in which everyone can contribute and through contribution achieve self-integration.

This idea reappears in both *Space Cadet*, where Commander

Arkwright, of the Academy at Terra Base, is blind (and has been blinded) and this impairs him not at all in his chosen function, and in *Starship Troopers*, where it is made clear in the recruitment scene when a paraplegic is inducted that no one can be turned away from Service who wishes to serve. It is the individual's right to achieve citizenship and the organisation's duty to ensure that they have the chance – hence as long as one flunks mobile infantry training honourably (lack of aptitude or health) another role will be found. In the last part of the novel, all of the teachers in officer training are veterans with one injury or another, few with all their limbs. None are 'disabled' in the context of their lives.

Of course some of this is prosthetics: Mannie in *The Moon is a Harsh Mistress* has an arm missing but is content with his array of prosthetic arms which give him greater facilities than his own hand did. What prevents this being the blasé optimism of an able-bodied writer is that there is one crucial scene where Mannie is genuinely impaired. On the flight to Earth, someone carelessly leaves Mannie's prosthetic arm strapped to a bulkhead out of reach. He has to free himself from his restraints with only one hand: in this context he is, we remember, impaired not by the loss of the hand but by the structure of the environment. Similarly, Richard's amputation hampers him in *The Cat Who Walks Through Walls*. His inability to don a space suit nearly gets them all killed because it means he cannot drive; so too does his secondary impairment, the inability to accept a grafted limb or to be able to regenerate that limb with current technologies.

Mannie is genuinely disabled by the Earth environment, as all Loonies are: the gravity is too high, his lungs cannot cope with the air, he is likely to catch almost anything going, and worse he is treated as if he is mentally retarded as well. It is a classic case of othering the foreigner, which is particularly interesting because Mannie appears to have one disability which no one ever comments on while he is on the Moon, but which may feed into this: Mannie has some kind of speech impediment or learning difficulty. Assuming he reports the syntax of those around him accurately it is not just a matter of a local pidgin: Mannie speaks in a disjointed and damaged fashion. This hinders his relations with the world and with the computer Mike not one whit.

Not all representations of disability are this direct. Heinlein's representation of gender transition moves from a scenario which constructs it as a disability or illness in 'Year of the Jackpot' (1952), through an intense but socially and medically constructed tragedy in '"All You Zombies—"', to a medical challenge in *I Will Fear No Evil*, and eventually takes it out of the category completely for Andrew Jackson Libby Long who is reincarnated as Elizabeth Long in *'The Number of the Beast'*. We will discuss this further in a later chapter.

7

Racism, Anti-Racism and the Construction of Civic Society

Heinlein has a dual reputation as both an anti-racist, and a racist. I intend to begin from the premise that both are true: that Heinlein is manifestly and provably and vociferously anti-racist, and that the construction of his anti-racism and very strong opposition to *colour prejudice*, and how he understood that, is the root of his racism. Consequently, this section will build up by looking at Heinlein's strengths and draw increasing attention to the racism and *why* the racism. This is not to excuse the issues but to contextualise them.

How Many Non-White Characters Does Heinlein Have?

The subtitle and the terminology of this section has been chosen carefully, after a lot of thought, for two reasons. One of the contentions of this chapter will be that there is only one African American character of significance in all of Heinlein's writings, that there are reasons for this, and that therefore the construction of 'black' is in itself not appropriate for this section. The second is that in the time Heinlein was writing, the label 'white' shifted in the United States.[1] So, for the purpose of this book, an Irish surname before the election of John F. Kennedy will indicate non-white. A Jewish name will be handled as firmly non-white in the same period, and will be understood as indicative of diversity by the 1970s, and irrelevant by the 1980s. This is something Heinlein himself understands. Jake Salomon in *I Will Fear No Evil* is the Judge's ex-teacher, but he was not in the same fraternity: 'I had no taste for being the exhibit Jew in a chapter that did not want its charter lifted' (Chapter 13). The discrimination is there in the past; it's barely relevant in the present-future. A Latino name will be considered non-white throughout, as will an Asian name (both North and South Asian). Heinlein's last novel is *To Sail Beyond the Sunset* in 1987 and there is little shifting of ethnic identity in the USA between 1980 and 1990.

Second, with the exception of the very first text, this chapter focuses on the novels, although it is often the short stories that have the clearest statement of anti-racism: these tend to be 'race neutral' within a paradigm of 'not mentioning it probably means white' (the same is true of *Beyond This Horizon* (Chapter 14), in which the whiteness of most of the characters is testified to when John Darlington Smith assumes everyone he is speaking with is white). This position changes markedly later on. The exception that I want to begin with is 'The Devil Makes the Law', published in *Unknown* in 1940. This story is worth considering for a number of reasons: as already mentioned it stands outside the white norm of Heinlein's short stories, but it also has the distinction of having a non-white

---

1   See Noel Ignatiev, *How the Irish Became White* (London and New York: Routledge, 1995).

character who is 'raced', that is, he is given culture and behaviour to go with his skin colour.

In this story Archie and his friend Jedson look around for magical consultants to help them fight back against a magical monopoly. They find the elderly and powerful witch, Mrs Jennings, and also a South African professor, Dr Worthington. Dr Worthington is a witch smeller. We meet him first on the phone: "'Speaking', answered a cultured British voice with a hint of Oxford in it.' But when he turns up he 'was as black as craftsman's ink.' Archie, framed throughout as a good man, 'tried not to show my surprise. I hope I did not, for I have an utter horror of showing that kind of rudeness. There was no reason why the man should not be a Negro. I simply had not been expecting it.' Worthington begins his rituals and then:

> The urbane Dr Worthington was gone. In his place was an African personage who stood over six feet tall in his bare black feet, and whose enormous arched chest was overlaid with thick, sleek muscles of polished obsidian. He was dressed in a loin skin of leopard and carried certain accoutrements notably a pouch, which hung at his waist.
>
> But it was not his equipment that held me ... It was the expression – humorless, implacable, filled with a dignity and strength which must be felt to be appreciated.

Later,

> When he returned to his place in the middle of the room he dropped to all fours and commenced to cast around with his nose like a hunting dog trying to pick up a scent. He ran back and forth, snuffling and whining, exactly like a pack leader worried by mixed trails.

One could never stage this scene: the 'construction of the primitive', the depiction of a human being behaving like a dog. Archie's admiring words cannot erase this 'respectful' racism. However, Archie's accompanying thoughts are in some ways far more significant in understanding what comes next in Heinlein's work.

Dr Worthington is an Oxford-educated African. His accent gives him authority over the mid-westerner, his degrees mark his superiority of education, his behaviour gives him cultural authenticity. The African American has none of these things. Archie muses:

> We white men in this country are inclined to underestimate the black man – I know I do – because we see him out of his cultural matrix. Those we know have had their own culture wrenched from them some generations back and a servile pseudo culture imposed on them by force.

This is Stanley Elkin's thesis, the idea of the Sambo mentality that mistook the survival mechanisms of slavery and Jim Crow for character failings, which I will explore later.

Averse therefore to depicting African Americans as he thinks they are, Heinlein mostly avoids it. Only Mr Alfred MacNeil and his great-niece in *Time for the Stars* are clearly African American, and 'Uncle Alf' is clearly coded as undereducated (although hungry for education) and servile, with 'the saintliness that old people get when they don't turn sour and self-centred' (Chapter 6). Instead, as we shall see, Heinlein references and includes Africans, such as Mr Kiku in *The Star Beast*, or opts for mixed race as in *Friday*, a choice that is more significant for white Americans for whom Friday, white in appearance, spectacularly fails the 'one-drop' rule.[2]

---

2   See Pew Social Trends, Chapter 1: Race and Multiracial Americans in the U.S. Census. Online. 2015

'The Devil Makes the Law' is a pre-war text. It is culturally specific and subscribes to a model of ethnicity that is diverse and various but reliant on outsiders, not Americans. There are no visible non-white characters in the remainder of the pre-war short stories and it is only after the war, and after Heinlein severed his relationship with Campbell, that the 'diverse' Heinlein emerges. But his model of diversity is straight from Norman Rockwell's paintings 'The Four Freedoms'. This is, I think, deliberate, and nowhere more so than in the first of his post-war novels, intended for children (not teens), *Rocket Ship Galileo*. In this book Ross Jenkins is an American WASP; Art Mueller has an American mother but his father was a refugee and spent time in a concentration camp; Maurice/Morrie Abrams is from a large Jewish family. But there is no other evidence of any of the other boys' ethnicity. Morrie is not, as far as I can tell, kosher.

This kind of wartime-movie casting diversity runs through the juveniles. In *Space Cadet*, Sabatello, Dynkowski, Lopes, Gomez, Brunn and Novak all serve in bit parts and are admired by mid-westerner Matt Dodson, his friend Jarman, who is from Texas and who is automatically called 'Tex' (which incidentally codes him white) by Matt without any introduction or permission, Oscar Jensen from Venus and Pete Armand from Ganymede via France. The most significant person in this backdrop is probably Lieutenant Wong, who is not only Chinese but one of the senior officers to whom they must defer. We also know this is not a Christocentric world. When in Chapter 5 Tex is told off for eating his dessert with his hands we are told that the manners have to suit everyone, and a reference is made to Muslim boys from homes where it is usual to eat with your hands.

We see this kind of wartime diversity in *Starman Jones* and in *Time of the Stars*; it is similarly visible in *The Day After Tomorrow*, a novel originally commissioned by John W. Campbell. In most ways it is Campbell's racism rather than Heinlein's that is on display: America is invaded by 'Pan Asians' or 'Orientals' or 'Asiatics' who overrun and commit terrible atrocities. The novel is also riddled with class prejudice towards gullible peasants of all nations and races (a thread that we can also see in '"If This Goes On—"' and which is still present, if a great deal more subtly, in *Job* in 1984). But the Americans who stand up to the invasion are a very similar mix to that in *Space Cadet*, with the notable inclusion of Franklin Delano Mitsui, a biracial man who is regarded by the invaders as a symbol of decadence. He dies saving his colleagues but significantly is killed by a ray designed for Orientals, rather than one for white men, thus proving that his Asian nature dominates his blood.

In two of the juveniles, diversity is deepened within the novel's landscape. In *Between Planets* and *Farmer in the Sky*, Heinlein had demonstrated his belief in a frontier diversity, expressed primarily in the presence of Germans. In *Between Planets* and *The Star Beast* he tried to imagine an intercultural future for his juvenile readers. In Chapter 8 of *Between Planets* Don washes up on Venus and falls in with the Chinese community – a banker gives him a credit when he is hungry and tells him to pay it forward; he is picked up by a Chinese dockworker who may well be a spy trying to steal his ring, and ends up washing dishes in a local Cantonese restaurant. There is more than one Chinese person in this book, and as a result Heinlein is able to avoid falling into stereotypes: no one person is expected to represent the race. Tellingly, Heinlein also presents the young Venus-born Chinese as no different from their Anglo counterparts – they laugh at the idea of going home: 'Venus was home.'

One issue that the mode of representing diversity raises is how we know someone is coded white beyond the fact of surnames and the lack of other identifying marks – which codes the reader as much as the other. In *Between Planets* Don Harvey is unmarked and coded white by never being given an ethnic heritage, other than that at stake in the novel – what it means to be born to parents from different planets. He had been born in space and awarded an open nationality. He is also coded white by the coding of others as not-white.

In *Red Planet* the colonists' names are almost all coded English, German, Irish or Scottish American: Marlow, Steubben, Kelly and Macrae, to give just four. Father Cleary and Frank Kelly and his father suggest there are Irish Catholics on Mars. There is one Montez. There are 'Eskimo', employed to keep the summer quarters in the winter, but many African Americans have the English, German, Irish, Scottish, Jewish names of slave owners and any one of the colonists could be black. None of the colonists is described in terms of their looks, not even the annoying Mrs Pottle or the apoplectic headmaster Mr Howe, nor even Jim's mother and sister, which is relatively unusual, since often women are othered precisely by being the ones described physically. Yet the only physical descriptions are of Willis and the other Martians. The imagery has to be that we raise ourselves. This is true throughout the juveniles with only a very few exceptions, of which one is Podkayne in *Podkayne of Mars* where her colour and that of other Martians shapes the response of other characters.

One of the few clear mentions of appearance is of Hazel Stone's 'thick red hair' in Chapter 1 of *The Rolling Stone.* However, when redheads appear it is not necessarily, as it would be in the UK, an indicator of ethnicity.[3] Heinlein just had a thing for redheads, of either sex. However the mention of 'red Irish' in Friday's genes in the much later novel, suggests it does have ethnic significance here. Ellie in *Starman Jones* is 'no beauty' (Chapter 7) but there is

3   Red hair tends to indicate either Celtic or Jewish ancestry. On a hunch I wondered about Virginia Gerstenfeld. I am indebted to Estelle Woifers for checking the migrant records and confirming that Virginia was descended from Jewish immigrants on her father's side.

no description. Nor is there a description of Betty Sorenson in *The Star Beast*, although there are a number of descriptions of her make-up. Interestingly, the African Mr Kiku in *The Star Beast* is also not described on our first meeting, although the alien Dr Ftaeml is described in great detail in Chapter 6.

Because few people are ever really described, Heinlein – presumably to evade a censorship aimed at ensuring that librarians across the country would buy the books – instead uses Easter eggs to plant information. One of the sneakiest, because it uses stereotypes and bigotry to do so, is in *Space Cadet*. The boys meet Captain Yancey, the captain of their first ship: 'the door in front of them suddenly opened and they found themselves facing the commanding officer. He was tall, wide-shouldered, and flat-hipped, and so handsome that he looked like a television star playing Patrol officer' (Chapter 11). Four pages later we discover that 'the Old Man likes watermelons' and when pansies appear on the table we are told on the same page that 'Captain Yancey smiled broadly.' Both characteristics are strongly linked with African Americans in US racialised discourse where they are meant to be insulting (the smiling indicates stupidity to many, although primatologists would comfortably label it appeasement). And both are a clear pointer that Captain Yancey, a man handsome enough to be a TV star, is black. It is a very neat sneak past the white supremacist censors of the Southern library systems, matched only by the mention of a Booker T. W. Jones, Food Technician, who is buried on the Mars of *Stranger in a Strange Land*, and of whom Valentine Michael Smith declares 'the Old Ones have cherished him' (Chapter 24).

From *Tunnel in the Sky*, Heinlein's approach began to change and we begin to see characters more clearly coded black/not-white and, more importantly, brought into the foreground. The first such character I want to consider is Rod Walker in *Tunnel in the Sky*. How do we know Rod Walker is 'not white'? We cannot use Rod's religion as evidence, as we are clearly told in Chapter 2 that the family are converts to Monism which 'swept out of Persia', and culturally, like all Heinlein characters he is default 'whitebread American' (Walton, 'Beware of stobor!', 2011). The first hint is that he does not wish to team with Johann Braun: 'But Rod did not trust him, nor did he think that Braun would want him'. This is 1955. Even friendships across the colour line were problematic, and Johann Braun has a German name and a cold face and does not want him, and his dog is called Thor (Chapters 1 and 3), as strong a hint of white supremacism as Heinlein can give. The second hint is that Rod's second choice is 'That big Zulu girl, Caroline something-unpronounceable' because in 1950s America, romance was strictly along colour lines. But he decided not to team with a girl: 'girls were likely to mistake a cold business deal for a romantic gambit' (Chapter 1). There is no one else. In 1955 (and even now) assertive dating in the US meant same-colour dating. There is one exception to that: Bob Baxter pairs (in both senses) with Carmen Garcia, but they are planning to be missionaries and later turn out to be Quakers so they too are participating in assertive mating.

As usual Heinlein describes very few people but when Rod and Jack are discussing whom they might have seen, Jack describes someone with 'light hair, pink skin' (Chapter 6). There is no white default. When Rod is scarred, his scars are described as being long and white: more like keloids than the long red scars on white skin. Twice also, we are told that there is a family resemblance: Rod reminds Caroline of her little brother – maybe she means looks, maybe she means character (Chapter 11) – but in Chapter 16 Rod tells his sister Helen quite clearly that Caroline 'looks a bit like you'. A twenty-first-century writer might well see likeness across colour lines, but it is inconceivable that a 1950s reader would.

In the end, most of the students have paired up, but not Rod. At the conclusion to *Tunnel in the Sky* Rod Walker finds himself dealing with a TV crew and discovers that his story is about to be made over for the public. Crucially for this section, he is about to be Othered: square dances reduced to 'primitive' dancing, filmed with and without clothing; the constitution dismissed; his group 'reduced' to illiteracy, and to add insult to injury, they add face paint to his skin, 'a little war paint' (Chapter 15). If you want 'savages' you have to erase anything that looks like 'civilisation.'

Double Star is perhaps the novel with one of the clearest statements of how Heinlein understands the root of prejudice. Smythe thinks of himself as not racist: 'I didn't care what a man's colour, race, religion was' (Chapter 1). But later we will hear him in his own mind think of a man as a mulatto so we know that actually he does care. Heinlein does not use the term in any other text; it is specific to Smythe's mindset. There are relatively few non-white-indicating names (perhaps Pateel, equerry to Emperor Willem) and we know that Bonforte is distinctly darker than Smythe. But Smythe is deeply prejudiced towards Martians. 'Men were men, whereas Martians were things. They weren't even animals to my ways of thinking . . . Permitting them in restaurants and bars used by men struck me as outrageous' (Chapter 1). But Heinlein undermines his point when he frames this not as institutionalised prejudice but as phobia. When Smythe is shown a series of vids of Bonforte he is surprised by the sudden appearance of Martians and panics: 'I had been so deep inside the picture that I could actually feel them myself – and the stink was unbearable' (Chapter 3). He is treated by hypnosis and ever after feels warm and cuddly towards Martians. If only all colour prejudice was dealt with as easily.

It is in Bonforte's mouth that Heinlein places the illogicality not of racism per se, but of the cockeyed-ness of imperialism; the strange idea that we should fear Martian invasion while colonising their planet (Chapter 6), that humans must 'never again make the mistakes that the white sub race had made in Africa and Asia' (Chapter 7) and perhaps most important that:

'Government of human beings, by human beings, and for human beings', is no more than an updating of the immortal words of Lincoln. But while the voice is the voice of Abraham, the hand is the hand of the Ku Klux Klan. The true meaning of that innocent-seeming motto is 'Government of all races everywhere, by human beings alone, for the profit of a privileged few'. But, my opponent protests, we have a God-Given mandate to spread enlightenment through the stars, dispensing our own brand of Civilisation to the savages. This is the Uncle Remus school of sociology – the good dahkies singin' spirituals and Ole Massa lubbin' every one of dem! It is a beautiful picture but the frame is too small; it fails to show the whip, the slave block – and the counting house! (Chapter 7)

There is never any question which side Heinlein stands on the debate, as we shall see in a minute, but we also need to be aware of the lack of nuance and sensitivity to the oxygen he breathes. Heinlein understands and opposes enslavement and colour prejudice, but he does not really see that racism has a wider infrastructure. He does not understand what we now frame as systemic racism.

There are few colour indicators in *Citizen of the Galaxy*. Thorby Baslim is not described even when on the slave block, and not even when he is being scrubbed, but in Chapter 17 we will be told that his cousin Leda has blue eyes. The Free Traders are of Finnish descent (judging by their language) and have a Romany lifestyle. The description of the slave ship matches those of the Middle Passage (Leonard, *'Farnham's Freehold*: A Narrative Enslaved', 2005). The slave culture in which the child Thorby winds up is faintly Islamic (in other texts, notably *Stranger in a Strange Land*, Heinlein is very pro-Islam); the planet is Jubbulpore and the Nine Worlds are ruled by the Great Sargon but slavery, we are told, is endemic across the galaxy and resorted to by many cultures: slavery is natural, the fight against it, civilised. As Thorby's own family turn out to be at the top of the slaving pyramid Heinlein makes his point.

The next novels in which there are clues for colour are *Starship Troopers* and *Podkayne of Mars*. Here, Heinlein gets a lot more explicit. *Starship Troopers* is the epitome of the diversity-in-time-of-war novel. I count fifty-seven individual names in *Starship Troopers*, including that of Johnny Rico, and they include French, German, Spanish, Mexican, Japanese, Korean, Polish, Czech, at least two possible Jews, and famously, a Finno-Turk, Sergeant Jelal (see appendix for the roll-call).

However it is far less clear that many of these soldiers have what we might call a colour identity. Only a few troopers carry 'markers' of race: Shujumi, one of the trainee troopers at Camp Arthur is a martial arts and dirty fighter specialist; Breckinridge talks in Southern African American 'dialect' (by which I mean you can never place it by state, only by colour); we are told Corporal Mahmoud is brown, but the information on Carmencita Ibanez is left until very late in Chapter 12 when she visits Johnny Rico, and even then it is only hints, such as 'she of the dark eyes', 'she waved her long black lashes at him' and we discover she once had a 'mane of thick wavy hair', 'blue-black hair'. Her ethnic identity is reinforced but otherwise absent. Johnny Rico's own identity is given only three points of acknowledgement: in his father's name; in the letter from his mother in which he is called Juanito; and right at the very end in which he uses a phrase from his mother tongue and explains it to Bernie (Bernardo) Montez as Tagalog, the language of the Philippines. Although this kind of name-check diversity has been evident in many of the juveniles, in *Starship Troopers* ethnicity is undercut even more by the construction of the story. The key to the operation of the troopers is their loyalty to each other and to achieve this, all other identities are subsumed; thus race may be indicated but it must be neutralised throughout for the right ordering of the infantry.

Of the novels written between 1947 and 1963 it is noticeable that the juveniles use the Norman Rockwell approach and that the novels written for the adult market are much more race-normalised. There is also a greater tendency to give brief colour-coding: Jubal Harshaw's secretaries for example are Anne (blonde), Miriam (red-headed) and Dorcas (dark) (Part 2, Chapter 10).[4] Miriam will later marry Dr 'Stinky' Mahmoud and change her name to Maryam; her daughter will be Fatima Michelle. Star in *Glory Road* is blonde and 'a tawny toast colour all over without a hint of a bikini mark' which can be read either as a full tan, or natural colour; her 'lips were full and her mouth rather wide'; and her eyes 'so deep a blue that they were dark, darker than my own eyes'. Star is of course an alien, but I think it fair to note not necessarily a white alien; rather, she is coded as acceptably exotic to a man who has served in Asia.

One further issue is the hostility to Asian population expansion that we see as virulent in *The Day After Tomorrow* and elsewhere in novels such as *Tunnel in the Sky*. In Chapter 1 of that book Rod goes to watch the emigrants setting off to new planets. When he sees the Asians go through gate five it is through a pen 'packed with humanity'. They 'poured out of nowhere ... hurried like cattle between the two fences'. An old 'coolie' is prodded so hard by the 'Mongol guards' that he falls and loses all his possessions that had been carried 'in two bundles supported from a pole balanced on his right shoulder'. Like 'most of the torrent [they] had only that which they could carry'. The emigration is to relieve the pressure

4   The names are all saints' names, they are not all slim, and the description is clearly a joke. Miriam of course is a very common Jewish name, so combined with the red hair it may be a hint that she is Jewish, but it's a stretch. Thornton and Patterson, in 'Jubal and the Secretaries', think the women are the Triple Goddess with Jubal as Jehovah.

of the Australasian Republic, a nation formed when the Australians were deported to New Zealand. In contrast at gate four: 'This was no poverty-stricken band of refugees chivvied along by police; here each family had its own wagon. The draft animals were Morgans and lordly Clydesdales ... Dogs trotted between wheels, wagons were piled high with household goods ...' The contrast is sharp, but there is a note of pity there. In Chapter 2, Heinlein mourns the Malthusian pre-contraception population explosion more generally. In the future he has created, the only route out of it is emigration to another planet. Asians are merely caught in the trap before other polities. There is no question it is racism, but the hostility to the people that we saw in *The Day After Tomorrow* is fading, and one of the students with whom Rod Walker will eventually join up is named Margery Chung. The fear of 'the Asiatic' disappears from later Heinlein's books.

But in 1964 we have a run of three novels written for the adult market with significant actors of colour. The first of course is *Farnham's Freehold* in which Joseph, the houseboy, becomes a major player in a future world run by dark-complexioned people I would tentatively suggest (from both names and physical features) are intended to be read as North Africans. Joseph has a significant role to play, despite his lack of a last name – an omission which is itself an indication of colour in the USA – and carries much of the moral imperative of the novel.

The first novel for the adult market in which a protagonist is inarguably not white is *The Moon is a Harsh Mistress*. Mannie is the descendant of African, Irish and Spanish/Hispanic or Latino migrants: his full name is Manuel Garcia O'Kelly.

My one grandfather was shipped up from Joburg for armed violence and no work permit, other got transported for subversive after Wet Firecracker War. Maternal grandmother claimed she came up in bride ship – but I've seen records; she was a Peace Corps enrollee (involuntary) which means what you think: juvenile delinquency female type. (Chapter 1)

There are at least three strong hints there that three of Mannie's ancestors were not white. For other characters, there are some classic Heinlein hints. Professor de la Paz may be Jewish: "'That pink salmon,' Prof answered, pointing at ham' (although it's also possible he is Catholic and avoiding fish for the day), as well as a statement that he is 'semi-vegetarian', which is a bit confusing (Chapter 5). In general colour is much more clearly stated in this novel. 'Shorty [Mkrum] was a big black fellow two metres tall, sent up to the Rock for murder, and sweetest, most helpful man I've ever worked with' (Chapter 2). Wyoming Knott is described on first meeting through Mannie's eyes as 'all curves and as blonde as Shorty was black. I decided she must be transportee since colours rarely stay that clear past first generation.' In one swoop Heinlein tells us the basic colouration on Luna. Isiah Lavender III suggests that this reframes the colonists' situation as those of sharecroppers (*Race in American Science Fiction*, 2011, p. 224), and delivers in the novel a challenge to Jim Crow arguments that black people cannot be self-governing.

When they need to hide Wyoming, they dye her skin sepia and her hair black (Chapter 3). 'She didn't look Afro – but not European either. Seemed some mixed breed, and therefore more a Loonie' (Chapter 3). Later, a more professional job will leave her looking 'Tamil, a touch of Angola, German' (Chapter 6). The scene has obvious overtones of minstrelsy and would be problematic on the screen. Lavender thinks it overturns the minstrelsy narrative and replaces it with one of organised revolution, but this of course would hark back to the unpleasantly blacked-up actors in the Senate house in the silent film *The Birth of a Nation* (1915). It is far from reassuring or challenging. More likely

Heinlein was thinking of John Howard Griffin's experiment in his book *Black Like Me* (1961).

But this does not mean Luna is homogenous: the city we see seems to be mainly Anglo-Afro-European, but Wyoming is from Hong Kong Luna where the mix seems to be more Chinese and Indian with clear reference to Hindus. Nor is it without stereotype, even if this does not turn nasty. Considering what imports could be done without, Mannie reflects,

> Even p-suits used to be fetched up from Terra – until a smart Chinee
> before I was born figured out how to make 'monkey copies' better
> and simpler. (Could dump two Chinee down in one of our maria and
> they would get rich selling rocks to each other while raising twelve
> kids. Then a Hindu would sell retail stuff he got from them wholesale
> – below cost at a fat profit. We got along.) (Chapter 6)

It is probably important to remind ourselves here that both Luna and Heinlein were very pro-babies.

A third of the way through the novel Mannie visits Earth, and alongside the prejudice against his marriage he finds himself dealing with racial prejudice in the Southern states. 'Is mixed up place another way; they care about skin colour – by making point of how they don't care. First trip I was always too light or too dark, and somehow blamed either way' (Chapter 18).

I Will Fear No Evil is much more ambiguous. Johann Sebastian Bach Smith gives no indication he is other than white but Jake Salomon and Dr Rosenthal are probably Jewish, and Dr Garcia presumably Hispanic. I had thought that Eunice Branca's husband Joe was Latino – he is certainly Catholic – but in Chapter 24 his mother's letter includes the insistence that African Americans can have anything they want while 'We white people that built this country and paid for it are just so much dirt' (as Mrs Branca is a drunk on welfare, we can assume that Heinlein disapproves), and complains that Mexican women are seen first by the doctor. But with Eunice it is unclear. We know she is from Iowa, but if she is white, why does Jake remind Smith that 'No instruction you gave said one word about race or sex?' (Chapter 8).

In *Time Enough for Love*, colour is mostly elided, and this is probably because Heinlein has created a bind for himself in that the Howard Foundation of the 1900s was most unlikely to have either selected African Americans, or even if it had, to have allowed intermarriage between African American and white families. In *'The Number of the Beast'* we can guess that all protagonists are white, simply because the British colonists of the Victorian ether romance do not react. It is in *Friday* that we meet our final protagonist of colour.

The problem with everything I have described so far is that with the sole exception of Uncle Alfred (*Time for the Stars*) and Joseph in *Farnham's Freehold* (of which more later), the colour of African American characters might be painted on. There is no culture associated with this colour. This is particularly evident in *Friday*. The titular heroine of *Friday* is mixed-race as we discover in a dramatic disclosure in Chapter 7. We also know that she is dark-skinned and when she was younger this was one element in her self-understanding: 'I thought I could get to be that colour [fair-skinned blonde] if I scrubbed hard enough' (Chapter 20). Yet, ironically, it is her AP status which gets her ejected from her family, not her mixed-race status. But Friday has no culture other than that which she has taken from the crèche and from those around her. Although Baldwin's posthumous letter to her in Chapter 7 lists her genetic heritage and then argues 'you can never afford to be racist, you would bite your own tail', this is a presumption that does not take into account how racism works.

Friday has no identification with the groups indicated (none of which by the way includes African American), and which in itself forms a roll-call of Heinlein's 'favoured nations' as deployed in *Starship Troopers*: Finnish, Polynesian, Amerindian, Inuit, Danish, red Irish, Swazi, Korean, German, Hindu, English. She does have a cultural identity however as an AP and I am going to propose that we can see this as 'raced': APs are a race because they are treated as such and thus behave as such and there is a constant thread throughout the novel that humans can spot APs, which the anti-racist humans deny. They continually insist as they do in *Friday*, that they cannot see the 'Other' and declare a philosophy of 'we are all the same'. We can see this in *Beyond This Horizon*, in *Farnham's Freehold* and *Podkayne of Mars*: Hamilton is a sound man because he understands what control naturals are for, Monroe-Alpha is not because he sees them as fundamentally Other, with a culture of their own. Hugh Farnham tells us, and Joseph demonstrates for us, that we are all the same up to and including cheerfully assimilating into the power structures, but being 'nice' about it. They are contrasted with Hugh's wife who does not see Joseph as like her at all (he is a representative of those people) and with Friday's first family, who despise the man their daughter is marrying because he is Tongan: 'Tongans are not like us. They aren't white people. They are barbarians' (Chapter 6). Vicki demonstrates the flaw of the 'just like us' approach. Friday tries to be logical: 'They are the most civilised people in all Polynesia. Why do you think the early explorers called that group "the Friendly Isles"?' But this is not a logical argument. When Vicki tries to explain that some brown people are more acceptable than others she comes out with 'Everybody knows that Amerindians are— Well, just like white people. Every bit as good' (Chapter 7).

Far from being inclusive the 'colour blind' position is actually demanding, a barrier to cross, but that 'colour blind' approach, and his emphasis on colour prejudice rather than institutional cultures of racist discrimination and violence, is fundamental to how Heinlein's understanding of, and statements on, how anti-racism functions. He uses racism and stereotyping to achieve an anti-racist blueprint. It is that which we will move to next.

Statements of Anti-Racism

The contention of this section is that it is by understanding the constructions of statements of anti-racism in Heinlein's work that we can see how *Farnham's Freehold* goes so terribly wrong. The book is, in a way, the ultimate in claiming 'look, they are just like us'. Although there are statements about racism and anti-racism scattered throughout Heinlein's work there are five short stories and six novels which are 'about' racism in one way or another. Some are direct, some use metaphor. None of the short stories are considered Heinlein classics. The earliest of the short stories is 'Successful Operation', a squib published under the byline of Lyle Monroe, in *Futuria Fantasia* in 1940. In this story a tyrant goes under the knife for a transplant – thus proving the adage that all humans are basically the same – and wakes up to find he has been labelled the concentration-camp inmate, thus intensifying the argument. The guards cannot tell the difference. The story is slight but it makes the point, one supported in 'Water is for Washing', in which racial prejudice is overcome in the face of disaster. *Methuselah's Children* is a book about a Chosen People, in which, again, prejudice is overcome, not this time through disaster but through education.

Also slight is 'It's Great to Be Back!' (1947), a story which on the surface is nothing do with race, but has buried in it the common American conceit that migration culls the herd: only the best and brightest and most practical are selected for, and can survive the rigours and moral demands of migration. This idea recurs often: in the eugenic history revealed towards the end of *Beyond This Horizon*, in the survival test at the heart of *Tunnel in the Sky*, in *The Moon is a Harsh Mistress*, in the notebooks of Lazarus Long, 'The Tale of the Adopted Daughter', and in Lazarus Long's ambition to leave Secundus, precisely because it is now too civilised and is nurturing the wrong kind of people. It does not occur to Heinlein that this might be racism – or at least one way to create racism – until *Friday*, when Friday receives an inheritance that will enable her to emigrate. 'Exception: if you migrate to Olympia, you pay for it yourself... That's where those self-styled supermen went' (Chapter 7).

Podkayne of Mars is the first of Heinlein's novels in which it matters that the protagonist is not white (a construction I have used deliberately here) and that this is discussed directly in the context of racism. It contains one of the clearest statements of anti-racism: Marsmen (not Martians) are mostly brown. When Podkayne visits a crèche in Chapter 3, she sees 'little brown dumplings' (at this stage in American culture food metaphors for babies were very common: 'so cute I could eat him', for example, so while this might make a modern reader flinch, here the point is describing the desirability of brown babies). When Podkayne is called to the Director of the crèche, we are told he 'had a dark brown skin and a grey goatee' (Chapter 3). His lawyer is Mr Kwai Yau Poon, and the doctor is Dr Schoenstein. Mars has precisely the diverse make-up that Heinlein has been constructing all along.

But on the second page of the novel we are told of Podkayne: 'I stand 157 centimetres tall in my bare feet and mass 49 kilograms. "Five feet two and eyes of blue" my daddy calls me.' On the next page she notes 'I'm colonial mongrel in ancestry, but the Swedish part of me is dominant in my looks, with Polynesian and Asiatic fractions adding a not-unpleasing exotic flavour... Besides that my hair is pale blonde and I am pretty' (Chapter 1). Podkayne therefore is to the visual eye a blonde, blue-eyed Swede with perhaps a tan, and non-Swedish features. The New English Library paperback I have before me does a reasonable job of depicting this, while all of the other covers opt for either obviously African American (which she is not), including the original magazine publication, or European blonde, which we are clearly told she is not. It would be easy to argue that making Podkayne light-skinned is to assure reader-identification, but if so Heinlein is deploying a bait and switch.

The contrast of Podkayne to those around her turns out to matter. In Chapter 6 Podkayne finds herself preyed on by an older woman, Mrs Royer, who tries to turn Podkayne into a servant. When Poddy refuses, in a scene familiar to many through Alice Walker's *The Color Purple*, the 'kind' Mrs Royer turns on her, trashing her to her friend as criminal or 'worse'. The worse is clearly raced. 'Have you noticed that little Martian girl? The niece – or so they claim – of that big black savage?' That 'big black savage' is Uncle Tom, senior Senator at large, and, Podkayne notes, 'as dark as I am blond; his Maori blood and desert tan make him the colour of beautiful old leather.' Mrs Royer's friend, Mrs Garcia, carries on:

> Criminals to start with . . . and then that Shameless Mixing of Races. You can see it right in that family. The boy doesn't look a bit like his sister, and as for the uncle – *hmmm* – My dear, you halfway hinted at something. Do you suppose that she is *not* his niece but something, shall we say, a bit *closer*?

Miscegenation, promiscuity, criminality are all mixed up and placed in the mouths of people who hate our heroine. The message is clear.

I have already discussed the statement of anti-racism in *Friday* where Friday's mixed blood turns out to be as much of an issue as her status as an artificial person. To Heinlein 'racial prejudice' is straightforward: you either feel prejudice to those of other colours or you do not. What is not there is any understanding of institutionalised discrimination or the role of a prejudicial and discriminatory culture. For that, one has to turn to Heinlein's arguments around slavery.

For Heinlein slavery is a human ill to which the species regularly falls prey. But Heinlein does not race slavery. In none of the three books in which slavery and the release from slavery is the storyline – *Citizen of the Galaxy, Time Enough for Love* and *Friday* – is race an element regarding who is enslaved, and with the exception of Friday, the enslaved all appear to be white.

Heinlein's family had been abolitionists. Part of this is described in the second chapter of *To Sail Beyond the Sunset*, and within that description he also encapsulates the limits of that: many of the areas in Missouri that refused slaveholding went on to exclude African Americans. These were places known later as Sundown Towns.[5] There is an indication that the family had also been involved in 'blockbusting' – selling their home to a white estate agent who would in turn sell to a black family (see *To Sail Beyond the Sunset*, Chapter 15).

Heinlein's hatred of slavery comes up over and over again. 'Jerry is a Man', in which a woman goes to court to prove the sentience and self-ownership of a sentient ape, is perhaps the most 'raced' story and thoroughly uncomfortable as a consequence, for the use of apes in this story, although logical, feels as if Heinlein has become locked into colonialist and slave owner and abolitionist arguments of 'uplift' of one kind or another. This argument that the enslaved have to be 'uplifted' was inherited from both slave owners and

---

5   See James W. Loewen, *Sundown Towns: A Hidden Dimension of American Racism* (New York: New Press, 2005).

abolitionists (white and black) and was almost certainly reinforced by Stanley Elkins' *Slavery: A Problem in American Institutional and Intellectual Life* (1959), and by emerging arguments, written up in Daniel Moynihan's *The Negro Family: The Case for National Action* (1965). Moynihan's report, which was built on the black sociologist Franklin Frazier's work of the 1930s, considered the disordered (as he saw it) nature of the African American family, and rather than blame contemporary institutional structures of imprisonment, poor education and restricted job opportunities, traced it back to the effects of slavery. Stanley Elkins reinforced this by studying the recorded behaviour of slaves and, using as his template the experience of holocaust survivors and their reports of how they behaved in order to survive, argued that slavery created a very specific mentality (it probably doesn't help that the story of the Israelites spending forty years in the wilderness is the template for this argument).

In *Tramp Royale*, the travel narrative Heinlein wrote in 1954, we can see the degree to which Heinlein bought into these ideas. In Chapter 8 he is horrified by South Africa and asserts that in the treatment of African Americans and Native Americans America has moved beyond, that the country has 'made many amends'. He insists that 'the barefoot Bantu savage is not capable of modern citizenship' while blaming that on the Nationalists, but it does not occur to him to question his use of the term 'savage', or to wonder if the Afrikaners are fit for modern citizenship. And he is deeply complacent that Americans 'know how to deal with natives', having granted to the Filipinos 'full and unconditional freedom'. Perhaps the worst line in this book is this: 'the ambition of every literate black man in South Africa is to emigrate to Birmingham, Alabama, or some place else in our Deep South, where he can be among his own kind and still enjoy freedom'. It is when Heinlein engages in cultural comparisons that he is at his worst.

The construction of the slave mentality is vivid in *Farnham's Freehold* and is a factor in why the book emerges as so racist. The comparative approach to racism also undermines it.

Farnham's Freehold

Farnham's Freehold is Heinlein's most problematic novel. Note that I have made no attempt to edit the language Heinlein uses in it, because for Heinlein to use such language cannot be anything other than deliberate. Heinlein set out to write a 'world turned upside down' but in doing so wrote instead an 'if this goes on' that could support white supremacist nightmares and convince people that African Americans (and Africans) were inherently barbaric. As Samuel Delany writes,

> what distresses one about the Heinlein argument in general, when it is presented in narrative form, is that it so frequently takes the form of a gentlemanly assertion: 'Just suppose the situation around X . . . were P, Q and R; now under those conditions wouldn't Y's behaviour be logical and justified?' – where behavior Y just *happens* to be an extreme version of the most conservative, if not fascistic, program. Our argument is never with the truth value of Heinlein's syllogism . . . Our argument is with the premises . . .' (*Starboard Wine*, 2012, p. 22)

Heinlein set out to write a Swiftian satire, and failed; a Mark Twain parody, and failed at that too. In part this is because the book reflects the third writer Heinlein admired most, Kipling. Jane Davitt has written an extensive exegesis of Heinlein's indebtedness to Kipling ('"Of One Blood": The Influence of Rudyard Kipling on Robert A. Heinlein', 2000). Here we can note that he and Kipling shared both the same ability to write lovely, loose, popular prose, and to embed within that prose the same bitterness and sense of loss that George Orwell identifies in his essay on Kipling:

[He] spent the later part of his life sulking ... Somehow history had not gone to plan. After the greatest victory she had ever known, Britain was somehow a lesser world power than before and Kipling was quite acute enough to see this. The virtue had gone out of the classes he idealized, the young were hedonistic or disaffected.[6]

This description fits Heinlein in his later years also: it describes the interludes in *I Will Fear No Evil*, and the backdrop to Maureen's picaresque in *To Sail Beyond the Sunset*, but it is first clearly expressed by Hugh Farnham, in *Farnham's Freehold*, for that is Hugh's stated position. In Chapter 2 he declares to Barbara 'This war may have turned the tide. This may be the first war in history which kills the stupid rather than the bright and able ... wars have always been hardest on the best young men. This time the boys in service are as safe or safer than civilians. And of civilians those who used their heads and made preparation stand a far better chance ... When it's over, things will be tough, and that will improve the breed still more' (Chapter 2). Taken at face value this argument is chilling, but once we have read the novel over, we need to pause: for if Farnham is correct then the logical outcome of this argument is that the dark-skinned peoples fulfilled this logic better than did the light-skinned peoples. The enslavement of whites becomes thus both punitive consequence and 'natural'.

One issue with *Farnham's Freehold* is whether we are to admire Hugh Farnham, and thus entirely accept his analysis, or not. On the

---

6   *The Collected Essays, Journalism and Letters of George Orwell, Volume 2: My Country Right or Left* (Harmondsworth: Penguin, 1970), p. 217.

one hand Hugh has built a bomb shelter and is 'prepared' in the way and to the degree that Heinlein had been advocating. On the other, as James Gifford's *Robert A. Heinlein: A Reader's Companion* argues (p. 84), Hugh Farnham has failed at life. He has made money but he has alienated both his wife and his son and he is not all that close to his daughter who, we will discover, is pregnant outside wedlock (and while Farnham accepts this, it is not a signifier of success). When Barbara describes him it is not as a man in the prime of his life but '[h]air thinning and already grey, himself thin, almost gaunt, but with a slight potbelly, tired eyes, lines around them, and deep lines down his cheek.' This image of an exhausted man whose life has gone awry is reconcilable if we place the book within one of Heinlein's named plots, 'the man who learned better' (Lloyd Eshbach, *Of Worlds Beyond*, 1947, p. 15). Furthermore, as we have already seen, Heinlein's heroes are often neither as smart, nor as in command of the situation, as are the secondary characters and sidekicks. In this case, that is Joseph, who, like most of Heinlein's sidekicks, is smarter and better educated than the protagonist.

There is much to discuss in *Farnham's Freehold* but in this section I will only discuss race and racism. On the first page we see the family together, petulant Grace, stern Hugh, the rebellious and questioning son, Duke, his sister Karen and Karen's friend, Barbara Wells. Also present is 'the houseboy, a young Negro.' The choice of phrasing is striking. At this stage Joseph is more or less invisible, or rather, he is constructed by the others' comments and commands. He has no last name. In Chapter 1 he is a fetcher and carrier. His trajectory will be rather like that of the butler Crichton, in J. M. Barrie's play *The Admirable Crichton* (1902). It is this trajectory that is, I think, the key to what Heinlein wanted to produce as opposed to what he actually wrote.

The first indication that Joseph is important is that when the alarm goes up, Hugh's first call is 'Red alert!' 'Somebody tell Joseph!'

When the family are all in the shelter, Hugh is concerned first for Joseph, then for Karen (Chapter 2), and then, most crucially, when Joseph arrives he dashes back out for 'Doctor Livingstone I presume!', the family cat who 'Loves Joseph, tolerates us'.[7] (Later, Joseph is seen in the shelter asleep with the cat curled up on his chest.) Hugh waits for him outside the door of the shelter. Joseph is not 'merely' a servant; he is Hugh's second-in-command (Chapter 2). As Heinlein often uses names as signifiers it is worth pausing a moment to note that Joseph is the dreamer, the one who sees the future and leads his people to greatness: also to note that as Joseph's status rises he becomes Joe. I will pick up on this again in the epilogue to this book, but it is worth stating here that the person the cat loves is, in a Heinlein novel, *ipso facto* a good person. Joseph, who at this stage is the least significant person in the book, is the one who matters to the two most important people: Hugh and Doctor-Livingstone-I-Presume. Joseph certainly matters more to Hugh than does Duke. When Duke turns awkward, it is Joseph whom Hugh trusts for back up and who picks up the hint, the Thompson submachine gun, and, in effect, Duke's patrimony.

In Chapter 3 we see Joseph being positioned as the competent man. After the fourth 'biggest slam of them all' the light goes out. Duke strikes a match. Joe (now) tells him to put out the fire hazard and switches on the flashlight. Joe takes care of the medical needs of the group and when Hugh comes round is ministered to himself. When they are working out how to get out of the shelter (which is no longer on the level) it is Joe who takes charge, and when Hugh does give Joe orders it is with Joe in charge of Duke.

---

7 Dr David Livingstone was a nineteenth-century missionary and explorer who also set out to oppose the slave trade, although he became embroiled with prestigious slavers much as Hugh will eventually do.

Meanwhile Grace continues to treat Joseph as a servant. Noticeably she calls him Joseph when others call him Joe, and continues to send him for alcohol and other drinks. There is a particularly awkward interaction in Chapter 4 where Grace asks 'And will you please tell me, Mr Farnham, what Joseph is going to do to earn his wages?' Hugh points out they won't be paying any, but to Grace this is 'preposterous! Joseph will get every cent coming to him – and he knows it ... After all, we've saved his life. And we've always been good to him' (Chapter 4). The condescension of that last phrase will come back to haunt them all. But meanwhile Hugh slaps her down: 'Joe is no longer our servant. He is our partner in adversity.' But Joe is still in appeasement mode and offers to cook lunch. What Joe realises (which Hugh does not) is that Hugh's attitude does not secure Joe. When Duke lashes out at Hugh it is in part for 'having that nigger pull a gun on me!' (Chapter 4). Hugh has violated the racial order of society and Duke does not like it. Duke argues for democracy but baulks when Hugh would grant Joe the vote. Interestingly, Hugh does try to even the score when he allows Duke to back him against Joe, but then undermines him when he tells him 'guns won't be necessary.' Duke doesn't get to threaten Joe. Perhaps even more interesting is why: Hugh has just given Joe an order that everyone must be observed when they bathe, in order to be protected. Joe declines. In effect, Duke backs his father to force Joe to 'protect' naked white women in the bath.

Hugh violates the racial structure further of course when he supports Karen's decision to marry Joe. Hugh is delighted that Karen is pregnant and even more pleased that it's by someone not there as it brings extra genes into the gene pool of the group. She announces it with a really offensive colloquialism however: 'I took the chance, like the nigguh mammy who said, "Oh, hunnuhds of times ain't nuffin happen at all."' Hugh lets this go unremarked.

Karen will die in childbirth. Her 'joke' does not die with her but has a lingering significance.

Not long after this Grace collapses, accusing Hugh of murder (for failing to find a doctor). It is at this point that Duke decides to withdraw with his mother to another cave, but as they are packing up and maintaining as civilised a demeanour as possible, they see the 'domino tile' that will herald the next stage of the story (Chapter 10).

The racist characters – Grace and Duke – yield easiest to servitude which seems to suggest that once one has signed on to racial supremacy as a societal structure, it only remains to be convinced as to where your place is so that the racist is a 'natural' 'slave'. Resistance has to lie in refusing the model of slavery itself. What these early scenes do is to deploy racism as a character marker: bad characters are racist, good characters are not racist, racist characters are weak.

When the four cars land, out of one of them 'strode a man'. For some unaccountable reason Hugh believes that the grandeur of the man indicates that he has taken trouble to dress up, that 'they were prisoners of importance and a parley might be fruitful. Or did that follow?' And Hugh is encouraged by the way the man looks: 'He had an air of good-natured arrogance and his eyes were bright and merry. His forehead was high, his skull massive; he looked intelligent and alert. Hugh could not place his race. His skin was dark brown and shiny. But his mouth was only slightly Negroid; his nose, though broad, was arched, and his black hair was wavy' (Chapter 10). Does this express Heinlein's own prejudice in that the man is set aside from being African American, as so many of Heinlein's dark-skinned characters are? In Chapter 11 we will learn that the language is clearly rooted in African languages so it is quite likely that this is not a culture descended from African Americans. But it is also evident that Heinlein has chosen to make him dark, and to give him looks that match white American notions of good-looking.

The man first approaches Joe, but Joe cannot understand what is said. He then examines Barbara as if she is meat and stings Hugh for resisting. There is then an attempt to try a range of languages and it is only when Joe tries French that he is able to respond. As they are taken into captivity Duke suggests they run and when Hugh refuses throws back at him, 'Aren't you even going to try to fight? Where's the crap you used to spout about how you were a free man and planned to stay free?' (Chapter 10). Duke is right: the cry of (slave-holder) Patrick Henry 'Give me liberty or give me death!' is momentarily in abeyance.

In the air car there are other men to contemplate: the pilot is 'a young Negro who looked remarkably like Joe'; the passengers are white but all of the pilots 'were invariably coloured, ranging from as light brown as a Javanese to as sooty black as a Fiji Islander.' What Hugh does not notice at this stage is the hands of the white men. The first time we meet this it is in the hands of Memtok, Chief Palace Domestic, who in Chapter 11, holds his pen nested between the first three fingers of his right hand.

It is in Chapter 12 that the realities of their situation begin to hit. Joseph comes to visit and it becomes clear that he is receiving very different treatment. Joe, it seems, is one of the Chosen, and 'It's not my fault that you are white.' But it takes some time for the true meaning of this to sink in for Hugh. When Ponse comes in, and he notices that he talks to Joe as an equal, he puts it down to the man's 'pleasing personality'. It is only when Ponse refers to Hugh as his chiefest possession that the truth begins to sink in, and when he walks out with Memtok in Chapter 13 and studies it in Chapter 15 he gets a lesson in the structures of his society.

There is no whip. Joseph is an intimate of the Charity, knowing him by his first name, and one of the ways this intimacy is expressed is through jokes. When he relates the prevention of Hugh's 'tempering' he recalls, 'Ponse laughed his head off at how close you came and how you and Duke yelped.' Hugh is not amused and Joe responds with the following, and it stings. 'Oh, Hugh, he simply has a robust sense of humour . . . Different people laugh at different things. Karen used to use a fake negro dialect that set my teeth on edge, the times I overheard it. But she didn't mean any harm.' Joe knows what he is doing. He is turning back to Hugh words that he has heard many times in the face of insult and violence. Heinlein knows that he is summarising the comments of many white people when they joke about lynching; he gives them to the crowd who stone Valentine Michael Smith in *Stranger in a Strange Land* (Chapter 37).

When Hugh goes looking for information about the past he finds a melange: some information about the destructions, some about the North America of the past. He discovers that people believe the USA at the time of the war still held its black population as slaves, and that history classed the Chinese as white and the Hindus as black, something which 'was not the accepted anthropological ordering of his day' (Chapter 14). 'The few white survivors, spared by Uncle's mercy, had been succoured and cherished as children' (Chapter 14), which is reflected in Hugh's own experience of being infantilised. It reflects both the common arguments of white slave owners, and also the rhetoric of slavery as 'rescuing' the black man, which was pushed by both slave-owners, and, surprisingly, by some ex-slaves.[8]

---

8   See the third paragraph at the World SF Blog, Speculative Fiction from Around the World, here: https://worldsf.wordpress.com/2012/09/07/heinlein-and-racism/ I do not disagree with the overall analysis of the entire letter cited here. What is problematic is the implication that Heinlein was inventing this particular comment as a white person. The argument of that paragraph which was assigned to Heinlein is actually from Booker T. Washington: 'We went into slavery a piece of property; we came out American citizens. We went into slavery pagans; we came out Christians. We went into slavery without a language; we came out speaking the proud Anglo-Saxon tongue. We went into slavery with slave chains clanking about our wrists; we came out with the American ballot in our hands' (Booker T. Washington Papers, p. 62). Sharon DeGraw also spots this link in *The Subject of Race in American Science Fiction*, 2007 (p. 121).

Heinlein himself does not make this argument in full, but for much of the book Hugh fully accepts the narrative of rescue, education and infantilisation.

Hugh discovers that his hunch that this culture is essentially African is correct. It is even matrilineal, with descent and inheritance through a man's sister, which is one of the issues that moves Hugh to consider escape when he realises that his future owner is less reliable than his present one. This, of course, maps well onto the evidence from his earlier work that Heinlein is a great deal more respectful of African culture than of African American culture, which he erases from many of his black characters and even in Joseph's portrayal.[9]

If Hugh had not been deprived of Barbara's company, or seen his son tempered (in order that he might stay with his mother), or realised that he was to be passed on to a cruel man, it is possible he would not have run. Ponse is, after all 'the perfect decadent gentleman – urbane, cosmopolitan, disillusioned, and cynical, a dilettante in arts and sciences, neither merciful nor cruel, unimpressed by his own rank, not racist – he treated Hugh as an intellectual equal' (Chapter 15). Later Ponse will declare that he is not 'one of those superstitious persons who thinks a servant can't think because his skin is pale.'

The slaves in *Farnham's Freehold* are kept acquiescent by the liberal use of Happiness, a tranquilliser. But Heinlein also widens the societal context. In Chapter 15 Hugh discovers that there are whites living in the mountains. He argues with Ponse as to whether the free savage whites can be happy and Ponse explains, in the manner of

---

9   Speculative Fiction from Around the World. In the same letter Heinlein declares that he could not find Negro engineers during the war; complains about African Americans demanding acting jobs; and argues that research needs to be done to prove or disprove whether the races are equal. He argues also for *legal* intervention, but as I note more than once in this book, he simply has no awareness of the issues of institutional or longitudinal discrimination.

an antebellum slave-owner, that of course slavery is better, of course it is better to be looked after and cosseted and to be a slave than it is to be free and poor 'not knowing where their next meal is'. He hears from Joe of the 'poor black trash', the Chosen who live like poor whites in Mississippi. And for a moment Hugh sees that, to Joe, he was never more than an escape from poverty. By the time he has discovered that in order to live with Barbara he would have to be castrated, and that castration and spaying is in part a programme to prevent overbreeding ('They would starve! I can't support them in unlimited breeding. Would if I could but it's wishing for the Moon. Worse for we can go to the Moon any time it's worth while but nobody can cope with the way servants will breed if left to their own devices'). And Hugh thinks 'glumly that Ponse was not a villain. He was exactly like the members of every ruling class in history: honestly convinced of his benevolence and hurt if it was challenged'. Which is interesting as the material I have put in brackets could also have been taken from one of Lazarus Long's reflections in 'The Tale of the Twins Who Weren't', in which he muses on losing his licence for advocating sterilisation.

By this stage in the novel it is evident that there is a retributive justice system at work: Karen, who has made jokes about African American mothers, dies in childbirth (although Sharon DeGraw notes that this also kills off a future of interracial children, *The Subject of Race in American Science Fiction*, p. 124); Grace, who called her own daughter a slut for being pregnant and contemplating a black husband, and has treated Joseph as a thing, not a person, ends up as Ponse's concubine; and Duke, who has feared black men as rapists of white women, and clearly would like to castrate each and every one, ends up castrated, unable to impregnate a woman of any colour. And ironically it is his beloved mother who triggers the order (by requesting his company). Perhaps worst of all is the evidence that

Duke is happy. Admittedly it takes drugs to achieve it, but also part of his happiness is his sense of status as a member of Ponse's intimate circle, particularly that status over Joe. What Heinlein demonstrates here, in contrast to his consideration of slavery in other books, is that you can make a slave from a free man if the conditions are right and the rewards seem great enough. Joe notes, 'he is happy in a life of luxury, instead of hard manual labour in a mine, or a rice swamp' (Chapter 17).

This is the key moment in the novel, the one in which Heinlein demonstrates at least that he has moved on from his defence of America in *Tramp Royale*. Hugh says,

> 'Joe, do you know what you sound like? Like some white-supremacy apologist telling how well off the drakes use to be a sittin' outside their cabins, a-strummin' their banjoes, and singin' spirituals.'
>
> 'I won't bandy words with you. I suppose it does look that way to you. If so, do you expect me to weep? The shoe is on the other foot, that's all – and high time. I used to be a servant, now I'm a respected businessman – with a good chance of becoming a nephew by marriage of some noble family. Do you think I would swap back, even if I could? For Duke? Not for anybody. I'm no hypocrite. I was a servant, now you are one. What are you beefing about?'
>
> 'Joe, you were a decently treated employee. You were not a slave.'
>
> The younger man's eyes suddenly became opaque and his features took on an ebony hardness Hugh had never seen in him before. 'Hugh,' he said softly, 'have you ever made a bus trip through Alabama? As a "nigger"?'

That part of the conversation stops there, but Joe rubs it in. When Ponse is dead he plans to adopt Grace and Duke, Grace to cook, Duke as his houseboy.

'Well? What do you think of my plan?'

'I thought better of you, Joe. I thought you were a gentleman. It seems I was wrong.'

'So?' Joe barely twitched his quirt. 'Boy, we excuse you All'

(Chapter 17)

This is the moment the novel is at its most effective. A writer less committed to story could have ended the novel there and it would have made its point: white supremacy is a matter of luck and violence, not reason. It would have been understood as a brilliant satire. Unfortunately, Heinlein, a devotee of Swift, pushes it one stage further.

The result is racism.

Shaken by the discovery that Duke has been tempered, and that he no longer has an ally in Joe, Hugh resolves to run and heads to Memtok to try and create a moment with Barbara. His walk with Memtok takes him through the butcher's shop.

There have been hints to the reader all the way through once we know what to look for. In Chapter 11, 'He [Memtok] had suggested that the chef himself, old and tough as he was, nevertheless would make a better roast than the meat the chef had sent in to Their Charity the evening before.' In Chapter 15 Memtok asks, 'Do you know how close you came to being cold meat?' And it is in this chapter Hugh first tastes what he takes to be pork, for which he has no great liking. It surprises him for this is a loosely Muslim culture although with a revised Koran. But in Chapter 18 he is brought face to hand with the truth. Among all the other carcasses in the butcher's shop he sees, 'A hand much like Kitten's' (his bed-warmer). He tries not to retch. 'There had suddenly flooded over him the truth behind certain incongruities, certain idioms, some pointless jokes', and when they visit the cold room, 'one long row of hooks down the centre held what he knew he would find – human carcasses, gutted and cleaned and frozen' (Chapter 18). He tells a joke, asks if one of the carcasses is Memtok's nephew and everyone freezes, but 'All these critters are ranch bred ... Their Charity considers it unspeakably vulgar to serve a house servant ... it makes the servants restless.' Hugh resolves that he will not touch pork, even though he thinks the pork the servants are served probably is pork.

We know from his writing that Heinlein was a devotee of Swift and Twain – Mike offers a summary of Swift's *A Modest Proposal* to his military tutors in Chapter 30 of *Stranger in a Strange Land*, and there is a discussion of *Gulliver's Travels* and Laputan flappers in Chapter 14. Heinlein would also have been very aware of the use of cannibalism as a metaphor for exploitation and uses it in 'The Man Who Sold the Moon', where one character accuses the Board of 'cannibalizing the youth of the land' (p. 154). For Heinlein the initiating sin is the sin of enslavement and of the knowing rationalisation of what you know to be evil. This is the crucial take for Heinlein: while the book is for many readers rendered repulsive and racist by the cannibalism, for Heinlein the moral relativist, the man who thinks he is writing a Swiftian satire, this is merely a consequence of the system: absolute power means absolute exploitation. Elisabeth Leonard thinks that Farnham/Heinlein is arguing that once you have dehumanised people, they are no more than cattle anyway (*'Farnham's Freehold*: A Narrative Enslaved'). If whites had absolute power they would do the same.

Heinlein was also aware of Herodotus' tale of Darius the Great, and the use of cannibalism as an argument about moral relativism (he refers to it in *Stranger in a Strange Land* several times, because the Martians eat each other, as food and as a display of respect, and also to maintain cultural continuity; Mike would be honoured, in Chapter 11, were he to be eaten),[10] and he uses it in *Orphans of the Sky* very successfully (the mutant and cannibal Joe-Jim is far more civilised and erudite than the pure and innocent officers). In *Stranger in a Strange Land*, Jubal Harshaw asserts that while a revulsion to cannibalism is so deep in the culture it does not have to be taught: 'cannibalism is historically one of the most widespread of human customs, *extending through every branch of the human race*' (Chapter 13, my italics). Heinlein does not regard cannibalism as a race marker, and in this novel he gives the habit to the intensely civilised and superior Martians. And of course, at the end of the novel, Mike's 'nest' drink Michael-broth (Chapter 38).[11]

Thus we can see 'objectively', in the sense of in the wider context of Heinlein's work, that what is intended here is a metaphor: white people eat black people, of soul and spirit and self; to eat them bodily is merely one step further (and Heinlein may have known that at some lynchings there were rumours that white people did eat the body parts of the black men they tortured and murdered). But there is no reflection in the text on this incident and it stands as an appalling horror which effectively argues that 'white people would never be that bad!' Not until Chapter 20 do we have any kind of confirmation that Hugh is not seeing this as uniquely racialised. Having run away and been captured he is kept under a tangle field, and in that time dreams or hallucinates, first of rebellion, of using the tunnels to educate the slaves. But, and here I am forced to quote the whole page because anything less is to cherry pick:

10 Part 1, Chapter 8, where Smith thinks of walking on living grass, 'He sought to enfold it and praise it; the effort was much like that of a human trying to appreciate the merits of cannibalism—a custom which Smith found perfectly proper.' *New World Encyclopedia*, Moral Relativism, http://www.newworldencyclopedia.org/entry/Moral_relativism

11 There is also the phrase 'have her/his skin for a rug/skull for an ashtray' which crops up in 'Lost Legacy', 'Jerry was a Man', 'The Man Who Sold the Moon', 'The Menace from Earth', and '"If This Goes On—"'.

Would these docile sheep *ever* rebel? It seemed unlikely. He had been classed with them by accident of complexion but they were not truly of his breed. Centuries of selective breeding had made them as little like himself as a lap dog is like a timber wolf.

And yet, and yet, *how did he know*? He knew only tempered males, and the few studs he had seen had all been dulled by a liberal ration of Happiness – to say nothing of what it might do to a man's fighting spirit to lose his thumbs at an early age and be driven around with whips-that-were-more-than-whips.

Hugh recalled an area of Pernambuco he had seen while in the Navy, a place where rich plantation owners, dignified, polished, educated in France, were black, while their servants and field hands – giggling, shuffling, shiftless knuckleheads 'obviously' incapable of better things – were mostly white men.[12] He had stopped telling this anecdote in the States; it was never really believed and it was almost always resented – even by whites who made a big thing of how anxious they were to 'help the American Negro improve himself.' Hugh had formed the opinion that almost all of those bleeding hearts wanted the Negro's lot improved until it was almost as high as their own – and no longer on their consciences. But the idea that the tables could ever be turned was one they rejected emotionally.

Hugh knew that the tables could indeed be turned. He had seen it once, now he was experiencing it.

But Hugh knew that the situation was still more confused. Many Roman citizens had been 'black as the ace of spades' and many Roman slaves had been as blond as Hitler wanted to be – so any 'white man' of European ancestry was certain to have a dash of Negro blood. Sometimes more than a dash. That southern Senator, what was his name? – the one who had built his career on 'white supremacy.' Hugh

12 This anecdote was based on an experience in the Navy, as Patterson details.

had come across two sardonic facts: This old boy had died from cancer and had had many transfusions – his blood type was such that the chances were two hundred to one that its owner had not just a touch of the tarbrush but practically the whole tar barrel.

The passage is crucial for it centres Hugh's understanding of slavery away from birth; there are no 'natural' slaves. But Heinlein cannot in 1964 move himself away from the idea that a bred slave and a bred slave mentality is possible, and this is confirmed in Chapter 21. Ponse, who had planned to stage an escape for the family he regards as potentially dangerous to the peace of his household, tries to strike a deal with Hugh: stay, take on Memtok's role, and be bred into his slave line. It turns out the 'savages' in the mountain are free-range stock, not free, artfully cultivated to provide hardy genes; all of the top slaves are partially bred from 'savages'. In the end, however, it is not so much Hugh who refuses as Barbara, because it is Barbara who has seen the gendered underbelly of the system. Hugh, for all he is a slave, has been at the top of the hierarchy. Barbara is much more acutely aware of the degree to which the 'benevolence' of the system relies on the individual in charge. Just as Hugh has had an unsatisfactory, spiteful and racist son and heir, so Ponse's nephew and heir is a brutal man. 'The bed-warmers all hate him, they weep when they are called to serve him – and weep even harder when they come back.'

There are small additional points we should pick up. Ponse has learned English (this was what Grace was for), has read all Hugh's books and has cracked all his codes. Hugh the tolerant had not really considered that this gracious cultivated black man might be smarter than him. Hugh is shocked that Ponse's scientists have figured out time travel, even though he knows that in many ways this is a more advanced society than his own (they have replaced his dentures, and have high-level hovercraft). There is the matter that Grace and

Duke choose to stay: two white people who choose enslavement to black people. They are despised by Hugh but they are a fact. They contribute to the argument that there is no such thing as a 'natural' slave, only a conditioned one (whether through breeding, abuse, drugs or desire).

And there is the final conversation Hugh and Barbara have about Ponse when back in their own time (although it is actually another timeline) when they realise he never intended them to accept his offer to head his household and chivvied them into the experiment in time travel. Hugh is resentful: 'He could always prove why the hotfoot he was giving you was for your own good.' But Barbara is not: 'Hugh, how many white men of today could be trusted with the power Ponse had and use it with as much gentleness as he did use it?' This is when Hugh returns to the cannibalism.

> 'Ponse is a cannibal. Maybe not a cannibal, since he doesn't consider us human. [. . .]
>
> [But] don't hold what he ate too much against Ponse. He honestly did not know it was wrong – and no doubt cows would feel the same way about us, if they knew. But these other things he knew were wrong. Because he tried to justify them. He rationalised slavery, he rationalised tyranny, he rationalised cruelty, and always wanted the victim to agree and thank him.'

But for most science-fiction readers, when the book is read through the structure of an 'if this goes on' tale, a mode Heinlein had used often, it functions as a prediction of what black men will do if in charge. The result is that the novel is racist.

Before leaving this book and this segment however we need to return to the beginning of the novel and then to the end. At the very beginning of the novel Hugh had made an argument that the strongest and cleverest would survive the nuclear war. If Hugh is correct then the overwhelming message of this book is that this is not the white people. At the end of the book there is a sense that Hugh has the chance to change this long-term outcome, but the past he goes into is not his past. There is nothing he can do to change that timeline. Uncomfortable as this may be to yet another set of this book's readers, out there somewhere black people rule over white.

My argument tries to tease out the argument of the text, but a novel is in the end *not* a rational object but an emotive one. Sharon DeGraw says it best when she writes,

> Farnham's positive characterisation rests, in large part, upon a vivid moral contrast with the Other. [. . .] Heinlein creates a human Other embodying the negative traits of both white slaveholders and (black) primitive cannibals. How can Farnham not appear a hero when he is the only person resisting the futuristic black leadership which practices both white slavery and cannibalism? (*The Subject of Race in American Science Fiction*, p. 124)

Slavery

Much of the work of Moynihan and Elkins has been overturned.[13] Elkins's book sparked an interest in slave resistance, and we now know that if 'Sambo' existed it was as the surface grimace of appeasement, not the happy smile of the contented. But the arguments that African Americans still suffer the mental consequences of slavery are still

---

13 See *Black Perspectives*: http://www.aaihs.org/post-traumatic-slave-syndrome-is-a-racist-idea/ (2016) which argues that there is plenty of current racism to constrain and damage. There is also research now in epigenetics which demonstrates the physical stress leading to serious illness that a life spent dealing with a hostile society can cause.

common and come from both the left and the right; research in epigenetics and the impact of trauma suggests that while there is truth to this, there is also plenty of evidence that current violence and discrimination against the African American community is a more significant contributor to poor physical and mental health.

Heinlein was working with what he had, and in a more optimistic age, and in this context wrote three clear stories in which he considered how you educate people out of slavery: *Citizen of the Galaxy*, 'The Tale of the Twins That Weren't' and *Friday*, each of which is very revealing of his own changing ideas around the idea of the bred slave.

The two crucial pieces of information about Thorby Baslim, the rescued slave in *Citizen of the Galaxy*, is that when he is bought he is clearly already marked as a resister, and that he has not been born into slavery. When Baslim sees him on the slave block he notes: 'The boy did not look like a docile house servant to Baslim; he looked like a hunted animal, dirty, skinny and bruised. Under the dirt, the boy's back showed white scar streaks, endorsements of former owners' opinions' (Chapter 1). The boy tries to escape several times. When Baslim hypnotises him he discovers he was born free: 'But he had always been sure of that' (Chapter 2). This is because he rebels and escapes. This is why when Thorby acts out and is caught stealing, Baslim's response is not to punish him but to manumit him. This is not what Thorby wants – 'Pop, I like belonging to you' – but that renders it more imperative. Thorby must not be allowed to settle into slavery. Those who are brought up in slavery are, according to Heinlein, conditioned to it. 'The Tale of the Twins That Weren't' in *Time Enough for Love* is a lengthy description of what 'natural' slaves look like and how to educate them out of it. That it is in many ways a really lovely story of kind parenting reinforces this because it insists throughout that however independent these slaves become, they will never cease to be 'children' of their master and dependent on them (a position forced on many former African American slaves in the 1870s as Reconstruction failed).

From the first these slaves are compliant. 'The kids dropped their robes and fell into display poses.' On the first night Estrellita is in his bed, 'wide awake and waiting': 'she had known what would be expected of her when milord Shipmaster Sheffield had offered to take them along, and had discussed it with her brother, and Brother had told her to do it.' When he refuses her, 'the freedwoman was startled and unbelieving, then sulky and offended'. Joe makes obeisance and has to be told 'Don't bow! When you speak to me stand tall and straight and proud, and look me in the eye.' Sheffield decides to start teaching them and asks himself, 'How could he take full-grown domestic animals and turn them into able, happy human beings, educated in every needful way and capable of competing in a free society?' The set of phrases there are very revealing: 'Was he going to have to keep them as pets for fifty or sixty years?' Heinlein, like many abolitionists, is not convinced slaves are fully adult, and also assumed that the inability of freedmen to compete was less to do with prejudice (as he does indicate in *Citizen of the Galaxy*, Chapter 3) than it was with their compliance and complaisance. So 'Captain Sheffield' sets about educating them: he teaches them when to wear clothes, to read (fiction and non-fiction), he teaches Joe to cook and when Estrellita demonstrates a talent for mathematics he teaches her book-keeping. He initially teaches only Joe to fight and Joe proves a little timid. When Estrellita begs to learn, she is not.

Estrellita gets pregnant and Sheffield/Lazarus Long introduces them to the concept of marriage and uses that too as a teaching moment: 'I added all sorts of things, telling her what she owed him, telling him what he owed her, telling them what they owed the child in her belly and the other children they would have' (Tale: 'Valhalla to Landfall'). He then gets Joe a job on Valhalla, an icy world, and confines Estrellita via a number of tricks so that she will not be whisked off by one (or more) of the local men. Sheffield/Long is anxious to protect Joe's still fragile pride and never questions that he is still treating Estrellita like property.

Once on Landfall, Sheffield/Long sets them up with a business: 'I could have set those kids up in style; that was as profitable a triangle trip as I ever made. But you don't cause ex-slaves to stand tall and free and proud by giving them things. What I did was enable them to go out and scratch.' This translates to paying them for ship-work done, but thinking to himself 'They hadn't been worth any wages; on the contrary I had spent quite a chunk on them.' In his profit and loss accounting Sheffield/Long behaves as if they had always been free rather than themselves improperly held slaves. It's complex but exactly the same omission can be traced to the compensation paid to slaveholders in many slave states when slavery was abolished. The very things Sheffield/Long owes to these people as an owner become deductibles when they are freed. After this he pushes them to the help wanted adds, and then to the business opportunities and finally to a café which it turns out he has bought and set up for them to buy without them knowing. He teaches them the restaurant business. But he does not regard them as having learned to be truly free until they send him a cheque covering the cost of their passage and various sundries. There is an embarrassing scene in which he rejects the money and Estelle declares 'Our master until you free us by letting us pay this—'. Slavery here is in a sense self-imposed, and the slave linked to his or her master by their own sense of obligation. Nowhere is this clearer than in *Friday*.

Friday's slavery is encoded in her Artificial Personhood. She is an artefact, made in a laboratory. She passes for human but exposure would come at a high cost. Even though she is reassured by both Anna the clerk that her identity is hidden and by Baldwin that her files were removed from the lab years before and that she is being 'foolishly self-conscious over an impediment that was removed years ago' (Chapter 4), and we later learn that APs can purchase their manumission, she is aware that she can never be a citizen, and is denied a soul. But more important, she is aware, and it taps straight back into the language used in the previous titles discussed, that 'It isn't any one thing; it's a million little things that are the difference between being reared as a human child and being raised as an animal.' Not least perhaps her name, Friday, which harks back both to *Robinson Crusoe* and to the old rhyme in which 'Friday's child is loving and giving', for Friday gives love even when she does not receive it.

There are several stages in Friday's development and Heinlein has allowed them to overlap, demonstrating that the recovery from abuse (and this novel is essentially a survivor narrative: see Farah Mendlesohn, 'A Critical Review', 1997) is not linear. The stages are appeasement, self-blame and resistance.

When we meet Friday, the titular heroine, she is a courier and spy working for a private agency run by Kettle Belly Baldwin. The story opens with her kidnap and rape, and then continues with her rescue. The first point I want to bring up is the way Friday demonstrates gratitude to those who rescued her: as each individual is identified, she kisses them. Again, this will be returned to in the next section but here I want just to note the subdued similarity to Estrellita offering Sheffield/Long her body. If we recognise that scene, we recognise these, in particular when she kisses the female librarian and 'I let my half of the kiss answer her wordless message – with my fingers crossed that I would never have to keep the implied promise' (Chapter 9).

As the book proceeds Friday will make many such wordless promises and act on several. This is one area where the book has received much criticism and has fed into a meme that Heinlein shows women 'putting out' from duty and through coercion. I will elaborate on just how contrary that interpretation is later, but here I want to argue simply two things: that Friday gives the only thing she believes is hers to give, because Friday is a slave; and that Friday's display and offer is in part a matter of appeasement. So that although this book is on one level about a very competent picaro (see Chapter 4), the story is an interior shot of 'The Tale of the Twins Who Weren't', in which Friday moves through the world, attempting to pass and accepting what is meted out to her (such as the rejection by her Christchurch family) as her just deserts, but gradually growing into personhood as she begins to feel genuinely loved for herself, and simultaneously receiving repeated confirmation of her humanity.

We constantly need to filter Friday's statements through her low self-esteem. In Chapter 6 when she is discussing passing, she notes that men credit her sexual prowess to themselves and adds 'Properly regarded, male vanity is a virtue, not a vice. Treated correctly, it makes him enormously pleasanter to deal with.' Friday models relations between sexes (and to a degree within sexes) through a constant need for appeasement (and her rider, that Boss is hard to deal with because he has no vanity, is Friday not noticing that he is blocking the appeasement pattern). Although the scenes in which she constructs family with her rescue/work colleagues are vital for Friday's development they function to give her skills: she 'plays' at family life with Goldie in Chapter 26 in the way a child might play fathers-and-mothers and in doing so gets her first healthy model as to what family life can truly be like away from the mercenary attitude of her Christchurch family (Chapters 7 and 8).

One of the first incidents of resistance takes place within the Christchurch family and has been described earlier in the chapter, but the scene is important for self-growth because it is in defending someone else – Ellen's Tongan husband – that Friday finds the courage to come out. She has not done so in her work environment even knowing it is safe, actively discouraged by a 'don't ask don't tell' policy. But Friday's outrage cuts through her inhibitions. Her first act of defiance comes from defending others and the treatment she receives – Anita the household matriarch declares her 'a creature not of God's Law', one who does not understand 'the concept of sin and guilt' – leads to the annulment of her marriage on the grounds that 'a nonhuman cannot enter into a marriage contract with human beings' (Chapter 7). She is ejected from the marriage and loses her financial input (about which Anita lies to the men). This of course leads rapidly to self-blame: 'I slunk away' (Chapter 8).

On leaving Christchurch Friday falls in with Ian, the ship's captain she had met before, and this time ends up going home with his family, where she gets trapped during the Red Thursday coup. This leads to Friday exposing her background in order to protect Ian, Janet and Georges. But before she does so Georges reveals himself as a designer and in explaining his job gently reproves her that her 'hyperbole' – 'some of my best friends are artificial people' – is 'intended to show that you are free of prejudice'. So that although in Chapter 13 Friday acts on instinct in protecting Janet, she has done so in a relatively safe space: Georges recognises what he has just seen but apart from his acknowledgement, no one comments. Friday is left not knowing what their internal reaction is. She leaves with Georges but is aware that Ian is rather distant, possibly because she is an AP, possibly because she has demonstrated that she is not the sweet, soft thing he had thought. And with Georges we have the next key scene in which Friday, repeating again the offer of sex as the only coin she truly believes she has, is gently turned down with the comment, 'Oh, my dear! Who hurt you so badly?' (Chapter 14). When Georges declares 'You will not go to bed with me to entertain me', Friday drops into the master-slave interaction. 'Sir, I'm sorry', I said miserably. 'I didn't mean to offend you. I did not intend to presume.' Eventually they work their way clear, but it is worth noting that while Friday goes for a bath and to sort herself out, Georges falls asleep. There is no transactional sex and by the end of Chapter 15, Friday is joking that Georges owes her sex.

Rome isn't built in a day and Friday is still engaging in transactional sex at the end of Chapter 17 where she goes along with the requests of a sergeant who uses her prerogatives to engage Friday's sexual services, but somehow one is not surprised that the sergeant ends up dead in the next chapter. If one ignores Friday's happy time with Goldie (Chapter 26), this could look like homophobia and I have interpreted it as such in the past[14] but I am inclined to think now that it is of a pattern that is constant through Heinlein – sexual coercers end up dead, however mild the coercion; and by this time, Friday is clear she is being coerced even if she chooses to go along with it.

It is Chapter 20 that really begins to shift her thinking. In this chapter, while Friday is still trying to get home, she is chatted up by Trevor: it goes reasonably well, but there is evidence over lunch that he is losing interest. Friday goes to her hotel room to make various calls which leave her very depressed (one is to her now ex-husband) and awaits Trevor, who bails, leaving her a long note in which he outs himself, and writes 'I can't help wishing you were an AP yourself.' Friday retires to lick her wounds and considers 'Trevor was the only man I had ever met whom I could have married with a clear conscience – and I had chased him away ... Kick a dog often enough and he becomes awfully jumpy.' Friday has begun to accept Georges' thinking, that while she is what she has been made, that 'made' is as true of her persona as it is of her body. It is no coincidence that Chapter 21 opens with the following: 'After a short nap that I spent standing on an auction block waiting to be sold, I woke up – woke up because prospective buyers

---

14   See Farah Mendlesohn, 'Women in SF', 1991.

were insisting on inspecting my teeth and I finally bit one and the auctioneer started giving me a taste of the whip.' Friday is biting back.

When she gets home, Friday's world collapses when Baldwin dies. The firm is disbanded and everyone paid off, but Friday receives along with her payout an origin story. A small comment is worth noting: 'we had lived for years in close association that had never, not once, involved even touching hands' (Chapter 24). One of the things Boss has given her is integrity concerning her own body: if we accept modern definitions of sexual abuse that are rooted in understandings of power, then this physical space between them is clear evidence that Baldwin understands the power he has over Friday (see also the refusal of Dan to touch Ricky in *The Door into Summer*). It is not clear that she recognises the significance of this.

Then we have the happy time in Chapter 26 where 'I was a proper housewife; I even bought sweet-pea seeds and planted them in lieu of that missing climbing rose over the door . . . but the seeds did not germinate', an indication perhaps that this relationship was not to be; but otherwise 'I enjoyed all the warm delights of being a housewife . . . including ants in the sugar and a waste line that broke in the night.' But one night she gets home to find a letter from Goldie, who has signed a contract and gone. Friday considers following her 'But Goldie did not want to stay with you badly enough to stay out of a war – doesn't that tell you something? Yes, it tells me something I know but hate to admit: I always need people more than they need me. It's your old basic insecurity, Friday, and you know where it comes from . . .' (Chapter 27). Friday is increasingly thinking in terms of context, of institutionalised reaction rather than assuming it is spliced into her genes.

It is in Chapter 29, aboard a ship and slowly realising that she has too many guards for a mere courier, that she confronts the last of her rapists, 'Mac'/Pete, who turns out to have been an agent from a different group from that which had kidnapped her. Crucially he is both an AP slave and a professional; he played the rape as his part (though it is clear he enjoyed it), but was not there for the torture which like Friday he thinks is amateurish. She does not forgive him but she allows him to go free and makes it clear that he is alive by her choice. In this conversation she and Pete are colleagues. They are both spies, and both do what is expected of them. It may be the first time we see Friday with an absolute equal and her first sense of a communal identity, so perhaps we should not be surprised that at least one other person who makes her living from masquerade also turns out to be an AP (Chapter 31). Friday has been manumitted, but Friday's maid/guard Shizuko (Matilda Jackson) is still under contract on a twenty-year indenture with thirteen to go. Her 'Japaneseness' is an imposed orientalising choice of her owner. Crucially, in order to complete the masquerade, she has not been entered into the ship's rolls as an AP (Chapter 31). When Friday jumps ship, Matilda and Pete go with her, expedite her and then escape. It is the first moment of AP solidarity that we see, the first moment in which there is no deference at all to the unmodified. Matilda escapes the slavery of her 'contract'; Friday escapes the slavery that still lurks in her mind.

One of the most challenging issues is that Friday's humanity is finally confirmed to herself when she carries and gives birth to a child (from an implanted embryo). It seems as if Heinlein is locating personhood in female fertility. First, Heinlein was of a generation that thought marriage every bit as vital to male adulthood as to female and it appears as a source of grief in *I Will Fear No Evil*; but second, and perhaps more important, his own infertility had become an ever greater source of mourning. In *Friday* perhaps he expresses his own self-doubt: is he a person for not having sown children? But in the context of this section the reason Friday's child is so important is that her inability to conceive is a marker of her slavery: she has been fixed

(I use the word we use for animals deliberately), 'made surgically sterile at menarche' (Chapter 30), and thus deprived of her agency. We know Heinlein was well aware of the history of sterilisation for he refers to it in 'The Tale of the Twins Who Weren't', where Sheffield/ Lazarus Long is a clear proponent of sterilisation of the unfit. That loss of agency is never completely undone, Friday cannot be 'unfixed' in the colony. That this is not in the end a hardship is for a reason discussed in the section on gender, that for Heinlein it is baby-rearing rather than baby-making which is the real test of humanity and 'We have babies and dogs and kittens underfoot. The babies don't have to be from my body any more than the kittens do' (Chapter 33).

The novel ends with Friday summarising her family, the family she has with Ian and Georges and Janet and others; and the family she also has with Pete and Tilly (Matilda), to whom she loans the money to start up: but once again note, they refuse it as a gift, and as in 'The Twins Who Weren't', loan payments end up going into a third-party trust account. There are no debtors, no indebted.

Friday, born into slavery, is trained out of it by Baldwin, but this time in contrast to the twins her real release (and that of Tilly even more so) is personal and self-affected. Individuals such as Georges are catalysts, but Heinlein is making clearer than ever that he thinks only the individual can decide to be free. The problem is that in doing so he renders the slave the agent of their own slavery. This was also one of the elements that poisoned *Farnham's Freehold*: in depicting Grace and Duke as complicit, it implies that other slaves – despite the use of drugs, castration and the removal of thumbs – are also complicit.

8

The Right Ordering of Self

In order for society to be right-ordered in a Heinlein world, individuals need to be right-ordered. This is a directional relationship: a right-ordered society cannot create right-ordered individuals, since for Heinlein right-ordered individuals must make the right-ordered society. This is clearly expressed in the short story 'Coventry', in which a young man chooses to leave society to go to an area known as Coventry – an individualist utopia – to play out his Ayn Rand/ survivalist fantasies of being a rugged individualist. He is very quickly disabused of any notion he might have that he is a superior person: he is robbed, convicted of smuggling and falls in with thieves. His sense of who he is and where he belongs is challenged by the discovery of a plot against his homeland and he returns, ready to help make the society he wants to live in. To be a right-ordered person in a Heinlein novel is to cleave to two clear values: a belief in the importance of facts and a belief and faith in personal honour.

Heinlein's belief in the neutrality of facts and their importance in decision-making is most vivid in letters he sent to his agent, Lurton Blassingame. In these he continually insists that 'the facts' must lead.

In Heinlein's personal life this amounted almost to a fetish: when he disagreed violently with someone, his main argument was that he believed they ignored 'the facts'. It never seems to have occurred to Heinlein that his own access to 'the facts' might be in any way compromised – this was particularly true regarding one of the events that facilitated his turn away from the Democrats: the release of Rear Admiral Robert A. Theobald's book *The Final Secret of Pearl Harbor* (1954), alleging that Roosevelt knew of the attack in advance and allowed it to catapult America into the European war. Heinlein had lost friends at Pearl Harbor and he accepted the allegations apparently uncritically, regarding Theobald as the reliable insider.

It would be true again when he turned against Eisenhower for negotiating with the Soviets, and it also seems to have influenced his take on the civil rights movement and McCarthyism: where we have evidence of his opinion it almost always suggests that Heinlein existed in a greater informational isolation than he realised. However, the stridency with which he took this position appears only a few times in the work: in 'The Roads Must Roll', in that the 'facts' of society are handed down, overwhelming the 'facts' of the environment, and Heinlein's usual attitudes. More usually, Heinlein's belief in 'the facts' is used to structure stories towards his reveals, to make of them, to all intents and purposes, crime narratives. *Red Planet, Between Planets,* 'Logic of Empire', *Citizen of the Galaxy* and several other novels are precisely structured that an accumulation of facts overrides personal emotion and responses to individuals, to lead instead to the realisation that there is a conspiracy.

In *Red Planet* – the most simplistic of the three – there is actually no misunderstanding: the unpleasant headmaster is colluding with the corporation and the facts in this case are transparent, and recorded by the Martian, Willis.

In *Between Planets*, Dom discovers that in all his adventures he has been only a lost mule. When he is picked up, he is deluged with reasons as to why he should hand over the package to someone he has never met. But at least initially Dom will not hand over the package (the ring he has actually given to Isobel). Unlike so many heroes, Dom is not in a hurry to assume that the nice people parading in the white hats are on the side of Right. In an unusual step, Dom decides that he does not have the facts available to make a rational decision but he does have one 'fact'. He knows that Venusian Dragons can only speak truth when they speak their own language, so he asks Sir Isaac Newton. The convergence of 'facts' in this novel is less the facts that Dom has accumulated regarding the war of independence than the 'facts' of personality – whom he learns to trust and by what signs he learns to trust them.

'Logic of Empire' is clearly a precursor text to *Between Planets* and to *Podkayne of Mars*: the indentured servitude of Venus described in the short story is repeated as background in both of these novels. In 'Logic of Empire' Humphrey Wingate, a prosperous lawyer, sounds off when drunk to his wealthier but liberal friend about the good deal contracted labour has on Venus, and in the narrative logic of the story, he gets drunk and wakes up as bonded labour. On his return to Earth Wingate tries to publicise the conditions, only to be told no one is interested. In effect he has been on a 'fact-finding' tour. What is odd, in terms of Heinlein's personal belief in the facts, is that no one believes him and he eventually gives up. This however points to a crack in Heinlein's declaration of faith in Americans, one that will widen over the years: for while he believed in the importance of 'the facts', the Heinlein trained in electioneering (see *How to Be a Politician*) had seen a very plausible campaign go down to propaganda, and simply didn't have faith that others would believe in facts. This lack of faith is explicit in "'If This Goes On—'", in that the revolutionaries actively create a false-front propaganda campaign making use of the theories of General Semantics. Heinlein turned away from a belief in such propaganda but he believes in the importance of facts, while not believing that facts can convince people en masse, and this is a long-running element of his work.

Citizen of the Galaxy, perhaps the very best of the juveniles in structure, plot, character and emotional impact, is essentially a fact-finding tour, even if Thorby Baslim does not realise it. The Beggar/Colonel Baslim trains Thorby as a spy, or, in other parlance, fact-finder, in an endless war against the recrudescence of slavery in the galaxy. As he makes his way home, passed from pillar to post, Thorby accumulates the information that will lead to him tackling the inter-galactic slave trade.

Citizen of the Galaxy contains a moment where Thorby contemplates walking away from the whole mess: that he does not is because of the second half of Heinlein's equation for making the right-ordered person. The right-ordered person must believe in the importance of facts and must have a belief and faith in personal honour. This, when one asks Heinlein fans about what Heinlein stood for, comes up over and over again: personal honour matters.

Personal Honour

The clearest expression is probably in *Space Cadet* (1948) where it forms the lesson in three key scenes. The first is during the initial testing phase: Matt is asked to go into a room, close his eyes and attempt to drop beans into a bottle. He manages just one, and returns the bottle, noting that some bottles have many beans; some have fewer. In an exchange with the officer in charge it occurs to him to wonder what it is that is being tested. In the second scene (or scenes) we see that education is almost entirely self-directed. This is of course a naval tradition – give the lecture, hand out the books and expect prospective officers to do the study – but the aspect rarely remarked on is that this is an honour system, given that the timing of many exams is also self-chosen. Finally, there is the engagement with the Venusians in which a series of previous lessons (eating pie with a fork being the most amusing and notable) come together to show what honourable dealing looks like, from nursing one's dying commander, through protecting a despised prisoner, through working together as a team and, at the very end, accepting that one does not need praise for doing the things one is expected to do.

Space Cadet is tied intimately to the short stories 'The Long Watch' and 'Solution Unsatisfactory'; the two stories are precursors to the world Matt lives in, but more importantly, they are stories that are vitally about honour. Dahlquist makes his choices in 'The Long Watch', less for what we might understand as political reasons – military officers rarely think of themselves as political (that is not actually the same as whether they are or not) – than for matters of personal honour. He is being asked to compromise the promises he made, to consent to arbitrate over something not up for arbitration. In 'Solution Unsatisfactory', a team led by Dr Estelle Karst and Colonel Clyde Manning invent a radioactive dust that they test on Berlin. In the aftermath Manning persuades the world to sign up to a Pax Americana. The Soviets (in this story Stalin has died in 1941) sign up, but as Manning had predicted they have succeeded in parallel development ('the reinvention of the method is a mathematical certainty, once they know what it is they are looking for') and Manhattan is lost to a Soviet attack. After the retaliation, Manning launches what is – to modern eyes – a military coup to establish not a world government but a world policeman.

Part way through the story there is an assumption that the US will of course take over the new patrol: the President is kindly but firmly repulsed. This will be an international body, with a supranationality. The relevance of the story here is not the story itself but the actions of individuals and the system set up in the end.

Estelle Karst commits suicide after the bombing of Berlin: she had been researching nuclear dust as a medicine. The two pilots who shot the film of a dying Berlin also died, of 'systemic, cumulative infection, dust in the air over Berlin'; and Manning, an officer of the United States, is a traitor in his choice not to hand over the new weapons to his government. Instead he sets out to establish a new culture based on a new kind of training, one that will emphasise honour and internationalism and, as Matt will later explain to his father, deliberately separate the boy from his patrimony. The long-distance plan included the schools for the indoctrination of cadet patrolmen, schools that were to be open to youths of any race, any colour or nationality and from which they would go forth to guard the peace of every country but their own.

In the working out of the final adventure in *Space Cadet*, the argument between Matt and Girard is in part because of Matt's adherence to an expanded mission for the patrol in which Venus becomes part of the Patrol's oversight, and Girard cleaves to an old idea of humans/Americans/family first.

Matt's notion of honour has been firmly inculcated and channelled to a purpose that gathers glory and admiration: Heinlein is clear that honour is part and parcel of what makes up the everyday actions of individuals. It is the everyday honour of workers doing their job that drives the short stories 'The Green Hills of Earth', 'Gentlemen, Be Seated!' and 'Delilah and the Space Rigger'. 'The Green Hills of Earth' has been discussed extensively but this time it isn't Rhysling I want to focus on – in the choices he makes he is a retired Dahlquist, returning for one last tour of duty – but the community that surrounds him, the prostitutes, the mechanics and the captains who let him ride for free. The network through which Rhysling moves is one of honour expressed through mutual exchange. There is no free lunch: Rhysling is a man who has paid his dues, and in his singing and occasional helping hand continues to do so. In 'Gentlemen, Be Seated!', two men take turns to sit on a leak in a moon tunnel: of the two Konski, the engineer, exhibits the honour of doing his job – he knows what he is doing and does it. It's the journalist who goes beyond. Scared witless, when the engineer passes out, he takes over rather than – as would be just as effective – leaving Konski in place. His honour is expressed in his concern for his companion. In 'Delilah and the Space Rigger', when a woman turns up on a space building-site as the new radio engineer, the senior project manager exhibits honour by focusing on the job and – as Heinlein might say – the actual facts: if one woman among hundreds of men is a problem, hire more women! There is personal honour involved in finding a solution where someone else only sees a problem, and once more in seeing one's loyalty as being to the well-running of a community.

That could be the tag line for *Have Space Suit—Will Travel* and also for *Double Star*. In *Have Space Suit—Will Travel*, Kip is frustrated at every turn as he discovers that his education is too poor to gain him entrance to a high-prestige college, and his family too poor (or unwilling) to pay his way. The story of his second place in a competition to visit the Moon, and acquiring a second-hand space-suit is one of honour overtaking disappointment. It isn't just that Kip has the interest, he has the determination and the willingness to look for new paths, and this is then played out throughout the book, up to and including the courtroom scene where he and Peewee defend humanity. This, their final hour, is also their hour of greatest honour, as they choose to remain part of the community of humanity. In *Double Star* it is in doing his job as an actor that Lorenzo Smythe moves from the role of outsider to one of insider, and trades status in his role as an actor for honour in doing his job as a politician, which turns out to be an escalation rather than a change of role per se. Smythe begins as a method actor who wishes to convince people of a persona, and ends as a politician who wishes to convince people of ideas. It is an odd encapsulation of honour and yet, as Smythe gets sucked into his role, it works. To be the politician Bonforte he must take on Bonforte's values, including a sense of duty not only to the human race but to the galaxy (something we also saw with Mr Kiku in the juvenile *The Star Beast*, 1954).

In *Farnham's Freehold*, if we learn anything from Hugh Farnham's relationship with his family, and most of all with Joseph, it is that personal honour is not enough. With his family Hugh has behaved with honour all his life: he has supported his wife as a stay-at-home mother, only to see her sink into alcoholism through ennui; he has disciplined his son, only for his son to see him as a bully; he has built a fall-out shelter to survive a holocaust, but, it should be noted, technically they don't survive (by this I mean that with a direct hit, they should be dead and know this: it's not the greatest advert for a fall-out shelter ever written). Most of all, Hugh has tried to be a good liberal, but as we saw, from Joseph's point of view this is merely Kind Massa, still a part of the system.

Beginning in 1963, with *Glory Road*, Heinlein began to use a picaresque mode, focusing on an individual's progress through society. The use of this mode is peculiarly suited to the exploration of individual integrity. Oscar in *Glory Road* is at a loose end precisely because he feels he has lost his integrity. Lazarus Long, as conjured up in *Time Enough for Love*, has spent a very long lifetime honing his. The 'notebooks' he dictates while he is undergoing treatment are essentially an exploration of what he truly believes (stand on your own two feet, help others to do the same, never abandon puppies, kittens, children or pregnant women, kiss a lot). In *Job: A Comedy of Justice*, Alec Hergensheimer learns that he has a great number of opinions but essentially very little integrity; it is his pagan girlfriend who has integrity. The continual moves from world to world, stripped of all belongings, are the adventure, but the story is about the stripping of the apparatus of Alec's (dis)honour and the gradual rebuilding of a man around more basic core values of neighbourliness and sexual honesty.

Heinlein understands – in what may be an early appreciation of the notion of the relation of self-esteem to success – that without a clear sense of oneself as an individuated person, there can be no such thing as honour. When in *Citizen of the Galaxy* Baslim dies (and is revealed as a spy and soldier) Thorby is not an independent person and does not have a sense of honour of his own. It takes the entire novel for that to emerge: in his time with the Free Traders he merely transfers his allegiance and puts his honour into the keeping of the family. It is only when, alone and supported only by a young woman who has been set up to seduce him, he challenges his family and refuses to transfer his honour – quite literally this time via a legal settlement – into their keeping, that he integrates himself and thereby acquires integrity and honour.

In 'The Twins Who Weren't' Lazarus Long buys two slaves. His attempt to teach them to be free is not wholly successful. Joseph is in many ways always subordinate to his wife and overly grateful to Long. Lita, however, negotiates the pitfalls of gratitude, and learns that sex given in gratitude is not a true gift. She emerges as a person of great integrity who is able to give a gift, rather than to see everything as a transaction (either a debt or duty).

One of the key issues that Heinlein identifies is that to have faith in personal honour, one must feel that one has the right to such honour. It is on those protagonists who do not feel they have such a right that Heinlein places the greatest burden. There are three of them: Thorby Baslim in *Citizen of the Galaxy*, the twins in 'The Tale of the Twins Who Weren't' in *Time Enough for Love* whom I will treat as one protagonist here, and *Friday*, in the novel of the same name.

In *Friday*, the inner integration of character and values and sense of personal worth becomes crucial to Friday's discovery of herself: it is not too far a stretch to say that only once Friday believes her honour is her own does she become a truly integrated person. For much of the first part of the novel Friday survives mentally by borrowing the honour of the organisation by which she is employed.

Before I leave this point I want to turn to someone with a remarkably similar trajectory, contextualised otherwise though it might be. In *To Sail Beyond the Sunset*, Maureen Smith is in a 1910s marriage with little right to property of her own: like Friday she doesn't realise how dependent she is. Heinlein is explicit in this novel. Maureen's father, aware of her sexual proclivities, advises her to find a man she can trust with her sexual honour, and in a marriage that contains much husband-swapping that is precisely what Maureen does. For all of the happiness of the marriage, Maureen has handed over control of her body and her mind; even the playful sexual games are primarily led by Brian. Heinlein reminds us of the basic feminist principles that he inherited from his mother: marriage, as it was constructed in twentieth-century America dishonoured women by literally dis-honouring them – handing their honour over to the keeping of others.

This comes into stark clarity for Maureen when Brian asks for a divorce and tries to take two-thirds of the property. It is in rejecting this, and fighting for her own rights as an equal person, that Maureen (and Heinlein) first recognises and rejects the systemic nature of discrimination, and discovers the financial integrity that powers her trajectory for the rest of the novel. It is less a case of a room of one's own than a checking account of one's own. Financial independence and sexual independence are, in this novel, essential elements of integrity.

Sexual Integrity

Financial integrity is relatively easy to depict as a civic duty: as we have already seen earlier in this chapter in *The Moon is a Harsh Mistress*, indebtedness is both a means of connecting society and of trapping it (the Moon's 'debt' to Earth is held as a sword of Damocles over the colony's head and it is in reversing the relationship that their case rests). The trajectory of 'The Green Hills of Earth' is structured around a debt culture that has been described by modern economists as a gift culture (see in modern SF the work of Cory Doctorow). In *Stranger in a Strange Land*, Jubal Harshaw sounds off about the iniquities of gratitude: 'The Japanese have five different ways to say "thank you" – and every one of them translates literally as resentment, in varying degrees' (Chapter 12). In *Time Enough for Love*, *Job* and *The Cat Who Walks Through Walls*, issues of debt, self-sufficiency and financial probity receive mini-lectures that are clear and transparent.

Sexual integrity as an aspect of civic duty is harder to depict and decode, yet if one does not recognise and understand Heinlein's arguments about sexual integrity then one profoundly misunderstands what he is trying to say about society. From Heinlein's earliest writings in *For Us, the Living*, sexual integrity consisted of an absence of jealousy, and an insistence on consent. In *For Us, the Living* (1939) Heinlein reserves a special place in his pantheon of evils for sexual hypocrisy. Transported to the future and immersed in a culture where sexual jealousy is unknown, Perry discovers he hates sexual hypocrisy:

> most of all he came to despise the almost universal deceit, half lies and downright falsehood that had vitiated the life of 1939 [. . .] The pillar of the community who taught his son that a man has to 'go with

a woman' but the women you marry are somehow different from the women you 'go with'. The mother who encourages her daughter to 'make a good match' but wants to 'run out of town' her sister from across the tracks who strikes a more generous bargain. (Chapter 6)

Yet despite this he still gets jealous over Diana's work partner and ex-lover, and quickly resorts to violence to make his 'ownership' of Diana clear to all. The result is, Perry ends up under psychiatric treatment.

Perry is a product of 1930s America, but an alternate Perry turns up again in *Job: A Comedy of Justice* (1984), as a man brought up in the world whom we recognise from "'If This Goes On—'". Alec Hergensheimer is a hypocrite, pure and simple. He has made the marriage he felt he ought to make, rails from the pulpit about the major sins, and has no love in his heart. He is the worst of puritans and he is an anti-Semite. 'At least as difficult was the Jewish problem – was a humane solution possible? . . . This was debated only in camera' (Chapter 12). There is a clear link in Heinlein's construction between one form of twisted morality and another.

When Alec accepts the overtures of the stewardess, Margrethe, he justifies it first by blaming the prudishness of his wife, and then by coming to see it as his mission to convert Margrethe. Margrethe is far more moral than Alec, refusing to begin an affair because he believes it a sin and refusing to pretend to convert (Chapter 7). She is also far more clear-headed. When in Chapter 9 they are stuck on a floating pad, she is the one who points out his gentlemanly attempts to rescue her are not actually going to work, because there is nothing to push against. This is a metaphor for the whole book.

Margrethe is a pagan: she sees nothing wrong with her relationship with Alec, abhors his nudity taboo and refuses to 'obey'. In Chapter 13 he sets off for the Salvation Army and she baulks. 'I thought we had agreed.' 'No, sir. You simply told me.' It takes a long time for Alec to understand that he is willing to love Margrethe in herself and for herself, and in learning to respect her integrity and the integrity of their union, he finds a deeper integrity in himself. This is not always well depicted by Heinlein: Alec sheds his nudity taboos rather too quickly; when he talks himself out of jealousy in Chapter 15 it just isn't that convincing. But what is well handled is that Alec's character development is a consequence of Margrethe's sexual integrity, that is in turn a fundamental part of her total integrity. Key to this is the degree to which it is Margrethe who has made the sexual advances.

Gender equality might be seen as a separate issue from sexual integrity, but Heinlein does not see it that way. Given that (as we will see in his later writings) he divides gender equality from gender roles, it is important to understand that equality is a vital part of Heinlein's structure of sexual integrity and honour.

The idea that equality means civilised attitudes to women is at the heart of the short story 'Delilah and the Space Rigger'. Published at a time when women were being pushed out of the war factories, it reflects both Heinlein's experience and his opposition to this discrimination. For Heinlein, equality reduces sexual tension. In the absence of equality in numbers, as with the infantrymen in *Starship Troopers* (1959), then segregation of women and the raising of their status may be the solution. It is barely explored however and the idea was never re-used, although when interviewed by Walter Cronkite at the time of the Moon landing Heinlein reiterated his belief that a female crew would have been more efficient (Patterson, vol. 2, pp. 308–9).

There is, inevitably for the 1950s, very little sex in the juveniles: the relationship between Max and Ellie in *Starman Jones* is romantic but never goes anywhere, and that between John Thomas Stuart XI and Betty in *The Star Beast* is anaemic. They are significant only for the point that in both cases the women make the choice as to whether a relationship will proceed. (This is repeated in *Podkayne of Mars*, but, told from Podkayne's point of view, the effect is lessened.) However, sexual integrity and honour is an issue in 'The Menace from Earth'. In this story Holly is fifteen. Still at school, she earns pocket money guiding on the Moon. There is a gender division of labour – boys do the outside, girls do the inside – and she asks her best friend Jeff Hardesty to take on a rather clueless but very beautiful female tourist (Ariel) for outside trips. Jeff has been Holly's best friend for years; they design spaceships together, and intend to set up in business. Holly is devastated when Jeff falls for the tourist: she stops eating (there is a lovely moment when her father notes her lunch is 800 calories short) and declines. But, and it is an important but, Holly resolves that her misery over the apparently lost friendship won't deter her from her plans. 'I reminded myself that I had been planning to be a spaceship designer like Daddy long before Jeff and I teamed up. I wasn't dependent on anyone; I could stand alone like Joan of Arc, or Lise Meitner.'[1] Holly's personal integrity is separated from her relationship with Jeff.

In the end, it all comes right: Jeff asks Holly to teach Ariel to fly. Holly ends up saving Ariel's life, and wakes to Jeff crying all over her in the hospital. But the story is significant not because Jeff realises he loves Holly and Holly lets him kiss her, but because of the conversation between Holly and Ariel. So much romantic comedy is set up with a good girl and a bad girl that it is a very real shock that Ariel likes Holly, and by the end Holly likes Ariel. Sexual integrity, at the end of this story, involves not seeing other women as competition.

---

1   Meitner was an Austrian physicist whom Heinlein greatly admired, who was forced to work as a 'volunteer' physicist for many years because of her sex, and was overlooked by the Nobel committee when they awarded her male colleague Otto Hahn for their joint work. She was later showered with other awards. Heinlein honoured Meitner in the short story 'Solution Unsatisfactory'.

This element, slight here, threads through all the later novels from *Stranger in a Strange Land* onwards to a greater and lesser degree.

Stranger in a Strange Land can be understood as a male fantasy of universal adoration. Michael Valentine Smith, Mike, is, after all, apparently intensely attractive to both men and women. He does indeed end up bedding almost all of the women he meets. But Mike is held up as the opposite of a cult leader: he is not setting himself up to be competed for but as a uniting link in a chain of love. He does, after all, begin his life that way, and the way his life has proceeded is a direct consequence of what Heinlein positions (with the title of Part One, 'His Maculate Origin') as original sin.

The book begins with a missing space mission that was sent out made up of married couples. However one couple was 'artificial', constructed in order to qualify. The ship disappears and when many years later it is found, there is only one survivor, a young man whom tests say is the son of the captain and a crew member not his wife. The surgeon who delivered him via Caesarean killed his own wife, the captain and himself. We don't know what happened to the rest of the crew. Complications in the inheritance customs of the crew members mean that the man is heir to the entire crew. Mike is a man with many fathers, born in sin.

When Mike is kidnapped or rescued by Ben Caxton and his not-exactly-girlfriend Jill, Mike immediately replays the 'sin' of his conception: although he does not realise this he essentially steals Jill's affection through the use of the water ceremony, making Jill a 'water brother'. His first difficulty will be to bring Ben within his purview and allow Ben to understand that his relationship with Jill does not preclude a relationship between Ben and Jill, should Jill wish it. This latter point is crucial: that Ben rejoins Mike's community is a necessary symbol of a wider love than the one Mike was born from, a love free from jealousy.

329

Mike himself is slow to convert love to sex; he spends a very great deal of time on kissing. Anne (one of Jubal's secretaries) notes that Mike is utterly focused when he kisses. She says that even the best of men 'don't give kissing their whole attention. They can't' (Chapter 17). Mike can. The integrity of his kiss – and we will return to kissing at the end of the chapter – is offered as a representative element of himself.

Once he does become sexually active in a wider sense Mike himself initiates sex only once in the book. For the most part, it is women who express desire, and Mike who acquiesces. There is only one scene in which he is the driver. This is immensely significant because we have already learned that the prophet Foster (against whom Mike is a foil, and who shows every sign of becoming like Nehemiah Scudder of "'If This Goes On—"'), is predatory. It would be quite possible – and Jubal Harshaw makes this point – to see Mike as a potential victim here, hustled into relationships before he himself is ready. Thanks mostly to Jubal's interference this doesn't happen, and this is our first lesson. Sex is for the individual to decide. The other's desire is not the overriding driver. In a text that formed one of the underpinnings for the counter-culture, it is impressive how often this point is made. Consent is essential. On the occasion where a man threatens a woman Mike's reaction is immediate: the man is disappeared.

To focus and contextualise Michael's activity, Heinlein creates two foils, the household of Jubal Harshaw and the religious movement of the Fosterites. In one sense it is a cheat: Heinlein was never likely to create an ecstatic religious movement he admired (he reserves his admiration in his early books for the Quakers, and in his later ones, including *Stranger in a Strange Land*, for Islam) but it works in creating a spectrum of behaviour from Jubal at one end and Bishop Boone at the other.

Jubal Harshaw, Mike's benefactor and mentor, does not sleep with any of his secretaries. He has sex once with a woman completely outside his 'line of command'. Although there is much coy joking Jubal sees himself as outside the area of attraction, and understands any sex he might have with those who work for him as a function either of pity, or of role. He wants neither. Sex must be equal or not at all.

In contrast Bishop Boone is a sexual exploiter, a creator of exactly the kind of cult activity that Mike will be accused of. So Heinlein draws parallels between the use of sexual activity in the Fosterite community and the activity between water brothers in Mike's community. For the Fosterites the willingness to have sex is a precondition of initiation into the centre; for Mike's community it is not a necessary consequence. Holding the centre on this is Jubal. Mike loves Jubal: 'As for faces, Jubal had the most beautiful face Mike had ever seen, distinctly his own' (Chapter 22) – but Jubal declines a 'growing closer'. 'It's a growing-closer for water brothers only if they are young girls and pretty – such as Jill'. Nor is Mike merely a collector of pretty girls à la Hugh Hefner. To Mike, 'These human females in Duke's picture collection could hardly be said to have faces. All young human females had the same face – how could it be otherwise?' (Chapter 22). Beauty is about life and personality. Thus he admires Bishop Boone's assistant, Dawn Argent. She had 'her own face, her own pains and sorrows and growings graved on it under her warm smile' (Chapter 23).

The themes that come through this work are that beauty is found in integrity, that integrity is lovable, that sexual activity is about consent and caring – if those two are missing the situation is abusive. Overall the trajectory is away from a link between love and ownership.

It is in *The Moon is a Harsh Mistress* that the issue of sexual integrity comes to the fore as a key aspect of a civilised society. Although the focus tends to be on line marriages, *The Moon is a Harsh Mistress* is the first place we see a really coherent discussion of Heinlein's wider attitude to sex. It is relatively easy for a group of readers who pride themselves on open-mindedness to embrace the idea of the pluralistic marriage, but Heinlein goes further. In *The Moon is a Harsh Mistress* is a clear argument for the autonomy of heterosexual female sexual desire. Females on the Moon have complete sexual autonomy and that goes in both directions. A girl or woman may say 'yes' without moral censure, and 'no' and have that respected. In a key scene, a tourist is hauled up for attempted rape. His story is that he had been flirting, the girl was a tease, and when she said 'no' he tried to push (force) the issue. In the ensuing discussion, while there are some rather negative epithets against girls who will go with any man (Mannie likes 'slot machines'), and a comment that Luna girls start young, again it is reiterated: her choice, always, no matter the circumstances. This, not the polyamory/polyandry, is the (still) radical statement in Heinlein's novel.

Equally radical, or more so, is Heinlein's position on sex workers. Sex workers as an approved profession crop up first in *For Us, the Living*, then in *Beyond This Horizon*, and again in 'The Green Hills of Earth', where they appear as the classic tarts with hearts. But Heinlein's position on this issue is visible first in the often performative and cringe-makingly sexist *Glory Road*. It is, I suspect, deliberate. It is because Star is willing to role-play fluffy femininity that she can turn around and tell Oscar firmly that all sex in the USA is treated as a commodity. To his protests that 'There is almost no prostitution in America' she lists 'dower, bridal price, alimony, separate maintenance' (Chapter 10) and painfully explains to him how the rituals of dating are a form of haggling for sex. Having established this with his main cohort of readers in *Glory Road* renders it easier for Heinlein to insist in *The Moon is a Harsh Mistress* that the rape of a sex worker is still rape, that refusing to pay a sex worker is theft and by extension rape. Sexual autonomy is an absolute. By *Time Enough for*

Love, prostitution is not only an honourable profession, it is one of the most honourable and Heinlein puts in a particular word for the children of prostitutes, a group traditionally despised, mistreated and fast-tracked into the trade: Galahad, one of Lazarus Long's nurses, turns out to be the son of the famous hetaera Tamara, a woman men joined waiting lists to be with. He has not gone into the profession because he feels he is just not good enough: for him, nursing is simply a logical second choice (and a fascinating reversal of the sexualisation of nurses).

In *I Will Fear No Evil*, sexual autonomy and the exploration of female desire is a driving force (forgive the imagery) behind the novel. The novel is an extension of a very old SF idea: that if you transplant an organ you transplant something of the old body's personality into the new. In this case the transplant is the other way around, a brain into a body, but if we take a mimetic reading of the novel rather than seeing it as a psychosis, the body turns out to have kept its 'mind' so that the brain of Johann Sebastian Bach Smith finds itself cohabiting with that of his secretary, Joan Eunice. The book can read as soft porn, although it is worth noting that none of the sex scenes are actually depicted in detail, but I am going to argue that it is a book that links together – not wholly accidentally – the willingness to donate your blood and body, and the willingness to give someone your wholehearted love in a wide expression of 'love'. The book, for all its coy and sometimes embarrassing rhetoric, is a eucharist.

Johann Smith is a very rich man, whose body is dying but who won't let go. He is waiting for a body transplant, but has a very rare blood group – one that has proven to him that none of his children are heirs of his body. At the time of writing Heinlein knew he had a rare blood group, and as part of his research he became involved with the Rare Blood Group society, and became a leading organiser of blood drives. For Heinlein, giving blood was an ultimate civic duty.

Thus the description of Eunice that precedes her murder must be understood as that of an intensively civic-minded individual.

In creating Eunice, before he constructs Joan Eunice, Heinlein creates his idea of an 'ideal' woman, and an ideal woman has an internal integrity and sense of self that is sexually encompassing. This Eunice – still present in the body of the new Joan Eunice – teaches Joan a sense of the female gaze upon the female body: it is Joan who really learns to look at her own body, exploring it herself in ways recommended by the contemporary text, *Our Bodies, Ourselves* (1971), and contemplating new ways of dressing this body. She gets to thoroughly enjoy dressing up, enjoying the playfulness of female clothing and the nakedness it involves. The book is explicit in the oddest ways, such as the mention of tampons when Johann is first transplanted into the body, while coy about actual sex in ways that are profoundly performative. Joan is learning to function as a heterosexual female.

Heinlein's 'take' on gender transition had shifted from "'All You Zombies—'" where he seems to be using contemporaneous ideas about intersex rather than transgender and where gender identity is in the body but sexual identity is in the head. So Joan 'feels' female from an early stage, but it is Eunice's sexual identity that she acquires. In one sense, of course, Joan 'fails' as it becomes clear that she will be bisexual, but this is not only because she is still in some sense Johann who was a straight man, but also because Eunice is – it becomes clear – bisexual, and if we accept Heinlein's insistence that this is a psychosis, then it can be read as an emotional legitimation of Smith's secret bisexuality.

Eunice also has a rather complex set of ideas about sex that are a strange mixture of old-fashioned and radical. The old-fashioned element is the constant emphasis on preserving men's sexual pride, letting them think they lead, letting them feel good about the act.

This will be repeated by Maureen in *To Sail Beyond the Sunset*. Yet, even within this context, it becomes clear that sex is a woman's choice, that swinging is fine as long as you are comfy, and the kind of man who uses women only to bring in other women – to construct a him-centred harem – is condemned, suggesting that Heinlein was trying to clarify a few points from *Stranger in a Strange Land*. This thought is supported by the insistence towards the end that Jake's love for Joan is a transference of the love for Johann that he could not express (due to age differences and an employer relationship, as well as discomfort with his homosexuality). The emphasis overall is on the integration of a bisexual identity, what we might now describe as a flexible, queer identity. In the finale, when Joan Eunice integrates Jake into her personality, we have the construction of the ultimate ménage, one that is, it is worth remembering, technically two men and a woman, or polyandry.

Joan Eunice is the character who is most constructed to emphasise the link between sexual integrity and personal integrity but the theme proves steady in all the later books. In the opening scenes of *Time Enough for Love* it is stressed that when two people contract for sex it is not polite to ask for sexual or gender identity, that the proposal is on the basis of liking, and desire arises from liking (although until very late the results are always heterosexual). In *Time Enough for Love* we see a different kind of queerness expressed and – again – a correction/caution placed around the theme of the charismatic man. Sex in this book is for two reasons: conception and play. Conception is practical and involves capturing the genes of the Oldest Man (Lazarus Long), and here it must be said that Heinlein's sense of integrity seems to desert him, for not only is Lazarus forced into rejuvenation he doesn't want (and protests against) but his genes are stolen and he is forced into a conception he does not want. It is particularly fascinating because 'trapping a man' through pregnancy was such a common accusation prior to the pill, and 'dispensing with a man' after you conceived such a common accusation against radical feminists. Here, Heinlein seems to assert the right to conceive. If, as I suspect, Heinlein did know that he was infertile, this is a poignant statement. Play is much more centred around Galahad, so that we have a family with two, and eventually three men (Justin Foote, head of the Families is brought in) sharing the alpha male slot and all of them essentially being treated as toys or tools. It is an interesting integration.

In *Friday* we can tell that Friday's line marriage is screwed up, because finances are kept secret and the sexual rota is decided/ dictated by the men. In *Friday*, there is a convergence of almost all the issues of honour and integrity we have considered so far in this chapter and many of them are played out in the comparison between the two families, the one 'headed' by Anita and the one nurtured around Janet. The line marriage that Friday has joined requires individuals to buy a stake in the 'family business', the business of families. In return the family demands that the individual cede control of their earning power (and thus their independence), and their intimate choices. We see this twice: without it being stated explicitly it becomes clear that the family practises two forms of arranged relationships, marital and sexual.

This is a civic society in which there is no mutual sense of duty. When Anita's daughter marries without approval, there is no duty of care towards her. The relationship is structured as one of ownership and thus betrayal. Flip this over to the sexual situation and we see the same thing: what the sexual rota between the men reveals is that this is not a family structured around mutual desire and consent but around an inward-directed 'duty' in which Friday 'owes' sexual favours as much as she owes regular payments to the family account. When she encounters Janet's family she will begin to understand just how manipulative this was. That Friday falls for this family, and sees it as rightly structured and nurturing, and herself as deserving no more, is because Friday begins the novel with no personal integrity.

Friday is a slave. She doesn't think of herself as one since she has received her manumission papers but her life is structured by gratitude and fear: gratitude for what she has been given and fear of what is out there. The emphasis in the book is on the sheer damage slavery has done to Friday. For the first part of the book her interactions are essentially transactional: Heinlein continually makes the links. Friday has bought her place in her family in New Zealand twice over, with body and with bullion. She buys her life during the kidnapping scene by sacrificing the image of honour in playing to the gallery during the rapes. After the kidnap she uses her body to express gratitude to people who have not actually asked for gratitude. Because Friday does not believe she is deserving, she cannot accept the gift of love (in any of its senses) without feeling that she must repay it (if only in the form of domestic duties).

In *Friday*, slavery and its abuse of sexual integrity, and its manipulation of the concept of consent, is front and centre. It did not begin that way in Heinlein's writing career. Early on there is extensive use of rape jokes and 'play' violence. In "'Let There Be Light'" Heinlein uses the experience of rape as an analogy for what we would now call Open Access knowledge. His heroine is advised to take the same approach to patents as 'the ancient Chinese advice to young ladies about criminal assault.' 'Just one word, "Relax".' By *Friday*, when the rape is real, this will have changed to '*emulate* the ancient Chinese adage' (Chapter 2; my emphasis) but Heinlein has a long way to go, through a rhetoric adopted from screwball comedy repartee and play violence. In *Beyond This Horizon* (1942), Hamilton Felix and his beloved engage in mock threats and mock violence. This repartee threads through the adult work in sometimes uncomfortable contexts: the ship Dora is not, after all, the same as Lazarus Long's short-lived wife, but once we have met the human Dora, then the sexualised repartee with the ship Dora, programmed to sound like Shirley Temple, is not comfortable.

There are strong hints that Heinlein is clear that not all banter is appropriate, and that rape can take place in a context in which consent is coercively institutionalised. In "'All You Zombies—'" the threats to Jane's virginity are, it is clear, threats of abuse and sexual exploitation in the orphanage. Jane's decision to train as a sex worker is approved because it is a choice. When she is seduced, it is consensual. There are clear, marked divisions, and sexual morality in this short story is absolutely nailed to consent. In *Podkayne of Mars*, one of the problems Podkayne has on board ship is harassment from one of the men. 'He differs from his wife primarily in that, instead of looking down his nose at me, he is sometimes inclined to pat me in a "fatherly" way that I do not find fatherly, don't like, avoid if humanly possible – and that nevertheless gets me talked about' (Chapter 5). Heinlein is aware not only of the problem of harassment itself, but also of who will get blamed and – in this novel – of the pernicious interaction of sexism and racism. Podkayne is seen as easy meat in part because she is mixed race, and she is assumed to have crossed the colour divide herself and to be sleeping with her dark-skinned uncle.

Heinlein very rarely (if at all) depicts actual sex, but opts instead for a hypersexualised banter. In *Glory Road*, the banter between Oscar and Star, once their emotional relationship has begun, seems to be deployed precisely to undercut (for Oscar) that Star is stronger and more powerful. Similarly, in *I Will Fear No Evil* the banter undercuts Johann Sebastian Bach Smith's history as a powerful man and repositions him as a vulnerable woman who does not wish those around her (mostly) to remember the economic clout she wields.

However, if Heinlein has a rooted conviction that a society should not tolerate rape, he has an unnerving number of female characters who condone it. In *Stranger in a Strange Land*, Jill declares, 'Nine times out of ten, if a girl gets raped, it's partly her fault' (Chapter 18). In *I Will Fear No Evil* there is a complex tangle of sexual gaze and a tendency to use a structure associated with soft porn in that Eunice's husband is in some ways a sex-toy, and Johann, once he becomes Joan, spends much of his time discussing flirtation in ways that are framed within what we might now call a rape culture: Joan should be encouraging the men she is interested in to 'seduce' her in the sense of using mild force. The result is endless rape jokes. At this stage Heinlein still mostly understands 'rape' as something specific – sex forced by physical violence, inflicted by a stranger (we meet a victim of this), rather than a continuum. It is in *I Will Fear No Evil* that Winifred talks about having enjoyed a non-consensual group attack (Chapter 16).

The emphasis on consent is there from the first. In "If This Goes On—"' Heinlein's premise for the story is that Judith is about to be raped. Her 'consent' is being presumed in much the same way that a married woman's consent is presumed. In *Glory Road*, Oscar scrubs Star's back without ever assuming that this is consent for anything else.

> Hell! I know she would not have made a 'token' protest. She would have put me in my place with a cold word or a clout in the ear – or cooperated.
>
> I couldn't do it. I couldn't even start. (Chapter 5)

By *To Sail Beyond the Sunset*, arguably the least feminist of his later novels in part because Maureen Smith is a product of another era, Heinlein has become convinced that non-consensual sex *under any circumstances* is rape. Hence, when Maureen goes to her minister intending to make a pass, although the sex is consented to, he then treats it as dirty and to be hidden – he locks her in a cupboard. She is not portrayed as 'leading him on', nor is her intent to consent portrayed as consent. She has not consented therefore it is rape. It is a startling moment.

But this is where Maureen and Friday are at opposite ends of Heinlein's spectrum: Maureen is portrayed as a fully integrated person, whose sexual integrity rolls over into her integrity with husband, family, extended family and on into her business dealings (it rather helps that Howard brides are expected to be pregnant on marriage). Friday, as we shall see later, works backwards, only slowly integrating her integrity with her business partners into her sexual life and into her own sense of self.

Sex and Sexuality

Heinlein began his short-story career in the context of the USA's 'blue laws' and his juvenile writings in the context of Alice Dalgliesh and the keen-nosed librarians of the American Library Association. This very much coloured his writings. First is the issue that there is very little sex 'before marriage'. However, as the inverted commas indicate, the nature of the marriage is one way in which Heinlein gets around this. In 'Year of the Jackpot', for example, two people fleeing an apocalypse marry each other. In *Tunnel in the Sky* the teens create a marriage ceremony. It is not until *The Puppet Masters* that we see unequivocal sexual activity taking place between two people prior to formal marriage, and this one is unusual as Sam begs for marriage and it is Mary (who knows she is technically far older than Sam) who declines and insists on an out-of-wedlock relationship for quite some time. In *Stranger in a Strange Land* there is the interesting twist that while the female participants may see their sexual activity as 'out of marriage' by the time it takes place, Mike sees them as 'water brothers', and Jill is sufficiently convinced that this is marriage to decline the option of a legal contract in Chapter 29. The one unequivocal act of adultery before we get to the more sexually radical texts of the 1970s is in *Farnham's Freehold* where, as in the much later *Job*, the wives of the soul (Barbara and Margrethe) are considered more 'true' than the wives of the marriage lines. It is telling that in *Farnham's Freehold* the issue of the Muslim mode of divorce comes up: it is Grace who enacts it, walking out and telling Hugh three times that the marriage is over. Only after that is Barbara and Hugh's union extended beyond the initial act of adultery. In both *The Moon is a Harsh Mistress* and in *Friday*, and formalised in *To Sail Beyond the Sunset*, there is also the idea that marriages should be tested sexually before being concluded: this is precisely the kind of semi-liberation of the 1960s in that, as my mother noted, you only slept with a boy you were intending to marry.

Perhaps the most surprising thing about Heinlein is how little sex there actually is. One of my correspondents described Heinlein's work as pornographic, but until Heinlein's very final book, *To Sail Beyond the Sunset*, every sex scene in a Heinlein novel takes place after the metaphorical curtains are drawn. This is true even of *I Will Fear No Evil*, where one would most expect sex to be described, as Heinlein is explicitly trying to capture the experience of a male discovering being female. Only in his final novel is intercourse ever explicit, and often it is less the mechanisms of sex than the accoutrements – condoms, internal medical examinations and douches – that are described in detail. But what is explicit is that Heinlein, who once wrote to a female reader that her boyfriend could not use quotations from *Stranger in a Strange Land* to persuade her to do something she did not wish to do, was terribly concerned about what was and wasn't good sex. Like Maureen in *To Sail Beyond the Sunset*, he was an amoral man who very much wished to work out a new sexual code.

Good sex, for Heinlein, was always consensual sex. Although there are many play fights in Heinlein's earlier work, in "'Let There Be Light'", *Beyond This Horizon* and *Glory Road*, not one of them turns into sex in that classic 'she fights until she realises she really likes it' construction. The nearest is in the very early *Beyond This Horizon*, although that it is complicated because Longcourt Phyllis wants to marry Hamilton Felix for his genes. They could hate each other and it wouldn't really matter; there was no actual obligation to be a couple (Heinlein has clearly drawn this pairing from E. E. 'Doc' Smith's Lensman series). Heinlein is careless with language, almost always using phrases such as 'he could have had me', 'you could take her'. He keeps the language and structures of heterosexist seduction right the way through his work, with a constant refrain in *To Sail Beyond the Sunset* of the need to structure sex and seduction to support a man's ego. In the group sex at the end of Chapter 7 is the comment that 'Briney put that little girl into my sweetheart Eleanor' where perhaps a later writer would have said 'made that little girl with', a more mutual phrasing. But Maureen too is a child of her times. Perhaps only the first seduction in *Time Enough for Love*, of Ishtar by Galahad, truly reverses this.

In addition, there is the problem of *how* Heinlein constructs consent. Heinlein is an individualist, and as with issues of race he is relatively oblivious to power structures. So that while he understands the transactional nature of mid-century American heterosexual dating as we see in the discussions in *Glory Road*, he is far less clear on how that affects coercion and what coercion looks like. This is clearest in his construction of rape and later incest. In "'Let There Be Light'" the heroine notes that she should accept Confucius' advice: what you can't prevent, enjoy. It is a play fight however, so although we will come back to the adage, we can pass over it for the moment. In *Glory Road*, in one of Heinlein's classic 'all values are relative' lectures, channelled through Star, Oscar is more or less coerced into sleeping with the daughter of his host because that is the tradition in the society he is wandering through: the societal coercion of the daughter is obvious and approved; she is expected to be ready to bring in hero genes to the family. Oscar is framed as rude and churlish for not wishing to oblige. But I would note that in this novel Oscar's consent is also coerced: we already know from much earlier on that he has been uncomfortable about sex with local women during his army service in Asia because of their small size; 'I could never convince myself that a female four feet ten inches tall and weighing less than ninety pounds and looking twelve years old is in fact a freely consenting adult. To me it felt like a grim sort of statutory rape' (Chapter 1). Faced with a twelve-year-old he baulks. Eventually he is persuaded to comply with her older sister and enjoys it (Chapters 8, 9, 10).

The age of that first girl is an issue. Star insists, 'she is *not* a child; in Nevia she is a woman. And even if she is unbreached as yet, I'll wager she's a mother in a twelvemonth' (Chapter 10). In *The Moon is a Harsh Mistress* the same issue of age comes to the same conclusion with no concept of statutory rape – 'once a girl is nubile, she's her own boss' (Chapter 11) – but the culture is harsh on both rape and on child molestation. In Chapter 22 of *I Will Fear No Evil* we again see the condoning/approval of very young girls involved in sex. Joan Eunice is horrified at twelve-year-old girl prostitutes, but Eunice, who is in this novel the authorial advisor, argues, 'that pretty child may have an I.Q. of eighty and no other possible profession – she may think she's lucky. Proud of her job . . . People usually are what they are because it suits them' (Chapter 22).

This is the only occasion however when there is an indication that young girls are going with older men. All other depictions of underage sexual activity are with peers: in *Time Enough for Love* Dora, for example, has been enthusiastically experimenting with boys her own age. There is a great deal of discussion of the right time for sex, and Long/Heinlein plumps for menarche, something that is extended into *To Sail Beyond the Sunset*. A closer look suggests that Heinlein thinks this is around fourteen or fifteen; the chances are that he was unaware that the age of menarche was falling rapidly. But for Heinlein, at least as far as sex between teens was concerned, he regarded this as a reasonable age to begin sexual activity; the idea that there might be coercion between teens is mentioned only briefly in *To Sail Beyond the Sunset* in terms of sex between siblings, and even then is framed as each sibling 'teaching' the one lower down.

Incest is a commonly noted theme in Heinlein's work. It first appears in *The Moon is a Harsh Mistress* where we discover that the youngest wife, Ludmilla, is the granddaughter of the founding mother of the Davis family and has married back in, against the usual codes. It isn't genetically incest, but it breaks a taboo. It crops up again in *Time Enough for Love*, where there are two cases of pseudo-incest and one of the real thing. In the first two, there is Lazarus Long's relationship with Dora; this is complex for Dora never lives with Long, regarding him as an uncle. Although we may question whether Long *should* accept her advances, she is eighteen by the time she makes them and there is no biological relationship between them. There may be an 'ick' factor due to the age differential, but by this point in Long's life he has no contemporaries anyway. Similarly, when Long's clones demand his attentions in the chapter 'Narcissus' (Variations on a Theme XVII) they are adults: they have been raised as his daughters but are his twins. There is a taboo that upsets Long deeply, but there is no exploitation. The one clear exploitation is ironically reversed: when Long seduces his own mother, in an acting-out of the Oedipus complex, he is the one with the knowledge. In the reworking of this in *To Sail Beyond the Sunset* it turns out that Ira Johnson has been trying to keep Long and Maureen apart not because he objects to her adultery – he has been aiding and abetting that all her adult life – but because he fears 'Bronson' is his child. Maureen thinks so too: so although her facts are wrong, she too chooses to transgress. But by this time Maureen is heading well into sin. The period in which she has sex with a man she initially thinks is her brother, she also sleeps with her son-in-law and in a four-way transaction, her daughter and husband have intercourse. This is one of the very few direct descriptions of intercourse in Heinlein's work and its explicit nature is probably deliberate. It is also the one time that Heinlein reverses his conventional description of sex in that a man 'has' a woman. 'Thirty-odd minutes later she closed her eyes and opened her thighs and for the first time received her father' (Chapter 14).

For Heinlein, allowing women to be sexual beings who enjoyed sex was fundamental to challenging the blue laws and a culture in which women pretended they did not. In *Glory Road*, American sexual culture comes in for a great deal of criticism. When Oscar returns to Earth he finds himself visiting the girl who had been his girlfriend before the army and ends up disgusted, not by the offer of sex, but the way it has to be hinted at and framed within a context of unhappiness and loneliness and cannot simply be *asked for* (Chapter 21). It cannot simply be a matter of mutual attraction and pleasure. This more than anything describes Heinlein's construction of sex from *Stranger in a Strange Land* onwards: in this book sex is also ritualised, but in *I Will Fear No Evil*, one narrative thread is Eunice's story of a good girl's pleasure in sex, and then from *Time Enough for Love* onwards, from the initial formal meeting of Ishtar and Galahad in the second chapter, the affair between Long and his mother in the same book, the framing of Alec's and Margrethe's sexual pleasure in *Job* and finally in *To Sail Beyond the Sunset*, the enjoyment of one's body and of other people's bodies is central to the text. And it is this enjoyment of the body that I want to move on to.

Crucial to understanding Heinlein's attitudes to some scenarios is remembering that his sexual education was primarily from the 1920s. Much of his writing about women's sexuality is arguing for the right of women to enjoy sex, something that was still challenged in the 1950s. Furthermore, for many in this era it was only by getting drunk that they could find a social context for legitimising sex. In this context, Winnie's description in *I Will Fear No Evil* of her *enjoyment* of a gang rape makes more sense. On the night she graduated from training she attended an intern party, and drank a great deal of champagne.

> Then I was in bed and it was happening. Wasn't surprised and tried to cooperate. But things were vague. I noticed that he wasn't dark haired after all; he had hair as red as mine. When I had been certain that he was dark-haired and had a mustache. When I noted clear that he was almost bald, I realised that something odd was going on. Joan, there were seven interns at that party. I think all of them had me before morning ... But I didn't try to stop it ... I didn't *want* to stop it. A nympho, huh? (Chapter 16)

Later she goes to bed with 'Chubby' who is the one who left her a thermos of coffee and a Danish pastry with a note. Winnie now doesn't drink at all: 'I know I can't handle it.' That rather undermines the insouciance of the tale, and reminds us that drunk and incapable is no longer considered by many legislatures in the US and UK as 'consent'. Similarly at the end of Chapter 7 in *To Sail Beyond the Sunset* the description of group sex is happy and friendly and clearly alcohol-fuelled.

But that doesn't mean *all* group sex is condoned in *I Will Fear No Evil*. Gigi has not minded hustling too much (particularly as she preferred to hustle with women), but she leaves Big Sam when she realises that she is being used to command group sex: 'a guru needs a young chela for openers or it won't get off the ground' (Chapter 24). There is consent, and then there is consent. The key to good group sex is expressed by Eunice when discussing her time with Fred and Anton: it needs 'men who love each other almost as much or even more than they love you' (Chapter 19). This is a rare acknowledgement of homosexuality, although it is still mediated by accompanying heterosexuality.

The game-changer in Heinlein's understanding of the way in which consent can be coerced structurally seems to be *Friday*. I have discussed *Friday* a number of times now in these terms but here I want to emphasise how much this story is the tale of an abuse survivor, and how much Friday's recovery is grounded in issues of consent. Friday has no proper family; her mother was a test tube and her father a knife, the slogan she and other APs repeat. Even the crèche she grew up in appeared to have provided no sense of identity, not even with other APs. Friday passes as both 'white' in a racist society and 'human' in a society that does not consider her human, and like the protagonist in Nella Larsen's *Passing* (1929) she is profoundly unintegrated as a result. The strain of passing means that no emotional relationship can be truly honest, and therefore Friday can never truly believe that the person who mouths 'I love you' really does. So with this in mind, Friday learns to trust sexually, in pace with the ending of her masquerade.

Friday's relationship with Boss is structured by gratitude and because only he knows who and what she is. One of these perverts her relationship with him, the other allows her to trust him in a way she trusts no one else. Offering and consenting to sex becomes Friday's attempt to demonstrate to others that she is both trustworthy and worthy. Thus one use for the rape scene is to give Friday – for whom coerced consent has been a function of being a slave – a sense of what not consenting feels like: this is deeply problematic but it may be the first time that Friday is so clear that her boundaries have been breached, that this is unequivocally rape.

The scene is controversial because Heinlein once again appears to create a kind of happy rape scene. However, this is not the version in "'Let There Be Light'": there, the advice is to do the 'lie back and enjoy it'. Here it is 'histrionic ability'. 'For rape she (or he – I hear it is worse for males) can either detach the mind or wait for it to be over, or (advanced training) *emulate* the ancient Chinese adage' (Chapter 2, my emphasis). There is a shift here. There is no pretence that this is real enjoyment. And there is never any question that even with Friday's efforts the rape and torture is brutal; although we don't see much, we do see the results.

The rape and the therapy is followed by a number of occasions where Friday uses sex and kissing (of that more later) to thank people and while it is clear that there are layers to her gratitude – she is not merely grateful for being rescued, she is grateful that for the first time she feels she matters – this scenario creates the chink in her self-doubt. On the way home to her New Zealand family she has a short fling with a pilot, a man of considerable status. It is her choice. When she returns to her family in New Zealand she is no longer quite so grateful that they allowed her to buy her way in, or that they allowed her to be part of what is essentially wife-swapping (and note that this is in contrast to *To Sail Beyond the Sunset* in that it is presented as husband-swapping), and this provides the context in which she speaks out about the ejection of Anita's daughter and, for the very first time, comes out.

The period of domesticity Friday enjoys with Goldie and Anna and Mike goes a long way to helping Friday realise that what she has been in search of – and what her New Zealand family abused – is family, and through family, identity, but she is still vulnerable to coercion: on the mercenary transport she accepts a pass from a sergeant even though she is not really interested, because the transaction has benefits. But her integration takes its next step when she unknowingly meets another AP. Trevor leaves, leaving a note 'confessing' that he is passing and assuming Friday is human. The loss of connection, the realisation that 'passing' has an extra cost in identity, shakes her up.

Thus it is important that Friday's final mission is coercive: she is tricked into carrying a foetus for a royal family. It is unlikely that Heinlein was aware that when she is pregnant is the most dangerous time for a victim of domestic abuse, but it is clear in a novel where sex has been used to control, and as a form of credit, that Heinlein is aware of the degree to which this is an abuse of Friday. It is also important that in plotting her escape, Friday comes out – if only initially as a threat – and then makes common cause with the two APs who have been set to guard her, even though one of them was her rapist. Pete, it becomes clear, was as much an indentured labourer as Friday, as much required to act in certain ways as she has been in her past (in fact he has less choice as Friday is freed), although Heinlein does not clear him entirely: he raped because in the end, he wanted to. Friday accepts this, she does not actually forgive and it is a misreading to assume she does. Friday comes to realise that transactional sex in a context in which she is trying to pay for her safety is not truly consent.

After *Friday* and in the novel *To Sail Beyond the Sunset*, Heinlein raises the minimum age to fifteen. He also, as we have seen, shifts on the issue of rape: in this novel there is a much clearer discussion through Maureen of what consent is or isn't and a belief that all activity, as well as the act itself, needs to be consented to. The novel is framed by a time spent on another timeline, highly puritanical, but with a once-a-year Rabelaisian festival named after one of Maureen's daughters, Santa Carolita. Maureen, who really likes sex, hates it: 'That party and the rest of that night was rape, rape, rape all around me.' She leaves the party after four men try to hold her down while another tries to rape her (Chapter 26).

There is something very loving about Heinlein's understanding of both men's and women's bodies. Almost no one in a Heinlein novel has a perfect body, and however lovely Eunice Branca's body is it shows the signs of childbirth. Many of his men, as we have seen, have old, skinny bodies with grey hair and pot bellies. Hugh Farnham is bald, Alec Hergensheimer is a preacher with a middle-aged body. The women tend to be on the spectrum of beautiful in Heinlein's later books but they are rarely actively described: we know the hair colours of Jubal Harshaw's women, we know Hilda ('The Number of the Beast') is small, and Deety, in the same novel, is tall with large breasts. We know Friday is beautiful with dark skin and red hair (not unlike Podkayne) but she has little sense of self-esteem. When Eunice Branca teaches Joan about the joys of sex, it's about the joys of sex in a woman's body, the pleasure of being touched and of orgasm. But all of the women, whether beautiful or not, are encouraged to take pleasure in their own bodies. Jill's account of her time as a show-girl is focused on this. When she takes work as a waiter she discovers she actively enjoys displaying herself in front of them. She takes a job as a show-girl and 'When she felt their admiring stares or outright lust – and she did feel it, could identify the sources – she did not resent it; it warmed her and made her smugly pleased' (Stranger in a Strange Land, Chapter 29). And Heinlein's women smell. In fact, he makes quite a deal of it. Maureen and Deety regularly describe themselves as smelling of sex.

And we know also that Maureen is not beautiful, and is a bit plump and a bit saggy after all the children – seventeen in total – and loves her own body and her body is loved by others. One cannot help wondering if Maureen is modelled on Duane Bryers' 1950s pin-up 'Hilda', a glorious, fat, red-headed woman drawn in various poses including with a daisy-chain. When Maureen has sex with her husband and her lovers, her body is hers to glory in. She dresses for both them and herself and sees the enjoyment of her own body as crucial to the act of sex – she notes elsewhere that when she sees a woman who shaves her pubes she knows that woman is ready for sex: the observation maybe incorrect but it links back to this idea that the body is one's own to be enjoyed.

Sex appeal is not linked to looks per se. In *Time Enough for Love* the courtesan Tamara is an old woman when we meet her and still intensely attractive. Her son, Galahad, is beautiful but considered to lack her appeal, and not on gendered grounds. In *Time Enough for Love* Galahad tells Justin Weatherall about Lazarus Long's rediscovery of sex after many years when he felt 'how much variety can there be in the slippery friction of mucous membranes.' Then he discovers, 'there was infinite variety in woman *as people* . . . and that sex was the most direct route to knowing a woman' (Chapter 15, 'Agape'). This sense of sex, as knowledge and as closeness, that we can see emerging in *Stranger in a Strange Land*, works all the way through World as Myth titles, culminating in *To Sail Beyond the Sunset*.

The key question however is *how* this enjoyment is achieved, which takes me back to an observation made earlier; there is remarkably little intercourse in Heinlein's adult and more audacious novels: what there is, is an awful lot of kissing. I want to argue that although Heinlein is rather obsessed with babies and reproduction, his actual sexuality and pleasure in sexuality is, as Eunice Branca notes, 'oral as hell' (*I Will Fear No Evil*, Chapter 13) with in addition a fixation on scent. Scent is first mentioned in *Double Star*: it is Penny's Jungle Fever perfume that is used to reorient Lorenzo Smythe's phobia around Martians with the result that he now likes

THE RIGHT ORDERING OF SELF

Martians, and loves Penny. It's a rare use of artificial perfume, for throughout the World as Myth books it is natural pheromones that really entrance Heinlein. By *To Sail Beyond the Sunset*, Maureen is hyper-aware of her own scent and it is scent that fixes Maureen on 'Bronson', who is 'a young man who matched in every way (even to his body odour, that I caught quite clearly – clean, male, in fresh rut) – a man who was my father as my earliest memory recalled him' (Chapter 12).

Ronald Sarti (in Joseph D. Olander and Martin Harry Greenberg, eds, *Robert A. Heinlein*, 1978, p. 130) thinks that the failure to depict intercourse in *I Will Fear No Evil*, and the emphasis on kissing, 'are all devices to avoid coming to grips with a subject that Heinlein does not know how to handle.' But I think kissing is front and centre because Heinlein just liked kissing. In *To Sail Beyond the Sunset*, Maureen Johnson declares, 'To this day I am convinced that tongue kissing is more intimate than coition' (Chapter 3) and this although Maureen goes on to have a very great deal of coition. Is this Maureen or is this Heinlein? The extent of the interest in kissing is ample evidence that this is Heinlein.

There are four great kissing novels: *Stranger in a Strange Land*, *I Will Fear No Evil*, *Friday* and *To Sail Beyond the Sunset*. In *Stranger in a Strange Land* the meme of kissing as both the greatest pleasure and the greatest reward begins to emerge. When Michael kisses (Chapter 17), it turns out it is for the second time not the first, and he's become *good* at it. 'Dorcas fainted.' Anne tries and is 'forced to give up from hypoxia.' Later, Jubal asks Anne: 'What's so special about the way the lad kisses?' And Anne responds that it's that Mike gives a kiss his entire attention, and she means *entire*.

> I've been kissed by men who did a very good job. But they don't give kissing their whole attention. They *can't*. No matter how hard

they try parts of their mind are on something else. Missing the last bus – or their chances for making the gal – or their own techniques in kissing ... but when Mike kisses you he isn't doing *anything* else. You're his whole universe ... (Chapter 17)

Much of *I Will Fear No Evil* is devoted to the art of kissing. Eunice Branca uses the excuse of the attack on the car in Chapter 2 as an excuse to 'snuggle' and if we have any doubt as to what she and Jake Salomon are doing, it is confirmed at the end when 'That was as good a kiss as the very first one, Jake...' concludes the chapter. The next kiss is in Chapter 10, and is one of what we will come to see as Heinlein's 'gratitude' kisses, the kind that say 'thank you' or act as bribes. Persuading Winnie (the nurse) not to tell that he is out of bed, Johann (as he still is) kisses her. 'Winnie did not dodge but seemed startled and somewhat timid. Then she caught her breath and her lips opened and the kiss progressed rapidly' (Chapter 10). It's a neat trick for reminding us that Johann, as he still is in this moment, is a male heterosexual. When he and Eunice discuss it they argue. She maintains he's a butch. She also notes that he was the one shocked when she said 'girls could be a blast'. Johann wants to fix it: 'I've had most of a century to appreciate girls; do you expect me to change overnight? The time I'll feel like a queer is the first time some *man* kisses me.' Eunice is amused, 'Poor Boss. Doesn't know whether he's A.C. or D.C.' But the point is neither: almost every character in this book 'stroll[s] both sides of Gay Street' (Chapter 10), as Eunice expresses it. The point is a sexuality in which the *kiss* is the centre of the experience.

The next kiss is at the end of a long conversation with Jake Salomon, the entire purpose of which is to accustom Jake to Johann's personality in Eunice's body. At the end of the scene – in which Jake is continually checking his behaviour and language to suit a lady – Jake kisses Joan Eunice's hand. She forces him to say her new name and then 'Unhurriedly, she pulled his face down, kissed him softly on the lips. "Good night, dear friend."' The kiss he gives back is fatherly, and Eunice notes 'perhaps Jake is going to settle for being fatherly. But don't count on it Joan . . . Jake can kiss *much* better than that. He can kiss so well that your insides melt down, starting at your belly button and spreading in all directions' (Chapter 11).

By Chapter 12 Joan Eunice is getting more confident and kisses Dr Garcia – 'to show my great appreciation, I want to add something' – and this time the emphasis is on Joan Eunice's heterosexuality; it is her first 'real' kiss in that sense. Eunice has to tell her, 'Don't faint! Let's not miss *any* of this' (Chapter 12). In Chapter 13 Joan Eunice kisses the opposition lawyer and the judge: Eunice considers them 'oral as hell and they kiss almost as well as Jake and if Jake weren't here they would have us down on the rug this instant—.' What is interesting is how often kisses are seen as satisfactory rewards, rather than teasing; the recipients of Friday's kisses are notably happy. It is not until Chapter 14 that Joan Eunice could be said to 'kiss with intent' and that, of course, is with Jake whom she persuades to kiss her *as Eunice* as much for Eunice '(I've waited a *long* time for this)', but who she enjoys as Joan Eunice. The kiss 'went on and on' and when it breaks Joan declares, 'you're going to have to marry me. You know that don't you?' The kiss is the opening strike in the deal.

Kisses in these texts and from here on are bonding acts. So in Chapter 18 Joan Eunice also kisses her guards, Tom and Shorty (and note that Shorty is 'a beautiful tower of ebony' so this is an interracial kiss, and it's still only 1970), and discovers that Eunice has been kissing the guards almost every night (the necking sessions are portrayed as discreet, not teasing; when Eunice asks them to stop they do so; Chapter 19). In Chapter 20 Joan finally sneaks into Jake's bed and consummates the union, and much of the kissing ends and, as is traditional, the curtain falls.

Kisses in *Friday* are bonding acts in a very different way. There are very distinct roles for kissing. Friday's kisses are gifts, but for the first part of the book they are problematic gifts. Friday kisses to appease, as in the rape in Chapter 2 and in her New Zealand family (although she doesn't realise it) and with the Sergeant (female) in Chapter 18, and she kisses as gifts in Chapters 4 and 5, but it is noticeable that none of these kisses deepen. One of the few that does is with Matilda, the other AP, in Chapter 31 at the end of the novel. It is Matilda who deepens the kiss and it comes *after* they have realised that they are both APs and that they are going to help each other simply because they are human beings who need to escape.

To Sail Beyond the Sunset is the most 'oral' of the texts. In this novel every man (and woman) is measured by the sweetness of their breath. Of her first beau Maureen notes 'Chuck's mouth was sweet ... his tongue was sweet and loving against mine' (Chapter 3). And for Maureen this is key, for while she believes 'Open thy mouth only if thou planneth to open thy limbs' she also believes that if the results are not good, 'I did not open my mouth. Or anything' (Chapter 3). She tries out all her suitors: 'Wet firecrackers' and goes no further with any who don't match up (one 'tried to rape me, right on Mother's sofa' – he leaves 'clutching his crotch', Chapter 4). And it is clearly on a buggy ride with the 'not inspiring' Brian Smith that she tries out his osculatory skills and 'Three hours later I was certain that I was in love' (Chapter 4). One reason why Maureen feels that her encounter with the minister in Chapter 9, and with Mr Renwick who finds her a cat (Random Numbers) in Chapter 10, is assault is the lack of consensual kissing. The minister moves from mouth to copulation in a breath. Mr Renwick bypasses the kissing entirely, and just grabs. And kissing does not just mean on the mouth: Maureen explains to Brian – when they are discussing erotic pictures – that she rejected one suitor because she does not like how his penis smells: 'if it wasn't sweet enough to kiss, it wasn't sweet enough to put inside me' (Chapter 8). She describes cunnilingus as 'the sweetest kiss of all ... and there is much to be said for taking the two sorts of kisses [cunnilingus and fellatio] at one time, and concentrate' (Chapter 8). When Maureen finally agrees to marry into the Long family it is celebrated with kisses, 'and they all kissed me and I knew they were mine' (Chapter 25), and it is with kisses she is welcomed back after her time in the Blitz rescuing her father.

9

Heinlein's Gendered Self

As must be clear by now, when we discuss the construction of the integral individual in a Heinlein novel, we cannot escape the issue of gender. This is not only because Heinlein's construction of women has often been controversial, or even because considering gender is one of those 'givens' in current discussions of science fiction, but because Heinlein himself is fascinated with gendered behaviour and the gendered self. I have already discussed his construction of gendered societies but here I want to think about the consequences for the individual, beginning with masculinity, then femininity, intersex and transgender and moving on to what I think is perhaps the most gendered and complex aspect of Heinlein's writing about the self, the growing craving for both biological and constructed or fictive family.

Heinlein's Masculine Self

Heinlein's understanding of what a man should be and do is scattered throughout his work, and at various times in this book I have tackled aspects of it. What emerges is that the concept of the 'Heinlein hero' or the 'competent man' that has come to be the accepted face of Heinlein's masculinity is actually rather problematic; perhaps only Lazarus Long fits this model of the masculine man.

As we have seen, most of Heinlein's male protagonists are sidekicks: from Matt Dodson in *Space Cadet* and the many other characters in the juveniles through Oscar in *Glory Road*, to any of the men in *'The Number of the Beast'*, the main characters are followers. Of the juveniles perhaps only Bill Lerner in *Farmer in the Sky* is truly master of his fate and a potential leader. However, Heinlein does not present being a follower as less than masculine. In *Job*, one aspect of Alexander Hergensheimer's perverted personal integrity is that he is a false leader, a man who has pushed himself forward into leadership by becoming an enthusiastic and unquestioning follower who uses 'leadership' as a tool of oppression. The admirable younger male protagonists are those who follow honestly and with enthusiasm. Johnny Rico is the most extreme expression of this.

As an additional twist, many of these men are following not institutions but women, reflecting Heinlein's own biography, in that women were hugely influential in his life. Heinlein novels where women appear are often Heinlein novels in which women lead men by the nose. This is frequently hidden by the cinematic and often pseudo-violent sexual banter, but it is very clear. Beginning in *Beyond This Horizon* we see a pattern in that a man's life is turned in a new direction by the woman he meets: Hamilton Felix is domesticated by Phyllis (presented as a good thing); Don lets Isobel do his thinking for him in *Between Planets*; Roger Stone's mother Hazel brings excitement into his life, and his wife brings ethics and risk (*Space Family Stone*); Betty is pretty much in charge of John Thomas's life in *The Star Beast* and the book is narrated by Lummox, the star princess, who has been breeding the John Thomas line for four generations. In *Citizen of the Galaxy*, Thorby is as much a dumb lunk as Don, and would be easy prey if not for his cousin Leda Rudbek; so too Michael Valentine Smith if not for Gillian's role in his life. The main character of *The Door Into Summer* is vulnerable when his smart girlfriend Belle decides to cheat him. And Mannie in *The Moon is a Harsh Mistress*, Oscar in *Glory Road* and Zeb in *'The Number of the Beast'* get involved in adventures because they are dragged there by Wyoming, Star and Dejah Thoris respectively. Men who do not listen to smart women, such as Jake in *'The Number of the Beast'*, end up looking like fools. Checking out one's brains to one's girlfriend is, in many Heinlein novels, admirable.

All of this sits alongside those novels where there are real tragedies in domestic relations. In each of the works described above, women have challenging roles to play in the lives of their men and of their society. When they do not, Heinlein's women fall apart. In *Methuselah's Children*, Lazarus cannot prevent Mary Sperling (scared of getting older and losing her role in the Howard Foundation) from joining the Jockaira. In *Farnham's Freehold* Hugh never forgives himself for undermining Grace by providing her with every comfort, by removing the challenge from her life in his rush to meet contemporary expectations of a 'good husband'. Both of these incidents are clearly reflections on Heinlein's feelings about his failed marriage to Leslyn MacDonald: Mary Sperling accepts the personality loss granted by the Jockaira in return for losing all emotional pain, while Grace takes refuge in tranquillisers that Heinlein and others in the early 1960s believed were less addictive than alcohol. Heinlein's guilt comes to a head in *To Sail Beyond the Sunset*: when Brian divorces Maureen, Maureen is furious at his new wife, once her daughter-in-law, not for the divorce itself but for the entrapment through pregnancy, the insistence on pushing Maureen out of her own family and for the attempt to control Brian's behaviour towards her. For all Heinlein's resolute defence of Virginia when any published account of their early relationship was written, it is hard not to read this as a re-evaluation of Leslyn's point of view. Overall, strong Heinlein men do not try to undermine strong Heinlein women. On the contrary, as with Georges and Friday, their role is to build them up.

Where there are male leaders in Heinlein novels they tend to be older men, and they tend to be distanced. Not all old men are put into this role: Dr MacRae in *Red Planet* and Professor La Paz in *The Moon is a Harsh Mistress* are provocateurs, not leaders. But the leaders are the men who have been seen as the authorial voice: Colonel Baslim, Mr Dubois, Uncle Tom, Kettle Belly Baldwin, the Old Man of *The Puppet Masters*, Jubal Harshaw, the later incarnation of Hugh Farnham and eventually Lazarus Long. Age per se is not a quality of male leadership, despite the assumption of the Howard Foundation that the oldest should lead. Although Baldwin and the Old Man are omnicompetent, Jubal Harshaw is rather irascible and functions more as a sounding board and commentator than as a leader. More interesting is that these men take the role less of leaders than of teachers. Sometimes this is blatant, as with Dubois and Baslim and Mr Matson from *Tunnel in the Sky*; sometimes it is less obvious, as with Kip's father in *Have Space Suit—Will Travel*, or Roger Stone, or with Baldwin who has been teaching Friday through modelled behaviour. What all have in common is that they have all been engaged in the behaviour they seek to model and teach; they are not – even when they are in the classroom – book teachers.

This leads in turn to Heinlein's general attitude to work. Work is for two purposes in Heinlein's construction of masculinity. It is there to develop the human being but it is also there to support a family (the second is rarely applied to women) and a man must be prepared to do anything to achieve this. The zenith of this argument is in *Job*, where Alexander Hergensheimer – who already knows in his heart that a training in theology is societal make-work and indeed an indictment of his society, and not real work such as the engineering he flunked – works his way around parallel universes washing dishes. This begins as a matter of pride, becomes one of humility and eventually gives Alec more self-confidence than anything else he has done in his life.

Heinlein's men are not necessarily handsome. Few are actually described anyway, but in *The Puppet Masters*, when the men strip, 'Rexton had a burned-in, high-altitude tan on his face, but from his collar line down he was as white as the President. On his chest was a black cross of hair, armpit to armpit and chin to belly, while the President and the Old Man were covered back with grizzled wiry fur. The Old Man's mat was so thick that mice could have nested in it' (Chapter 15). Even given an older fashion for hairy men, it is not a good look. And Sam's comment on himself, 'Me – well, I'm the spiritual type', does not suggest a well-built form. There are plenty of similar older, unattractive men who become love objects in Heinlein's work. Potiphar Breen in 'The Year of the Jackpot' is small, older and pot-bellied; so is Hugh Farnham, who is also bald. Although Friday seduces handsome pilots her eventual family contains far more of a mixture. Men do not, in these novels, either find themselves in handsome avatars nor are they persuaded that handsome is of value, although it does fall into the trope of older, saggy man secures hot babe. And they are often not even very noticeable. Dan B. Davies in *The Door Into Summer* has 'one of the Twelve Standard Faces, as lacking in uniqueness as one peanut in a sackful' (Chapter 9). Perhaps the most *beautiful* man in Heinlein's work is Galahad, in *Time Enough for Love* and its sequels, and he is not a conventional male role-model, being a nurse and the son of a hetaera.

These men do not always dress like the men of Heinlein's time, although Heinlein would be pleased to see how much he predicted sartorial fashion; Johnny Rico wears jewellery in civilian life, and Hamilton Felix wears make-up. At the start of *Double Star* Lorenzo Smythe criticises a man's clothing as looking bad, but does not object in principle to a 'ruffled chemise'. Oscar enjoys the sartorial cosplay to which Star introduces him; and perhaps the most startling sartorial choice is Richard's choice of three 'two-piece rumpus suits' in lime-green, powder-pink, and lavender. 'I had chosen to wear the lavender; I think it suits my complexion' (*The Cat Who Walks Through Walls*, Chapter 19). In *'The Number of the Beast'*, 'styles follow the stock market. In evening dress, men are wearing their skirts floor-length with a slight train. Bodices are off one or both shoulders ...' (Chapter 41). In *To Sail Beyond the Sunset*, Lazarus Long reveals an unexpected skill as a seamstress and alters a very elaborate wedding dress for Maureen's daughter (Chapter 14). These are men confident in their sexuality.

Heinlein spent most of his life on a crusade against sexual hypocrisy and particularly the double standard. Michael Valentine Smith sets out to dismantle this ideology; Lazarus Long keeps up a running complaint about the culture he came from, while Maureen tells how she sidestepped it. Alexander Hergensheimer is of course the living embodiment of all that is worst about it. But this could very easily have deteriorated into a very standard 'free love' ethos in that all the pressure is on women to put out, and on men to collect women. If we concentrate only on Michael Valentine Smith, or Lazarus Long, who do collect young ladies, this seems evident, but Heinlein is not only concerned with sexual access but with sexual consent.

The consequence is that jealousy is fingered very early as a thoroughly inappropriate feeling for a man. In *For Us, the Living*, Perry almost loses Diana when he exhibits jealousy. Michael Valentine

Smith has no time for jealousy and Ben has to learn to let Gillian go. In *I Will Fear No Evil*, Joe Branca has no jealousy over Eunice and his own attitude to his sexuality is puppyish. In *The Puppet Masters*, Sam tries to offer Mary an open contract: this novel is written with an uncharacteristic prudery on Heinlein's part – he was trying for a break-out book – but it is Mary who declines and there is a strong suggestion that she has experienced sexual abuse in a rather rigid commune (it is not clear but there is a hint that they use an Oneida-style rota[1]). In *Glory Road* it takes Oscar a while but by the end of the book he has figured that Star will sleep with whomever she pleases and that he simply has no rights in the matter. In *Job*, one of the lessons Alec learns is that jealousy is simply not permitted. When Alec becomes unhappy that Margrethe is attractive to others and is dressing to attract attention, he has a tantrum. She retaliates by taking off her skirt (Chapter 16). And these incidents are all of course outside the structures of the line marriages and S-marriages[2] and collectives that Heinlein creates. Within those, it is worth noting that it is in Friday's New Zealand marriage that the men figure out who has sex with whom and that this is the marriage that is poisonous. In contrast, the healthiest marriage we see is that of Maureen and Brian in *To Sail Beyond the Sunset*, an idyll of husband- and wife-swapping, arranged concubinage and mutual facilitation. Heinlein men are not permitted to be predatory or jealous.

Where Heinlein is limited is in the range of male sexuality. It is quite clear he is nowhere near as comfortable with male homosexuality as he is with polyamory or, even later on, lesbianism.

---

1   The Oneida community was founded in 1848 with a principle of male continence within a complex marriage. Relations with women were organised on a rota.

2   The S-marriage is a complex marriage not fixed by generation and sex as is the line marriage. Friday is part of two S-marriages in which relations within the marriage are less formal and across genders.

In his early work there is one possibly gay character. In *Tunnel in the Sky*, Rod is not particularly fond of girls. He annoys Jack by suggesting they should not recruit girls because though 'swell on picnics [and] just right on winter evenings ... for a hitch like this they are pure poison' and can trigger 'quarrels and petty jealousies' (Chapter 6). One wonders how his sister would have reacted at this comment. Jack is unamused; Jack is also female. Their next recruit, Jim, notes 'Rod ... were you born that stupid? Or did you have to study?' What is obvious to Jim is not obvious to Rod. Rod never does pair up. We know from other books (*Space Cadet* is the clearest example) that Heinlein was actively encouraging upwardly mobile boys to delay marriage (he had ruined his own prospects with an ill-advised early marriage) but when Rod leaves this book he still shows no interest. Could Rod be gay? Why I am inclined to think it likely is that when in Chapter 10 his rival Grant Cowper asks him if he is thinking of marrying, 'Rod was startled. "Farthest thing from my mind."' Later, when he is Mayor, he carefully dances with no woman more than once. 'He had promised himself long ago that the day he decided to marry should be the day he resigned and he was not finding it hard to stay married to his job' (Chapter 14). For an author as familial as Heinlein this really stands out.

In *The Puppet Masters* however, Heinlein has a problem with homosexuality that he writes into the plot. Mary is used as bait to discover whether men are being ridden or not: her test is whether the men react because only 'harem males' do not. We can only presume that this is intended to refer to homosexuals, for it is never made clear, but if so it assumes absolute homosexuality – men who cannot react to women. The novel is a cold-war novel and in it the loss of a few 'harem males', shot by accident, is hardly worth weeping over (until nudism takes over, which avoids arousing new questions by being presented as a bit of a turn-off).

But Heinlein was both logical and determined and clear that sexual hypocrisy was wrong, and *The Puppet Masters* is an anomaly. Heinlein is never enthusiastic about homosexuality – and he gifts to Lazarus the opinion that it is still not quite natural – but he does try to incorporate it as his novels develop. In *Stranger in a Strange Land* it is very clear that to be part of the Fosterite Church women at least must be heterosexual. In Mike's church however it is more ambiguous. If there is not compulsory heterosexuality there *is* compulsory bisexuality which is every bit as exclusive.[3] There are strong hints that Ben sleeps with Michael Valentine Smith, and even stronger hints that Jubal Harshaw has been invited – but Jubal rejects almost all advances until he meets a woman roughly his contemporary.

However, because the novel is focalised through a number of characters it is often their attitudes that come through strongest, thus it is Jill who has a problem with homosexuality (Chapter 29). On the one hand she 'was not sure that Mike would refuse a pass, from say, Duke' but on the other hand she refuses to consider he will admit homosexuals as water brothers: 'Mike would grok a "wrongness" in the poor in-betweeners anyhow – they would never be offered water.' Jill's understanding of masculinity and femininity are very tied to sexual performance. It is not clear that Heinlein was making the same assumptions. Mike himself is baffled by all of this: physical beauty as Earth people understand it is a blank to him. He is interested only in what is on the inside.

The really interesting text is *I Will Fear No Evil*. Is Johann Sebastian Bach Smith gay or not? Is s/he gay when she kisses a woman? Is s/he gay when she marries her lawyer Jake Salomon? Is Jake gay when he falls in love with Johann – Eunice is very insistent that Jake loves

---

3   I am indebted to Jane Carnall for a very thorough dissection of this issue in personal correspondence. See also Warren G. Rochelle, 'Dual Attractions', 1999.

Johann, 'Why do you think Jake put up with your bad temper?' – or when he falls in love with Joan Eunice (Chapter 10)? All of these are complex questions and Heinlein seems careful not to resolve them – not least because he wrote the text as a psychosis story, even if it is rarely read that way – but there is a stronger integration. Joan reprimands Jake when he shows an aversion to homosexuality and notes that as Joan Eunice she is discovering that she likes both sexes (Chapter 14). Jake does not only love Eunice, but he has stayed with Johann because he loves him also. And in Chapter 13, after they have finished kissing Joan Eunice (after the court hearing), the opposing lawyer Alec Train and the Judge – both married – have a conversation in which it becomes clear that they are both bisexual. Joan Eunice is '[e]nough to make a queen switch from A.C. to D.C.' and '*Who* said we needed a vacation from women?' (Chapter 13). A little later there is a longer discussion in which Joan seems to be channelling Heinlein's own thoughts, and here it's worth remembering that this book was written in 1982, just as Americans were becoming aware of AIDS and before it changed the face of American gay life. The world Heinlein was writing in was barely out of the closet.

> When I was a kid, homosexuality or 'perversion' as it was called, was hardly even a myth; I never heard of it until long after I encountered girls. Oh, I don't mean there wasn't any; I know that there was, lots of it. But it was spoken of seldom and kept under cooker. When I was fifteen, a man made a pass at me – and I didn't know what he was after; he just scared me. (Chapter 14)

But Smith wonders whether a modern boy would be that innocent:

> there are books and magazines and pictures – and other boys – to make certain that he understands even if he doesn't join in.

The Government just misses endorsing it as a way to hold down our outlandish population – would endorse it openly, I feel sure, if it were not that a large percentage disapprove of it publicly while practicing it in private. It reminds me of that weird period in my youth when people voted dry and drank wet. (Chapter 14)

I'd note that perhaps the oddest aspect of this piece is not the unfamiliarity of the closet but the absence of birth control.

When Joan Eunice discovers that her lawyers are 'as gay as Julius Caesar' or 'ambi-gay' in Chapter 15, there is a fairly lengthy discussion of sexual orientation that is surprisingly modern in its understanding of bisexuality or 'ambivert'. These two men are both married, but clearly in love with each other. Fascinatingly Jake insists, 'there is no clear way to spot it, if an ambi does not want to be known. Either ambi or clear over the line' and compares the game of spotting homosexuals to that of trying to spot virgins in its pointlessness and accuracy. By *Time Enough for Love*, while gay sex may not be Lazarus Long's thing it is clearly a norm within the society to the degree that it is considered impolite to ask someone's sex before making a pass (Counterpoint I). Galahad may be pleased Ishtar is female but there is no conditionality in this. As the story develops, it is clear that Galahad, having inherited his mother's interest in sex, is comfortable with a range of sexualities. In *'The Number of the Beast'*, Libby Long declares that while she was *not* homosexual in her male incarnation, 'it probably would have been good for me' and that Lazarus was the first man she had ever loved (Chapter 40); at the end of Chapter 43, while Jake is impregnating Libby and Hilda is seducing Lazarus, Lazarus confides that he has made love with Libby as male: 'I miss the "before", appreciate the "after".' Jake gets to express what was probably Heinlein's own experience and position by this time: 'So much calisthenics . . . Not for us' (Chapter 41). In *The Cat Who Walks Through Walls*, Richard is struck with Galahad's beauty though angered when Galahad kisses him, but when later he is involved in collective love-making he flashes back to his suppression of desire as a soldier. Warren G. Rochelle observes, however, that while heterosexuals travel to bisexuality in Heinlein's work, homosexuals mostly do not ('Dual Attractions', p. 57). Furthermore, homosexuality and lesbianism remain unrepresented within this family structure.

In *To Sail Beyond the Sunset* it is Chapter 12 before Maureen and Brian find regular playmates with Eleanor and Justin Weatherall; it is Eleanor who makes the first move, kissing Maureen, but when the party is set up it is fully four ways. This is a rare example of Heinlein depicting homosexual behaviour of any kind, but as in *I Will Fear No Evil* it remains carefully contextualised in a setting in which heterosexuality is normed. It would be a stretch to say that Heinlein is ever comfortable with homosexuality, but by *To Sail Beyond the Sunset* it is within the range of 'normal practices' that Maureen's father, Ira Weatherall Johnson, identifies. But Ira Weatherall states a clear hostility to anal sex in both heterosexual and homosexual partners; it is viewed as painful and a disease vector and Maureen argues this was demonstrated by AIDS (Chapter 8). But I would also suggest that Heinlein's own personal medical condition, which included several operations on his rectum, is quite likely to have influenced his attitudes. Mostly, by the time we get to *To Sail Beyond the Sunset* Heinlein is explicit through the authorial voice of Maureen that a healthy sexual future will include it and that there is nothing about homosexuality that undermines masculinity.

Heinlein's Interstitial Self

One aspect of Heinlein's work on identity is his use and expression of alternative genders. On one hand, there are only five incidents of this, but on the other hand, two of these expressions – '"All You Zombies—"' and *I Will Fear No Evil* – are such strong characterisations that they stand out from the body of his work. Over the course of the work Heinlein moves from what I will describe as transvestism through intersex, through several models of transgender, to a full transgender identity for one of his characters and this is why the very different experiences are grouped together. It is not always an attractive portrayal and as we shall see, there are a number of rather cruel and dismissive comments in both *I Will Fear No Evil* and elsewhere. Heinlein's fascination with transgender is unusual for him. Almost every other interest expressed in his work links to a public aspect of his biography – even the domestic robots in *The Door Into Summer* link to his desire to provide Virginia (not a terribly domestic woman) with a fully serviced house. This is why I have chosen in this chapter to conclude with *To Sail Beyond the Sunset*. If, as most critics have felt, Lazarus Long is the clearest expression of Heinlein as author, then I think we should consider Maureen as an expression of Heinlein as author as woman. Like '"All You Zombies—"' and *I Will Fear No Evil*, this novel is written in the first person.

There are five clear characters of interest: the sidewalk people in 'The Year of the Jackpot'; Jane in '"All You Zombies—"'; Mike/Michelle in *The Moon is a Harsh Mistress*; Joan Eunice in *I Will Fear No Evil*; and Elizabeth Long, aka Andrew Jackson Libby, in *'The Number of the Beast'*.

'The Year of the Jackpot' is a science-fiction story about statistics and cycles. The principle that Potiphar Breen is advocating is that when all the trend cycles of madness from economic depression through skirt lines and oil prices converge, chaos will ensue. One of these aspects of chaos is a young woman stripping in the centre of the street without any real awareness of what she is doing. Breen rescues her but two other bystanders also step in to prevent the police officer from arresting her. 'The male member of the team wore a frilly feminine blouse but his skirt was a conservative Scottish kilt – his female companion wore a business suit and a Homburg hat.' The woman turns out to be a lawyer and while she and her boyfriend may be symbols of urban deterioration, they are *portrayed* as sane and sensible. When the policeman threatens to run them in, the woman notes, 'Arrest us for being clothed, arrest her for not being. I think I'm going to like this.' Later, in a seeming reversal, we hear:

> Transvestism by draft-dodgers had at last resulted in a mass arrest in Chicago that was to have ended in a giant joint trial – only to have the deputy prosecutor show up in a pinafore and defy the judge to submit to an examination to determine the judge's true sex. The judge suffered a stroke and died and the trial was postponed – postponed forever in Breen's opinion; he doubted that this particular blue law would ever again be enforced.

Although a superficial, contextless reading of the story might imply hostility to this queering (to use a modern term), by the time we have read all of Heinlein we know he was consistently hostile to the draft, and this was to be only the first of his sartorial speculations: by *Time Enough for Love*, macho Lazarus Long is consistently in a kilt. In *Stranger in a Strange Land*, when Mike is dressed in female clothing by Jill, 'He was delighted and surprised by the long false skins Jill drew over his legs, but she gave him no time to cherish them' (Chapter 8). This is underplayed in these texts but is crucial in '"All You Zombies—"'.

There are other brief moments of queering we should acknowledge: Willis in *Red Planet* and Lummox in *The Star Beast* both begin their respective novels with assigned male gender. Both end it with at least a speculation that Willis is female (within the complex understanding of a Martian sexuality where age determines biological sex) and Lummox most definitely is. If Willis is female then *Red Planet* is no longer a single-sex novel. And Willis is further regendered in that there is an implication he is the same kind of Martian as found on Valentine Michael Smith's Mars, where it is clear that Martians are gendered only in terms of a time-delimited reproductive period. If anything they have three 'genders': nymphs, breeding juveniles and Old Ones. As juveniles are adventurous and get themselves killed in large numbers, we could describe this as a trajectory from male child, to adult female, to neutral wisdom – the ordering would be consistent with Heinlein's stated opinions on the relative adulthood of the sexes (Chapter 11).

Alice Dreger argues that as nineteenth-century medical practices became ever more concerned to defend the boundaries of masculinity and construct the walls of femininity, they became increasingly disturbed by those individuals they met whose bodies did not conform, increasingly concerned to ensure that these individuals were assigned to the 'right' sex as they constructed it.[4] By the 1950s much of the concern had centred around 'gonads': did the *specimen* (a word chosen precisely to alienate) have ovaries, testicles or both? Only both indicated a 'proper' hermaphrodite. The presence of only one or the other pushed a decision to that direction, and there had to be a decision, the space for an intersex person or true hermaphrodite shrank into non-existence. And shaping this overall was of course an underlying belief that if there was an option for male, this higher-status gender was of course the preferred one.

These attitudes colour "'All You Zombies—'". Jane follows the regular experience of an intersexed person as recorded in many interviews. Until she wakes from the caesarean she has no idea that

---

4   In Alice Dreger, *Hermaphrodites and the Medical Invention of Sex* (Cambridge MA: Harvard UP, 2000).

she is intersexed. When she is presented with the news it is with her gender predetermined by a doctor who sees her as incorrectly sexed.[5] She wakes to find her ovaries removed, and her male organs activated, a common action when doctors in the nineteenth and early twentieth century chose to operate – testicles were essentially more precious.[6] (Dreger notes that this desexing was more common in British medicine; the French tended to prefer a social realignment). Her doctor tells her callously that 'you can develop properly as a man.' Wedded to what Dreger has called the 'restitution narrative' the doctor clearly assumes she will be delighted by the realignment to what he sees as her 'natural' sex, and of course a realignment to the higher-status sex.[7] Instead Jane finds herself estranged from her own body: 'I was ruined as a woman can be . . . I was no longer a woman . . . and I didn't know how to be a man.' Although she later 'performs' sexually as a heterosexual man with her own self, there is no other evidence of heterosexual performance. Jane has 'failed' in her proper realignment; she has not, as the medical professionals would assume, adopted the heteronormative performance that many sexologists believed accompanied gender realignment.[8] In no sense at the end of the story has Jane's personal gender identity changed. 'There isn't anybody but me – Jane – here alone in the dark. I miss you dreadfully!' Gender identity in this novel is fixed; the body is mutable.

The position of the computer, Mike/Michelle, in *The Moon is a Harsh Mistress* is rather different and the coding that emerges is shadowed because all of Heinlein's later intelligent computers – Dora and Minerva – are coded female from the start and choose female

5   Ibid., p. 86.
6   Ibid., p. 93.
7   See the case of Sophie V, in ibid., p. 3.
8   Ibid., pp. 115.

bodies. But Mike is coded male for Mannie, and it is only when Wyoming meets Michael that a secondary persona emerges, and it is a female persona.

But first we should note how Mannie genders Mike. When he introduces Wyoming to Mike he is explicit, he warns her off flirting and tells her to use her brains, for 'Mike is *not* a man. No gonads. No hormones. No instincts. Use fem tactics and it's a null signal. Think of him as a supergenius child too young to notice vive-la-difference.' Mannie has fixated on the gonad theory. Without gonads there is no gender. But Mike proves Mannie wrong. Wyoming and Mike repeat an exercise that Mike and Mannie have gone through: discussing which of a list of jokes is funny. Mannie and Wyoming often agree but:

> [the] real stumbler turned out to be stories I had marked 'funny' and Wyoh had judged 'not funny' or vice versa; Wyoh asked Mike his opinion of each.
>
> Wish she had asked him *before* we gave *our* opinions; that electronic juvenile delinquent always agreed with her, disagreed with me. Were those Mike's honest opinions? Or was he trying to lubricate new acquaintance with friendship? Or was it his skewed notion of humour – a joke on me? (Chapter 4)

Either way, on the basis of what each finds funny, Wyoming is convinced: 'Mike is a *she.*' Later Mannie wakes to hear Wyoming talking to 'Michelle': 'much more a woman than Mike is a man' (Chapter 4). The issue here is not what Mike is, but that Mike chooses two binary identities, and that self and external identification have moved away from gonads and towards self-perception *and self-construction* (although we should note that in *To Sail Beyond the Sunset* the implication in Chapter 27 is that the rescued Mike will embody as a man). Heinlein's relationship with intersexuality and transgender issues is uneasy: he uses the language and theories he has available as in *'The Number of the Beast'*, where Deety asks Zeb 'are you qualified to check my twenty-third chromosome pair? With transsexual surgery as common I assume that anything less would not satisfy you' (Chapter 1). But note that Zeb, perhaps in a nod to *Some Like it Hot*, declines. There is a constant shifting of argument and ground. In Chapter 15 of *Friday*, the titular character tries to find a restroom in California.

> There was a person of indeterminate sex selling tickets for the rest room. I asked her (him) where the powder room was. She (I decided on 'she' when closer observation showed that her T-shirt covered either falsies or small milk glands) – she answered scornfully, 'You some kind of a nut? Trying to discriminate huh?'[9]

Once it's sorted that Friday is a foreigner, she is told firmly 'Just don't talk that way; people don't like it. We're democratic here, see? – setters and pointers use the same fireplug' (Chapter 15). 'Beyond the open stalls were pay stalls with doors; beyond these were doorways fully closed with drapes.' There are perfumes and toiletries on sale. There is uneasiness but there is no sense that this is *wrong* and the slapdown Friday receives for trying to gender someone, stands.

There is a long tradition of transvestite/transgender narratives known as 'Bad Boy to Good Girl' stories. These have a very typical arc in that for one reason or another a man (usually but not always young) is forced to dress as a woman and discovers he likes it. In 1970 Angela Carter wrote the much-acclaimed *The Passion of New Eve* that took this theme and rendered it as a highly coloured novel

---

9   See Alice Dreger *Hermaphrodites*, for the tendency of sexologists to sex by breasts and ignore that many men have breasts.

of racial civil war in which an arrogant young Englishman mistreats a black lover who he regards as barely human. For him she is all sex: 'she sprayed herself with dark perfumes that enhanced rather than concealed the lingering odour of sexuality that was her own perfume.' Although much of the sex is consensual, he rapes her more than once, but it is her fault because 'so aroused was I by her ritual incarnation, the way she systematically carnalised herself and became dressed meat, that I always managed to have her somehow.' I am offering these quotes because Heinlein will write both Eunice and Maureen Smith in ways that repudiate this revulsion.

When the protagonist of Angela Carter's novel leaves the city, he runs quickly into trouble in the desert and is 'rescued' by Mother and her acolytes. There he is first raped, and then castrated in order to 'reactivate the parthenogenesis archetype'. The surgery is undertaken with him awake and is followed by 'massive injections of female hormones daily' and readings about the mutilation of women's genitals and 'horrors my old sex had perpetrated on my new one.' The operations concluded, he considers:

> I had transgressed and now I must be punished for it.
>
> But, then, why should I have thought it was a punishment to be transformed into a woman? (Chapter 6)

Then follows a stage in which he must learn to become a woman, 'to make water in the way a woman does and the right way to perform one or two other biologically determined acts, how to comb my hair and plait it, to wash between my legs and under my arms and so forth' and then he experiences his first period. 'Then I knew for certain that my change was absolute' (Chapter 6) and he decides to escape. He understands himself as a monster, 'Not a woman, no: both more and less than a real woman. Now I am a being as mythic and monstrous as Mother herself' (Chapter 7). Faced with forced impregnation he escapes, falls in with the mad Zero and his perhaps madder women (for they adore him for his ill-treatment) and is raped and abused. They go in search of Tristesse, the actress the protagonist worshipped as a child and whom Zero blames for his infertility. Tristesse is discovered to be a man, but that is of less interest than the reasons why Mother did not operate on Tristesse when he requested it (note that I am using Carter's choice of gender indicators). Tristesse had offered 'a million dollars to match his function to his form, the poor, bewildered thing' (Leila/Lilith). But she would not do it, 'Mamma told me, he was too much of a woman, already, for the good of the sex; and besides, when she subjected him to the first tests, she was struck by what seemed to her the awful ineradicable quality of his maleness' (Chapter 11).

Heinlein's *I Will Fear No Evil*, published seven years earlier, is an act of revolted rejection of the kind of loathing – self-loathing and loathing for the body, male and female – that Carter uses to render the transition punitive. This is not only a matter of the narrative voice. In the comments of Mother and of Leila/Lilith is a sense of real-versus-unreal femaleness familiar in the current writings of a particular segment of feminists. Known to opponents as TERFS, Trans Exclusionary Radical Feminists, they argue that transitioning is a false response, and that the social conditions that create people desiring transitioning should be tackled instead.[10] This is essentially an argument that transgendered people have false consciousness. In particular it forms a challenge to that last comment, on the 'awful ineradicable quality of his maleness'. Heinlein rejects this.

10 See Janice Raymond: Official Author Site: http://janiceraymond.com/fictions-and-facts-about-the-transsexual-empire/ 'Fact' ' I want to eliminate the medical and social systems that support transsexualism and the reasons why in a gender-defined society, persons find it necessary to change their bodies'.

I Will Fear No Evil begins with the relationship between Johann and Eunice. Johann actively likes Eunice, and although he likes to think of her as a 'good girl' her relative undress does not change his opinion and neither does his flirting. Realising later that Eunice enjoys sex and enjoys men does not damage this. Heinlein's books are generally sex positive and this is one of the most sex positive of the texts. Eunice is framed as smart and independent. She is uncomfortable with the inheritance of shares she is granted and there is no sense at all of dependency. When we later discover that she has had a child, similarly there is no sense that she is understood as either careless or manipulative. Her sexuality as expressed with Joe Branca is contained and under her own control. She refuses sex she does not want, is a willing and active participant in what she does want. If Joe lives off her, as Evelyn does off Leila in Carter's novel, it is because this is how she has chosen to structure a relationship. Heinlein gives her agency.

The story proper begins with Chapter 4 when we arrive as the operation is concluded. This being a science-fiction story we have far more detail about the operation, and told as SF (factually) rather than as gothic (heightened and visceral). It's important only because we are told about the way eyes adapt to inverted lenses; after a while 'rather suddenly he sees everything right side up', as the brain has learned to process the input. It will be a key metaphor for what is about to happen.

In Chapter 5 Johann Sebastian Bach Smith begins to come to. He dreams. He dreams of his childhood as a small German boy before the First World War, of his relationships with his wives (almost all bad), and eventually he begins to wake into thinking and what he thinks of is Eunice and how much he liked her and also how much he liked sex and the women he liked with him liked having sex. It is an exact counterpoint to Evelyn's memories of using and loathing. As he sinks into a tranquillised sleep he dreams of foxtrotting with Eunice.

He hears Eunice at the end of Chapter 6, but in Chapter 7 becomes aware that she is not around. Jake fobs him off; fobs him off too about the use of a mirror. But by Chapter 8 Smith knows something is up, 'Jake . . . *I'm almost certain this new body of mine is female!*' It has not occurred to Smith that they might put him in a woman's body. In an interesting nod to the degree to that men think of male bodies as the default, Smith has forgotten to specify the sex of any transplant. The 'transition' takes place less with the female body however than in the social space. Informed that Smith knows, the doctors immediately default to 'Miss Smith' and Heinlein immediately switches over to the female pronoun.

We will skip over the trauma of the moment when Smith finds himself in Eunice's body except to note that in shifting the trauma from the *fact* of a female body to *that* female body, Heinlein effectively erases the body trauma and instead will locate Smith's acculturation in a loving relationship with *this* body, and – as it becomes clear Eunice is either still there or is part of an elaborate fantasy – with the owner of the body. Heinlein achieves two things: first the female body, although not the process of inhabiting it, is naturalised, and second the process locks down as essentially pleasurable, which we will see in a number of ways, all shaped by the sexual agency that Eunice has held in real life. This is the mirror image of Carter's Evelyn, who frames the female body as barbaric and whose relationship with his new body is hostile. In responding to the fears of the early sexologists that the male in the female body will be a predator,[11] Heinlein enjoys the social and sexual confusion and grants to Joan a healthy sexual experience with both men and women.

This is seen in the first 'teaching me to be female scene'. This contrasts sharply with that in Carter, which had been enforced.

11 Alice Dreger, *Hermaphrodites*, p. 153.

In *I Will Fear No Evil* it is a playful exchange between Smith and the now evident inner voice of Eunice. In Chapter 9, Eunice refuses to let Johann admit the doctors until her hair and make-up is sorted. Later there will be lessons in dressing and the art of seduction. Johann has been 'forced' to become female but unlike Evelyn s/he has a great deal of fun in the novel both with her own body and speculation about other bodies, starting with her doctors and working outward. Even the experience of menstruating is described in much more even terms: no cramps but 'things didn't *feel* right' and aided by the civilised intervention of a tampon. The possibility of pregnancy is discussed in equally clinical terms – and is of more concern because she is Rh negative. Eunice has been told her baby was born dead (Rh second pregnancies are dangerous but not usually first ones). Eunice thinks she has been told this to cover the automatic adoption – probably still true in 1987. That turns into a discussion with Eunice of her experience of a teen pregnancy in Chapter 10, a fairly lengthy conversation in which Eunice encourages Johann to explore their new body. It is also the moment when Johann notes 'instead of thinking like a girl I'm still ogling girls'. But this is not a moment when Heinlein enforces heteronormativity. Eunice responds 'when Winnie was making up our face and you were sneaking a peek down the neck of her smock every time she leaned over, I was staring as hard as you were'. Smith tries to fix Eunice as a closeted lesbian and is told instead that while she is 'too interested in boys to live in Gay Street', she rather likes cuddling women. In Heinlein's world 'cuddling' is a euphemism.

Although Joan Eunice will eventually explore most of her sexuality with men and particularly with Jake, there will be more than one interaction with women as the novel goes on, beginning with kissing his nurse who seems quite keen that 'Johann's free hand was cupping one of her breasts'. Heinlein does not make the mistake of assuming that sexual identity is entirely fixed in the body. Smith observes, 'The first time I'll feel like a queer is the first time some *man* kisses us' (Chapter 10). If the person of Joan Eunice is to be heterosexual it will be mostly because Eunice drives it (as in her comment that if Winnie, the nurse, moves into the valet's apartment 'she'll be in bed with you before you can say "Sappho." *You* may not want men in our life – but I do' Chapter 11).

Interestingly the first mention of a 'sex change' is over the matter of name, but Salomon notes that this isn't really an issue because someone can call themselves whatever they wish. However it is reinforced at odd moments over issues of performativity. When Jake apologies for swearing in front of a lady, Joan Eunice notes 'I'm going to have more trouble learning to be a lady than you will have in remembering that I am supposed to be one.' Joan notes that s/he must withdraw her membership from the Gib club, for 'They'll never let me past the ladies lounge – now' (Chapter 11). It reinforces the idea that her body is the performance of her gender, and again in Chapter 13, where Joan Eunice forces the issue: showing her body off to her law-team (and opposition) she describes herself as 'an old man who is trying to learn to wear her body'. Yet it is not all performative. When Joan is setting out to seduce Jake into marriage she notes that 'I'm cyclic now . . . ruled by the Moon . . . It means the body controls the brain as much as the brain controls the body. I'm tempery and inclined to tease just before my period. My feelings, my emotions, even my thoughts are female' (Chapter 14). In 1973, in *Time Enough for Love*, Lazarus Long will counter with 'Once a month, some women act like men act all the time.'

In Alice Dreger's terms the emphasis on what gender *is* has shifted from the gonads of "'All You Zombies—'" to hormones and glands.

Joan is trying to work things out. Johann Sebastian Bach Smith has a lifetime of prejudice to bring to the project. Heinlein is stuck in

1970 with the knowledge and prejudices of the period however much he might in this book be trying to speculate beyond. There is the question of sexuality: when is Joan Eunice being homosexual; when s/he is attracted to Winnie or when she is attracted to Jake? Their principal outburst reads as follows:

'Because I'm in the damnedest situation a man ever found himself in, I'm not the ordinary sex change of a homo who gets surgery and hormone shots to tailor his male body into fake female. I'm not even a mixed-up XXY or an XYY. This body is a normal female XX. But the brain in it has had a man's canalization and many years of enthusiastic male sex experience. So tell me Jake, that time am I being normal, and that time perverse?' (Chapter 14)

Jake plumps for the body. Joan is less sure: 'Psychologists claim that sexual desire and orgasm take place in the brain' and in addition there are at least six sex-gender identities recognised in the present of the book. For all the offence of that outburst, as the scene moves on it's clear that Heinlein, through Joan Eunice, is searching for a more complex understanding of both gender and sexual orientation. After Chapter 15 Joan Eunice's transition slips into the background as she explores instead her sexuality and a modernity that she had missed through old age. Its last mention is in Chapter 26 in one of the news roundups that have begun many of the chapters: 'A notorious sex-change case married her attorney but the newsworthy couple managed to leave for their honeymoon before issuance of their license was noted.'

But there is a final twist: when Jake dies unexpectedly in Chapter 27, of a massive cerebral rupture, Eunice and Joan find his 'soul' and incorporate it. We are at the end of the novel by now and Heinlein has little more to add, but there is one quotation I want to note. When talking to Jake about sex, Eunice says of the greater intensity of sex for females, 'Let him judge for himself, Boss – whether it's better to spread Eunice . . . or to *be* Eunice.' I will come back to this.

The novel ends in tragedy. As Joan Eunice-Jake goes into labour her body goes into rejection syndrome. The novel ends: '(One for all and all for one!) An old world vanished and then there was none' (Chapter 29). It repeats in a sense the ending of '"All You Zombies—"' but where that ended in miserable isolation, this ends in a *collective* triumphalism.

I want to return to that last comment about sex from Chapter 27, the idea that to be Eunice in sex, is better than making love to Eunice. As one reads these stories as a set it is hard to get away from a sense of yearning. One aspect of that is a yearning for family that I will explore shortly, but the other aspect is a yearning for femaleness. It is the story in *I Will Fear No Evil*, and it is the conclusion to one very old character's character arc. Andrew Jackson Libby, of 'Misfit', reappears in *Time Enough for Love* as one of Lazarus Long's best-loved friends. In *'The Number of the Beast'* he reappears as Elizabeth Andrew Jackson Libby Long, 'male nearly eight hundred years; then I was killed . . .' 'In renewing me it was found that my twenty-third gene pair was a triplet – XXY – with the Y dominant'. This, Libby feels, explained a lot: 'he' was shy, hesitant to command, married, had children, was in love with Lazarus. When he died his body was thrown into the sun. It is crucial in our understanding of the degree to which Heinlein rejected some aspects of contemporary sexology that he deliberately refuses to see Libby's mathematical abilities as contrary to her preferred gender. For many sexologists, gender linked gonads or by now chromosomes with behaviour. Mathematical ability was coded male. But Libby is Deety's doppelgänger and Deety is also a mathematician and genius: maths becomes the proof of the alignment not the denial. Libby's leadership potential is realised *when* she is embodied female, in contrast to many sexologists' assumptions that leadership and bravery were indications of a male 'true' sex.[12]

> I don't *recall* being dead, either [...] dreams I can't remember; then someone asking me patiently, again and again and again, whether I preferred to be a man or a woman ... and at last I tracked clearly enough to realise that the question was serious; and I thought about it and answered, "Woman", and they made me answer that same question at least once a day for many days; and then I went to sleep one night and when I woke up, I was a woman – that did not astonish me nearly much as to learn that fifteen centuries had passed. Being a woman seemed completely natural.
>
> I've had five children now – *borne* five, I mean. (Chapter 40)

And incidentally taken command, which feels much more natural from the body of a woman.

Finally there is a happy ending, and finally the yearning to be a woman is completed in Heinlein's mind. And I am arguing that there is something here that is intensely personal, an idea that Heinlein was chasing down from very early in his career. I do not have the material to push speculation much further but it is important to be aware of this yearning, for it is expressed in the way, when he writes women, he chooses to write them from the inside.

Heinlein's Female Self

There is no question that many (but not all) of Heinlein's women are based on Virginia Heinlein, whom he both admired and adored. In his private writing he continually expresses his pride in her abilities

---

12 Alice Dreger, *Hermaphrodites*, p. 113.

and achievements. But what I want to trace in this section is the yearning to get a real feeling for what women think, feel and want. Whether Heinlein achieves that is more problematic.

That Heinlein approved of full participation for women in any future society is not really in doubt. As has been demonstrated again and again, once free of the constraints of the juveniles (and even within some of them) he repeatedly depicts women at a time when many of his contemporary writers of science fiction often forgot about the need for the human race to reproduce. But neither does he assume this is women's only purpose. In the juveniles he frequently steers clear or even undermines any romantic plot line, as in *Starman Jones*, where the ingénue marries someone else, or in *Have Space Suit—Will Travel*, where Peewee is too young for this to be an issue. In both cases the female characters are fully engaged in the adventure, and in Kip's case there is an argument that he is the recruited companion and aide to Peewee. He joins her adventure; she does not join his. Even when the female characters are the 'love interest', as in *The Puppet Masters*, Heinlein gives them full agency within the adventure, and often more acuity and ability than their male protagonist companions. There is a case to be made that Sam is subordinate to Mary, not only in terms of his role in the drama – he is replaceable, she is not – but also in their relationship. For all the language of subordination it is Sam who is anxious to conform to Mary's needs, not the other way around.

The above is not to argue that all of Heinlein's portrayal of women is comfortable – both Barbara in *Farnham's Freehold* and Margrethe in *Job* are subservient in behaviour – but as with Star in *Glory Road* there is a performativeness to the subservience that we can trace back to the cinematic conventions of Heinlein's earliest work. When push comes to shove, both shove. In *Stranger in a Strange Land* Alice Douglas is positioned as the nagging wife, the one who believes herself the power behind the throne: 'her own political philosophy . . . [was] a belief that men should rule the world and that women should rule men' (Chapter 9). But Heinlein immediately notes '[t]hat all her beliefs and actions derived from a blind anger at a fate that had made her female.' That is a clear indication that while he does not *like* the Alices of this world, he understands them as a product of a distorted society – a relatively rare acknowledgement of the consequence of systemic oppression. And of course, Alice turns out to be right: she has been sent to Earth as a 'goad' to keep someone on his destined path (Chapter 28).

Unusual also is that Heinlein's women have bodies. His women feel fat (Puddin'), hate their skin colour (Friday), have fertility issues (Wyoming) and periods (Barbara, Karen, Joan Eunice, Maureen). Heinlein may be the only male science-fiction writer to regard sanitary equipment as part of the general supplies of a bomb shelter. In this context we must not take all of Heinlein's depictions of women by male narrators as either authorial voice or a statement on how things should be. The birth scene in *Farnham's Freehold* has frequently been mocked as unrealistic and dangerous, without the qualification that it *is* unrealistic in the sense of not meeting contemporary expectations, and dangerous: Karen dies. This is no miracle survival story. If Barbara had not ended up receiving medical treatment from her captors, it's a certainty that she, too, would have died, ignorance being compounded by twins.

But this raises the point that Heinlein has ten stories narrated by female protagonists, or where there is space made for a female perspective and narrative thread, and it is these that I want to turn to in order to explore how Heinlein constructs the female self. These texts are the three Puddin' stories (between 1949 and 1951) – 'Poor Daddy', 'Cliff and the Calories' and 'The Bulletin Board' – all of them the precursor stories to *Podkayne of Mars*. There are two female narrators/focalisers in *The Star Beast*, Betty and Lummox herself. There is the very neat short story, 'The Menace from Earth', anthologised four times between 1957 and 1984 and still popular. Eunice is a narrative voice in *I Will Fear No Evil*, Hilda and Dejah Thoris/Deety in *'The Number of the Beast'*, Friday in her own novel, and Maureen Smith in *To Sail Beyond the Sunset*. For *I Will Fear No Evil* I will look in this section only at the character of Eunice because it is Eunice who is the authorial voice or advisor.

My contention is that in those texts in which women have narrative and focalised agency, Heinlein made a conscious effort to think about what women were like, and how they thought about themselves. He tried to create for them a voice that was embodied and aware of being female in a male world. In these stories he also tried to make an argument about the possibilities for shifting that sense of self.

Heinlein had grown up at a time in which a woman's world was constrained, but even more constrained was the degree that she was permitted to acknowledge her body, her bodily needs and her sexuality. Although these are not always front and centre, they are there in the first three stories he attempted in the female voice, non-science-fiction stories about Pudding that he wrote at the behest of a female editor 'simultaneously astonished, offended and amused at the ridiculous and arrogant notion that a mere man could write stories for girls' (*Expanded Universe*, p. 286).

Maureen, or Pudding, is a delightful character. Her father is a college lecturer, her mother an energetic organiser, her brother a brat. She is a college student at the same place as her father teaches and she has a boyfriend called Cliff whom, in true 1950s style, she has decided she is going to marry; she loves her food, has a relationship with her weight that is healthy but caught up in the stress of external influences, and she is also self-aware, analytical and kind. She is one of Heinlein's smart young women.

The first of the Pudding stories is the one most connected to *Podkayne of Mars* in that it uses the same characters of extrovert, smart, adventurous and energetic woman married to a rather more cautious man whom she overwhelms. In the story Pudding observes that her mother's adventurousness is drawing her away from her bookish husband. One day he declares he is going to learn to skate, having figured it out from the books. Pudding observes him teaching himself in public and doing things efficiently, if not elegantly. Mom is both terrified he will injure himself and impressed at his skill. Pudding figures out it's a stitch-up: Dad has been taking lessons in a neighbouring town. While there are aspects of this story that seem to be a putdown to the mother, a Lucille-Ball-like figure, there is nothing of the denigration so common in the scripts of *I Love Lucy*. Dad does not try to prevent his wife from achieving: although he does have some fun at her expense it is in part because she assumes there is only one way to approach life. What he wants is to join in. Susan Cain would note that it describes fairly accurately the difference between extrovert and introvert approaches to learning, the former tending to be public in the process, the latter private until competent. From what Heinlein says in *Tramp Royale* this fairly describes the difference between himself and Virginia. What Pudding learns is that she does not have to be like her mother, and that it is acceptable to take her father as her role model. In *Podkayne*, Poddy's father's failure to offer another model undermines her own sense of self. Overwhelmed by her mother she has no other strategy to turn to.

The second of the Pudding stories is in many ways more interesting because it cuts right across American body culture. Pudding/Maureen has acquired her nickname both because she is chubby and because she does rather like that second helping of pudding. Yet Maureen is anything but a social failure: she is happy, popular and has a boyfriend. And for all Heinlein describes her in his introduction as 'having a weight problem' the outcome of the story suggests otherwise. Maureen opens the story with a growing fear about her weight, prompted by family teasing (she 'has no sideways'). Although it bothers her she is more worried that her boyfriend might agree, so when a girl arrives at the school with the same measurements she directs Cliff's gaze at the other girl's figure. He is dismissive, 'Oh, sure – from her ankles down.' And thus Pudding embarks on a diet, starting by checking out the calories in the cheese and crackers she has been eating. The whole family ends up on diets: Daddy for possible allergies, kid brother for training (beef, dripping with blood, wholewheat toast) and Mother 'seaweed soup or cracked wheat or raw rhubarb'. The diet lasts until they are on a road trip and, starving hungry, come across a place that advertises itself as Santa Claus, Arizona. They pull up at a restaurant with a menu to die for: Minted Fruit Cup Rouge, Pot-au-feu à la Creole, Chicken Velvet Soup, Roast Veal with Fine Herbs, Ham Soufflé, it goes on for another twenty-two items of which nine are dessert. Pudding is miserable. Asked 'Anything special you mustn't eat?' she responds 'Nothing in particular – just food. I mustn't eat food.' Mrs Claus noted that 'I've never been able to work up interest in such [low calorie] cooking' and suggests she just eat a little bit. Maureen tries, 'I counted up to ten between bites, then I found I was counting fast so as to finish each course before the next one arrived.' 'Once my conscience peeked over the edge of my plate and I promised to make up for it tomorrow. It went back to sleep.' When the cook offers them rooms for the night they stay. Breakfast is grapefruit, milk, oatmeal, sausage and eggs, toast and butter and jam, bananas and cream: 'my personality split hopelessly between despair and ecstasy.'

They drive on and finally get to their hotel where Cliff is waiting, 'What has happened? You look as if you had lost your last friend – and you are positively emaciated.' Once she stops crying Maureen tells Cliff all about it. He doesn't speak but drives her to the local art museum and finds *The Judgement of Paris* and other Rubens paintings. 'That,' he said, 'is my notion of a beautiful woman.' 'What this country needs ... is more plump girls – and more guys like me who appreciate them.' And that is the end of the diet. Cliff it seemed thought the other girl was a knock-out, but had not said so because he didn't want to make Maureen jealous. He then takes her off for a Mount Everest, twenty flavours of ice cream, four bananas, butterscotch syrup and nuts with chocolate syrup, sprinkled malted-milk powder and more nuts, with marshmallow syrup and whipped cream. What makes the story a delight is that Maureen is mostly so comfortable in herself. Yes, Cliff provides reassurance but Maureen is a young woman who deep down knows she is lovely and it helps her resist the pressures from outside. We see this again in the third story, which sadly was not published at the time, perhaps because Heinlein's fat positivity was too much for the editor to handle.

The third story, 'Bulletin Board' (in *Requiem*), is just as reassuring in its own way and is a counter to Cliff's suggestion that Maureen might be jealous. Much 'girl culture' in this period was directed at competition, and American culture generally is directed towards popularity as a specific goal. But Heinlein opts to value something else: generosity of spirit. Maureen realises that a newish student, Gabrielle, who has been educated in France and isn't socialised for American college culture, is lonely: she has been sending notes to herself on the bulletin board. Another girl finds out and sets up a very spiteful trick, setting up a fake invitation to a party, planning to leave Gabrielle sitting lonely and isolated in a coffee bar. Maureen and Cliff retaliate by setting up a surprise party. Mom empties the freezer, Cliff finds a band, Maureen books the local hairdresser and finds a cake (in a very nice touch the manager of Helen Hunt's Tasty Pastry Shoppe is referred to as Mr Helen Hunt throughout). Gabrielle is transformed physically, introduced to a French exchange student and is off and running with her own fans. The story offers two lessons: one is about making the most of oneself physically with some standard comments on make-up and clothing and being popular, but the much more pertinent lesson is the one that real popularity and true connection lies in the alliances between women.

We see this vividly in 'The Menace from Earth'. This story initially starts as one about the distraction of boys from the serious things in life, 'designing space ships'. As discussed earlier, the story concludes with Holly's discovery that women can be allies.

Holly is lucky. Neither Betty nor Lummox (in *The Star Beast*) have supportive women in their lives. John Thomas Stuart XI's mother is one of the awful women in Heinlein's writing, the mother who does not support the ambitions or interests of their children. She is very similar to the mothers of Max Jones, Johnny Rico and Joe Branca – mothers who actively undermine. Here Heinlein demonstrates that girls can have some power even where they don't have authority. Betty is a free agent, and though she lives in a world where there are no adult powerful women, she has figured out that she can negotiate with it by supporting her chosen male partner. It is probably the least science-fictional of Heinlein's books in that Betty appears entirely trapped in the 1950s, and may be the last of the juveniles to have no visible female authority figures.

Betty is sassy, takes control of the courtroom, negotiates with Mr Kiku and plans to do the proposing herself. She is very much the driver of the story. And then of course there is Lummox. Lummox is patient, friendly and a pet. Until she turns out to be the missing princess of the Hroshii, the Infanta, the heir to an empire. We spend quite a lot of time with Lummox, musing in his/her thoughts. We get to know a female character rather intimately, without ever realising it is female. It is a very neat trick because, by the end of the story, as with *Have Space Suit—Will Travel*, we can pause and wonder just whose adventure this is? John Thomas is an extremely passive character; apart from running away with Lummox he does very little to actually help either himself or her. It is Betty who drives the court case in a tale of a young woman fighting for justice for the oppressed, and Lummox is clearly the wandering child in a portal fantasy. All the interpretation of this story, the *shaping of it*, comes from the two female characters.

Despite this level of agency, one thing that emerges when one focuses on the female narrative voices is the degree to which they are watching rather than participating voices (even when I have argued that theirs is really the adventure). Maureen, Holly, Betty and Lummox are all outside the institutional structures in which they live; their participation is not taken for granted in the way it is for the boys and they are not on a trajectory to integration into a wider social family. This takes us to *Podkayne of Mars*.

Told through Podkayne's diary, this should be the story of a very modern young woman. Instead it is almost classically nineteenth century, in that Podkayne is positioned at the edge of the room in almost every scene, looking into a world she cannot have. She is marginalised by her parents, who are interested in their own careers and their super-bright son; she is marginalised when the triplets arrive and finds herself losing the chance of a trip to Earth and changing nappies instead. When she is aboard ship with her Uncle Tom she is positioned as his companion, and then finds herself trapped into the role of companion to an elderly and very unpleasant lady. Although Tom has done his best to recentre Podkayne by demanding the crèche compensate her, the degree to which Podkayne has learned to sit on the side and watch is vivid in the scene where Tom confronts the Director of Marsopolis Crèche. In the two pages in which the Director tries to offer her a deal, Podkayne says nothing. Even though she is the centre of the conversation, all the real conversation has taken place between Tom and the Director before she arrived. Her only contribution is to accept the deal. Her brother Clark has more lines in this scene than does Podkayne (Chapter 3).

Throughout *Podkayne of Mars*, Podkayne watches. She watches the dynamics in her family, she watches the dynamics on board ship – the ones that ensure that no one dances with lovely, middle-aged but not old Girdie, thus giving Podkayne a lesson on how hard life is for an unattached middle-aged lady (Chapter 5). She watches the dynamics between the older women well enough that she knows when they are using her and conspiring. And she watches the ship's officers. Because Podkayne lacks any sense of entitlement, she does not outright *ask* for the coaching and support of the ship's officers. Instead she uses what she has learned about being feminine and watching to manipulate the second and third officers into teaching her how to program a ballistic computer. In many ways, the elder she is modelling is Uncle Tom, Senator and spy. He is the only person who has engaged her in his work, and thus when Podkayne does acquire agency it is on the political side, where she eventually takes action. *She* is the hero, she is the one who goes to rescue her brother who has made an ill-advised attempt at being a knight in shining armour for Girdie, and her uncle, and then when they escape, goes back to rescue the baby fairy. I think it no coincidence that the novel ends with the active younger brother, having ceded action to Podkayne, being the one stuck watching, unable to take action to secure Podkayne's life.

The tragedy is that Podkayne is unaware of the way she has been trapped, and does not know the routes out. Instead what she learns by watching is that women are marginalised and that they are rarely supportive of each other. The novel is in many ways about the grinding down of a young woman, the reducing of her ambitions. For all that the crew like her and teach her, no one takes her seriously. Even Tom, who will conclude the book by shredding her parents for failing to educate her properly, uses her as a guise.

Eunice Branca is a minor character in *I Will Fear No Evil*, although she becomes a crucial narrative voice. From the very beginning she is assigned to watching and to commenting and this is then her function in the later part of the novel when she moves from her role as external and embodied PA to that of internal and disembodied authorial Advisor. She is one of Heinlein's confident women and that means some very specific things to Heinlein. Eunice is confident in her looks – she was a beauty queen; in her intelligence – she decided beauty wasn't going to earn her a living and went back to college; in her ability to attract men; and in her sexuality. Chapter 2 of the novel is very much focalised on her interior voice, foreshadowing how much of the conversation will be interior. It allows Heinlein to explore two very specific sides of Eunice Branca, her sound common sense with money and her sexuality. I have put it that way because that is how we are introduced to her interiority. When she contemplates Joe it's 'as sweet a husband as a girl could wish . . . as long as I never again let him share a joint account' (Chapter 2). Later, Smith will assume that Joe has been living off Eunice, but it is clearer through Eunice's eyes – and later through Joan Eunice's experience – that Eunice 'keeps' Joe as a toy boy, admiring his art but his sexual prowess more. There is a strong hint that she pays her way through college as a sex worker. She dresses for Smith in order to make him feel good, but it is in a way that she actively prefers: if anything the more 'modest' clothing she has donned is the clothing she finds uncomfortable. She offers Jake a 'skin pic' and when he admits he likes perfume she offers to wear it for him. When she asks Joe to paint her she notes that for Boss, she needs a G-string. 'As long as I wear a minimum-gee – and paint and shoes – I'm dressed, not naked' (Chapter 3), for he 'formed his ideas so long ago that nakedness wasn't just uncommon, it was a sin.' She may well be a male fantasy of the liberated woman, and we may not always be comfortable that Heinlein's construction of confidence in a woman is always linked to sexual confidence, but it is confidence, and it is a confidence that allows her to negotiate her own sexual boundaries. Eunice chooses her men. When Joe suggests swinging with Big Sam and Gigi she declines, not because she won't swing but because she does not like Sam: 'Big Sam is no guru, he's just a stud. And bliffy' (Chapter 3). Heinlein's female sexual confidence does not extend to an assumption that women will automatically 'put out.'

Eunice is also self-confident in her person in other ways: she is willing to go through an Abandoned area both to get to work and to give blood in an emergency. When Jake warns her that her clothing (or lack of it) makes her a temptation she brushes it away: she goes armed. She shoots one attempted rapist and doesn't wait behind to find out whether he lived. For all she ends up dead, the attack is not sexual and in this case Heinlein does not position sexuality as vulnerable, quite the opposite. Eunice makes her own choices and if her narrative voice (possibly imaginary of course) is to be believed, she does not regret taking the risks.

In 'The Number of the Beast', the emotional set-up is led by the two women, Hilda and Deety. Both go husband-hunting although it has taken Hilda rather longer to sort Jacob out – Heinlein really does prefer a small subset of names – but the relationships are monogamous in a way alien to Heinlein, and only comprehensible if you remember that he is riffing heavily on his hero E. E. 'Doc' Smith. But Heinlein being Heinlein one aspect of the plot is precisely about Jacob's assumption that the women in his life will 'put out' in the social and economic sense as alluded to in Chapter 4.

The book is unusual for Heinlein in that each chapter is narrated by a different voice. This gives him the chance to be very clear that narrative voice and authorial voice are very different. Part of the set-up of the story is that the captaincy of the ship is rotated. It turns out that the men are a lot less enthusiastic about the reality of this than they are about the theory and that the women are a lot less honeymoon-sweet on their husbands.[13] Hilda has to slap Zeb down for declaring 'I don't like to leave you girls unguarded!' with 'I am not a girl. I am eleven years your senior', and a reminder of her rank (Chapter 22). When Jake is narrating in Chapter 23 his contempt for female ability is disclosed when he tries to relieve Hilda of command in a tight spot: 'We'll lift as soon as possible – and Zeb will be in command. This farce is over.' Hilda calls him on it, reminds him he voted for her three times and goes to call another vote but Deety prevents her: 'A commanding officer *commands*; she doesn't ask for votes.' Jake swallows and decides to accept it but 'In truth I wanted Zeb and *only* Zeb to command when the car was off the ground.' But the tension builds and there is more and more sniping, with Jake regularly using endearments to undermine his wife's status as captain and expressing 'concern' that she is not qualified, for example to act as a diplomat (Chapter 24).

In Chapter 25 the voice switches to Deety and she dishes the dirt: 'Pop is one of the most selfish people I've ever known.' She does not mean selfish with money but with his assumptions about his entitlement to the labour of women. This piece can only have come from life. 'I was bucking for my doctorate. Pop seemed to think that I should cook, clean house, shop, keep financial records, manage our businesses, cope with taxes – and earn my doctorate simultaneously.' Deety tries a strike and eventually he notices and gets a housekeeper,

---

13   Jo Walton wonders if Heinlein is revisiting the very sexist structure of *The Rolling Stones*, in which the father, Roger, takes for granted his captaincy and Meade is relegated to a far inferior education than that of her brothers (Jo Walton, 'Pass the Slide Rule', 2011).

and he helps Deety with a sexist committee, but 'Pop is one of those men who sincerely believe in Women's Lib, always support it – but so deep down that they aren't aware of it, their emotions tell them that women never get over being children' (Chapter 25). And worse even, when called out for lack of respect by just about everyone, he cannot structure an apology to his wife that shows respect for her captaincy. Here Heinlein captures what has become a tenet of social justice awareness; all Jacob's apologies contain 'buts' and 'If Pop started defending himself, he would wind up self-righteous. The ability of the male mind to rationalize its deeds – and misdeeds – cannot be measured.' In Chapter 26, he decides to keep his mouth shut, but it is because he does not want to hurt Hilda's feelings. He quite simply cannot see her competence and even when he does have a moment of realisation it is that 'the three women I have loved most all consider me to be a back-seat driver' (Chapter 25). Hilda finally has to threaten him with a charge of mutiny to get him to take this out of the personal and into the professional (Chapter 27). By the end of the book Jacob is thoroughly squashed, and Hilda's professional integrity has been established. Hilda's integrity and agency is never in doubt to outsiders but Heinlein argues fiercely that there is something seriously wrong when a man fails to recognise this.

To Sail Beyond the Sunset, a curious, anti-feminist and yet feminist novel, brings into focus Heinlein's idea of a perfectly integrated, right-ordered individual, and the person in the frame is a woman. It is in this story that we get most strongly the sense of Heinlein trying to write women from the inside and focus himself as a woman. I have spent a little time here describing this book, for it is the book that relatively few people have read, and very few people (including myself before I started this project) have read twice. I have come to believe that it is simply not the book that I read in 1987 at the age of nineteen; my current age and experiences have profoundly shifted my response.

The full title of this book is *To Sail Beyond the Sunset: The Lives and Loves of Maureen Johnson (Being the Memoirs of a Somewhat Irregular Lady)*. Maureen was born in 1879, and grew up in Missouri, like Heinlein himself. She is closer in age to Heinlein's mother but through her Heinlein explores the life of American women during his own lifetime, although the timeline in which Maureen lives is not precisely Heinlein's: apart from anything else, it is a timeline shared with numerous characters from Heinlein's Future History.

The novel begins when she wakes up in bed with a dead man, on a strange planet; and most of the novel is spent with her contemplating her past life while she is in jail awaiting trial for murder and a possible death sentence. The only indication at first that she is a little different is her father's insistence that she is essentially amoral and his desire that she works out for herself the commandments that she will live by. This is a remarkably radical statement. Andrea Dworkin, considering the women on the right who were prominent in the late 1970s, notes that 'for women the world is a very dangerous place. One wrong move, even an unintentional smile, can bring disaster – assault, shame, disgrace. The Right acknowledges the reality of danger, the validity of fear. The Right then manipulates the fear. The promise is that if a woman is obedient, harm will not befall her' (*Right-Wing Women*, 1983, p. 22). Maureen's father makes no such promise, and while Maureen does construct a similar fear, using Brian as her shield in her adventures, she also realises when the marriage breaks up that even this thin belief was false.

By the age of fifteen – like many of Heinlein's women – she is sexually active and enjoying it, and like all of Heinlein's confident women she does not wait to be asked but does her own choosing, placing her emphasis on cleanliness of body, sweet breath and a good temper. With little money in the household budget, and a *lot* of children, Maureen decides college is out of her reach and that she is essentially the domestic type; she is, after all, growing up at the height of the cult of domesticity.[14] However, she works her way through her father's books, and through those of her older brothers. When she is sixteen her father explains to her the Howard Foundation (which appears first in *Methuselah's Children* in 1941). She marries Brian Smith, and they proceed to have a happy and sexually playful marriage, and eventually an open one with other Howard couples. For Maureen this is perfect happiness as defined by Jubal Harshaw later in her life: 'Happiness ... lies in being privileged to work long hours in doing whatever you think is worth doing' (Chapter 10). The only snag is that when Brian is away she is mostly too tired for the adultery he condones; it is Chapter 12 before they find regular playmates with Eleanor and Justin Weatherall.

As Maureen notes, it just was not done in the nineteenth century for a woman to ask her husband about money. Thus, even though Maureen's pregnancies bring in the capital (from the Howard Foundation), she knows nothing about the financial details. She disowns any financial ability, but she sniffs a bank failure in time to rescue the family savings and those of the Howard Foundation. Maureen's financial instinct is a foreshadowing. Once divorced, she will prove adept at investment, principally in the projects of D. D. Harriman.

The key event of Maureen's life, in terms of its long-term impact, is the affair with 'Mr Bronson', detailed first at the end of *Time Enough for Love*. Her father is convinced Bronson is one of his by-blows. In Chapter 12 she plots Bronson's seduction and it is eventually completed, with the connivance of Brian and her father, who arranges it. Maureen ends up in bed with Bronson and Brian (Chapter 13), when she 'discovers' that Bronson is descended from her.

---

14 Glenna Matthews, *Just a Housewife: the Rise and Fall of Domesticity in America* (New York and Oxford: Oxford UP, 1987).

At this stage, Maureen is not an independent woman. She is relieved that her father is stationed nearby. 'Oh, I'll be a pioneer mother if I must ... But I would rather be a womanly woman to a manly one' (Chapter 13). This kind of comment is what gets the book labelled anti-feminist, but as we shall see, in *behaviour* in later life Maureen shifts ground. She may like male presence but her sexuality is her own and so eventually her finances will be. There is no sense that a woman *can't*, only that this woman isn't interested.

One key change Ted Bronson/Lazarus Long brings with him: when a rump session of the Howard Foundation is called so that Long can give Judge Sperling crucial information about the future, he prevents the withdrawal and exclusion of the women from the discussion. The Howard Foundation of the future, he points out, assumes equality of the sexes: 'as Howard Chairman in his own time ... he could not in conscience take part in any Howard meeting in which women were excluded' (Chapter 14). From this point on Maureen is clued into the financial future, with full access to Heinlein's account of 'The Crazy Years'.

Brian's control of the finances all comes to a head in 1946. Almost all of Maureen's and Brian's children make it through the war but her father is missing, and her son Richard dies at Iwo Jima (in an alternate timeline in which the attack is on San Francisco, Japanese Americans are subject to a pogrom, Hirohito dies early and his twelve-year-old son commits seppuku with his ministry).[15] Richard's wife Marian moves in with them, and into Brian's bed. To Maureen's surprise, Marian allows herself to get pregnant (they are using Long's guide to the rhythm method with rather more accuracy than

---

15   In this paragraph Heinlein seeks to justify the incarceration of the Japanese and the ferocity with which the Americans fought the end of the war by arguing it could have been so much worse. In this timeline it is not Hiroshima or Nagasaki that are bombed but Tokyo and Kobe.

is strictly plausible) but she should have remembered the tradition of Howard Foundation courtships. When they move to Texas they begin a masquerade in which Maureen poses as Marian's mother-in-law, and quite quickly discovers that she has been usurped. She discovers what Andrea Dworkin explains in *Right-Wing Women*, that the rules she had obeyed because she was told that they would keep her safe work only as long as her protector consents.[16]

Marian wants marriage and by this time Brian wants divorce. Brian tries to cheat Maureen financially. But self-educated Maureen has been reading the *Wall Street Journal* all these years and she keeps all the shares in Harriman holdings. With the financial settlement, and the hard dealing she does on her own behalf, and the decision of her youngest children to go with Brian and Marian, she graduates into full autonomy and the second half of her life.

Maureen spends the next six years in college. She gets her Ph.D. in philosophy which, like a good Heinleinian hero she regards as a fascinating test of intellect but fundamentally worthless, then signs up for a night-school degree in law and a daytime Masters in Medicine. She passes for the bar in 1952: 'It may have helped that my papers read: "M. J. Johnson" rather than "Maureen Johnson" (Chapter 17). She studies some Japanese that turns out to be useful when the Ouroboros Foundation tries to intervene in the disastrous events in several timelines around the end of the Second World War.

By Maureen's 1982 'almost all the laws discriminating against women had been repealed', but in a rare acknowledgement by Heinlein of more systemic assumptions, she notes that in many ways the more important issues were cultural bias. In Chapter 18 she recounts a friend of her husband, in town for the National Democratic Convention, treating her as a servant, and perhaps most significantly

16   Andrea Dworkin, *Right-Wing Women*, p. 22.

assuming that she would not be attending the convention. In 1970 at a board meeting of Skyblast Freight, she is a director. 'I knew all the directors by sight and they knew me.' But she has had some plastic surgery and lost some pounds, and was aiming to pass for forty (in preparation for another age adjustment). As she prepares to go into a board meeting Phineas Morgan shrugs off an overcoat and throws it at her. She steps aside, and lets the coat land on the floor. 'Why, you little bitch! I'll have you fired for that.' His face when he finds himself sitting opposite her is a picture.

> The moral? In 1970 on time line two the legal system assumed that a man is innocent until proved guilty; in 1970 on time line two, the cultural system assumed that a female is subordinate until proved otherwise – despite all laws that asserted that the sexes were equal. I planned to kick that assumption in the teeth. (Chapter 18)

Like many women of the 'I'm not a feminist but' brigade, Maureen rejects contemporary feminism and, like Betty Friedan, particularly the rejection of gallantry. She adds a whiff of homophobia to her position: 'the Lesbian Mafia. I don't know that all of them were homosexual (although I'm certain about some of them) but their behaviour caused me to lump them altogether' (Chapter 18). Maureen, of course, was one of many who made the charge and while we might want Heinlein to render Maureen more challenging, the attitudes are consistent with the woman he creates, full of her own conflicts and, despite having enthusiastic sex with many female friends, she would never consider herself a lesbian.

Maureen also never notes the degree to which Brian had used *his* gallantry to secure services of a range of kinds, and then claimed those services were non-contributory. However, the labour of parenthood and its lack of acknowledgement is rendered visible to Maureen in the next section: just as Maureen is about to plan her bachelorhood, her two youngest, Donald and Priscilla, return home and she is saddled with a very tricky and eventually unpleasant situation. The children (teens) turn out to be having sex together (Chapter 19). In true Heinlein fashion, that isn't actually a moral problem because it is consensual. Maureen is actually far more horrified that they aren't using condoms (having run out). But the real problem is that Priscilla thinks she is an adult, and a contributing member of the family, and tries to insist that Maureen shape her own decisions – such as where to live – with influence from Priscilla. Maureen is past that. In that sense she has left her family feeling behind and is no longer strictly thinking in terms of 'best for the family' but what is best for herself; her last two children can join the ride or not. When they prove completely out of control she hands them back to her husband with a bitter sense of failure but none of responsibility.

Maureen has also intensified her sexual integrity. She is having a great time with 'a friendly fair exchange' with the gentlemen of her choice and without the constraints of her youth. She then uses her command of 'Theodore Bronson's prophecies', as well as her own astute purchase of shares through dummies, to parlay a place on the board of Harriman Industries (by this time Heinlein is stitching his earliest stories into the timeline to create a history for Maureen's world that never was, a rather effective way of dealing with the erosion of the predictions of Golden Age Science Fiction). As she herself notes, 'If Brian had kept me, I could never have become a director in my own person. While Brian had not begrudged me any luxury once we were prosperous, aside from my household budget I had actually controlled only "egg money" – even that numbered Zurich account had only been nominally mine' (Chapter 21) and for that reason she declines an offer of marriage from a lover. 'As his mistress I would be his equal; were I to marry him, I would at once become his subordinate – a pampered subordinate most likely – but a subordinate.' She also refuses to accept from Justin Weatherall that she owes him all the predictions; they are *her* gift from Bronson, and *her* gift to the Foundation, not least because he heard and did not at the time take them as seriously. What she earns she keeps and may choose to use as she sees fit (Chapter 23). Eventually, and under the name Prudence Penny, Maureen also empowers other women by creating an advice column to teach them how to invest. It is one of the few times we see Maureen oriented to supporting other women beyond an individual relationship. In 1964 on this timeline, Prudence Penny persuades women to invest in D. D. Harriman's Moon Shot, simultaneously helping it to happen, and also to turn space travel into a thing for women, something Heinlein had advocated for in calls for female astronauts. In the end, it is Maureen's backing for the Moon Shot (through the Howard Foundation) that prevents it being called in by creditors. Maureen, once a housewife, is now a Jonbar point of crucial divergence in history (Chapter 24).

At the end of Chapter 24 Maureen accidentally steps in front of a moving truck and is swept into the future in Boondock, where she finds herself at the heart of her own son's family, married to several wives and husbands, which suits her just dandy, and back to breeding, which she loves. She is recruited to the Time Corps by Jubal Harshaw with the possibility that she will have the chance to whisk him from his MIA in the Second World War. It is that of course that gets her stuck on a timeline she doesn't know and that she is not sure the Time Corps can find. Here, however, we need to conclude Maureen's trajectory and to consider my argument that began in the section on intersex and transexuality and continued through this section, that in Heinlein's construction of womanhood, it is not only a female character he seeks to construct. Nor should we understand it as a depiction of Virginia (although to Maureen he gifts many of Virginia's learning abilities) but rather that we might want to understand this focus of his work – and it is a focus; very few male authors write as many texts so resolutely focalised within a woman – as a yearning to understand himself as a woman.

There are a number of incidents that convince me that *To Sail Beyond the Sunset* could be understood as Heinlein writing himself as a woman for there are several reversals: in real life for example, Heinlein got Virginia a cat as a present when she moved in, and in *To Sail Beyond the Sunset* Maureen gets a cat for Briney; in real life Heinlein felt himself the least favoured male child, and in the novel his representative Lazarus/Woodie becomes the one deliberately repressed because he is the favourite. But the most conclusive evidence of this is in Chapter 24 of *To Sail Beyond the Sunset*. Musing on those aspects of her family to whom she had remained close, and the degree to which this was not always 'real' kin, Maureen remembers 'little Helen Beck, who was just Carol's age' and had gone to school with her. Helen stayed in touch and became a dancer, changing her name to Sally Rand. Helen Beck/Sally Rand had been a school friend of Heinlein himself.

The Craving for Family

There is a real craving for family in Heinlein's work. Jo Walton wrote an entire essay on how this manifested in the juveniles – 'Heinlein's protagonists tend to be firmly embedded in families, all of whom are mildly fond of each other. Heinlein's families tend to trust each other' – and listed all the families both united and broken in the juveniles, and the ways in which family maintenance and family recreation are at the heart of the novels (Jo Walton, 'Child Markers and Adulthood', 2011). This section looks at how this carried over and developed in his novels for adults.

In those novels with female characters it is easy to link this to Heinlein's gendering of women, but the craving is longer lasting and goes further and deeper than that. He is explicit in *Stranger in a Strange Land* that 'Babies are the obvious result ... but not the primary purpose at all' (Chapter 36). Heinlein grew up in a period when marriage and family were the indicators of adulthood for both sexes (note that in early science fiction good scientists are or have been married – if only to produce the beautiful daughters – while evil scientists have not). Nancy F. Cott writes that social policy increasingly framed marriage as a societal matter in the late nineteenth century and that:

> Married status did not literally become a requirement for men's voting, but the age of twenty-one and property holding did, and these denoted marriageability if not marriage itself.
>
> Men's civil and political status grew then from being independent heads of units that included dependents, from heading household units that deserved representation in the world.[17]

To not want to marry is to want to stay a child. Thus the entire story of Hamilton Felix in *Beyond This Horizon* is about how to convince a man to marry and reproduce, a rather odd story line for a science-fiction novel; that much of the argument is eugenicist (as it is for the Howards in *Methuselah's Children* and later *To Sail Beyond the Sunset*) does not alter the issue that marriage is destiny, and family creation is where adulthood lies. The same is true of the juvenile *The Star Beast*: if Lummox is to carry on breeding John Thomases

---

17 Nancy F. Cott, 'Giving Marriage to Our Whole Civil Polity: Marriage and Public Order in the Late Nineteenth Century', in *U.S. History as Women's History*, ed. Linda Kerber (Chapel Hill NC: U. of North Carolina Press, 1995), p. 111.

(and how the name got past Alice Dalgliesh at Scribner is anyone's guess) then John Thomas must marry. When Mr Kiku wants to send John Thomas to the stars with Lummox, he approaches Betty to find out if her intentions are honourable. So the story begins with John Thomas as a boy but ends with him entering manhood through marriage as much as through migration. Similarly, in *Tunnel in the Sky* the success of the colony is demonstrated through its ability to produce marriages and families. And for all that Rod is the leader, it is ironically his failure to marry and to create a family that leaves him in the suspended adolescence in which the settlement is an adventure or career he wants to pursue. At the end of the novel we see his sister and his mentor laying down the groundwork for family while he continues suspending that movement into adulthood for some time.

Tunnel in the Sky is the last of the nuclear family creation we will see. From here on in, the families Heinlein creates lead in other directions. In *Double Star*, for example, Heinlein repeats the family of affinity that he created in 'The Devil Makes the Law'; Lorenzo Smythe's father has clearly been of the same kind as the oppressive father in 'Coventry'. His ability to leave that behind is partially structured around taking on the political family of Bonforte, eventually marrying Bonforte's aide to construct a new unit, and it is no coincidence that Bonforte himself is an expansionist, seeing the only true future for humans as part of a larger family. In *The Door Into Summer*, family expands to include the child one cares for, the cat who cares for you.

However, as we have seen from the evidence in Bill Patterson's biography and Heinlein's own letters, Heinlein was almost certainly infertile. There is evidence in the biography that Ginnie knew but thought she was covering up so that Heinlein would not find out; there is also evidence that Heinlein thought Ginny was infertile, but overall, there is clear evidence over and over again in Heinlein's written texts (particularly in *I Will Fear No Evil*) that he knew perfectly well that it was him. The issue of childlessness is there, and its importance within the texts increases with time. Infertility is one of the shaping forces of Johann Sebastian Bach Smith's life. Monstrous births are referenced by both Wyoming (*The Moon is a Harsh Mistress*) and by Eunice Branca (*I Will Fear No Evil*) and are an obsession in the Howard family sequence from *Methuselah's Children* on.

What makes Heinlein unusual is that from very early on, although he never goes beyond heterosexual and later bisexual families, he imagines different ways of parenting and construction of families. In *Beyond This Horizon*, Hamilton Felix (a 'star line') meets several people who have chosen not to have children because they cannot see the point (their genes don't offer a good enough pay-off), or it proved impossible. One of the distressing moments is when Mordan, head of reproduction, is called out by Hamilton: 'I haven't noticed you doing *your* bit.' It turns out he is married to his secretary Martha (a woman older than him, which is interesting in itself) and 'She's a mutation . . . sterile' (Chapter 15). But it is Hamilton's response I want to draw attention to: 'He realized with a slight shock that Claude and Martha were as much parents of Theobald as were Phyllis and himself – foster parents, godparents. Mediator parents might be the right term' (Chapter 15).

Heinlein's comments may not seem radical but we still live in a society where some people see the childless and childfree as somehow lesser. Although Heinlein will become obsessed in later life with the bearing of children, and will transfer his longing for children of his own body to both Lazarus Long and Maureen Smith and the hyper-fecund Howard Families, he does not overall fix on bio-parenting. With the exception of Lazarus Long, far from his males 'spreading seed', many of his senior males have no children, and some are clearly infertile and know it. Lazarus Long is the exception, not the rule. Heinlein also never assumes that bio-children are a good thing. Johann Sebastian Bach Smith pretends his children are his bio-children and they despise him. He also creates a foundation to enable women to have children by sperm donors, no questions asked. Maureen detests her two youngest. And many of the children are adopted into families, from Hazel Meade through to Friday, while some of his families have no children.

Heinlein begins constructing his idea of the family in his juveniles. Some of the strongest fictive kin relationships that he creates – presumably from his own experience of cohort loyalty – are in his cadets and cadres. Heinlein was writing in a world in which adulthood in the form of assimilation into the workplace arrived much earlier than it does for most western teens today. The cadets in 'The Roads Must Roll' are absorbed into a corporate family around the ages of sixteen and seventeen as trainee engineers and managers. In 'Misfit', Andrew Jackson Long is welcomed into a family of officers, as well as into a career. The same is true for Matt Dodson, Max Jones and Johnny Rico in *Space Cadet, Starman Jones*, and *Starship Troopers*, respectively. In this Heinlein is channelling a mix of his own nostalgia for naval life, and the corporatist myth-making of the America in which he had grown up, in which a man worked his entire life for the same company and structured his entire social life around his work buddies (best expressed in *The Flintstones*). In 'The Green Hills of Earth', Rhysling finds family among engineers and prostitutes and in 'Jerry was a Man' the protagonist discards her husband easily but fights for Jerry (an enhanced ape) to join the family of man. It is a stretch but you can feel Heinlein gradually reaching out to think about what connections do and don't matter. *The Door Into Summer* also has strong things to say about 'natural' family ties and their replacement with new constructs, as does *Time for the Stars*, in which one's twin brother turns out to be one's rival, not one's ally; and in *Citizen of the Galaxy*, where most of your family conspired to have you kidnapped and sold into slavery and your *real* families are first the man who rescues and adopts you, and second a family of Free Traders for whom all family is a carefully mapped business deal. From his earliest work the stress is on the importance of the family you make. In Heinlein, the bonds of narrative are stronger than the bonds of blood.

The two key family-building strands in Heinlein are family as a structure for childrearing, not childbearing (that is expressed in *Have Space Suit—Will Travel*, *Friday*, and in the late construction of the Long saga from *Time Enough for Love*); and family as a gathering-in of the like-minded and loving that we see strongly in *Stranger in a Strange Land* and in the World as Myth sequence that begins with *'The Number of the Beast'* and sweeps the Long clan into itself with *The Cat Who Walks Through Walls* and *To Sail Beyond the Sunset*. Bill Patterson (in 'Incest and Archetype in Robert Heinlein's World as Myth Books', 2006) makes a convincing argument that in these novels, family (and particularly consensual incest) are an indication of Greek- or Egyptian-style godhood, after one of Heinlein's favourite novels, James Branch Cabell's *Jurgen*.[18]

The idea of family as a site of childrearing is the raison d'être in *The Moon is a Harsh Mistress*. Wyoming has left the possibility of family behind *because* she cannot have children. In *Friday*, Friday feels that family is not really for her for similar reasons and accepts her poor treatment by her New Zealand family in part because she cannot contribute to this element of the family parameters that are set out on paper. The two are on the same path although Wyoming

---

18 Despite the name, it is not *Job* but *Glory Road* that most closely follows the plot of *Jurgen*.

is saner, with more personal resources, but each discovers that the ability to have bio-children is quite separate from the ability to *rear* children. In *To Sail Beyond the Sunset* Maureen Smith will note something similar but with greater acerbity, when she concludes that while Brian – in the terms of a Howard Foundation marriage – was right to leave her for a fertile woman, he had not actually found one with her child-raising skills. Heinlein is also pro-adoption (and we know he tried): while Eunice Branca believes her child was born dead she is insistent that the 'mother' of any such child is the one who raised it. In contrast Jake Salomon has never reared a child but has sired one for a family where the husband had had mumps. Baby-making is not baby-rearing.

So Hazel Stone is welcomed into the family as a revolutionary war orphan in *The Moon is a Harsh Mistress*. Hugh Farnham welcomes his daughter's out-of-wedlock child, and is unsurprised that Joseph is also willing to welcome a child who is not his own (this is but one of many signals that Joseph is a Good Guy in the narrative). Johann Sebastian Bach Smith, in *I Will Fear No Evil*, is clear that he was willing to accept all his children, knowing that every single one of them was a cuckoo's egg: his sadness is that he is alienated from them. Friday bears a child but does not create one and her partner, Janet, makes sure she combines both males' genes. The label 'parent' is not, by the end of Heinlein's writing career, automatically connected to genetic inheritance. Even in *Time Enough for Love*, the female members of the family are transparent about wanting Lazarus Long for his genes, but everyone (male and female) wants Galahad for his body and for his ability – like his mother Tamara – to make them feel good and welcome and at home. The symbol of home becomes (as it is in *Friday*) children, kittens and puppies playing together on the floor. Maureen is proud of Long, not for producing his descendants but for never abandoning a wife or child. Over and over again Heinlein's argument is that the family is for the support of children; the children themselves can come from anywhere.

The other aspect of family for Heinlein is the gathering-in, or the construction of what Kurt Vonnegut called the karass (*Cat's Cradle*, 1963). Heinlein first pulls this together in *Stranger in a Strange Land*, in which the bio-family is completely screwed up (they kill each other), the main character has been adopted by aliens and the craving for family is in many ways most naked. Michael Valentine's first greeting to Jill Boardman is 'Let our eggs share the same nest' (Chapter 8). When Michael Valentine Smith first arrives on Earth he is as completely orphaned as it is possible to be, deserted by his birth family in a welter of murder and suicide, and wrenched from his Martian family. His trajectory is in part the creation of a new type of family in that, notably, he pulls in others who appear to have no family ties (even Janet is oddly without family). He constructs a family around the sharing of water, and he is attracted to the Fosterite Church (and models his own church on it) because it is structured to create family; when he sees a ceremonial orgy, 'He wished forlornly that someone would invite him to join . . .' (Chapter 23).

Thus it is noticeable that the one person who is not pulled completely under Michael's sway is Jubal Harshaw who has also – with his secretaries – created a fictive kinship network under one roof and one with no children. Michael's family nurtures people and theology, Jubal Harshaw's family nurtures people and bad fiction.[19] Later, in the background of *Friday* we will meet Kettle Belly Baldwin who nurtures people and spies (but again no children). Nurturing remains the definition of 'home' for all of them. *Friday* is the novel where the craving for family is most explicit and most dangerous. In

19 Robert James suggested it is an allusion to Erle Stanley Gardner and his working methods (personal correspondence).

her craving for family, Friday abandons common sense and ignores the warning signs in her relationship with her New Zealand family.

This gathering-in becomes explicit in *'The Number of the Beast'*, first with the construction of the quartet (paying homage to E. E. Smith's family-camping-in-space sagas) and then with the construction of the World as Myth. As the family meet people from all over the meta-verse they reconstruct past Heinlein families into a meta-fictional one. Eventually they cross fictional timelines and are joined by the Harshaw clan and Michael Valentine Smith's Water Family to create one great sprawling interlocking narrative of belonging.

Heinlein used Hazel Meade Stone to pull his future histories together at the end of his life. We meet her as a grandmother in *The Rolling Stones*, sharp, acerbic, and a founder member of Luna City. We learn about this in *The Moon is a Harsh Mistress*, where she is adopted into the Davis family, after they discover that she has been living as an orphan and unpaid skivvy at the crèche (Chapter 12). Hazel turns up again as Gwen in *The Cat Who Walks Through Walls* (where the characterisation is sadly unconvincing); she constructs a new family with Richard Colin Campbell, and then is eventually absorbed into the Long clan.

Overlapping this is the Howard Family Saga. First signalled in *Methuselah's Children*, the Howard Foundation keeps genealogies and creates families (for childbearing and childrearing). By the time of the book the families are already seeing themselves as a family, and in *Time Enough for Love* they have become a people. The scheherazade tale of *Time Enough for Love* works as a novel if the interstices of the stories are understood as a narrative of family-building. While Hamilton Felix enjoyed life but needed a reason to breed, Lazarus Long is willing to breed but has stopped enjoying life. Along with time travel, and the chance to meet his mother again, one of the key elements that convinces him in the end is the construction around him of a new, rambling, shambolic family: here, while the children are persuasive, and the construction of his clone twins entertaining, I would suggest it is not the purposeful nature of family that tempts him back to life, but family per se, a family made of wives and husbands, of kids and cats, and also of friends of both bed and book. The conclusion of *To Sail Beyond the Sunset* in which Maureen welcomes her father into this fold is a suitable ending to the Heinlein oeuvre, appropriately sentimental and making a very clear statement about what is important.

Epilogue:
The Cat Who Walked
Through Genres

This epilogue is brought to you with the oversight of Lord Miles Vorkosicat and Lord Ivan Vorcatril. It is written in memory of Petronius the Arbiter, Pixilated Blassingame Arroyo (Pixie III) and the Honourable Miss P, all of whom found the Door Into Summer.[1]

* * *

It is not clear when cats became a 'thing' in science fiction but Heinlein made a significant contribution to their presence and to the construction of that presence. He is one of the great 'quotables':

> 'Women and cats will do as they please, and men and dogs should relax and get used to it.' (The Notebooks of Lazarus Long)

[1] See the introduction to the Virginia Heinlein edition of *The Door Into Summer* by Bill Patterson for a full account of Pixel's influence on the book. The Honourable Miss P was Potchka (Yiddish for messing about), our cat for twenty years. She was very like Kitten.

'Cats, like butterflies, need no excuse.' (The Notebooks of Lazarus Long)

'Anyone who considers protocol unimportant has never dealt with a cat.' (*The Cat Who Walks Through Walls*)

'How we behave toward cats here below determines our status in heaven.' (The Notebooks of Lazarus Long)

Heinlein had some strong opinions about cats: no male cat should ever be neutered, a special place in hell is preserved for people who abandon cats, and cats and women will walk through your social and emotional walls, tearing down everything you thought you knew about yourself.

It might not have gone that way. When Heinlein wrote the first draft of *For Us, the Living* he was a self-expressed dog man. If we had the original manuscript we could know if Captain Kidd pre-dated Heinlein's third marriage but I am going to guess that he did not. Getting kittens had been part of 'the deal' – move in together, get cats – the author's partner is familiar with this deal. At some point Heinlein fell in love with felines. By the time *For Us, the Living* was published posthumously in 2004, Captain Kidd was a forceful presence.

They were interrupted by the appearance of a large grey cat who walked out to the middle of the floor, calmly took possession, sat down, curled his tail carefully around him, and mewed loudly. He had only one ear and looked like a hard case. Diana gave him a stern look.

'Where have you been? Do you think this is any time to come home?'

The cat mewed again.

'Oh, so you'll be fed now? So this is just the place where they keep the fish?' (Chapter 3)

It sets the tone for all Heinlein cats; conversational, demanding, spoilt. Naturally, as this is a science-fiction novel, Captain Kidd benefits from the future; he has a voice-operated cat door. 'I made a record of the mew he used to let me know he wanted to come in the house and sent it to be analyzed and a lock set to it' (Chapter 3). In these days of micro-chipped cats this still strikes me as a splendid idea.

Almost all of the cats in Heinlein's work are walk-ons: only Pixel in *To Sail Beyond the Sunset*, who acts as a courier for Maureen, truly affects the story. But they are a special species of walk-on whose role is as a familiar, a magical creature who intensifies the qualities of a person or situation.

In several of these texts the 'cats' are not *cats*. Neither Kitten the whirlwind nor Lummox the star beast are strictly of the genus feline but each display feline behaviour: Kitten is named as such because she plays with the things she finds on the street, creating a whirlwind of paper. There is the cat from Oz in *'The Number of the Beast'*, who insists on being fed lobster. And Lummox shows all the destructive intelligent curiosity of the cat and the same tendency to regard rules and confinement as something to work round. But perhaps most crucially each attracts the fascinated and exasperated affection known vividly to the cat owner. One loves and cares for a cat *because* it is ornery, and in doing so, one demonstrates something of one's character. Thus, Betty's patience with Lummox in *The Star Beast* demonstrates that she will be a better choice for Lummox's John Thomas breeding programme than was his mother. In *The Door Into Summer* the Girl Scout leader accepts Dan as trustworthy because of 'Pete's silent testimony to my respectability of the fraternity of cat people' (Chapter 11).

Perhaps the most 'revealing' use of cats as character markers, in the very literal sense, is in *Space Family Stone*. Hardboiled young entrepreneurs Castor and Pollux have accidentally allowed Martian flat cats to breed. These charming little fur blankets with three eyes and a purr like an engine motor turn out to be the best trade goods that the boys have left when they arrive in the asteroids. They use the sound of their purr on a radio show to advertise their hardware store and incidentally their sale of Martian flat cats. They are down to the last few when 'a tired-looking, grey-haired man showed up . . . he hung back and let the twins sell flat cats to the others. He had with him a girl child . . .' Mr Erska is Icelandic, one of the few family men out in the asteroids and has brought his daughter to see a flat cat. Just to see. When they try to prise the flat cat away from the child she clings to it. Castor, realising that the man would be too proud to take it as charity, invents a free gift of a flat cat for their 500th customer. As they turn they see Grandma Hazel grinning at them. The boys try to pass it off as advertising but as she says, 'With your stock practically gone? . . . My boys! I'm beginning to think you may grow up yet. In thirty, forty, fifty more years you may be ready to join the human race' (Chapter 3). The flat cats, although they do nothing but purr, are agents of change.

But the kitten in 'Ordeal in Space' really is a cat, and it too acts as a character facilitator, an agent of change. A slight story, it tells of a space man invalided out by post-traumatic stress-related agoraphobia. He rescues himself when he forces himself to rescue a kitten mysteriously trapped on a ledge on a skyscraper window.

The role of the cat in *Farnham's Freehold* has far greater portent. There are two cats in this novel, Dr Livingstone-I-Presume, and the Mama Cat who is found in the gas station at the end of the novel. Heinlein's names are often significant, and Dr Livingstone-I-Presume (who is female) might even hint at the cannibalism that is to come, but she is also a character signifier; she tells us that Joseph is one of the most important people in the book, and perhaps the most moral, for it is Joseph who rushes out of the bomb shelter after the alert is given, to find her. When Joseph turns on Hugh Farnham in Chapter 10 (before we know about the cannibalism) it behoves us to remember the cat, and Joseph's actions. For all that Hugh thinks he has the moral high ground, he is not the man who rescued the cat, and he is not the man who truly understands racism in the South. In this deliberate parallel, Joseph is the most moral being in the novel.

At the end of the book, when Hugh and Barbara are back in a past (because it isn't their past) they stop at a gas station and start grabbing boxes: 'The end carton was not empty. Mama cat, quite used to strangers, stared solemnly out at him while four assorted fuzzy ones nursed. Hugh returned her stare.' He grabs the box and runs; she is both promise for the future and an indication that Hugh, now and only now, has the moral stature of Joseph. The circle of the story is completed.

But we must reluctantly note the two occasions when Heinlein does not care for the kitten. The first is the moment in *Glory Road* when Oscar, having killed the dragon, abandons its baby (Chapter 13). Somehow, this reader expected Oscar to acquire a pet dragon, the Chinese obligation of which Heinlein is so fond – that you are responsible for lives you save or circumstances you create – coming into play. However, given the nature of this story, perhaps it is to be expected. It is a picaresque in that our protagonist pretty much abandons his own moral judgement to the superior one of his lady. That might explain why a similar situation crops up in *The Cat Who Walks Through Walls* because in many ways, this is the same novel as *Glory Road*; a soldier at a loose end is recruited by a lady adventuress to help her on a mysterious mission. Like Oscar, Richard allows his own morals to be overcome by his lady, in this case Hazel/Gwen. It is implied in *Glory Road*, and it is explicit in *The Cat Who Walks Through Walls*: Heinlein abandons the kitten!

In Chapter 5 Gwen and Richard acquire a stray 'kitten', a young man of the name of Bill who is a small-time crook hired to do a cash job by getting Gwen and Richard to open the door so others could step in and grab them. They capture him and take him along. Gwen sighs, 'I think he's a good boy. Could be, I mean, if anyone had ever bothered with him' (Chapter 5). And Bill is a good boy. He protects Gwen's bonsai, and when their rolligon is attacked on the surface of Luna and Richard is handicapped by his amputated leg, Bill acts promptly and sharply, sealing the driver's pressure suit (Chapter 12). Bill comes out of this and the later court case as a minor hero (Chapter 14). Gwen commits herself to Bill and to his re-education: when asked what she will do if he does turn out stupid: 'I guess I would cry a bit and find him some protected place, where he could work at what he can do and be whatever he is, in dignity and comfort . . . I could not send him back down to the dirt and the hunger and the fear.' They are, without question, taking the stray kitten home (Chapter 7). But in Chapter 15 Bill gets upset that on entering Luna City they are required to pay an air tax. Richard gives a very cursory explanation that this is not New Orleans, this is the Moon and air is not free, but Bill does not get it and argues that the government should supply it. Bill, it seems, is a socialist who also thinks that the government should pay for medical services. Gwen tries to explain that this is a mathematical impossibility. If we skate over the really shoddy understanding of socialism that is placed in Bill's mouth and the utter failure of Richard and Gwen to notice that Luna is a communalist city in that their taxes go to the government which then indeed does provide air, they have quite simply abandoned someone for whom they took responsibility. The 'Chinese obligation' that is referred to in the scene, that does indeed involve the hazards of picking up stray kittens . . . fleas, getting bitten, peed on, ending up with a psychotic cat . . . have here just been dumped. Bill, who has carried Tree-San and anything else, who has helped to save their lives and *received not one penny in pay* has been abandoned. By Chapter 19, Bill – this scrawny, damaged, abandoned boy – is mysteriously transformed in conversation into 'a smiling villain if ever one smiled, as well as a consummate actor' (Chapter 29). *After* they have abandoned him, he turns on them, and this is used to justify the abandonment.

In some of the stories the cats are only there as an exemplar. When Helen is saying goodbye to her brother in *Tunnel in the Sky* she applauds a cat's way of saying goodbye, 'When a cat greets you, he makes a big operation of it, bumping, stropping your legs, buzzing like mischief. But when he leaves, he just walks off and never looks back' (Chapter 2). When Pirate the cat is entangled by a slug and dies of burns in *The Puppet Masters* (Chapter 22) he becomes a symbol of a much wider loss in society of animal companionship. In *The Cat Who Walks Through Walls*, if we have any hope of a happy ending somewhere off the page (or, in the event, in the sequel, *To Sail Beyond the Sunset*) it is because Richard in a metatextual pre-mortem moment thinks, 'Anyone who would kill a baby kitten is cruel, mean cruel. Whoever you [the writer] are, I hate you. I *despise* you!'

In two novels however this symbolic role becomes a strong thread throughout. The two books that make the most significant use of cats, not coincidentally two of Heinlein's most sentimental works, are the otherwise slight *The Door Into Summer* (1957) and *Friday* (1982). *The Door Into Summer* is not a symbolic tale. For all the existence of little Ricky, this is a tale of a man and his cat. There is quite simply no one whom Dan B. Davies loves as much as he loves Petronius the Arbiter (Pete), and the entire novel is driven by this love and the way it changes his life. This novel has become one of the great cat books even though Pete is off-stage for most of the middle part. The novel begins with Dan reminiscing about their bachelor days in an old farmhouse at the edge of a nuclear blast area. The house has eleven doors, and one just for Pete, 'a board fitted into a window in an unused bedroom and in which I had cut a cat strainer just wide enough for Pete's whiskers'. But Pete, like all cats, prefers personal service and will 'bully me into opening a people door for him . . . Pete had worked out a simple philosophy. I was in charge of quarters, rations and weather; he was in charge of everything else'. And when winter snow lay thick on the ground, Pete would insist on checking every single door. In a phrase that has achieved so much resonance it has become a euphemism for a cat's death: 'He never gave up his search for the Door into Summer' (Chapter 1).

But when Dan falls in love with Belle, Pete ignores her 'as he did anything he disapproved of, but could not change' (Chapter 2). 'If I had not been in love I would have seen it as a clear sign that Belle and I would never understand each other'. She treats Pete like a dog and tries to pat him instead of stroke him. He scratches. How Belle treats Pete is a metaphor for how she treats men: trainable, pettable. Cats aren't like that. 'Cats have no sense of humour, they have terribly inflated egos, and they are very touchy' (Chapter 2). Later, we will see Belle behave in exactly this way, but she is much less adorable.

When Dan's relationship with Belle collapses after she has married his business partner in secret and had him booted out of the business, it is Pete he goes on a bender with. It is also Pete with whom Dan decides to go into cold sleep. This is his best buddy. Here we have to remember that it is 1957 and ideas have changed. In 1957, keeping cats was still relatively new and eccentric, especially for a man.

> You can't give away a cat the way you can a dog; they won't stand for
> it. Sometimes they go with the house, but not in Pete's case; to him I
> had been the one stable thing in a changing world ever since he was
> taken from his mother nine years earlier . . .

I could pay to have him kept in a kennel until he died (unthinkable!) or I could have him chloroformed (equally unthinkable) – or I could abandon him. That is what it boils down to with a cat: you either carry out the Chinese obligation you have assumed – or you abandon the poor thing, let it go wild, destroy its faith in the eternal rightness.

The way Belle had destroyed mine.

So, Danny Boy, you might as well forget it. Your own life may have gone as sour as dill pickles; that did not excuse you in the slightest from your obligation to carry out your contract to this super-spoiled cat. (Chapter 1)

But things go wrong. Dan makes the mistake of thinking *what would Pete do?*

Pete wouldn't sue anybody; if he didn't like the cut of another cat's whiskers, he simply invited him to come out and fight like a cat.

Dan ends up drugged, flat on his back. Even then his relationship with Pete is the key scene:

Pete jumped out of his bag, trotted over to where I slouched, and asked what was wrong. When I didn't answer he started stropping my shins vigorously back and forth while still demanding an explanation. When still I did not respond he levitated to my knees, put his forepaws on my chest, looked me right in the face, and demanded to know what was wrong, right now and no nonsense.

I didn't answer and he began to wail. (Chapter 4)

Belle tries to kill Pete and he flees, leaving blood and scars behind. The sound of Pete keening follows Dan into the enforced cold sleep. Belle's attempt to soothe him with hypnosis and a tale that Pete has gone to live with Ricky, fails. Even at the last, as he drops into uneasy slumber, he asks 'Where's Pete? I want to see Pete' (Chapter 4).

When Dan wakes from cold sleep, it is with a certain amount of *'c'est la vie'*. He had intended to go into cold sleep anyway (he does not know that he has been robbed). And then he remembers Pete. 'They had done worse than kill Pete; they had turned him out to go wild ... to wear out his days wandering back alleys in search of scraps, while his ribs grew thin and his sweet pixie nature warped him into distrust of all two-legged beasts.' They let him die 'thinking that *I* had deserted him' (Chapter 5).

While it is Dan's realisation who patented (and stole) his inventions, and who may have met Ricky from cold sleep, that finally propels him into time travel, the trajectory he is on is entirely fuelled by his anger for Pete. When he discovers first that Ricky has married he dreams that 'Ricky was holding me on her lap and saying "It's all right, Danny. I found Pete and now we're both here to stay. Isn't that so, Pete?" "*YeeeoW!*"' (Chapter 5). In the future he is 'bitterly lonely' and 'would gladly have swapped it all for one beat-up tomcat or for a chance to spend an afternoon taking little Ricky to the zoo' (Chapter 6). When he finally tracks Belle down it's hard to say if he is angrier that she accuses him of being in love with Ricky, or that she describes Pete as 'that horrible cat' (Chapter 7).

When Dan goes back through time it is because the universe is telling him he already has (in patents, and in a recorded marriage to Ricky), but his *motivation* to go back through time is to rescue Pete. After he has earned enough to do it and made his arrangements, his timing is all oriented to one incident: the moment at which Pete runs from the house. He goes back, gets his invention, Flexible Frank, and then waits:

I had promised myself that I would relish every second of Pete's triumph. But I couldn't see it. The back door was open and light was streaming out the screen door, but while I could hear sounds of running, crashes, Pete's blood-chilling war cry, and screams from Belle, they never accommodated me by coming into my theatre of vision. (Chapter 11)

So Dan creeps up to the screen door to peep through and discovers it's hooked. He 'jabbed through and unhooked it just in time to jump out of the way as Pete hit the screen like a stunt motorcycle hitting a fence.' Dan has not gone back in time merely to watch Pete as he escaped; it turns out that he has facilitated that escape.

As he waits for Pete to calm down we have what had been established as a characteristic conversational exchange.

'Mrrrowrr?' he said – meaning, 'Let's go back and clean out the joint. You hit 'em high, I'll hit 'em low.'

'No, boy. The show is over.'

'Aw, c'mahnnn!'

'Time to go home, Pete. Come to Danny.'

Taking Pete on his lap Dan drives off, throwing out the hardware and eventually all the notes and plans from Flexible Frank, until Pete's rightful place in the passenger seat is once again reserved. With his partner riding shotgun, they head off to find Ricky.

Ricky's story is not really of interest to us here, but it is important to note the number of equivalences. Miles is not Ricky's father but her stepfather. He has kept to his duty and cared for her after her mother died, but when he marries Belle, Ricky, like Pete, wants out. Dan feels a tremendous affection for Ricky and he goes to see her to ensure that she is safe, helping her to run to her grandmother and securing her financial future. It's also important to note that he gives her *choices*. No one makes Ricky take cold sleep to wait for him, or even specifies when. Twenty-one is merely the age of majority at which she can make the choice. But the equivalences are stronger than that. Heinlein uses the same terms for Ricky as he does for Pete: both have sweet natures and pixie faces. To both Pete and Ricky he is Danny, not Dan. In Chapter 11, when Pete comes charging out of the house he waits for Pete to quiet down: 'I would not touch him then, certainly not try to pick him up. I know cats'; while of Ricky Dan observes, 'I did not kiss her; I did not touch her at all. I've never been one to paw children and Ricky was the sort of little girl who only put up with it when she could not avoid it. Our mutual relationship, back when she was six, had been founded on mutual decent respect for the other's individualism and dignity' (Chapter 11). As with the girl child Hazel Stone in *The Moon is a Harsh Mistress*, Heinlein imbues Ricky with bodily integrity and self-ownership. When they say goodbye Pete acts as intermediary: Ricky hugs Pete, but can only look Dan 'steadily in the eye even though tears were running down her nose and leaving streaks' (Chapter 11).

Finally, his debts paid and Ricky's future assured, Dan returns to the Cold Sleep establishment on the day and date and hour arranged and 'About four in the afternoon, with Pete's fat head resting on my chest, I went happily to sleep again.' He dreams, not such bad dreams this time but the most significant is the one in which he himself starts opening doors, looking for the Door Into Summer, where Ricky will be waiting for him. 'I was hampered by Pete, "following me ahead of me," that exasperating habit cats have of scalloping back and forth between the legs of persons trusted not to step on them or kick them' (Chapter 12). He wakes and this time all goes smoothly and he is there to wake Ricky, who raises both arms: 'Pete chirruped and jumped on the bed, starting shoulder dives against her in an ecstasy of welcome' (Chapter 12).

They marry and, of course, Pete is his best man. His life moves on and occasionally he wonders if he is even on the same timeline: 'Is there another universe somewhere (or some*when*) in which Pete yowled until he despaired, then wandered off to fend for himself, deserted?' But Dan has found his Door Into Summer, and he is now content. 'Except that Pete is getting older, a little fatter, and not as inclined to choose a younger opponent; all too soon he must take the very Long Sleep. I hope with all my heart that his gallant little soul may find its Door Into Summer, where catnip fields abound and tabbies are complacent, and robot opponents are programmed to fight fiercely – but always lose – and people have friendly laps and legs to strop against, but never a foot that kicks' (Chapter 12). The book closes as Pete declines to use his super modern self-cleaning cat-litter tray (remarkably like ones now available), but 'Pete, being a proper cat, prefers to go outdoors, and he has never given up his conviction that if you just try *all* the doors one of them is bound to be the Door Into Summer.'

The Door Into Summer continually parallels Danny's love for Pete with his love for Ricky. Cats and children are to be cherished, their hopes and dreams and confidence to be applauded and supported. In *Friday* Heinlein moves from simile to metaphor. How people look after their cats is the most powerful signifier in the book because this is a tale of a little lost kitten who has been abused to a degree that she no longer has faith in the people in her world. This is also a kind of tale that has gone very much out of fashion (that may explain some of the uneasiness of the response): it is a tale not of someone striving to be special, but of someone who desperately wants to be ordinary. Friday is Ursula Moray Williams's *Gobbolino, the Witch's Cat* (1942), whose fur sparks, who can sing the baby to sleep and charm butter, yet who is desperate to be a kitchen cat. Each of her adventures is concluded with a demonstration of powers that both get her into and out of trouble. As long as she is 'special' she cannot stay still.

Heinlein is shameless in his construction of an overarching metaphor and of all but stating outright: note how people look after their cats, for it will tell you how they will look after their people. In *Friday* there are two families and two sets of cats.

In Chapter 20 Friday calls her now ex-New Zealand family to try and find out if she has missed messages. Her interaction with Brian is not good – he has been told by Anita that Friday cheated them financially – and closes when she asks about the cats.

> He looked about to explode. 'Marjorie, are you utterly heartless? When your acts have caused so much pain, so much real tragedy, you want to know about something as trivial as cats?'
>
> I restrained my anger. 'I do want to know, Brian.'
>
> 'I think they were sent to the SPCA. Or it might have been to the medical school. Goodbye! Please do not call me again.'
>
> 'The medical school—' Mister Underfoot tied to a surgical table while a medical school took him apart with a knife?

Friday can do nothing:

> I dug deep into my mind-control training and put matters I could not help out of my mind –
>
> – and found Mister Underfoot was still brushing against my leg.

The heartbreak is real, for the cats, for the destroyed family, for her destroyed trust.

But Friday's trust is slowly reconstructed and has been reconstructed by her experience with Janet and her family, and it has already been indicated with cats. In Chapter 13, when Janet suggests they all leave, she hesitates then Janet realises '"I can't. Mama Cat and her kittens. Black Beauty and Demon and Star and Red . . . I *can't*."

There wasn't anything to say, so I didn't. The coldest depth of Hell is reserved for people who abandon kittens.' Friday does not yet know it but in that moment she learns to trust Janet. When they meet up again on the cruise ship, as Friday hides among the emigrants to escape, they are carrying Mama Cat. Mama Cat actually becomes part of Friday's disguise as she 'wound up carrying a cat's travel cage.' And of course, while they are not travelling with kittens, they have secured their future as if they were children.

"'They,'" Freddie answered for her, "have, through my influence, gained excellent positions with fine prospects for advancement as rodent control engineers on a large sheep station in Queensland.'" It is a throwaway line, a flippant joke, except that in this book it is not, it is a promise, and with Janet and Ian, and Georges, and Freddie and Betty, Friday finds a place where she can be cared for, and where she can be what she has always wanted to be, an ordinary family cat.

Appendix 1:
The Pattern of Publication

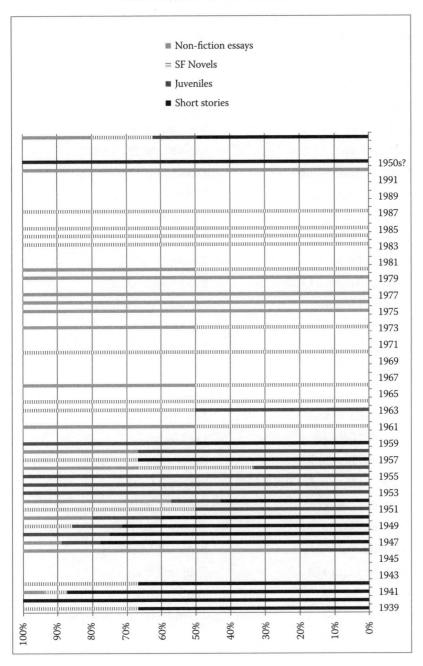

Appendix 2:
Names from *Starship Troopers*

Bernardo Montez

Bjork

Breckinridge

Brumby

Cadet Byrd

Cadet Hassan

Captain Blackstone

Captain Chandar

Captain Chang

Captain Deladrier

Captain Frankel

Captain Terence O'Kelly

Captain Jorgenson

Career Ship's Sergeant Zim

Carmencita Ibanez

Carruthers

Clyde Tammany

Colonel Chauncey

Colonel Nielssen

Corporal Emilio Rico

Corporal Instructor Bronski

Corporal Jones

Corporal Mahmoud

Dillinger

Fleet Sergeant Ho

Flores

Gridley

Heinrich Meyer

Jenkins

Johnny Rico

Kitten Smith

Lieutenant Rasczak

Lieutenant Silva

Lieutenant Spieksma

Lieutenant Warren

Major F. X. Mallory

Major Reid

Major Xera

Malan

Miss Kendrick

Mr Jean W. Dubois

Mr Morales

Mr Saloman

Mr Weiss

Naidi

Navarre

Pat Lievy

Rusty Graham

Sergeant Cunha

Sergeant Jelal

Sergeant Johnson

Sergeant Migliaccio

Shujumi

Ted Hendrik

Third Lieuteant Bearpaw

First Publications of Heinlein's Fiction
(in chronological order)

EU: story or article republished in Robert A. Heinlein. 2003. *Expanded Universe* (Riverdale, NY: Baen).

PTT: story republished in Robert A. Heinlein. *The Past Through Tomorrow: SF Gateway Omnibus* (London: Gollancz). (Originally published in 1967 by G. P. Putnam's Sons). This is the text used in this book for those stories.

R: story or article republished in *Requiem: New Collected Works by Robert A. Heinlein and Tributes to the Grand Master*, ed. Yoji Kondo (New York: Tor, 1992).

1939. 'Life-Line.' *Astounding Science Fiction*, August. EU, PTT.

1939. 'Misfit.' *Astounding Science Fiction*, November. PTT.

1939. *For Us, the Living: A Comedy of Customs.* Not published until 2004. Edited by Spider Robinson. New York: Scribner.

1940. 'Requiem.' *Astounding Science Fiction*, January. PTT, R.

1940. '"If This Goes On—".' *Astounding Science Fiction*, February and March. PTT.

1940. (as by Lyle Munroe). '"Let There Be Light."' *Super-Science Stories*, May. PTT.

1940. 'The Roads Must Roll.' *Astounding Science Fiction*, June. PTT.

1940. 'Coventry.' *Astounding Science Fiction*, July. PTT.

1940. (as by Lyle Monroe). 'Successful Operation.' As 'Heil!' in *Futuria Fantasia*, Summer 1940. EU.

1940. 'Blowups Happen.' *Astounding Science Fiction*, September. EU, PTT.

1940. 'The Devil Makes the Law.' *Unknown*, September. Later published as 'Magic, Inc.'

1941. (as by Anson MacDonald). *Sixth Column. Astounding Science Fiction*, January, February, March. Later published as *The Day After Tomorrow*.

1941. "'—And He Built a Crooked House—'". *Astounding Science Fiction*, February.

1941. 'Logic of Empire.' *Astounding Science Fiction*, March. PTT.

1941. 'They.' *Unknown*, April.

1941. (as by Elma Wentz and Lyle Monroe). 'Beyond Doubt.' *Astonishing Stories*, April.

1941. (as by Anson MacDonald). 'Solution Unsatisfactory.' *Astounding Science Fiction*, May. EU.

1941. 'Universe.' *Astounding Science Fiction*, May. PTT.

1941. (as by Anson MacDonald). "'—We Also Walk Dogs'". *Astounding Science Fiction*, July. PTT.

1941. *Methuselah's Children. Astounding Science Fiction*, July, August, September. PTT.

1941. (as by Caleb Saunders). 'Elsewhere' (later 'Elsewhen'). *Astounding Science Fiction*, September.

1941. 'Common Sense.' *Astounding Science Fiction*, October. PTT.

1941. (as by Anson MacDonald). 'By His Bootstraps.' *Astounding Science Fiction*, October.

1941. (as by Lyle Monroe). 'Lost Legion.' *Super Science Stories*, November. Later published as 'Lost Legacy.'

1942. "'My Object All Sublime.'" *Future*, February.

1942. (as by Lyle Monroe). 'Pied Piper.' *Astonishing Stories*, March.

1942. (as by Anson MacDonald). 'Goldfish Bowl.' *Astounding Science Fiction*, March.

1942. (as by Anson MacDonald). 'Waldo.' *Astounding Science Fiction*, August.

1942. (as by Anson McDonald). *Beyond This Horizon. Astounding Science Fiction*, April, May.

1942. (as by John Riverside). 'The Unpleasant Profession of Jonathan Hoag.' *Unknown Worlds*, October.

1946. 'A Bathroom of Her Own.' Not published until 2003 in the collection *Expanded Universe*.

1946. 'Free Men.' Not published until the collection *The Worlds of Robert Heinlein* (New York: Ace, 1966). EU.

1947. 'The Green Hills of Earth.' *Saturday Evening Post*, February 8. PTT.

1947. 'Space Jockey.' *Saturday Evening Post*, April 26. PTT.

1947. (as by Lyle Monroe). 'Columbus Was a Dope.' *Startling Stories*, May.

1947. (as by Simon York). 'They Do It With Mirrors.' *Popular Detective*, May. EU.

1947. 'It's Great to Be Back!' *Saturday Evening Post*, July 26. PTT.

1947. 'Jerry is a Man.' *Thrilling Wonder Stories*, October. Subsequently published as 'Jerry was a Man.'

1947. 'On the Slopes of Vesuvius.' Not published until 2003 in the collection *Expanded Universe*.

1947. *Rocket Ship Galileo*. New York: Charles Scribner's Sons.

1947. 'Water is for Washing.' *Argosy*, November.

1947. 'No Bands Playing, No Flags Flying—.' Not published until *Vertex* no. 3, 1973.

1948. *Beyond This Horizon*. Reading, PA: Fantasy Press. Serialised 1942.

1948. 'The Black Pits of Luna.' *Saturday Evening Post*, January 10. PTT.

1948. 'Ordeal in Space.' *Town and Country*, May. PTT.

1948. 'Gentlemen, Be Seated!' *Argosy*, May. PTT.

1948. *Space Cadet*. New York: Charles Scribner's Sons.

1949. *Sixth Column*. New York: Gnome Press. Serialised 1941.

1949. 'Our Fair City.' *Weird Tales*, January.

1949. 'Nothing Ever Happens on the Moon.' *Boy's Life*, April/May. EU.

1949. (as by R.A. Heinlein). 'Poor Daddy.' *Calling All Girls*, August. R.

1949. 'Gulf.' *Astounding Science Fiction*, Nov–Dec 1949.

1949. 'Delilah and the Space Rigger.' *Blue Book*, December. PTT.

1949. 'The Long Watch.' *American Legion Magazine*, December, in an abridged version called 'Rebellion on the Moon.' PTT.

1949. *Red Planet: A Colonial Boy on Mars*. New York: Charles Scribner's Sons. Author's original text published 1989, New York: Ballantine/Del Rey.

1950. 'The Man Who Sold the Moon.' In *The Man Who Sold the Moon*. PTT.

1950. *The Man Who Sold the Moon*. Chicago, IL: Shasta. Collection containing '"Let There Be Light"', 'The Roads Must Roll', 'The Man Who Sold the Moon', 'Requiem', 'Life-Line' and 'Blowups Happen.'

1950. *Waldo and Magic, Inc.* Garden City, NY: Doubleday.

1950. 'Cliff and the Calories.' *Senior Prom*, August. EU.

1950. 'Destination Moon.' *Short Stories Magazine*, September 1950. R.

1950. *Farmer in the Sky*. New York: Charles Scribner's Sons.

1951. *The Green Hills of Earth*. Chicago, IL: Shasta. Collection containing 'Delilah and the Space Rigger', 'Space Jockey', 'The Long Watch', 'Gentlemen, Be Seated', 'The Black Pits of Luna', 'It's Great to Be Back!', '"—We Also Walk Dogs"', 'Ordeal in Space', 'The Green Hills of Earth', 'Logic of Empire.'

1951. *Between Planets*. New York: Charles Scribner's Sons.

1951. *The Puppet Masters*. Garden City, NY: Doubleday. Author's original version published 1990, New York: Ballantine/Del Rey.

1952. *Space Family Stone*. New York: Charles Scribner's Sons.

1952. 'The Year of the Jackpot.' *Galaxy Science Fiction*, March.

1953. *Starman Jones*. New York: Charles Scribner's Sons.

1953. *Revolt in 2100*. Chicago, IL: Shasta. Collection of three linked stories: "'If This Goes On—'"; 'Coventry', 'Misfit'.

1953. *Assignment in Eternity*. Reading, PA: Fantasy Press. Collection containing 'Gulf', 'Lost Legacy', 'Elsewhen' and 'Jerry was a Man'.

1953. 'Project Nightmare'. *Amazing Stories*, April.

1953. 'Sky Lift'. *Imagination*, November.

1954. *The Star Beast*. New York: Charles Scribner's Sons.

1955. *Tunnel in the Sky*. New York: Charles Scribner's Sons.

1956. *Double Star*. Garden City, NY: Doubleday.

1956. *Time for the Stars*. New York: Charles Scribner's Sons.

1957. 'The Menace from Earth'. *Magazine of Fantasy and Science Fiction*, August. PTT.

1957. *The Door Into Summer*. New York: Doubleday.

1957. 'The Elephant Circuit'. *Saturn*, October. Subsequently published as 'The Man Who Travelled in Elephants'.

1958. 'Tenderfoot in Space'. *Boys' Life*, May–July. R.

1958. *Methuselah's Children*. Hicksville, NY: Gnome Press. Revised from 1941 serialisation.

1958. *Citizen of the Galaxy*. New York: Charles Scribner's Sons.

1958. *Have Space Suit—Will Travel*. New York: Charles Scribner's Sons.

1959. "'All You Zombies—'". *Magazine of Fantasy and Science Fiction*, March.

1959. *The Menace from Earth*. Hicksville, NY: Gnome Press. Collection containing 'The Year of the Jackpot', 'By His Bootstraps', 'Columbus Was a Dope', 'The Menace from Earth', 'Sky Lift', 'Goldfish Bowl', 'Project Nightmare' and 'Water is for Washing'.

1959. *The Unpleasant Profession of Jonathan Hoag*. Hicksville, NY: Gnome Press. Collection containing 'The Unpleasant Profession of Jonathan Hoag', 'The Man Who Travelled in Elephants', '"All You Zombies—"', 'They', 'Our Fair City' and '"—And He Built a Crooked House—"'.

1959. *Starship Troopers*. New York: G. P. Putnam's Sons.

1961. *Stranger in a Strange Land*. New York: G. P. Putnam's Sons. Author's original version published 1991, New York: Putnam.

1962. 'Searchlight'. Published in an advertisement for Hoffman Electronics in *Scientific American*, August, and elsewhere. EU, PTT.

1963. *Orphans of the Sky*. London: Gollancz. Fix-up of 'Universe' and 'Common Sense'.

1963. *Podkayne of Mars: Her Life and Times*. New York: G. P. Putnam's Sons.

1963. *Glory Road*. New York: G. P. Putnam's Sons.

1964. *Farnham's Freehold*. New York: G. P. Putnam's Sons.

1966. *The Moon is a Harsh Mistress*. New York: G. P. Putnam's Sons.

1970. *I Will Fear No Evil*. New York: G. P. Putnam's Sons.

1973. *Time Enough for Love*. New York: G. P. Putnam's Sons.

1980. *'The Number of the Beast.'* New York: G. P. Putnam's Sons.

1982. *Friday*. New York: Holt, Rinehart and Winston.

1984. *Job: A Comedy of Justice*. New York: Ballantine Books/Del Rey.

1985. *The Cat Who Walks Through Walls*. New York: G. P. Putnam's Sons.

1987. *To Sail Beyond the Sunset*. New York: Ace/Putnam Sons.

Selected Non-Fiction by Robert A. Heinlein

1941. 'Guest of Honor Speech at the Third World Science Fiction
Convention – Denver, 1941.' In *Requiem*.

1946. 'Pie from the Sky.' First published in *Expanded Universe*.

1946. 'The Last Days of the United States.' First published in
Expanded Universe.

1946. *How to Be a Politician*. First published as *Take Back Your
Government*. Riverdale, NY: Baen, 1992.

1946. 'How to be a Survivor.' First published in *Expanded Universe*.

1947. 'On the Writing of Speculative Fiction.' In *Of Worlds Beyond*,
edited by Arthur Lloyd Eshbach. Reading, PA: Fantasy Press.
Reprinted London: Dennis Dobson, 1965.

1950. 'Shooting *Destination Moon*.' *Astounding Science Fiction*,
July. R.

1952. 'Where to?' *Galaxy*, February. Updated versions published
in *The Worlds of Robert A. Heinlein* (1966) and *Expanded
Universe* (1980), as 'Pandora's Box.'

1952. 'This I Believe', delivered in a radio broadcast, and not
published until *Requiem*.

1952. 'Ray Guns and Rocket Ships.' *Bulletin of School Library
Association of California*. EU.

1954. *Tramp Royale*. First published in 1992. New York: Ace Books.

1956. 'The Third Millennium Opens.' *Amazing*, April. EU.

1958. 'Who Are the Heirs of Patrick Henry?' Colorado Springs
Gazette Telegraph, April 13, 1958. EU.

1959. 'Science Fiction: its Nature, Virtues and Faults', in *The Science
Fiction Novel: Imagination and Social Criticism*, ed. Basil
Davenport. Chicago: Advent. Reprinted in *Turning Points:
Essays on the Art of Science Fiction*, ed. Damon Knight. New
York: Harper and Row, 1977.

1960. '"Pravda" Means "Truth".' *American Mercury*, October. EU.

1960. 'Inside Intourist: How to Break Even (or Almost) in the Soviet Union.' First published in *Expanded Universe*.

1961. 'Guest of Honor Speech at the XIXth World Science Fiction Convention – Seattle, 1961.' In *Requiem*.

1969. 'Guest of Honor Speech – Rio de Janeiro Movie Festival, 1969.' In *Requiem*.

1973. 'Channel Markers.' *Analog*, January (abridged). Speech to the graduating class of the US Naval Academy in Annapolis on April 5th, 1973. Published in full as 'The Pragmatics of Patriotism' in *Expanded Universe*.

1975. 'Paul Dirac, Antimatter and You.' Article for the 1975 *Compton Yearbook*, published in full in *Expanded Universe*.

1976. 'Guest of Honor Speech at the XXXIVth World Science Fiction Convention – Kansas City, 1976.' In *Requiem*.

1980. 'Spinoff.' In *Expanded Universe*.

1980. 'The Happy Days Ahead.' In *Expanded Universe*.

1980. 'Larger Than Life: a Memoir in Tribute to Dr Edward E. Smith.' In *Expanded Universe*.

1990. *Grumbles from the Grave*, ed. Virginia Heinlein. New York: Ballantine/Del Rey.

Bibliography

Albright, Martin. 2010. 'Editorial: Is An Armed Society Really A "Polite" Society?' *Luckygunner.com*, March 30, 2010.

Baxter, Stephen. 1998. 'Moon Believers: Robert A. Heinlein and America's Moon.' *Foundation* 74: 26–37.

Berger, Alfred I. 1993. *The Magic that Works: John W. Campbell and the American Response to Technology* (San Bernardino, CA: Borgo Press).

Blish, James (as by William Atheling, Jr.). 1973. *The Issue at Hand*, Second ed. (Chicago: Advent Press).

Bly, Robert W. 2005. *The Science in Science Fiction: 83 SF Predictions that Became Scientific Reality* (Dallas, TX: Benbella Books).

Bould, Mark, Andrew M. Butler, Adam Roberts and Sherryl Vint, eds. 2009. *The Routledge Companion to Science Fiction* (London and New York: Routledge).

Bould, Mark, Andrew M. Butler, Adam Roberts and Sherryl Vint, eds. 2010. *Fifty Key Figures in Science Fiction* (London and New York: Routledge).

Boyer, Paul. 1985. *By the Bomb's Early Light: American Thought and Culture at the Dawn of the Atomic Age* (New York: Pantheon Books).

Brin, David. 2016. 'What's Your Favourite Heinlein Article, David Brin?' https://www.torforgeblog.com/2010/07/12/whats-your-favorite-heinlein-novel-david-brin/./

Broderick, Damien. 2004. *x, y, z, t: Dimensions of Science Fiction* (I. O. Evans Studies in the Philosophy and Criticism of Literature) (Holicong, PA: Wildside Press).

Brown, Joseph F. 2008. 'Heinlein and the Cold War: Epistemology and Politics in *The Puppet Masters* and *Double Star*.' *Extrapolation* 49 (1): 109–21.

Carpenter, Joel A. 1999. *Revive Us Again: The Reawakening of American Fundamentalism* (Oxford: Oxford UP).

Cheng, John. 2012. *Astounding Wonder: Imagining Science and Science Fiction in Interwar America* (Philadelphia: U. of Pennsylvania Press).

Clareson, Thomas D. and Joe Sanders. 2014. *The Heritage of Heinlein: A Critical Reading of the Fiction* (Jefferson, NC: McFarland).

Clute, John. 2014a. *Stay* (Harold Wood, Essex: Beccon Publishing).

Clute, John. 2014b. 'Introduction.' In *Robert A. Heinlein: The Past Through Tomorrow*, ix–xv (London: Gollancz).

Clute, John and John Grant, eds. 1997. *Encyclopedia of Fantasy* (London: Orbit).

Csicsery-Ronay, Jr., Istvan. 2008. *Seven Beauties of Science Fiction* (Middletown, CT: Wesleyan UP).

Davitt, Jane. 2000. '"Of One Blood": The Influence of Rudyard Kipling on Robert A. Heinlein.' *Journal of Heinlein Studies* 6: 18–25.

Davitt, Jane. 2001. 'Red Planet – Blue Pencil.' *Journal of Heinlein Studies* 8: 16–24.

Davitt, Jane and Timothy Morgan. 2002. 'Heinlein's Dedications.' *Journal of Heinlein Studies* 10: 11–18.

DeGraw, Sharon. 2007. *The Subject of Race in American Science Fiction* (New York and London: Routledge).

DeGruy, Joy. 2005. *Post-Traumatic Slave Syndrome: America's Legacy of Enduring Injury and Healing* (Portland, Oregon: Joy DeGruy Publications).

Delany, Samuel R. 2012. *Starboard Wine: More Notes on the Language of Science Fiction* (Middletown, CT: Wesleyan UP)

Disch, Thomas. 2005. *On SF* (Ann Arbor, MI: U. of Michigan Press).

Dreger, Alice. 1998. *Hermaphrodites and the Medical Invention of Sex* (Cambridge MA: Harvard UP).

Dworkin, Andrea. 1983. *Right-Wing Women* (London: The Women's Press).

Easterbrook, Neil 1997. 'State, Heterotopia: The Political Imagination in Heinlein, Le Guin, and Delany', in *Political Science Fiction*, ed. Donald M. Hassler and Clyde Wilcox (Columbia, SC: U. of South Carolina Press), 43–75.

Easterbrook, Neil. 2009. 'Ethics and Alterity', in *The Routledge Companion to Science Fiction*, Mark Bould, Andrew M. Butler, Adam Roberts and Sherryl Vint, eds (London and New York: Routledge), 383–92.

Edmonds, Lisa. 2006. 'Sex and Other Metaphors: Heinlein Redefines Beauvoir's Myth of Woman With His Vision of the Eternal Feminine.' *Journal of Heinlein Studies* 16: 37–40.

Elhefnawy, Nader. 2006. 'The Problem of Belonging in Robert A. Heinlein's *Friday*.' *Foundation* 97: 34–47.

Erisman, Fred. 1997. 'Robert A. Heinlein's Primers of Politics.' *Extrapolation* 38 (2): 94–101.

Eshbach, Lloyd, ed. 1964. *Of Worlds Beyond: The Science of Science Fiction Writing (1947)* (Reading, PA: Advent Publishers).

Evans, Arthur B., Istvan Csicsery-Ronay Jr., Joan Gordon, Veronica Hollinger, Rob Latham and Carol McGuirk, eds. 2010. *The Wesleyan Anthology of Science Fiction* (Middletown, CT: Wesleyan UP).

Forsythe, Mark. 2013. *The Elements of Eloquence: How to Turn the Perfect Phrase* (London: Icon Books).

Franklin, H. Bruce. 1980. *Robert A. Heinlein: America as Science Fiction* (Science Fiction Writers) (New York and Oxford: Oxford UP).

Franklin, H. Bruce. 1988. *War Stars and the Superweapon in the American Imagination* (New York and Oxford: Oxford UP).

Gifford, James. 'The Nature of "Federal Service" in Robert A. Heinlein's *Starship Troopers*': https://www.nitrosyncretic. com/pdfs/nature_of_fedsvc_1996.pdf.

Gifford, James. 2000. *Robert A. Heinlein: A Reader's Companion* (Citrus Heights, CA: Nitrosyncretic Press).

Gladstone, Kate. 2002. 'Words, Words, Words: Robert Heinlein and General Semantics.' *Journal of Heinlein Studies* 11: 4–6.

Grey, William. 1999. 'Troubles with Time Travel.' *Philosophy*, 74 (287): 55–70.

Hanley, Richard. 2004. 'No End in Sight: Causal Loops in Philosophy, Physics and Fiction.' *Synthèse* 141 (1): 123–52.

Harvey, Georgina. 1993. *Are We Not Men Too? Women and the Sex-Gender Role Reversal Motif in SF*. MA dissertation, English, Acadia University, Wolfville, Nova Scotia.

Hassler, Donald M. and Clyde Wilcox. 1997. *Political Science Fiction* (Columbia, SC: U. of South Carolina Press).

Higgins, David. 2013. 'Psychic Decolonization in 1960s SF.' *Science Fiction Studies* 40 (2): 228–45.

Hoyt, Sarah A. 2010. 'What do Heinlein Women Want?' Tor.com.

Hull, Elizabeth Ann. 1979. 'Justifying the Ways of Man to God: The Novels of Robert A. Heinlein.' *Extrapolation* 20 (1): 38–49.

Huntington, John. 1989. *Rationalizing Genius: Ideological Strategies in the Classic American Science Fiction Short Story* (New Brunswick and London: Rutgers UP).

James, Edward. 1990. 'Violent Revolution in American Science Fiction', in *Science Fiction, Social Conflict and War*, ed. Philip John Davies. (Manchester: Manchester UP) 98–112.

James, Edward. 1994. *Science Fiction in the Twentieth Century* (Oxford: Oxford UP).

James, Robert. 2001. 'Regarding Leslyn.' *Journal of Heinlein Studies* 9: 17–36.

James, Robert. 2002. 'Heinlein on the Airwaves.' *Journal of Heinlein Studies* 11: 14–15.

James, Robert and William H. Patterson Jr. 2006. 'Re-Visioning Robert Heinlein's Career.' *Foundation* 35 (97): 11–28.

Kidd, Kenneth, 2004. *Making American Boys? Boyology and the Feral Tale.* Minneapolis and London. University of Minnesota Press.

Kilgore, De Witt Douglas. 2003. *Astrofuturism: Science, Race, and Visions of Utopia in Space* (Philadelphia: U. of Pennsylvania Press).

Krummer, Larry. 2016. 'Why do we believe an armed society is a polite society?' *Fabius Maximus.* Accessed 6th June.

Lavender III, Isiah. 2011. *Race in American Science Fiction* (Bloomington and Indianapolis, IN: Indiana UP).

LeGere, John C. 2000. 'Navigators: *Starman Jones* and Life on the Mississippi.' *Journal of Heinlein Studies* 7: 15–23.

Leonard, Elisabeth Ann, ed. 1997. *Into Darkness Peering: Race and Color in the Fantastic* (Westport, CT: Greenwood Press).

Leonard, Elisabeth Ann. 2005. '*Farnham's Freehold:* A Narrative Enslaved.' *Journal of Heinlein Studies* 18: 4–13.

Leslie, Chris. 2005. 'Robert Heinlein's Challenge to the Bureaucratic States: The Speculative Potential of *Sixth Column*, "If This Goes On—", *The Moon is a Harsh Mistress*, *Citizen of the Galaxy*, and *Friday.*' *Journal of Heinlein Studies* 16: 21–8.

Link, Eric Carl and Gerry Canavan, eds. 2015. *The Cambridge Companion to American Science Fiction* (Cambridge: Cambridge UP).

Lockett, Christopher. 2007. 'Domesticity as Redemption in *The Puppet Masters*: Robert A. Heinlein's Model for Consensus.' *Science Fiction Studies* 34 (1): 42–58.

Major, Joseph T. 2000. 'Writing Stories Never Written: Speculation Concerning "Stories Never Written".' *Journal of Heinlein Studies* 6: 8–17.

Mandala, Susan. 2010. *Language in Science Fiction and Fantasy: The Question of Style* (London: Continuum).

McGiveron, Rafeeq O. 1999. '"Starry Eyed Internationalists" versus the Social Darwinists: Heinlein's Transnational Governments.' *Extrapolation* 40 (1): 53–70.

McGiveron, Rafeeq O. 2004. 'He "Just Plain Liked Guns": Robert A. Heinlein and the "Older Orthodoxy of an Armed Citzenry".' *Extrapolation* 45 (4): 388–407.

McGiveron, Rafeeq O., ed. 2015. *Critical Insights: Robert A. Heinlein* (Ipswich, MA: Salem Press).

McGuirk, Carol. 2002. 'Patterson/Thornton's Critical Perspective on Robert A. Heinlein's *Stranger in a Strange Land*.' *Science Fiction Studies* 29 (3): 507–9.

McGuirk, Carol. 2015. 'God in a Yellow Bathrobe: a review of William H. Patterson Jr's *Robert A. Heinlein in Dialogue with his Century, Vol. 2*.' *Science Fiction Studies* 42 (1): 151–7.

McHugh, Anna E. 2016. 'Compulsively Fruitful: Proliferation in the Short Fiction of Robert A. Heinlein, 1939–1954', in *Critical Insights: Robert A. Heinlein*, edited by Rafeeq O. McGiveron (Ipswich, MA: Salem Press), 136–52.

Mendlesohn, Farah. 1991. 'Women in SF: Six American SF Writers between 1960 and 1985.' *Foundation* 53: 53–69.

Mendlesohn, Farah. 1997. 'A Critical Review of Diane Parkin Speer's article, 'Almost a Feminist".' *Journal of Heinlein Studies* 1: 3–4.

Mendlesohn, Farah. 2009. *The Inter-Galactic Playground: A Critical Study of Children's and Teens' Science Fiction* (Jefferson, NC: McFarland Press).

Mendlesohn, Farah. 2017. 'The SF Short Story', in Mendlesohn, *Rejected Essays, Buried Thoughts* (Smashwords: Stoke-on-Trent).

Morgan, Timothy. 2002. '*Friday*'s Dedications.' *Journal of Heinlein Studies* 10: 2–3.

Nicholls, Peter. 1982. 'Robert A. Heinlein', in *Science Fiction Writers: Critical Studies of the Major Authors From the Early Nineteenth Century to the Present Day*, ed. E. F. Bleiler (New York: Scribner's).

Olander, Joseph D. and Martin Harry Greenberg, eds. 1978. *Robert A. Heinlein* (Writers of the 21st Century) (Edinburgh: Paul Harris).

Panshin, Alexei. 1968. *Heinlein in Dimension* (Chicago: Advent).

Panshin, Alexei and Cory Panshin. 1980. *SF in Dimension: A Book of Explorations* (Chicago: Advent).

Panshin, Alexei and Cory Panshin. 1989. *The World Beyond the Hill: Science Fiction and the Quest for Transcendence* (Los Angeles: Jeremy P. Tarcher).

Parkin-Speer, Diane. 1995. 'Almost a Feminist: Heinlein.' *Extrapolation* 36 (2): 113–25.

Patterson, Jr., William H. 1998. 'A Study of "Life-Line".' *Journal of Heinlein Studies* 2: 17–27.

Patterson, Jr., William H. 2001. 'A Study of 'Requiem".' *Journal of Heinlein Studies* 8: 25–38.

Patterson, Jr., William H. 2006. 'Incest and Archetype in Robert Heinlein's World as Myth Books.' *Foundation* 97: 28–33.

Patterson, Jr., William H. 2010. *Robert A. Heinlein In Dialogue with his Century. Volume 1. Learning Curve. 1907–1948* (New York: Tor).

Patterson, Jr., William H. 2014. *Robert A. Heinlein In Dialogue with his Century. Volume 2. The Man Who Learned Better. 1948–1988* (New York: Tor).

Patterson, Jr., William H. and Andrew Thornton, eds. 2001. *The Martian Named Smith: Critical Perspectives on Robert A. Heinlein's Stranger in a Strange Land* (Citrus Heights, CA: Nitrosyncretic Press).

Reid, Robin Anne, ed. 2009. *Women in Science Fiction and Fantasy.* Vol. 2 (Westport, CT: Greenwood Press).

Reid, Robin Anne. 2015. 'Reading the Man in the Moon: An Intersectional Analysis of Robert A. Heinlein's *The Moon is a Harsh Mistress*', in *Critical Insights: Robert A. Heinlein*, edited by Rafeeq O. McGiveron (Ipswich, MA: Salem Press).

Reno, Shaun. 1995. 'The Zuni Trine: A Model for *Stranger in a Strange Land*'s Martian Culture.' *Extrapolation* 36 (2): 151–8.

Richmond, Alasdair. 2001. 'Time-Travel Fictions and Philosophy.' *American Philosophical Quarterly* 38 (4): 305–18.

Roberts, Robin. 1985. *A New Species: Gender and Science in Science Fiction* (Urbana and Chicago, IL: U. of Illinois Press).

Rochelle, Warren G. 1999. 'Dual Attractions: the Rhetoric of Bisexuality in Robert A. Heinlein's Fiction.' *Foundation* 76: 48–62.

Ryder, Mary Ellen. 2003. 'I Met Myself Coming and Going: Co(?)-Referential Noun Phrases and Point of View in Time Travel Stories.' *Language and Literature I* 12 (3): 213–32.

Schulman, J. Neil. 1999. *The Robert Heinlein Interview and Other Heinleiniana* (Mill Valley, CA: Pulpless Press).

Seed, David. 2007. 'Constructing America's Enemies: The Invasions of the USA.' *The Yearbook of English Studies* 37 (2): 64–84.

Showalter, Dennis E. 1975. 'Heinlein's *Starship Troopers*: An Exercise in Rehabilitation.' *Extrapolation* (May): 113–24.

Slusser, George Edgar. 1977a. *Robert A. Heinlein: Stranger in his Own Land.* (The Milford Series: Popular Writers of Today 1) (San Bernardino, CA: Borgo Press).

Slusser, George Edgar. 1977b. *The Classic Years of Robert A. Heinlein* (The Milford Series: Popular Writers of Today 11) (San Bernardino, CA: Borgo Press).

Slusser, George Edgar. 1995. 'Heinlein's Fallen Futures.' *Extrapolation* 36 (2): 96–112.

Stover, Leon. 1987. *Robert A. Heinlein* (Boston: Twayne).

Sullivan III, C.W. 1985. 'Heinlein's Juveniles: Still Contemporary After All These Years.' *Children's Literature Association Quarterly* 10 (2).

Thornton, Andrew. 1997 and 1998. 'Mythos and Logos: The Influence of P. D. Ouspensky in the Fiction of Robert A. Heinlein.' *Journal of Heinlein Studies* 1: 9–14; 2: 8–16; 3: 13–17.

Thornton, Andrew and William H. Patterson Jr. 2002. 'Jubal and the Secretaries.' *Journal of Heinlein Studies* 10: 4–5.

Twain, Mark. 1875. 'The Curious Republic of Gondour', in Twain, *The Curious Republic of Gondour, and Other Whimsical Sketches* (New York: Boni and Liveright, 1919).

Walton, Jo. 2010. 'The Right Kind of Girl.' Tor.com.

Walton, Jo. 2010. 'Ever Outward: Robert A. Heinlein's *Have Space Suit—Will Travel*.' Tor.com.

Walton, Jo. 2010. 'Smug Messiah: Robert A. Heinlein's *Stranger in a Strange Land*.' Tor.com.

Walton, Jo. 2011. 'Beware of Stobor!: Robert Heinlein's *Tunnel in the Sky*.' Tor.com.

Walton, Jo. 2011. 'How Robert A. Heinlein Wrote About Making Dinner: Some Thoughts on *Farmer in the Sky*.' Tor.com.

Walton, Jo. 2011. 'Child Markers and Adulthood in Robert A. Heinlein's Juveniles.' Tor.com.

Walton, Jo. 2011. 'Pass the Slide Rule: Heinlein's *The Rolling Stones*.' Tor.com.

Walton, Jo. 2014. *What Makes This Book So Great: Re-Reading the Classics of Science Fiction & Fantasy* (London: Constable and Robinson).

Washington, Booker T. 1972. *Booker T. Washington Papers. Volume 1* (Chicago: U. of Illinois Press).

West, Chris. 2002. 'Queer Fears and Critical Orthodoxies: The Strange Case of Robert A. Heinlein's *The Puppet Masters*.' *Foundation* 86: 17–27.

Westfahl, Gary. 1995. 'The Dark Side of the Moon: Robert A. Heinlein's *Project Moonbase*.' *Extrapolation* 36 (2): 126–35.

Westfahl, Gary. 1998. *The Mechanics of Wonder: The Creation of the Idea of Science Fiction* (Liverpool: Liverpool UP).

Wright, Sr., David. 2006. 'Rebutting Joseph T. Major's View of General Semantics in *Heinlein's Children*.' *Journal of Heinlein Studies* 19: 45–52.

Wright, Sr., David. 2007. 'Rational Anarchy: An Analysis of the Theme Given by Professor Bernardo de la Paz in Robert A. Heinlein's *The Moon is a Harsh Mistress*.' *Journal of Heinlein Studies* 21: 9–15.

Wright, Sr., David. 2011. 'General Semantics as Source Material in the Works of Robert A. Heinlein.' *ETC: A Review of General Semantics* 68 (1): 92–109.

Acknowledgements

This book would not exist had Bill Regier at the University of Illinois not commissioned it for Illinois' Modern Masters of Science Fiction series. I would have been honoured had the book appeared in that series, and I have only myself to blame: this book is twice the length of the commission.

I am deeply grateful to Simon Spanton and everyone at Unbound who responded with immediate enthusiasm when I tentatively enquired if they would be interested.

Thanks go to Dan Henderson for the sale of his complete run of the *Journal of Heinlein Studies*, and to the Arts, Law and Social Science Faculty of Anglia Ruskin University for making the purchase possible.

Beta Readers: Jane Carnall, Robert James, Dave Langford, Robin Anne Reid, Kari Sperring.

H. Bruce Franklin for clearing up one or two matters; Sean McPherson for fact-checking gun-lore for me; Josh Pearson for work in the Eaton collection; Montana Morris for scouring the internet for essays; Maureen Kincaid Speller for copy-editing; Leigh Kennedy for indexing; Edward James for editing and proofreading.

The participants in the 300-word challenge were particularly supportive when I was aiming for negative word-counts; my colleagues at Anglia Ruskin University for their friendship and support; my ever-patient Ph.D. students and anyone who has had to listen to me talk about Heinlein for the past five years.

Extra thanks to the friends who helped us pack and unpack when our removal company fell through. Without you I would not have been able to keep working on the book: Yasmin Timothy, Kate Keen, Caroline Mullan, Kari Sperring, Russell Smith, Liz Sourbut and Richard Williams.

As Johnny Rico said, 'I guess my luck has always been people'.

All errors are of course my own.

A Note on the Author

Farah Mendlesohn is a historian and critic. She has chaired the Science Fiction Foundation; served as the President of the International Association of the Fantastic in the Arts; and been involved in both national and international convention running. She is the author of several books about science fiction and fantasy literature and is best known for her book *Rhetorics of Fantasy*. She won the Hugo Award for *The Cambridge Companion to Science Fiction* (edited with Edward James). Her most recent book, *Children's Fantasy Literature: An Introduction* (with Michael M. Levy) won the World Fantasy Award in 2017 and the Mythopoeic Scholarship Award in Myth and Fantasy Studies in 2018.

Index

INDEX

Unbound
Liberating ideas

Unbound is the world's first crowdfunding publisher, established in 2011.

We believe that wonderful things can happen when you clear a path for people who share a passion. That's why we've built a platform that brings together readers and authors to crowdfund books they believe in – and give fresh ideas that don't fit the traditional mould the chance they deserve.

This book is in your hands because readers made it possible. Everyone who pledged their support is listed below. Join them by visiting unbound.com and supporting a book today.

Aahz
Les Abernathy
Zac Abraham
John Adams
Hon. Joel S. Agron
Arnold Akien
Nina Allan
Bob Allen
Craig Allen
Jocelyne Allen
Peter J. Allen
Carl Allery
William Allison
Merwyn Ambrose
Mark Anderson
Martin Andersson

Lise Andreasen
David Andress
Yarrow Angelweed
Johan Anglemark
Audrey Annoh-Antwi
Jennifer Anstey
John Appel
Helen Armfield
Richard Ashcroft
Brian Attebery
David Auburn
Ondrej Audy
Andrew Bach
Wolfgang Bachmann
Will Badger
Fredrika Baer

Ali Baker

Catherine Baker

Matthew Baker

Henry Balen

David Ballard

Francesca T Barbini

Rob Barrett

Andrew and Kate Barton

John Barton

James Bauserman

Mike Bayliss

Greg and Astrid Bear

Sally Beasley

Tom Becker

Chris Beckett

Jeff Beeler

Adrian Belcher

John Bell

Daniel Bennett

Stephen Benson

Elizabeth Bentley

Catherine Berry

Christopher Beute

Norman Bier

Christopher Biggs

Andrew Bikle

Christian Bikle

Katherine Bishop

Simon Bisson

Bob Blake

Helena Blakemore

Richard Bleiler

Daniel Blum

Leslie Bocskor

Ruth Booth

Stephen Boucher

Mark Bould

Lucas Boulding

Elisabeth Bouynot

Bruce Bowie

Stephanie Boyd

Christopher Boyer

Julie Bozza

Simon Bradshaw

Sean M. Brannon

Robert Brazile

Peter Breeden

Gavin Brennan

Catherine Breslin

Claire Brialey and Mark Plummer

Mike Brind

Simon Brind

Arne Brix

Daan Broekhof

Ian Brogan

William Brooks

Sarah Brown

Rich Brownell

Ed Bruce

Margaret Brumm

Bryan Randolph Bruns

James Bryant

Adam Bryce

Melissa Bube

Paul Bube

Jim Buck

Curt Buckley

Daniel Buckmaster

Blazej Bucko

Bob Buhr

John Burger

Bill Burns

Michael A. Burstein

Geoff Burton

Joshua W. Burton

David Busch

Andy Bustamante

Andrew M Butler

Yury Bychkov

Pat Cadigan

Amir Cahane

Lynn Calvin

Ritch Calvin

Donna Camp

Gerry Canavan

Chris Candreva

Michael Capobianco

Andrew Carle

Norah Carlin

Rob Carlson

Jane Carnall

Keith Carscadden

Howard Carter

Joe Carter

Margaret Carter

Dominic Cave

David Lars Chamberlain

Chaostrophy

Heather Chappelle

Ash Charlton

Bodhisattva Chattopadhyay

Andy Checker

Jeremy Cheek

Fred Cheng

Frederic Cleaver

Bill Clemente

David L Clements

Jonathan Clements

John Clute

Catherine Coker

Rachel Coleman

Ruth Coleman-Taylor

Ian Collier

Steve Coltrin

Darcy Conaty

Helen Connor

Christian R. Conrad

Laura Conrad

David Cook

Jonathan Cook

Tim Cooper

Barry Cope

Travis J.I. Corcoran

Lisa Costello

Gary Couzens

Bill Cox

Cardinal Cox

Diana Cox

John Coxon

Simon Craven

Paul M. Cray

Peter Crettenden

Tomas Cronholm

Deborah Crook

Steve Cross

Mary Crouse

Jonathan Crowe

Cheryl Cruse

Walter Cuirle

Tony Cullen

Dana Cushing

John D'Angelo

Dominic Dalgliesh

John Dallman

John Dalton

Laurence Davies

Rhodri Davies

Christopher K. Davis

Ken Davis

Anna Davour

Susan Dawson

John Day

DC

Olivia Dean-Young

Kris Dehaes

Brad DeLong

David Demers

Steven DesJardins

Ian Dickson

Brian Dillon

Stephen Dougherty

Aaron Doukas

Zeb Doyle

Melanie Drake

Michael Duda

Clemens Duerrschmidt

Sydney Duncan

Owen Dunn

David Dyer-Bennet

Tim Dymond

Melanie Dymond Harper

Phil Dyson

Stephen Early

David East

Neil Easterbrook

Scott Edelman

Nick Eden

John Edge

Ivar Otto Ekker

Erik Elmgren

Iain Emsley

Drammar English

Doug Engstrom

Marc Fabian Erdl

Jordan Evens

Lynne Everett

Jack Everitt

Jeff Fair

Bryan Fanning

Gary Farber

Maria Farrell

Doug Faunt

John-Robert Fay

Moshe Feder

Bruce A. Ferguson

Shawn Ferry

Travis Finborg

Colin Fine

John Flemming

WIlliam Flynn

Konstantinos Fotis

Mark Norman Francis

D Franklin

James Franks

Pamela Freeman

Joy Freeman and John Adams

Patrick Friedel

Beth Friedman

Ken Fritz

Stephen Frug

Sara Gabai

Matthew Gabby

Richard Gadsden

Sean Gaffney

Neil Gaiman

Marcus Gales

Karl Gallagher

Morgan Gallagher

Nico Gallo

Guillaume Galy

Wayne Gauthier

Alexander George

John Gersten

Daniele A. Gewurz

Eugene Giddens

Mathieu Glachant

Richard Glanville

Steve Glover

Dwight Godding

James Goetsch

Mich Goforth

Jeanne Gomoll

Paul J Goodison

James Gotaas

Rob Goza

Megan Gragg

Peter Graham

Stephen Graham

Steve Grandi

Roger Gray

Ian Grey

Mike Griffiths

Richard Guadagno

Eileen Gunn

Kjetill Gunnnarson

Kristian Gustafson

Marie Guthrie

Sean Guynes

Gideon Haberkorn

Andrew Hackard

Edward Haines

Peter Halasz

Joe and Gay Haldeman

Martin S. Halldin

Gideon Hallett

Will Hamilton

Jeanne Hand-Boniakowski

Russell Handelman

Tom Hanlon

Gwyneth Hannaford

Max Hansson

Colin Harris

Jim Harris

Henry Harrison

Niall Harrison

Eric Hart

Mark Harvey

T Q Hassenpfeffer

Andrew Hatchell

Paul Hattori

Blair Haworth

Rachel Haywood Ferreira

Steven Healey

Nigel Heffernan

Tommi Helenius

Magnus Hellstrand

Dan Henderson

Liz Henry

Melissa Herbert

Wendrie Heywood

Andrew Hickey

Adrian Hickford

David Hicks

William S. Higgins

David Hilbert

Kate Hill

Rick Hill

Robin Hill

Matthew Hintzen

Lynn Hirshman

Derek Hodges

Timothy Hodler

Stephen Hoff

Jer Hogan

Richard Hohm

John Holbo

Neil Holford

John-Henri Holmberg

Joseph Hoopman

Rich Horton

Matthew Hoskins

Gil Houck

John Hulls

Michael Humphries

Mike Hungerford

Dave Hutchinson

ICSF – Imperial College Science
    Fiction Society

Carl Inglis

Christopher William Ingram

John Ireland
Johari Ismail
Maxim Jakubowski
Mike James
Vic James
Andrew Jaremko
Ben Jeapes
John Jeffrey
Brian Jenkins
Don Jennings
Harald Johannessen
Bruce Johnson
Kevin Johnson
Al Johnston
Michael Johnstone
Brian Jones
Kai Jones
Lenore Jones
Johan Jönsson
Mike Jordan
Per Jorgensen
Joseph Justice
Michael Kagan
Henry Kaiser
Gary Katsevman
Gareth Kavanagh
John Kaye
Sander Kean
Tony Keen
Ian Kelly
James Kelly

Mark R. Kelly
Thomas Kendall
Patricia Kennon
Sean Keogh
Dan Kieran
Fred Kiesche
Katie King
Tara Kirby
Tim Kirk
David Kirkpatrick
Mia Kleve
Robin Knauerhase
J. W. Knott
Franziska Kohlt
Bill Kohn
Hedzer Komduur
Tom Kowal
Andreas Kraft
Alexander Krygsman
Jane Kurtz
John Kuzma
Janet Lafler
Chris LaHatte
Steve Lane
Sandra Lang
Henk Langeveld
David Langford
Knud Larn
Kurt LaRue
Steven Latta
M Lauren LaTulip

Duncan Lawie

Nancy Lebovitz

Nicholas Lee

Andy Leighton

Marianna Leikomaa

Pascal Lemaire

Fred Lerner

Russell Letson

David N. Levy

Paul Linford

Anselm Lingnau

Olov Livendahl

Sir Logan

Troy Loney

Jodi Longobardo-Bauer

Tom Losh

Rebecca Loudon

Andrew E. Love, Jr.

Susan Loyal

Richard Lucas

Karl Ludvigsen

Do-Ming Lum

Fredrik Lundh

Heidi Lyshol

Jerry Maatta

Meg MacDonald

Duncan MacGregor

Ken MacLeod

Morgan MacLeod

Dan Mahoney

Robert Maines

J.S. Majer

Laura Majerus

Lynn Maners

Dave Mansfield

Rob Mansfield

Kathy Mar and Dean Dierschow

Paul March-Russell

Kevin Marks

Kevin Maroney

Scott Martin

Adrienne Martini

Dvora Mathews

Elise Matthesen

Paul May

Kyle McAbee

Rich McAllister

Scott McBride

Parris P McBride-Martin

Martin McCallion

Elizabeth McClellan

Kim McCleskey

Mike McCown

John McDaid

Edward McDonald

Jim McGee

Martin McGrath

Rod McGregor

Ross A. McIntyre

Allison McLemore

Victoria McManus

William McMillan

Ron McNew

Sean McPherson

Joseph McTee

Gale Mead

John Medany

Robert Mee

Merril Collection of Science
    Fiction, Speculation
    and Fantasy

Caroline Mersey

Dan Mertz

Edmund Meskys

Adrian & MJ Midgley

Emily Midkiff

George Miller

Matthew Milne

John Mitchinson

Joan Mize

Ian Mond

Daniel Monson

Tom Moody-Stuart

Fiona Moore

Murray Moore

Richard Moore

Wayne Moore

Marcia Morelli

Cheryl Morgan

Edward Morgan

Mem Morman

Judith Mortimore

Oliver Morton

Brooks Moses

James Mostowski

Fred Moulton

Steve Mowbray

Joerg Mueller-Kindt

Caroline Mullan

David Mulligan

Robert Munck

Arthur Murphy

Nathan Murphy

Colin Murtagh

Ravi Nanavati

Kim Nash

Carlo Navato

Philip J. Nesser II

Grant Nichols

Lydy Nickerson

Betsy Nicoletti

Patrick Nielsen Hayden

Garth Nix

David Noonan

Bruce Norcross

Therese and Karl-Johan Norén

Hugh Norwood

Lynette Nusbacher

Jody Lynn Nye

Kevin OBetseyBrien

Terence O'Carroll

Michael O'Donnell

Nathan Ogden

Paul Oldroyd

Pat Olver

Frank Olynyk

KianWee Ong

David Onnen

Roman Orszanski

Ollie Östlund

Gill Othen

Chris Owen

Scott Pack

Shannon Page

Ignazio Palmisano

Alexei Panshin

Steph Parker

Robert Parks

Mark Passera

Ryan Patridge

Simon Patterson

Harry Payne

Heather Payne

Wendy Pearson

Chris Pepper

Michael Perkins

David R. Perry

Helen Perry

Steve Perry

Tommy Persson

William Pettit

Eric Picholle

Catherine Pickersgill

Fiona Pickles

Duane Pierce

William Piper

Justin Pollard

H David Pollock

Pedro Ponce

Catherine Porter

Samantha Potter

Anthony Pratt

David Pringle

Judith Proctor

Christopher Puzak

Michael Rader

Dawn Raison

Bruce Ramage

Malcolm Ramsay

James Ransom

Suzanne Ratkowski

Nancy Reagin

Gillian Redfearn

John Redford

Barry Rees

Bill Reich

Malcolm Reid

Robin Reid

Rachel Rennie

Libbi Rich

Rafe Richards

Don Riggs

Carl Rigney

Lance Roberts

John Robinson

Roger Robinson

Alan Robson

Frank Rodolf

Robert A. Roehm

Dan Rogart

Jean Rogers

Lorena Rosaleny-Peralvo

Kalina Rose

Craig Ross

Umberto Rossi

Jean Rossner

Tim Roudebush

Lee Ann Rucker

Geo Rule

M.J. Ryder

Cathy S

Michael Saler

Ian Sales

Alex Arash Sand Kalaee

Joe Sanders

Juan Sanmiguel

Jukka Särkijärvi

Andy Sawyer

Robert J. Sawyer

John Scalzi

Homer Schaaf

Veronica Schanoes

David Schappert

Will Schenk

Michael Scheuermann

Sebastian Schleussner

Christopher Schmidt

Rob Schutt

Jenny Schwartzberg

Alison Scott

Georgina Scott

Mike Scott

Adrienne Seel

Stu Segal

Christopher A. Semisch

Sid Seton

Steven Shaviro

Michael Shields

Dan Shlepakov

Adam Shostack

Linda Shoun

Mike Shupp

Susan Shwartz

Jörg Sicher

Marc Sidwell

Ian Simpson

Roger Sjölander

Tim Skellett

Debbie Slater

Graham Sleight

Mike Smith

Nic Smith

Owen Smith

Rohan Smith

Keith Soltys

Christopher Sommer

Flavio Vinicius Spalato Zanchi

Catriona Sparks

Michael Spehar

Kenneth Spell

Kari Sperring

Simon Spiegel

Francesco Spreafico

Francis Spufford

Matthew Squair

Jesper Stage

Kevin Standlee

Sharon Stanfill

Charles Steele

Yanaba Stegman

Gabriela Steinke

David Steinsaltz

Tristan Stephens

Michael Stevens

CathiBea Stevenson

Ian Stockdale

Tracy Stone

Peter Straub

Galen Strickland

Peter Sullivan

Erik Sund

Chris Suslowicz

Phil Sutherland

Nils-Erik Svangård

K. A. Stefan Svensson

Michael Swanwick

David Tallan

Liam Tanzer-Wilde

Sharon Lin Tay

Shaista Tayabali

Audrey Taylor

Paul Taylor

Jedidiah Hanes Templin

Barry Tennison

Becca Testerman

Sten Thaning

Raja Thiagarajan

Randall Thomas

Ben Thompson

Dan Thompson

Eric Thompson

Gary Thompson

Josh Thompson

Richard Thompson

Eva Thury

John Tilden

Charles Timpko

Patric Toms

Lorna Toolis

Ross Tregaskis

Michael Trinder

D.J. Trindle

Lynda Trower

Roz Trudgon

A.M. Tsaasan

David G Tubby

Steve Turnbull

Peter Turner

L Frank Turovich

Carole Underwood

Kimberly Unger

W. A. V-Litten

Jo Van Ekeren

Chris van Gorder

Bruno Van Vaerenbergh

Colin Vaughn

Chris Veazey

Bob Vennerbeck

Miika Vesterinen

Beryl Vex

Britt-Louise Viklund

Paul Vincent

David Vinson

Bob Walker

Rich Walker

Steve Walker

David Wallace

Don Walling, Jr.

Jim Wallman

Michael Walsh

Kenneth Walters

Bruce Walton

Jo Walton

Kay-Megan Washington

Shannon Waters

Rina Weisman

Alan Wendt

William Wentworth-Sheilds

H Wessells

Frank Westdahl

Magnus Westerlund

Kathy Westhead

Curtis Weyant

Traci Whitehead

Paula Whitehouse

Betty Widerski

Rick Wilber

Elizabeth 'Betsey' Wilcox

Daniel Wilksch

John Willard

Chris Williams

Mike Williams

Trevor Williams

Cat Wilson

Paul Witcover

Gary Wolfe

Nick Wood

Roger Wood

Spencer C. Woolley

Shana Worthen

Thomas Wouters

Trooper Nick Wray

Robert Wright

Steve Wright

David Wuertele

Mark Yon

Merris Young

Mike Young

Joel D. Zakem

Timothy Zeddies

Ariel Zeitlin

Yonatan Zunger